AFTER
ONE HUNDRED
YEARS

CORPORATE PROFITS, WEALTH & AMERICAN SOCIETY

JOSEPH J. DUNN

#7769030072

ISBN: 1466249544
ISBN: 13: 978-1466249547

Contents

Prologue

He sat alone. The last of the staffers had finally departed. The enormity of the next few days was finally sinking in. On this small desk, he had put together a manifesto, mainly copies of speeches he had given during the campaign. Each focused on a specific issue, depending on the audience. At the American Legion convention, he called for an administration that would finally give adequate care to those who had risked all in defense of our country. For those who had lost their hard-earned savings, as many had, he pledged new regulations on banks and an end to unbridled speculation. There were calls for more efficient government, for balanced budgets, for national unity. Everywhere, he had promised hope and reminded Americans that they had endured in the past and would endure again. The publishers would have this on the shelves within weeks, and sales would ride the crest of popularity that comes with the inauguration of any new president. These introduction pages, just typed, would pull it together nicely. It would commemorate the election campaign to reinvigorate those who had been with him all along and enlist those among the opposition who were now, whether out of citizenship or seeking some favor, prepared to follow.

He had used the media well. His speechwriters had provided plenty of memorable sound bites that people loved to repeat whenever they talked politics, letting the phrases sink in and grow warmer and more comfortable in their minds with each repetition. That was the process for winning millions of votes. But this was for the readers, the people who considered the whole text, and thought it through. He had their allegiance, too. They knew, as he had written here, that "Nothing is more striking than the simple innocence of the men who insist whenever an objective is present, on the prompt production of a patent scheme guaranteed to produce a result. Human endeavor is not so simple as that." So, he had made the speeches and won the election. Tomorrow, to Washington. He took up the pen and signed: "Franklin Delano Roosevelt, Hyde Park, March 1, 1933."

Introduction

Nothing is more striking than the simple innocence of the men who insist when-
ever an objective is present, on the prompt production of a patent scheme guaran-
teed to produce a result. Human endeavor is not so simple as that.

S o wrote Franklin Delano Roosevelt on March 1, 1933, three days before
his inauguration as president of the United States in the midst of the Great
Depression.[1]

Roosevelt had no patent scheme, but he was committed to "bold, persistent
experimentation," as he had declared during his 1932 campaign for the Democratic nomination.[2] He had an amazing propensity for action, the likes of which
had not been seen since the administration of his cousin, Theodore, in the first
years of the twentieth century. Since then, Americans had been experimenting
with the relationships between government, business, and nonprofit organizations. Every experiment had been an attempt, in the words of the Constitution,
to promote the general welfare.

Now, in the wake of the 2008—2009 Great Recession, we are searching
anew for paths to innovation, to new jobs, to rebuilding the prosperity of the
middle class and the security of those in need. Today, we have the benefit of one
hundred years of experimentation. The story of those experiments can take us
beyond the strident calls of those who offer patent schemes or rely on simple

---

1   Franklin Delano Roosevelt, *Looking Forward,* p. viii.
2   Oglethorpe University Commencement Address, May 22, 1932; President's Master Speech File (Box 9); Franklin D. Roosevelt Presidential Library.

axioms. It provides a basis for civil discourse. Learning from a century of experiments, we can find the way forward. From the early days of the twentieth century, American Telephone and Telegraph Company, United States Steel, Ford Motor Company, and other big, publicly traded corporations and wealth—profits accumulated by their owners—have influenced our health care, education, environment, civil rights, and the standard of living of wage-earners and those without work.

During the same century, the nonprofit sector in America has grown from mainly local associations into thousands of local, national, and international organizations. Early in the twentieth century, the American Red Cross was struggling to build an identity and mission that would survive its aging founder. University education was only for the well-to-do, with few exceptions. Hospitals and aid to the hungry or unemployed were largely funded by local donations. The quality of services depended entirely on the energy and good intentions of founders and staff, with no government oversight and little knowledge on which to base standards of professional care. Today, as in the past, nonprofit organizations deliver essential aid to those in need. They play a major role in our nation's higher education and health care, in the arts, and in scientific discovery. They press us on to new concepts of fairness and experiment with solutions to ancient problems.

Government, particularly at the federal level, has grown from a small number of workers focused on a few federal issues—national defense, the postal service, issuing patents—into a major employer with regulatory powers affecting every type of business and nonprofit activity. Federal revenues were collected mainly through tariffs until 1913, when a tax on personal incomes was permitted by the Sixteenth Amendment. Every tariff and every change in taxes has been an experiment.

Each sector of our society—business, nonprofit, and government—impacts the general welfare of our people. These sectors interact in ways that are even more complex. The interactions produce results that may be intended or unintended, proximate or remote. They affect the number and quality of available jobs, advances in medical research, access to higher education, innovation for energy efficiency and environmental safety, and even the price and quality of our food. These are the issues of our day. These are social justice issues. Progress depends on our understanding these interactions.

Experiments, as Franklin Roosevelt surely knew, produce successes and failures. Noble intent does not guarantee good results. Successful experiments bring prompt acclaim, but failed experiments also have value. They show us what does not work—and that knowledge brings us a little closer to discovering what does work. The process of experimentation and discovery is tedious. Some discoveries are reported as spontaneous flashes of brilliance when in fact they are the products of years, even decades, of trial and error. We learn relatively little by gazing at the experiment in progress; we learn a lot by reviewing the results. The initial certainty of a new technology or new cure is sometimes displaced when longer experience reveals hazardous effects. Experimentation and honest, dispassionate assessment of immediate and long-term results are steps on the hard path to successful innovation in the physical sciences: chemistry, metallurgy, physics, medicine, etc.

We must be equally diligent in reviewing the results of our experimentation with corporations, government, and nonprofits. After one hundred years, we can step back and see what changes have occurred within and beyond the walls of factories and offices, among wage-earners and their families, for those without employment, and in the general welfare of our people. We must review the notes and look at the data that tell us what worked and what did not.

After a century of experimentation, we still have questions. How can we best promote innovation and create new industries that offer new jobs? The federal courts ordered the dissolution of the Standard Oil trust in 1911, but ExxonMobil earned $40 billion in profits in 2006, as was widely reported, plus another $28 billion you didn't read about. Where did all those billions go? Who really directs the actions of large corporations and holds them to account for their actions? Government has been redistributing income, corporate profits, and wealth for almost one hundred years, yet there are wide differences in the distribution of wealth and income. How has that happened? What tax structure would raise the most money for vital government programs? What major factors promote or inhibit the work of nonprofits? How do we make more money available for these important works? We want answers. This book provides them, drawing on our century of experimentation.

The notes and data from our experiments are found in government investigations, in corporate reports, in the wills and estate plans of the world's wealthiest few, and in the letters and testimonies of those in need and those who devoted lifetimes to their aid. Human endeavor—the interaction of people in corporations, government, and nonprofit groups—is not simple, but the records of the endeavor have value. They reveal the actions that advanced or retarded our social progress.

Michael Novak, a philosopher and theologian, presents some interesting statistics:

> Among the 139 million civilians employed in the United States, 24 million work for Fortune 500 companies, the largest industrial corporations, about 50 million, are employed by businesses with fewer than 100 employees, and almost 10 million people are primarily self-employed. About 20 million work for government—federal, state, and local. About as many—20 million—work for nonprofit organizations such as churches, hospitals, clinics, libraries, museums, schools, universities, research institutes, foundations, the Girl Scouts, the Sierra Club, and thousands of other nonprofit associations and activist groups.[3]

Each of us conducts our own experiments. We develop ideas about how to achieve a higher standard of living for ourselves and for others in our society. We buy new products to replace old ones, and we start new companies or take up new jobs. We elect new politicians who pass new laws. We give to charities, walk or run in the 5Ks, and join organizations to take up new causes. We save and invest, or we decide not to. Our decisions as consumers, voters, investors, and philanthropists propel the interactions of businesses, government, and nonprofit organizations. Those decisions tip the scales of social justice. They affect the general welfare. Good decisions bring progress; mistakes waste resources and cause human misery. The lessons from one hundred years of experiments show the way forward to innovation and new opportunity.

This book requires no prior knowledge of business or economics. The best prerequisite would be concern for promoting the general welfare, and honest curiosity about how to make advances and avoid setbacks in the quest for a stronger economy and social justice. If we are comfortable in our present knowledge and the axioms we hold dear, we should remember Albert Einstein's response when asked how he had made his great discoveries: "By challenging an axiom."[4]

The best way to understand how corporate profits and wealth impact society is to follow the trail of money. During the 1970s, two *Washington Post* reporters suspected, but could not prove, that the Nixon administration had played a role in a burglary of the Democratic National Committee headquarters at the Water-

---

3   Michael Novak, *The Universal Hunger for Liberty—Why the Clash of Civilizations is not Inevitable,* 69.
4   *The Autobiography of Lincoln Steffens,* 816.

gate Office Building in Washington, DC. An anonymous source encouraged the reporters to "follow the money," to learn who benefited from the break-in and who was responsible.[5] As they followed the money trail, the truth became clear, and on August 9, 1974, Richard Nixon resigned the presidency. By following the money, we will learn how corporate profits and wealth impact American society. That knowledge has value for those who would move forward.

Whatever your current or future employment, and whatever your views on corporations and social justice issues, you will meet new people, learn new facts, and acquire new perspective as you read.

---

5   Thirty years later, the anonymous source identified himself as W. Mark Felt, deputy director of the FBI at the time of the Watergate scandal. The *Washington Post* corroborated his identity.

I

CUSTOMERS

Chapter One

Customers

Every dollar of corporate profit comes from the pocket of a customer. Customers—people who make purchases—are the driving force of business activity. You pick the clothing you wear, what you eat for breakfast, the soft drink you sip, and the websites you visit. You chose the remedy for your last head cold. Which artists are on your MP-3 player? Do you subscribe to basic cable or premium channels? Kindle, Nook, or iPad? Your college major? Did you get to your current location by bus, train, car, bike, or foot? Those are consumer choices. Some are trivial, others are important. Cumulatively, over the course of months, years, or decades, these are lifestyle choices. Any decision you make *not* to purchase a product or service is also a consumer decision.

In 1900, after four years of solid economic growth, many Americans felt confident about the future. In November, they elected William McKinley to a second term as president of the United States.

Ten million Americans, a third of all workers, made their living farming or ranching. More than 750,000 worked as seamstresses, tailors, or dressmakers. Six hundred thousand worked on the railroads; half a million people worked in mines and quarries. Another three hundred thousand were iron or steel workers. A quarter of a million people worked in cotton mills. More than two hundred thousand were blacksmiths.[6]

---

6   *Statistical Abstract of the United States, 1907,* Table 81 (data for 1900).

The last decade of the nineteenth century had seen a rapid increase in the number of multistate corporations, and corporate bureaucracies expanded accordingly. The number of bookkeepers and accountants in the country grew 60 percent between 1890 and 1900; the number of stenographers and typists more than tripled.[7]

New technologies were producing new jobs. The 1900 census counted fifty thousand electricians. Ten years earlier, there had been too few to bother counting.[8] The work of these electricians had its origins in the patents that Thomas Edison obtained for his incandescent light bulb in 1879 and his construction of the first municipal electric generating station in New York City in 1882. In the twenty-four years that had passed since Alexander Graham Bell obtained his patent on the first telephone, more than one million telephones had been installed in American homes, businesses, and government offices. In 1900, twenty-five thousand people worked for American Telephone and Telegraph Company and its "Bell System" affiliates.[9] By 1910, the number of phones in use jumped to almost eight million, and 105,000 people were employed delivering phone service.[10] Many others supported the telecommunications industry, making telephone poles, switching equipment, and copper wire.

The Pittsburgh Reduction Company produced aluminum for industrial products and kitchenware at its mills in Niagara Falls, lured there by cheap hydroelectric power. Carborundum Company was there also, making drills, saws, and grinding wheels from new material patented just a few years earlier. There were customers overseas as well, and ships were needed to transport products. The New York Shipbuilding Company opened its shipyard at Camden New Jersey in August, 1900, with 1,350 employees.[11] And all those workers had money to spend.

Department stores in the big cities did a booming business helping the armies of accountants, lawyers, managers, and skilled tradesmen obtain the accoutrements of middle class life. In May 1901, Isador Straus announced that R. H. Macy & Co. planned a new department store in New York City to replace its twenty-year-old Fourteenth Street and Sixth Avenue location. The new ten-story store, on Broadway from Thirty-third to Thirty Fourth Street, would provide 750,000 square feet of space. The four escalators and thirty-three elevators could accommodate forty thousand people per hour. The eighth floor restaurant

---

7   *Statistical Abstract of the United States, 1907,* Table 81.
8   *Statistical Abstract of the United States, 1906,* Table 13.
9   *Statistical Abstract of the United States, 1905,* Table 184.
10   *Statistical Abstract of the United States, 1910,* Table 158.
11   David Cannadine, *Mellon,* 36.

seated twenty-five hundred.[12] Four thousand sales clerks, buyers, bookkeepers, and cleaners were employed to attend to all these customers. In 1910, another floor was added to the building to provide more floor space.

Philadelphia's shoppers browsed through a downtown shopping district anchored by three huge department stores—Lit Brothers, Gimbel Brothers, and Strawbridge and Clothier—each occupying a corner at the intersection of Eighth and Market Streets. Boston had Filene's. Chicagoans marveled at the goods on display at Marshall Field's store on State Street. In Cleveland, Halle Brothers Company presented its wares at the corner of Euclid Avenue and E. Twelfth Street. In San Francisco, Gump's on Post Street competed with I. Magnin & Co. on Market Street. Pittsburgh had its Kaufmann's and Horne's stores. Atlanta had Rich's and Chamberlain's. Belk Bros. offered its wares on a "cash only, no credit" basis to keep prices low in Charlotte. In each of these and hundreds more throughout the country, sales clerks gushed over customers. Inventories were constantly updated and entire stores refurbished to meet the ever-growing demand.

Rural America was served by general stores in towns and through the mail-order catalogues of Sears, Roebuck and Company and Montgomery Ward, which delivered all the latest fashions and home furnishings by railroad networks that stopped at every village and crossroad.

Some of these white-collar workers and skilled technicians put aside a few dollars and went looking for newer, larger, and nicer homes. On the edges of industrial cities, developers filed plans for new subdivisions to accommodate these upwardly mobile families. Middle class housing was undergoing a major evolution. Indoor plumbing was the norm. Electric lighting began to replace kerosene lamps, and even some homes that had been built a few years earlier with gas piping for "modern" lighting were converting to electric. New electric interurban trolleys offered reliable, quiet transportation to the business districts from these new residential areas. In New York City, construction was starting on a network of subway lines.

For the wealthy, at least for those who craved the latest technology, there was something new. In Ohio, the new Packard Motor Car Company sold out its entire production of automobiles in 1901 and 1902. The Olds Motor Works produced 425 Oldsmobiles in 1901 and an astounding 2,500 in 1902.[13]

Not everyone was spending all their earnings on new luxuries. Some used their extra income to afford their children the new educational opportunities.

---

12 *New York Times,* September 28, 1880, May 16, 1901, and November 9, 1902.
13 Douglas Brinkley, *Wheels for the World,* 34, 42.

The University of Chicago was founded in 1890 and drew many of its professors from the much older universities in the East. By 1900, its library of three hundred thousand volumes rivaled those of Yale and Columbia universities; with thirty-five hundred students, it was among the largest universities in America. Leland Stanford Jr. University in Palo Alto was still building its original campus buildings, but it had already established an excellent faculty. Its president, David Starr Jordan, was lured from Indiana University when the school opened in 1891. One of Stanford's first graduates, in the class of 1895, was a mining engineer named Herbert Hoover. By 1900, he was working in China. In the spring of that year, Franklin Delano Roosevelt graduated from the Groton School in Massachusetts. In the fall he entered Harvard University.

A few used their discretionary income in really novel pursuits. In September 1900, Wilbur Wright took leave from his brother's bicycle store in Dayton Ohio to spend six weeks at Kitty Hawk, North Carolina, experimenting with new design features on a glider he had built in the back room of the shop. A few years of strong sales of bicycles, the latest fad product, had given the brothers enough economic flexibility that Orville hired a full-time manager for the store and joined his brother at the test site.[14]

Early in 1901, a twenty-six-year-old visiting from Italy was searching the east coast of Cape Cod for a location suitable for his wireless receiver tower. Guglielmo Marconi had convinced the directors of his firm that he could transmit telegraph signals across the Atlantic Ocean without using undersea cables. His company had already built a transmitter at Cornwall on the English coast. He found the perfect receiver site at South Wellfleet.[15]

———

The one event of 1901 that tore Americans from their daily routine was the shooting of President McKinley on the afternoon of Friday, September 6. For several days, he seemed to be recovering well enough from emergency surgery. On the tenth, the vice president was advised that all was well and he should join his family on vacation in the Adirondacks. Then the president's condition worsened. Medical bulletins were followed closely. Crowds gathered at telegraph stations and scrambled for each successive newspaper edition. On the afternoon

14   John Evangelist Walsh, *One Day at Kitty Hawk: The Untold Story of the Wright Brothers and the Airplane,* 41-46.
15   Calvin D. Trowbridge Jr., *Marconi: Father of Wireless, Grandfather of Radio, Great-Grandfather of the Cell Phone,* 140, 150.

of Friday the thirteenth, the vice president was summoned to come at once back to Buffalo. The next morning, the fourteenth, the nation awoke to the news that the president had died during the night.

McKinley was buried in his hometown of Canton, Ohio, on the following Thursday, after ceremonies in Buffalo and Washington, DC. The next morning, newly-inaugurated President Theodore Roosevelt went to his office in the White House. People went back to their routines.

Three months after McKinley's assassination, the social season in New York City was in full swing. On December 17, the Honorable William C. Whitney, former Secretary of the Navy, gave a ball in honor of his step-daughter Miss Adelaide Randolph at his home at 871 Fifth Avenue. There were five hundred guests for supper, which was served just after midnight as most of the guests had attended dinner parties earlier in the evening. Dancing followed. The mansion was adorned with floral decorations, mainly palms and begonias, which gave a lively contrast to the heavy draperies, the formal portraits of Charles I by Van Dyck, and other art treasures. Three weeks later, Mrs. Astor, the acknowledged leader of New York society, held her annual ball at her home just three city blocks north of the Whitney residence. This event was the annual high point of the social season. That year, almost eight hundred guests attended. The menu included filet of beef, terrapin, canvasback duck, and pate de foie gras. The large assembly was easily accommodated by removing sections of the walls that separated Mrs. Astor's house from the adjacent home of her son, Col. John Jacob Astor. This feature had been thoughtfully planned when the homes were built in 1895.[16]

Some of these New York City fortunes were vested in families that had arrived in Dutch colonial days. Others were the profits amassed by nouveau riche industrialists. Socially, these two groups rarely mixed. But they shared a talent for spending money on a grand scale. Mansions on and near Fifth Avenue were part of the sprawl that moved ever northward on Manhattan Island, each competing with its neighbors in size and opulence. Amazing wealth was on display in Pittsburgh, Chicago, Cleveland, Baltimore, San Francisco, and most other cities.

Whenever the Whitneys or Astors gazed through the front windows of their homes, they saw the beauty of Central Park across the street. Just a fifteen minute walk through that park, about a mile away, were some of the most crowded tenements of New York City. Here lived the families of hundreds of thousands of unskilled and low-skilled workers. Most were new arrivals; 95 percent of the

---

16 *New York Times*, December 18, 1901, and January 7, 1902.

tenement dwellers were foreign-born or had parents who were foreign-born. Their neighborhood, too, was undergoing major change.

In 1894, a commission chaired by Richard Watson Gilder documented the living conditions in great detail and publicly announced names of some slumlords. Some were people of limited means who had saved enough to buy a building and use it as a cash cow, extracting the maximum possible rent while spending nothing on maintenance or improvements. There were surprises. Trinity Church Corporation owned more than 350 of the tenements and owned the land under many others. Many of the four- and five-story buildings had no running water above the basement, few windows, and dark wooden stairways. Many of the three-room apartments were occupied by more than one family, all pooling their resources to pay the rent. When the Health Department ordered the corporation to install the required plumbing in several buildings, the corporation refused and went to court to vacate the order, arguing that the Health Department's order was an excessive exercise of power.[17]

The Gilder Commission found its voice in Jacob Riis, a reporter who had long advocated housing improvement. A reform mayor had won election in the same year, and a new bipartisan Board of Police Commissioners was appointed. The president of the Board of Police Commissioners, Theodore Roosevelt, had long been an admirer of Riis. By 1895, Riis and Roosevelt were visiting the tenements together by night and pressing for code enforcement by day.[18] The worst of the New York City tenements were torn down by order of the Health Department under a new municipal ordinance. Downtown, in the neighborhood known as Little Italy, the notorious Mulberry Bend tenement was taken over by the Health Department and demolished. The owners were compensated with $1.5 million in city funds. A park was built on the site, now known as Columbus Park.[19]

Several wealthy individuals constructed new buildings specifically for low-income families to demonstrate that decent housing could be built and maintained while affording the investor a 5 percent income on the funds committed, and some of these were proving successful. Housing advocates hoped that this early success could be maintained. If so, affordable housing would be in ample supply, and the slums would disappear. Others converted old mansions into shelters for homeless men. Government played no role in financing, building, or

---

17   *New York Times,* December 9, 24, and 27, 1894.
18   *The Autobiography: Theodore Roosevelt,* 199.
19   *New York Times,* December 7, 1894.

operating low-income housing. Enforcement of building or fire codes, where they existed, depended on the political bosses. Few states (Massachusetts was a notable exception) employed career inspectors directed by professional boards committed to public safety.

In 1900, the low-income housing situation in New York State was still the most abysmal in the country. Families taking in boarders or sharing their apartments with another family or two were so common that, while there were 4.4 people in the average family, seven people lived in the average dwelling.[20] In Manhattan and the Bronx, the average dwelling (counting rich, poor, and in between) had 20.4 occupants.[21] Every other city in America had similar neighborhoods. These were the homes of semiskilled and unskilled wage-earners. Some stayed only long enough to save for a better home. Others skipped from apartment to apartment when the rent was due but they couldn't pay because of a layoff or strike, accident or illness, or alcohol or gambling.[22]

The destitute—those with no income and no place to live—found lodging nightly in police stations or longer-term in almshouses financed by charity or municipal government.

A survey conducted in 1904–05 tracked the income and expenses of two hundred families in New York City's Gramercy Park neighborhood. The author of the study, Louise Bolard More, concluded that $720 per year was needed to supply a family of five with food, decent housing, clothing, sundries, and enough life insurance to cover funeral expenses.[23] More observed that some of the families borrowed to make ends meet, while others on the same income were able to save a little. By making different decisions about spending, some families were able to move ahead while others with the same income fell behind. With the money that remained after paying for necessities, a wage-earner could decide to spend on some new convenience, move to a nicer home, save for the future, or donate to a church or charity. That difference in dollars between income and expenses— discretionary income—allowed a man or woman to reach for their dreams.

John Curtis Kennedy, of the University of Chicago Settlement Board, directed a team of social workers who carefully tracked the living expenses of 184 families living in the Chicago stockyard district over the period between April 1909 and March 1910. Each family kept a log of its spending, and a case worker

20 *Statistical Abstract of the United States, 1910,* Table 36, statistics for 1900.
21 *Census of the United States, 1900.*
22 Jacob Riis, *Battle for the Slum,* 41, 54, 56.
23 Louise Bolard More, *Wage Earners' Budgets: A study of Standards and Cost of Living in New York City,* Table II, 51.

visited weekly to help ensure the accuracy and completeness of the record. For the year, the typical expenditures for rent of a four-room apartment, heat, light, and food totaled $533.12. Clothing, laundry supplies, union dues and society memberships, newspapers and children's books, and $10 for doctor bills and medicines added $210 per year. Kennedy then added $63 to cover Christmas presents, alcoholic beverages, barber visits, tobacco, entertainment, ice cream and candy, and the occasional but considerable expenses of weddings, births, and funerals. Thus he concluded that a family of five might subsist for a limited period of time on less, but that "even with the most intelligent expenditure of money and the most economical management of the household, it would be impossible for a family of five to live on less than $800 a year."[24] Kennedy's social workers found that many families took in boarders to earn the difference between their wages and a subsistence living.

Residents of rural areas had their own housing challenges. A survey of housing conducted from 1912 to 1915 in 770 counties across eleven southern states showed that less than 1 percent of rural homes had sanitary arrangements that state authorities deemed satisfactory. Half of the farmhouses visited had no latrine or privy of any kind. Open fields served as their sewage disposal system. In some communities, hookworm was diagnosed in more than 40 per cent of the population. Hookworm spreads when microscopic worm larvae are absorbed through the skin—children walking barefoot in southern climates were especially vulnerable. The larvae settle in the intestines and are carried in feces. Human waste in the fields was the vehicle for spreading the disease. It could also be the vehicle for dysentery and typhoid fever. Hookworm infection can be fatal. It lowers the hemoglobin level in the blood. That leaves the infected person more vulnerable to the ravages of malaria, tuberculosis, and pneumonia.[25] Some children missed 20 percent of school days. Adults were often unable to work. The disease had existed in warm climates since ancient times. It was documented during the 1870s, but few understood how it was transmitted, and cures were still experimental.

The average salary for a teacher in New York (rural and urban areas) in 1900 was $552; in Ohio, $350; in Illinois, $440; in Texas, $266; in South Carolina, $134; and in Georgia, $179. California had the highest average teacher salary in the nation at $709.[26] President McKinley was paid $50,000 per year, plus an allow-

---

24   John Curtis Kennedy, *Wages and Family Budgets in the Chicago Stockyard District: With Wage Statistics,* 79.
25   *Annual Report, 1917,* The Rockefeller Foundation.
26   *Statistical Abstract of the United States, 1933.1, Fifty-Fifth Number,* Table 106, United States Department of Commerce.

ance for expenses at the White House. The governors of New York, New Jersey, and Pennsylvania earned $10,000; governors of Texas and Michigan, $4,000; and South Carolina and Mississippi, $3,000. Members of Congress received $5,000 annually.[27] John D. Rockefeller received approximately $11.7 million in dividends from his shares of Standard Oil stock.[28] There was no federal income tax.

———

Consumer action has sometimes been a powerful force for change in societal issues even without government action. During the 1890s, Consumers Leagues were organized in a number of large cities. The guiding principle of the organizers was that "the purchaser is responsible for the conditions under which goods are made and distributed." Initially, the women who formed these local clubs wanted better working conditions and higher wages in stores, especially for women and children employees. The first objective was to get stores to close at noon on Saturdays, but clubs quickly became interested in minimum wages, prohibition of workers under fourteen years old, restriction of work hours for children under sixteen, and provision of adequate and sanitary lunch rooms and rest rooms.

League members met with owners or managers to discuss improvements. The group always brought facts and figures to the meeting, gathered during inspection tours allowed by management. Some members made detailed observations while employed by unsuspecting employers. One of these quiet investigators was an eighteen-year-old named Eleanor Roosevelt, niece of the president of the United States. "Investigate, record, agitate" was a strategy that produced results.

An informed, positive approach was important since the labor laws in many states were weak, and the enforcement in almost every state was weaker. The leagues printed and circulated "white lists" naming stores that implemented the changes. There were no "black lists" or boycotts of nonconforming merchants, but many customers looked to the list when deciding where to shop. Women's social clubs invited league members to speak about the movement. Some clergy spoke from the pulpit, promoting the reforms. In some cities, wealthy women added clout. A letter from a valued customer always got attention. College women supported the cause, volunteering time and channeling their purchases. Wellesley and Vassar Colleges had their own leagues.

---

27   Henry W. Ruoff, *The Century Book of Facts.*
28   Charles R. Morris, *The Tycoons,* 332.

Before long, the larger stores were inviting league inspectors to visit and attest to their good practices.

Interest quickly spread to conditions in factories where women's garments were manufactured. In 1899, the local leagues organized a National Consumers League, which quickly suggested that a white label be sewn into all garments produced by employers who met the League's workplace standards: all goods were manufactured on premises; all state factory laws were met; no overtime was worked; and no children under sixteen were employed. The League had enough influence with merchants and consumers that the manufacturers paid the costs of making and attaching the labels to the garments and signed written contracts attesting to their continued conformance.[29]

Progress was slow but steady. In 1905, the Retail Merchant's Association in New York City had a rule that no member should sell goods bearing the National Consumers League label. But as more customers became aware of the League and its programs, merchants and manufacturers saw participation in the League's "white list" as a competitive necessity. The power of the pocketbook prevailed. Retailers competing to attract the socially aware customer invested in new, safer, more attractive stores that also provided amenities for workers. In 1909, Jacob Gimbel laid the cornerstone for a new $17 million store at Broadway and Thirty-second Street in New York City. The new thirteen-story building featured "fireproof" construction and a roof-top garden for employees. Speakers at the ceremony included Dr. Edward T. Devine, professor of social economy at Columbia University and general secretary of the Charity Organization Society, a leading New York City philanthropy. Two other social workers also spoke, praising the enlightened approach to employee welfare that was becoming evident among the major retailers.[30]

By 1910, the National Consumers League was looking for a new leader for its New York City operations. Thirty-year-old Frances Perkins was completing a master's degree in political science and already had experience working at nonprofit organizations. Frances took the job. The $1,000 annual salary and the promise of a full-time secretary were powerful incentives.

The National Consumers League became more influential. During World War I, the group convinced Woodrow Wilson's administration to include specifications of workplace conditions in the contracts for military uniforms. In 1933, Frances Perkins became the first-ever female Cabinet member as Secretary of

---

29   *New York Times,* August 28, 1899, and August 25, 1901.

30   *New York Times,* March 24, 1905.

Labor in Franklin Roosevelt's administration, and she was a major architect of the New Deal.[31] The League proposed detailed wage and hours standards for use in the National Industrial Recovery Act industrial codes, a key part of Roosevelt's efforts to end the Great Depression.[32]

———

Prohibition was America's most expansive experiment with consumer protection legislation. For decades, the Women's Christian Temperance Union, the Anti-Saloon League, and other advocates had professed that abstinence from alcohol would rid the country of drunkenness and largely eliminate profligacy, poverty, wife-beating, child abandonment, and most other forms of violence. Alcoholic beverages, it was widely believed, were at the heart of all these problems. Many states had already enacted their own prohibition statutes. By January 1919, the Eighteenth Amendment to the Constitution had been ratified by the requisite three-fourths of the states. It prohibited the manufacture, sale, or transportation of intoxicating liquors for beverage purposes throughout the United States, as well as the export or import of such liquors. Congress passed the Volstead Act to implement the provisions of the Amendment, over President Wilson's veto. The Act authorized both federal and state enforcement of its provisions. Any beverage with more than 0.5 percent alcohol, including beer and wine, was banned, although individuals were permitted to keep or drink alcohol within their own homes and serve it to their guests. Physicians could prescribe up to one pint per month for medicinal purposes, to be dispensed by a licensed pharmacist.

This noble experiment proved a dismal failure. Thirsty consumers found sources for the prohibited drink. Neighborhood taverns closed and secret "speakeasies" opened. Organized crime networks took control of manufacture and transport. Each gang protected its neighborhood, county, or city by extortion and murder. Violent crime surged, and public health records showed no statistically significant outbreaks of sobriety. In 1928, voters elected the "dry" candidate, Herbert Hoover. By 1932, voters had changed their minds and made their preferences known to their representatives. The Twenty-first Amendment was ratified the following year. The federal experiment with prohibition was ended. Henceforth voters in each state would make their own decisions about alcohol regulation.

---

31   Kirsten Downey, *The Woman Behind the New Deal,* 26-29.
32   *New York Times,* November 10, 1929, December 10, 1933.

After World War I and a brief but sharp recession in 1920–21, Americans resumed their frenzied acquisition of all the goods that modern technology provided. Between 1921 and 1930, ten million radios were brought into American homes.[33] Early adapters could buy a kit and build their own receiver as early as 1908, but the consumer product of the 1920s came ready-to-use in a fine wooden cabinet, an attractive piece of furniture as well as a source of news and entertainment. By 1930, there were more than twenty-six million motor vehicles registered in the states.[34] In the same decade, Sears, Roebuck and Company was the country's largest retailer, and sales grew at an annual rate of 11.7 percent.[35]

———

Consumer boycotts are rare, but they have played a powerful role. Rosa Parks boarded a bus one day in 1955 in Montgomery, Alabama, for her homebound commute. She eased into a seat near the middle of the bus. Later, after all the seats were filled, a white man boarded the bus and the driver demanded that Mrs. Parks give up her seat. She refused, thereby violating a municipal ordinance that required blacks to surrender their seats to whites if so instructed by the driver. A policeman was summoned, and Mrs. Parks was arrested and fined for violation of the city ordinance. At this point, Mrs. Parks's action was an act of civil disobedience—an act of bravery and merit but, like others before it, ineffective in changing discriminatory laws and customs.

But then the black citizens of Montgomery decided to boycott the municipal bus system. They vowed not to ride the buses again until the discrimination ended. Blacks who had relied on the buses for daily transportation started walking, in some cases many miles, to and from work. Those who had cars shared a ride with others. Churches used station wagons to transport people who normally relied on the buses, and temporary taxi systems were organized. Since blacks had represented about 75 percent of the bus ridership, the daily revenues of the bus system fell sharply.

Before long, the ongoing costs of all those busses, plus salaries for the drivers, mechanics, and other employees, exceeded the revenues from the fare boxes. After two months, the bus company was forced to increase fares for the

---

33   *Historical Statistics of the United States: Colonial Times to 1970.* U.S. Department of Commerce, vol. 2, 695-96, 796.

34   *Statistical Abstract of the United States, 1933,* Table 372.

35   Boris Emmet and John E. Jeuck, *Catalogues and Counters: A History of Sears, Roebuck and Company,* 301, 650.

remaining riders by 50 percent. Six months after the boycott started, the bus company had laid off half of its drivers and several of its office and maintenance personnel. Within a year, the company was facing bankruptcy.

Merchants in the midtown business district saw their business decline and quietly pressed for a resolution.[36] The city government now had a business decision to make. It could repeal the discriminatory laws and allow black riders the same privileges as all other riders, or it could allow the bus company to enter into bankruptcy, which would bring adverse financial consequences to the entire city. The black citizens of Montgomery, rallied by Rosa Parks's brave action, were using their economic power as customers to compel the repeal of racist laws and customs. In November 1956, the U.S. Supreme Court ruled that racial discrimination in public transportation violated the Constitution. The following month, the discriminatory practices were dropped, and the boycott ended. While the Supreme Court decision resolved the issue before the city's finances were ruined, the effectiveness of the economic boycott was already quite evident.

Consumers still exercise major influence over the social behavior of big businesses. MSNBC and CBS Radio dismissed the well-known talk-show host Don Imus after his insulting comments about the Rutgers University women's basketball team, while rap musicians who use the same words in their lyrics maintain their multimillion-dollar contracts from major entertainment corporations. Why?

The answer lies in consumer power. Imus was ousted because General Motors, Procter & Gamble, and other Fortune 500 corporations canceled their sponsorship contracts upon realizing that so many Americans objected to Imus's language.[37] These sponsors worried that their products' reputations would be tarnished if associated with the insulting language. Most of the sponsor cancellations came shortly after the team coach, C. Vivian Stringer, described the slurs as offensive to all women and invited society at large to consider how offensive these remarks would be if directed toward anyone's daughter. Her thoughtful and powerful speech, and the dignified, articulate comments by team members, raised the likelihood that Americans, and possibly many beyond our borders,

---

36 *New York Times,* January 8, 1956; June 30, 1956; December 22, 1956.
37 *Fortune* magazine publishes every year a list of the 500 largest corporations, ranked by sales, and a separate Global 500 list.

would find the sponsors' products just a little less desirable. The sponsors were convinced they could no longer associate with Don Imus. With sponsors canceling, and the difficulty associated with obtaining new sponsors for an Imus show, the networks quickly fired Imus. The private sector—corporations, responding to their customers—had acted to cancel Imus sponsorship contracts within days.

In contrast, the typical purchaser of rap music seemed unaffected by the incident. Imus's words were part of their normal vocabulary. With no hint of a consumer backlash among customers of rap music, the major entertainment corporations continued business as usual, recording and selling rap music and paying the artists. So by these two very different reactions, each consumer group exercised powerful influence on corporate actions. Consumers do not speak with one united voice. They act in millions of individual decisions.

Why were the customers of huge corporations like Procter & Gamble so powerful? After all, P&G makes Tide and Gain soaps, Pampers, toothbrushes, Crest toothpaste, Gillette razors, Folgers coffee, Duracell batteries, and similar everyday household products. They are on the shelves of supermarkets around the world. Millions of customers buy these products month after month.

The power of consumers arises from their ability to impact a corporation's profits. P&G and many other large companies are "mass marketers." They have billions of dollars invested in plants, manufacturing equipment, and distribution facilities. Every sale is important to cover these fixed expenses. That is why these companies spend millions of dollars on customer research and more millions of dollars on advertising. When the Imus controversy arose, P&G executives considered the math.

The dynamics are interesting, so let's follow the money. Procter & Gamble had, on December 31, 2006, $18.8 billion in plant (e.g., manufacturing facilities, offices, product research labs, etc.) and equipment expenses. Those are called "fixed expenses" because they do not subside or go away if sales volume falls. Also, P&G had 138,000 employees. Sales that year totaled $68 billion. Profits were $8.7 billion. If sales dropped by just one percent, or $680 million, and all of those expenses continued, profits would fall by about $680 million. That assuming that just one customer in one hundred changes brands. Loss of market share is a serious threat to any mass-market business because it leads directly to lower profits.

Now consider a more drastic scenario. What if 10 percent of P&G's customers decided to buy similar products made by Colgate-Palmolive or Clorox or any of its other competitors? You can be sure that Procter & Gamble senior managers were doing quick calculations of the possible financial impact. If P&G's sales fell by 10 percent even for one quarter,[38] the lost revenue would be $1.7 billion (annual sales of $68 billion x .25 x .10). The company could not possibly react quickly enough to trim its "variable expenses"—mainly raw materials and employees—in the same quarter, so profits would be lower by roughly $1.7 billion—a drop of 20 percent for the entire year, just from a 10 percent sales drop lasting just three months. The loss of customers and profits would not be short-lived. A customer, once lost, rarely returns. Management quickly concluded that sponsoring the Imus program presented a serious risk with no reward. The sponsorship contracts were cancelled.

———

The largest consumer movements are often invisible to those not watching quarterly and annual sales figures. Some managers see falling customer-retention statistics and a competitor's growing market share, but fail to heed the message in the numbers.

The collapse of General Motors and Chrysler during the financial crisis of 2008–2009 may have seemed sudden. Some headlines blamed the sudden surge in gasoline prices. Others pointed to the inability of consumers to get car loans in a tight credit market. But the end of GM and Chrysler probably started decades earlier, with decisions made by just a few car-buyers.

Grady and Mabel Jones were among these "early adapters." Grady was a skilled machinist. Mabel worked in a book bindery. They had no children, so a small car met their needs. In 1960, they purchased a new, red Volkswagen "beetle." Mabel appreciated the economy, and Grady praised the clever design and solid workmanship. The Volkswagen cost less than the least expensive American models. It was highly reliable and far more fuel-efficient. The rear-mounted engine gave it superior traction in snow. The top speed of fifty-two miles per hour posed no problem for their daily commute to work in Philadelphia. The weak heater and absence of an air-conditioner were acceptable privations, fair exchange for the fuel economy of a four-cylinder, air-cooled engine. For Mabel and Grady, low purchase price and fuel economy were the purchase-decision factors, and they trumped any concerns about country of manufacture, style (no

---

38   "Quarter" refers to calendar quarter, or a three-month period, e.g., January 1 through March 30. Corporations report their financial results on both a quarterly basis and an annual basis.

tail fins, minimal chrome, purpose-built bumpers), or keeping up with, well, the other Joneses.[39]

Later in the decade, college students began buying foreign-made economy cars. Opel, made in Germany, competed with Volkswagen for American customers. Datsun models from Japan also gained a following. When the Baby Boomers[40] graduated, their first cars were more frequently foreign-made. Born after the Second World War, they brushed aside whatever anti-German and anti-Japanese sentiments their parents still harbored. A new generation of purchasers entered the market and made its mark. Slowly, over several decades, more customers shifted to Toyota, Honda, and other carmakers that established reputations for quality and fuel efficiency.

No corporation has unlimited capital to pursue every customer's desire. So every corporation chooses how to concentrate its available money. The process of matching available resources to management's vision of future customer needs and preferences is "strategy." Toyota and Honda executives believed that at some point higher fuel costs would cause more customers to buy small cars and hybrids. Toyota particularly committed capital to continuously improving its production methods. The goal was to make smaller, fuel-efficient vehicles that produced a profit for the company while selling at competitive prices. Toyota and Honda offered gas guzzlers, too. But their corporate profitability did not rely upon vehicles that became "too big to fuel." By 2007, Toyota was enjoying market share equal to GM's.

General Motors' management had established a different strategy. Sales data showed that customers, in spite of publicity about global warming and the volatility of fuel prices, were buying SUVs and pickup trucks at prices that were high enough to generate big profits for the manufacturers. These buyers were not just construction workers, farmers, ranchers, or others who needed the large cargo space or towing capability. Many soccer moms and office workers also preferred the "gas guzzlers" over small cars and hybrids. Those large profit margins on gas guzzlers became essential to General Motors' corporate profits by compensating for thin profit margins on smaller vehicles. Every manufacturer selling in the U.S. had to meet federal standards for average fuel efficiency measured across their entire fleet of cars and light trucks.

---

39   The author recalls riding to high school every day of freshman year in the back seat of said Volkswagen, which can best be described as functional. But wherever you are, Mabel and Grady, thanks for the ride.
40   Baby Boomers, as the term is used by demographers, marketing specialists, and politicians, includes all people born between 1946 and 1964.

When gasoline prices rose sharply to $4 per gallon in 2008, more consumers started trading in the pickups and SUVs and buying smaller, fuel-efficient cars. Toyota and Honda were able to survive on the profits from their fuel-efficient models, including hybrids. General Motors finally had to shut down four major plants that had manufactured pickups and SUVs. Capital—money—would be redirected to research on smaller electric-motor cars and hybrids to meet the consumer demand, which had been shifting for decades.[41] Too late. A financial crisis occurred just as fuel prices peaked, and vehicle sales plummeted, limiting the options available to both General Motors and Chrysler.

Changes in business strategy take time to implement and do not produce results in days, weeks, or months. Customers, each one making his or her own decision about how to spend their own money, had brought General Motors— one of the largest corporations in the world—to bankruptcy.[42] But the change in topography of the automobile market had resulted from glacial changes in customer decisions as much as from any sudden earthquake of gasoline prices or the credit crunch. The cumulative effect of individual customer purchases determines the fate of even the largest corporations.

Customers also influence corporate decisions about donations and the use of company assets for community projects that do not directly benefit the company's business. In one well-publicized case, Berkshire Hathaway, the holding company formed by Warren Buffett,[43] ceased a long-running program that permitted its stockholders to designate organizations that would receive donations from the corporation. Some prolife customers of Pampered Chef, a Berkshire subsidiary, decided to boycott independent associates of the firm because some Berkshire donations were going to Planned Parenthood. Berkshire's announcement suspending shareholder-nominated donations stressed that its board could not jeopardize the businesses of associates in favor of corporate giving, whatever the merits of the gift recipients. In this case, consumers used their power to buy, or not buy, products

---

41   General Motors news release, June 3, 2008
42   The process in which new technologies, products, or manufacturing processes replace older ones was termed "creative destruction" by the Austrian economist Joseph Schumpeter in the1930s.
43   Warren Buffett is not just your average CEO. He was listed in *Forbes* magazine as the wealthiest person in the world in 2008 and is consistently among the wealthiest few.

to send a powerful message to stockholders. The chairman—one of the wealthiest people in the world—heard it. Corporations willing to support nonprofit organizations face the tricky problem of deciding which organizations to support. But customer purchase decisions affect corporate actions far more powerfully than buying a few shares of stock and introducing a shareholder resolution.

––––––

Business leaders know that to grow sales and profits they cannot simply wait for a competitor to fumble. Some corporations are especially gifted at anticipating, perhaps even influencing, customer preferences. Apple Inc. produces amazing new products that customers find innovative. The most successful corporations are those that repeatedly act in ways that make their customers happy. Starbucks took coffee—a commodity—and elevated it to an experience that delights customers. CarSense made a national business out of selling used cars by providing a no-haggling, clearly posted price strategy some customers found appealing. Other corporations develop ways to produce established products at lower cost, making them affordable to more customers. Companies must offer a genuinely attractive product or service every day. Customers enforce that rule with millions of decisions every day.

Firms that meet consumers' wishes tend to grow as more people learn about the product or service and decide that it meets their need also. Products that lose their appeal fade from the scene. So do the companies that make them. Competition ensures that customers get the best product or service at the lowest price.

This competition for customer dollars is also an effective antidote to corporate greed. Simply, any company extracting an excessive profit soon finds itself confronted by a competitor who will charge a lower price, or deliver a better value to customers, to attract their business. The greedy company must either improve its product to match the new rival's or cut prices to meet the competition. Failure to do so results in loss of customers. If uncorrected, loss of customers leads to bankruptcy. Corporate executives understand all this. They believe it. They act on it. Some, but not all, succeed at it.

––––––

Competing to attract customers requires innumerable estimates about what customers will want next. The restaurateur orders food for next week's menu.

The auto manufacturer needs to think several years in advance. Merchants use bar codes and membership cards to detect the latest craze. They order more while cutting prices on items that linger on the shelves. Supply chain management is a specialty discipline. Companies sometimes get it wrong, and sometimes the entire economy gets supply and demand out of balance. How does that happen?

A story provides valuable insight into business cycles. The Andrew W. Mellon Foundation has long been a supporter of graduate programs. The Foundation's 1988 Annual Report discusses a boom/bust cycle in the number of PhD degrees earned in the United States, which accompanied an "extraordinary proliferation of graduate programs. That overexpansion of graduate education—which was both too large in scale and poorly timed, in that it started too late and lasted too long—led subsequently to the oversupply of aspiring academics that in turn contributed to a general disenchantment with graduate study in many fields during the 1970s." Much of the disenchantment was caused by the inability of these PhDs to find employment in their chosen field, after so many years of study.

How did this happen in an arena untouched by any corporate profit motive? University presidents had plenty of notice that college enrollments would soar, beginning in 1964, when the first Baby Boomers would finish high school. Colleges would need more professors with doctoral degrees to teach the coming wave of students. Colleges would also need to build more dormitories, add classroom buildings, and expand libraries and science labs, etc. But the "long-lead" item, that which required the longest preparation, was developing an adequate number of PhDs to teach the undergraduates when they arrived. Most candidates need four to six years of post-college study and research to complete the PhD requirements. So universities geared up to find, encourage (through fellowships, part-time teaching assignments, etc.), and train larger numbers of graduate students. Each university set its own agenda and determined the size of its own programs both at the graduate level and in planning for the coming surge of undergraduates. At many colleges, the build-up involved spending millions of dollars.

The number of PhDs awarded annually in the subjects defined as "letters," mainly subjects such as English and American language and literature, comparative literature, classics, and philosophy, more than tripled between 1958 and 1972. Universities were expanding their graduate programs and awarding scholarships to draw top students. In mathematics, the number of PhDs awarded increased more than six-fold, from just over two hundred per year in 1958 to more than twelve hundred in 1972. The overproduction of PhDs became apparent when many newly minted doctors could not find professional employment. As college students learned of the situation, fewer opted to pursue doctoral degrees. From 1972 to 1982, the number of PhDs awarded in the letter subjects fell by more than one third. In mathematics, the number fell by 50 percent. The boom had turned into a bust.

All the careful planning by university presidents and trustees, and meetings with alumni and major donors and more than a few independent planning consultants, still resulted in overproduction of PhDs. Once colleges and universities had hired all the professors they needed, the remaining newly minted doctors could not find employment. These student-customers had spent a great deal of money and time pursuing a worthy goal, only to languish for years in second-choice careers. As word spread, bright students chose careers in business or other fields with better employment prospects.

Customers (in this case, those seeking PhD degrees and eventual professorships) and providers (universities offering to train these future professors) created a supply/demand imbalance similar to those that occur periodically in business. Perhaps cycles of boom and bust are a function of human behavior not unique to the for-profit sector.

———

In the following chapters we'll see how some companies outperform others at meeting customer needs. How corporations act is fundamental to how they interact with the other sectors of society. We follow the money from the customer's pocket into the accounts of large corporations.

CORPORATIONS

Chapter Two
A Primer on Profits

News Release, February 1, 2007 9:08 a.m.
Irving, Texas

Exxon Mobil Corporation Announces Estimated Record 2006 Results

Net income of $39,500 million ($6.62 per share) was a record and increased $3,370 million from 2005. Net income for 2006 included a special item of $410 million for a tax-related benefit.

Exxon Mobil's Chairman Rex W. Tillerson commented: "Full year 2006 earnings excluding special items were a record $39,090 million, driven by strong results in every business segment. ExxonMobil continued to leverage its globally diverse resource base to bring additional crude oil and natural gas to market."[44]

No corporate earnings announcement has produced as much discussion, reaction, and from some quarters, outrage as this. Shareholder-owned corpora-

44   Exxon Mobil Corporation news release, available at www.businesswire/portal/site/exxonmobil/index.jsp?ndmViewId=news_view&ndmConfigId=1001106&newsId=20070201005687&newsLang=en.

tions announce their profits or losses every quarter. A few words of accounting language help to understand the full impact of this announcement—and all corporate profit announcements.

Revenue consists of all money coming into the corporation. For most companies, sales of goods or services are the largest component of revenue. Companies also receive interest on bank deposits, and some receive investment income. Investment income may be a relatively large component of revenue for insurance companies, as they invest some premium dollars to pay claims that may arise in the future out of policies written today. Some corporations that own patented technology grant licenses to other companies to use that technology for a fee. Those license fees are revenue to the company owning the patent. All revenue received by the corporation in the quarter (or year, as in the example below) is added together and reported on the top line of the "income statement" for that period. Then all the expenses for the same period are totaled.

Expenses include all payments of money in conducting the business. For manufacturers, the largest expense is often "cost of goods sold," in other words, raw materials and component parts made by others that form part of the corporation's products. Payments for utilities, insurance, wages and salaries, bonuses and sales commissions, employment taxes (mainly the employer's share of Social Security and Medicare taxes), rent paid for facilities owned by others or property taxes on owned property, sales and advertising, and postage and printing are expenses.

Profit is calculated by subtracting total expenses for the period from total revenue for the same period. Profit is reported on the bottom line of the income statement. The terms "earnings" and "income" are sometimes substituted for profit, as in ExxonMobil's news release above. Companies, whether large or small, calculate profits in the same way. They use an "income statement" to report their financial performance during a certain period of time. The income statement may also be referred to as an "earnings statement" or "profit and loss statement" (a.k.a. "P and L statement"). Here is an income statement for a hypothetical company, XYZ Corporation, showing the revenues, expenses, and resulting profit for the year 2005.

Income Statement
XYZ Corporation

January 1 to December 31, 2005
($ thousands)

Revenue
Sales, net of refunds	2,395,615
Patent license fees	20
Total Revenue	2,395,635

Expenses
Cost of goods sold	1,317,588
Compensation (wages, bonuses)	658,794
Employee benefits	197,638
Insurance	21,042
Utilities	12,950
Fed & State Income taxes	73,173
Total Expenses	2,281,185

Profit	114,450

Our hypothetical corporation has total revenue of $2.4 billion (in round numbers), and profit was $114 million. That does not quite get to the Fortune 500 list, but it is certainly a substantial company. The income statement gives a summary of the company's performance. This document doesn't show details such as how much was spent on the employee picnic or the CEO's pay. Those are included in the line items shown. For many purposes, this is all one needs to know. If you want to lend money to this firm (perhaps as a supplier) or buy shares in it, you would want much more detailed information. For now, we simply want to understand that profit is what is left after the company has counted all its revenue and covered all its expenses.

"Earnings per share" are calculated by dividing the profit reported on the income statement by the number of shares of stock outstanding. When discussing total dollars left after subtracting expenses from revenue, the terms profit and earnings are interchangeable. If two hundred million shares of stock were issued by our hypothetical XYZ Corporation to its owners, then earnings per share is calculated by dividing the profit for the year by the number of shares:

$$\$114,450,000 \div 200,000,000 \text{ shares} = \$.57 \text{ per share.}$$

It's that simple in principle. In practice, the bookkeeping and accounting functions in a major corporation involve hundreds, if not thousands, of people.

Then there are the internal audit staffs that check on the accuracy of the book-keepers, accountants, inventory managers, and anyone else who handles corporate money, property, or contracts. The internal audit department enjoys a rather unique status, since it has direct access to the audit committee of the board of directors—no need to go first to the chief financial officer (CFO) or president or even the chief executive officer. Internal auditors have access to all corporate facilities and operations.

The corporation's board of directors engages the services of an independent certified public accounting firm—sometimes referred to as independent auditors. The board's recommendation of independent accounting firm is usually presented for approval in a shareholder vote. Note the division of duties. The corporation's executives, management, and employees are responsible for keeping the records, conducting the financial operations of the company, and preparing the financial statements that are distributed to shareholders and government regulatory agencies, including the Securities and Exchange Commission (SEC). The independent registered accounting firm plans and conducts a review—audit—of the evidence supporting the facts and figures contained in the financial reports. Has the inventory been properly counted and valued? Are sales figures documented by invoices and shipping orders? Independent auditors contact banks to confirm balances reported, as well as suppliers to confirm prices paid for materials. The audit firm's role is to assure that management has systems and processes in place to assure that the financial reports are free of material misstatement.

The purpose of the accounting and auditing work is to provide company managers with reports on which to base business decisions, detect misuse of company funds, and assure that current or potential investors and tax authorities have an accurate picture of the corporation's financial position.

The following chapters explore the profitability of corporations in a variety of industries. Financial results for the years 2002 to 2006 are particularly relevant for two reasons. First, these were years of economic growth. The brief recession that followed the dot-com crash was receding, and the country was beginning to recover from the shock of the September 11, 2001, terrorist attacks. Second, we now know that a new recession started in the second half of 2007 and a financial panic struck in 2008, the combined effect being a sharp decline in corporate profits. So the years 2002–2006 provide a more "normal" time frame for consideration and a first step in examining the impact of profits on society.

Chapter Three

Big Oil

ExxonMobil is the largest publicly[45] traded oil company in the world, based on sales, which in 2006 totaled $334 billion. The company traces its history to 1882, when John D. Rockefeller and other investors established Standard Oil Company of New Jersey.

Profit is the reward for a successful risk-taking investment, so to measure just how successful the venture has been, we really need to consider the profit in relation to the equity invested—in other words, placed at risk—to produce it. In ExxonMobil's case, shareholders placed at risk (as of December 31, 2005) $111 billion. Investors always have options. Each stockholder had the option, at that date and throughout the following year, to sell shares of ExxonMobil stock and buy some other stock or investment, deposit the funds in a bank account, or spend the money. The risk/reward ratio is, in accounting terms, expressed as "return on equity," or "ROE," by simply dividing the profit dollar amount by

---

45   Publicly traded, or public, corporations are those whose common stock can be bought and sold on stock markets or stock exchanges by members of the public. Shares of most large corporations in America are publicly traded. Private corporations are those whose stock is not available to the public. In some cases, the stock is held by one or a few people, and any shares being sold by one of the stockholders may only be purchased by an existing stockholder. These firms are referred to as privately held or closely held. Whether the shares of a corporation are traded publicly or privately, the shareholders own the corporation.

the dollars of shareholder equity at risk during the period in which the profits were earned.

$$\frac{\text{Reward}}{\text{Risk}} = \frac{\text{Return (after-tax profit)}}{\text{Equity (what shareholders have placed at risk)}}$$

So for ExxonMobil in 2006, the calculation is:

$$\frac{\$39.5 \text{ Billion (after-tax profit)}}{\$111 \text{ Billion (equity at risk)}} = .35 = 35\% \text{ return on equity}$$

Is this a good result? Is the equity being well used? Would another company have been a better steward of this invested capital? To answer these questions, we look at the ROE produced by other similar corporations. Two other very large integrated[46] oil companies, BP (once known as British Petroleum) and Royal Dutch Shell, are used for comparison. Also, a five-year average ROE is presented for each of these corporations, to determine whether Exxon Mobil's 2006 success is an aberration or part of a longer-term trend.

	Sales 2006 (Billions)	Net Profit 2006 (Billions)	Shareholder Equity on 12/31/05 (Billions)	ROE 2006 %	Average Annual Profit 2002-06 (Billions)	Average Shareholder Equity 2002-06 (Billions)	5-Year Avge ROE 2002–2006
Exxon Mobil	$334	$39.5	$111	35.1	$25	$98.3	24.7
BP	$266	$21	$88	24.4	$15.5	$80.8	19.2
Royal Dutch Shell	$319	$25	$106	24.1	$17	$83	20.8

---

46   Integrated oil companies are involved in exploration, extracting, refining, and marketing. Some oil companies specialize in one or a few of these activities, e.g., Schlumberger and Transocean specialize in exploration; Valero and Sun specialize in refining and marketing. These different business strategies appeal to different investors.

ExxonMobil's 35.1 percent ROE for 2006 far surpasses the competitors' returns. The five-year average return for ExxonMobil is also substantially better. Looking at 2006 alone, ExxonMobil's sales were 4.7 percent higher than Royal Dutch Shell's, and the amount of shareholder equity at Exxon Mobil, at year-end 2006, was only 4.7 percent larger than Royal Dutch Shell's. Each company has exploration, extracting, refining, and marketing operations. So we have two major corporations of approximately equal size in terms of sales and shareholder equity with similar operations. But ExxonMobil profits were 58 percent higher. ExxonMobil has made substantially better use of the shareholders' money than its two key competitors, in both one-year and five-year comparisons. Past results do not ensure future success, and an investor would want to understand better the reasons for the obvious performance differences. This example shows why ROE is so important to potential investors. Corporations that have produced high return on shareholders' equity over a period of years are generally preferred over those with weaker returns. No one has unlimited funds to invest, so it makes sense to choose wisely. Some call that savvy investing, others call it optimizing use of funds, still others refer to it as good stewardship. Profits make headlines; return on equity is the heart of the story.

The main factors in deciding where most of us buy gasoline are price and convenience. Most people can easily select from gas stations owned by Exxon-Mobil, Shell, BP, from a number of large refining companies such as Valero or Sun, or the Venezuelan government–run Citgo. A service station offering easy access from a busy intersection may be able to charge a few cents more than a less-accessible station nearby. But that daily competition at the pump limits the price that Exxon Mobil can charge. This reflects a basic principle of economics, that in a free market, a commodity-seller is a "price-taker," that is, they must sell the gas, oil, or whatever at the "going price" in the geographic area, and they must find ways to keep costs low to make a profit. So how does ExxonMobil produce ROE so much higher than its competitors are able to produce?

The answer probably lies in several strategies that have directed ExxonMobil management for many years and keep expenses lower than competitors' costs.[47]

---

47   Within any company, the words "cost" and "price" have different meanings, and the difference is important. Cost is the amount of money paid by the company for raw materials, parts, hardware, etc., (all of which are reported as "Costs of goods sold" in financial reports) and electricity and other utilities, rent paid to others, insurance, wages, employee benefits, etc. Price is the amount of money that a customer pays for the product or service offered by the company. So a "low-cost" strategy involves keeping costs to a level that is

The company has extensive laboratory and research facilities that continuously improve the methods used to find, extract, transport, refine, and sell the products. But ExxonMobil's competitors have research labs also. The company also plows profits back into the business to make the most efficient use of all the possible derivatives of its basic ingredients, which are crude oil and natural gas, as do the other integrated companies. Differences in strategy that may account for superior ROE include ExxonMobil's long practice of locating its chemical plants next to refineries, so that byproducts of the refining process such as sulfur can be further processed without the cost, time delay, and potential accidents of moving refinery byproduct to a distant chemical plant. ExxonMobil management also claims to use a more disciplined approach to selecting which business opportunities to pursue. Making consistently superior decisions about investment of money, over a period of years or decades, would certainly provide superior return on equity. No company has unlimited funds to invest. Every dollar of capital used well contributes to a superior ROE, and every dollar wasted lowers ROE. The Annual Report contains exhibits of ExxonMobil's industry leadership in worker safety, spill prevention, and other activities that demonstrate a commitment to low-cost, efficient operations. The charts and numbers indicate that at ExxonMobil, high shareholder returns are attained with, and perhaps caused by, management attention to the safety of employees, property, and the environment.

Industry-leading ROE defines ExxonMobil as making the best use of every dollar of shareholder equity, compared to its competitors. ExxonMobil prefers "organic growth," which is finding new potential drilling sites or building new plants by its own efforts, often on a joint-venture basis with another oil company or government of a foreign country. Capital—money—is committed only to those projects that offer the highest available return. This is a very focused stewardship of corporate funds by the Board of Directors, chief executive officer (CEO), and management.

ExxonMobil rarely engages in mergers or buy-outs of other companies. These always create anxiety and friction among the workforce, but they often fail to deliver the "strategic synergies" that are confidently predicted when such acquisitions are announced. The buying company often overpays.

Some point to BP's commitment of one billion dollars into research in alternative fuels and environmental protection. But BP incurred several serious refinery fires and explosions in recent years, and the major explosion and spill

---

less than competitors' costs, but says nothing about pricing strategy relative to competitors. Think of it this way: the *price* you pay for an item is almost always higher than the producer's *cost* of making the item.

in the Gulf of Mexico. They resulted in several deaths, property damage, and interrupted operations, as well as environmental damage. The entire process of drilling for, transporting, and refining crude oil and gas, and distributing the products, is inherently hazardous. It is reasonable to ask if BP's operations would be safer, and ROE higher, if its vast oil and gas operations received the attention of management undistracted by billion-dollar investments in alternative energy. Would the shareholders be better served, and the development of alternative energy sources progress more efficiently, if the billion dollars were returned to BP shareholders, allowing them to invest in corporations specializing in alternative energy? We will look at several corporations that specialize in that business.

———

Is there a conspiracy to fix prices in the oil industry? Absolutely yes. The Organization of Petroleum Exporting Countries (OPEC) coordinates the production and sale of crude oil from its member countries.[48] The oil reserves in those countries are either wholly or partly owned by the state. The oil ministers or other authorized representatives from the member countries meet several times each year, often in Vienna, Austria, to discuss conditions in the world oil market. As stewards of their nation's reserves, each wants to maximize the benefits that his country derives from its natural resource, both now and in the future. Their principal concerns are how much demand is likely to exist in the coming months from customers around the world, how much production their country can sustain, and how much customers can afford to pay. They rely on statistics and estimates made by well-educated staff members who study these trends. In these meetings, the ministers agree on production quotas, assigning how much crude oil each member country should sell in coming months. Setting the amount of crude oil available for sale directly affects the price of each barrel.[49] These are sovereign countries, and they meet outside the U.S. Approximately 44 percent of the world's crude oil is produced in OPEC countries, and about 13 percent is produced in Russia. Only 7 percent is produced in the U.S.[50]

---

48   OPEC members in 2007: Algeria, Angola, Ecuador, Indonesia, Iran, Iraq, Kuwait, Libya, Nigeria, Qatar, Saudi Arabia, the United Arab Emirates, and Venezuela.

49   Arrangements such as this, wherein parties agree to coordinate their production, prices, target markets, or other factors to maintain profits, are known as cartels.

50   Data from US Department of Energy, Energy Information Administration.

One key factor that causes energy prices to be so volatile, and to trend generally upward, is the lack of reserve production capacity—the ability to deal with surges in demand, or disruptions of existing drilling and transportation activities. Thus the sudden, rapid price increases when, for example, a hurricane threatens the Gulf of Mexico rigs or international tensions rise in the Middle East. In 2003, there was about 5.2 million barrels per day (bpd)[51] of spare production capacity in the world. By 2007, there was only about 2 million bpd spare capacity on most days.[52] The world's appetite for oil is growing faster than facilities for producing it.

From 1997 to 2007, global crude oil production—what was pumped out of the ground or from under the sea—increased by 13.9 million bpd, from 74.2 million bpd to 84.5 million bpd, an increase of 14 percent. Over the same years, global petroleum demand—what people used—rose from 73.9 million bpd to 86.3 million bpd, an increase of 17 percent. With consumption rising faster than production, the amount of "spare" production capacity is shrinking.[53]

This growth in oil demand reflects an important change. Paul Collier, professor of economics and director of the Center for the Study of African Economies at Oxford University, writes: "Since 1980, world poverty has been falling for the first time in history."[54] Billions of people who had lived just above the subsistence level started to see their hard work elevate their lifestyle into somewhat better conditions. A generation later, after the collapse of communism in Eastern Europe and with a more market-driven (less regulated) economy in India, plus China's gradual accommodation of private ownership of capital and production in some industries, the number of people living in extreme poverty has fallen to about 1 billion. Today, more than five billion people are using and bidding for energy resources that were shared by about one billion people less than thirty years ago.

As Thomas Friedman, foreign affairs columnist for the *New York Times*, predicted in 2006:

> If millions of people from India, China, Latin America, and the former Soviet Empire, who for years had been living largely outside the flat world, all start to walk onto the new flat-world platform—each with

---

51   One barrel of oil is 42 gallons.

52   *Short-Term Energy Outlook,* U.S. Energy Information Administration, November, 2007.

53   Data from US Department of Energy, Energy Information Administration.

54   Paul Collier, *The Bottom Billion,* Oxford University Press, x.

his or her own version of the American dream of owning a car, a house, a refrigerator, a microwave, and a toaster—we are, at best, going to experience a serious energy shortage.[55]

That prediction is already playing out. We need to find new sources of energy, as well as much more efficient methods of using energy, to welcome these new participants in the world economy.

World Petroleum Production and Demand (million barrels/day)

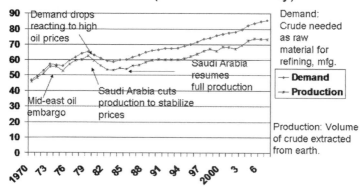

Is there a conspiracy among the big, multinational oil companies to control prices and award themselves big profits? There have been numerous congressional investigations to discover such a conspiracy. Imagine the political windfall that a member of Congress would gain if he or she uncovered such a conspiracy. Imagine the financial whistleblower award that an oil company employee or independent auditor, or any citizen, would earn by disclosing such a conspiracy. Surely a Pulitzer Prize and lucrative book and movie contracts await any investigative reporter who discovers such activity. In spite of the incentives, and all the effort, no such conspiracy has been uncovered.

When we follow the money, evidence points to the nonexistence of such a conspiracy. As we discussed earlier, the big oil companies have very different ROEs. Why would executives of British Petroleum or Royal Dutch Shell conspire with ExxonMobil to accept such dramatically lower ROEs than ExxonMobil? The CEOs of BP and Royal Dutch Shell would fiercely resist it, since their own livelihoods are being hurt by the lower ROEs. ExxonMobil, as current and

---

55   Thomas Friedman, *The World Is Flat*, 2006 edition, 495.

multiyear winner of the ROE competition, would reject any conspiracy, since it would only help a competitor. Could BP and Royal Dutch Shell somehow conspire to compete more effectively against ExxonMobil? No evidence to suggest any such activity between these two has been found, and if such a conspiracy were to exist, it is proving terribly ineffective. ExxonMobil's performance is significantly better than that of its competitors.

There is another problem with the conspiracy theory. Although ExxonMobil is the largest publicly traded oil company in the world, it has drilling rights to less than 3 percent of the world's crude oil reserves. BP and Royal Dutch Shell have even smaller percentages. Saudi Arabia, through its national company Saudi Aramco, controls 25 percent, and through its participation in OPEC, it influences additional crude oil supplies. The numbers just don't support the theory of "greedy shareholders driving oil prices up to boost profits." Saudi Arabia and the other OPEC members have the market share needed to influence the price of crude oil, but the investor-owned major oil companies just don't have the market share needed to influence oil prices.

That leaves us to consider what government does, or should do, to control the price of oil. Many people earnestly believe that "the government" or "the president" should lower the price of crude oil or the price of gasoline. But facts present a problem. American consumers rely on imported crude oil for a large amount of the gasoline, jet fuel, diesel, and petrochemicals (which include pharmaceuticals, artificial flavors, and dyes) that we use every day. Foreign countries with crude oil to sell know that every day consumers around the world will need crude oil, gasoline, and other oil products. Americans use far more than we produce, so ours is not a strong bargaining position.

Our position gets worse every year. Since 1970, U.S. demand for oil has increased 40 percent, but U.S. oil production has dropped 47 percent. World demand for oil has grown more than 50 percent during the same time. America produces 7 percent of the world's crude oil and uses about 25 percent. We use more crude oil and petroleum products, per person, than any other country in the world, about three gallons per day for every American.[56] For comparison, other Organization for Economic Cooperation and Development (OECD) countries consume 1.4 gallons per day per capita, and countries outside the OECD use 0.2 gallons per day per capita. On a typical day, we use about fourteen million barrels more than we produce. We depend on imported crude and

---

56   Demand, production, and consumption per-person data from Energy Information Administration, U.S. Department of Energy, September 2009.

refined products for that difference—fourteen million barrels, every day. Our crude oil imports alone average ten million barrels per day.

In the U.S., unlike most other countries, two-thirds of our crude oil consumption is for transportation, and two-thirds of that is used as gasoline. What you drive, and how many miles you drive, counts far more than any other factor in our dependency on imported crude oil. Regarding supply, every barrel of crude oil produced here is one less imported from abroad.

Crude Oil Production & Demand
United States (million barrels/day)

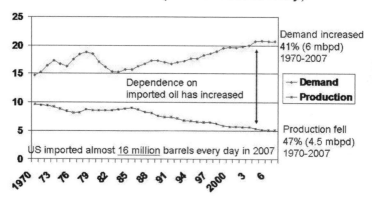

Our government does not control foreign oil; foreign governments do. The supply and demand numbers tell us that we need to put aside the myth that the U.S. government, or the president, controls oil prices or that some high-level meeting, or new energy program, will bring quick relief at the gas pump or in the monthly utility bill. Oil prices are controlled by supply and demand in a global market. Demand in the U.S. and around the world has been rising faster than production, and reserve production capacity has been falling.

———

Let's shift to a different issue. Imagine you are a university president and a member of the board of directors of a hypothetical integrated oil company[57]

---

57   Almost every Fortune 500 corporation has a university president, provost, or distinguished professor on its board of directors. Such "independent" board members (not employees of the corporation) often serve on the compensation committee. Shareholder-owned corporations list their directors in the proxy statement and usually in their Annual Report.

the same size as Royal Dutch Shell, and with the same ROE. As a director, you are painfully aware that ExxonMobil, a company of essentially the same size and in the same business, is performing much better on behalf of its shareholders. Financial analysts who follow the stocks of oil companies are pointing out the ROE differences in their research reports.[58] A few of your corporation's major shareholders, including a major union retirement fund, have sent letters to the board complaining about the company's poor performance compared to other corporations in the same industry. Recognizing your duty as a director to the shareholders of the corporation, you conclude that a new approach to the business is needed to improve your company's ROE. After much discussion, you and your board colleagues decide that the corporation needs a new CEO to improve performance. The chairman of the board dismisses the current CEO, with appropriate announcements to the press, employees, and shareholders, and appoints a search committee to meet with candidates. Senior executives from inside and outside the corporation are considered, and an executive search firm provides two additional names. Meanwhile, the board's compensation committee, of which you are a member, must determine an appropriate package of salary, benefits, and incentives to be offered to the successful candidate. Salary is easy to set—that will be similar to the salaries earned by CEOs at the other similar-size integrated oil companies. But what about the incentive package? Those vary greatly from one oil company to the next.

You consider several relevant bits of information. First, you calculate how much the improved ROE would be worth to the corporation's owners, the shareholders. The board is targeting ROE equal to that of ExxonMobil. Since the amount of shareholder equity for the two corporations is about equal (roughly

---

58   Financial analysts are professionals who study corporations in order to make informed estimates of future profits the corporation will earn. Sales and profit numbers already reported are important considerations, but analysts also study the corporation's current business plans and attempt to estimate the number of customers who will buy the products, whether the corporation will be able to raise prices or be forced to lower them, whether costs of raw materials and wages are growing or shrinking, and ultimately the amount of profit the corporation will be able to earn in coming quarters and years. Analysts may be independent, i.e., employed by companies that sell the analysts' reports to investors and do no investment banking business, or analysts may be employed by investment banks and/or major stock brokerage firms. As many as fifteen or twenty analysts may "follow" (study) a Fortune 500 corporation, each with his or her own methods, arriving at different estimates of future earnings and different investment recommendations, e.g., buy, sell, or hold.

$110 billion), your corporation's profits need to increase from the current $25 billion to $39 billion per year. That's a 56 percent increase. This level of profits has to be sustained. Your shareholders are demanding long-term growth of earnings, not just a one-year aberration. Five years of additional profits at $14 billion per year totals $70 billion.

But the value to the shareholders actually exceeds $70 billion. That is because a major factor in the price of any common stock is the price-to-earnings ratio (P/E ratio). Quite simply, investors buying a share of stock are buying the right to a future stream of earnings. For the stock of a major integrated oil company, investors will typically pay a share price equal to ten or twelve times current earnings per share. That means investors would value the company at about ten or twelve times its annual profits. A $14 billion increase in the company's annual profits, using the same amount of shareholder equity, would very likely produce an increase between $140 billion (10 x $14 billion) and $168 billion (12 x $14 billion) in the valuation of the company once the higher level of profits and ROE is recognized as sustainable. Even the humble gain of $140 billion in share equity would more than double the starting point equity of $110 billion. Current shareholders would be quite pleased with that, since the price of every share would reflect that increased value!

How much incentive award or bonus should the CEO receive for that achievement? You recognize your responsibility to get someone who can do the job and get the required financial results. The incentive plan should tie the CEO's reward to just how much the profits, and share price, improve over the years ahead.

What part of the $140 billion should be considered as the CEO's bonus for designing and driving this achievement? Just one tenth of one percent of the total would be $140 million! Shareholders are saying they are tired of getting "second-best" results. The board wants to get the best possible person for this job. To succeed, the new CEO will have to devise a new strategy or find some other way to dramatically boost performance. The eighty thousand–plus employees around the world need a leader who can motivate them to produce their best work.[59] The few really top candidates are already well-paid. Some are probably being sought by other corporations, including your competitors. The candidates and the competing companies have all the same information regarding profits, ROE, etc.,[60] and they can do the math. They understand the impact of profits on

---

59   ExxonMobil and BP have eighty thousand employees. Royal Dutch Shell has one hundred thousand employees.

60   Every shareholder-owned corporation in the U.S. is required to prepare an annual report to shareholders and file a copy with the Securities and Exchange

share price. They know that achieving those results will take real skill and leadership. Your offer needs to be very attractive indeed.

You also need to prepare a severance package for your prospective CEO. All of the candidates know that the average tenure of a CEO in a major corporation is six years, since boards are increasingly aggressive in removing CEOs for weak performance.[61] The candidates are all in their early or mid-forties, and losing a CEO job would end their career long before normal retirement age. What will you and your compensation committee colleagues recommend to the board? So much depends on getting just the right person, not another "second-best." Later chapters will identify those shareholders and explore their eagerness for profits.

————

How does the 35.1 percent return on equity that ExxonMobil earned in 2006, or the 24.7 percent five-year average ROE, compare to the ROE of corporations in other businesses? We'll look at some "alternative energy" companies, and then at several other industries, to make this comparison.

Commission, as well as quarterly reports. Each of these must present financial statements prepared in accordance with generally accepted accounting principles (GAAP). The financial controls must be audited by an independent certified public accounting (CPA) firm. The CPA firm, after conducting tests of the firm's accounting and financial management systems, and confirming such items as it deems appropriate (bank balances, inventories, etc.), signs a statement that the financial reports present accurately the condition of the corporation during the period or specific date shown on the report. If the CPA firm disagrees with management's presentation of the financials, the disagreement will be described in the auditor's statement. As noted earlier, within specific industries, there are many independent analysts who scrutinize and "second guess" these reports and publish their own estimates of the corporation's likely future financial results. This may not be a perfect system, but it is regarded as one of the best in the world, and it is, as they say, the coin of the realm. People rely on this information. You can find the annual and quarterly reports on the corporation's website.

61   National Bureau of Economic Research, Working Paper 12465, by Steven N. Kaplan and Bernadette A. Minton.

Chapter Four
Alternative Energy

	Sales 2007 (Billions)	Net Profit 2006 (Billions)	Shareholder Equity on 12/31/05	ROE 2006 %	Average Annual Profit 2002–2006 (Billions)	Average Shareholder Equity 2002–2006 (Billions)	5-Year Average ROE '02–'06
Suntech Power	$.599	$.106	$.402	20.1	N/A	N/A	N/A
First Solar	$.135	$.004	$.013	0.9	N/A	N/A	N/A
SunPower	$.237	$.027	$.259	5.4	N/A	N/A	N/A

Innovation creates new opportunities and new challenges. Many companies of various sizes are developing solutions to the world's need for less expensive, cleaner forms of energy. Suntech Power, First Solar, and SunPower are just three of the numerous companies making photovoltaic cells and solar panels, which convert sunlight into electric power. Photovoltaic cells assembled into solar panels are becoming popular as a "clean" source of energy (e.g., no greenhouse gas output) and as a method of generating electricity in remote parts of the world.

Suntech Power Holdings Co., Ltd., commenced operations in 2002. The company was first organized in China, and its operating headquarters are still there. To expand its manufacturing facilities, the corporation needed to raise capital from investors outside China. A holding company was established in the Cayman Islands, and it went public by selling twenty-six million shares of stock at $15 each in 2005. Anyone with $15 could become a part-owner of the corporation, and the shares would then be traded on major stock exchanges. The company now has manufacturing facilities in Shanghai and in Goodyear, Arizona, and sells its photovoltaic panels in eighty countries.

SunPower Corporation was founded in California in 1985. Twenty years later, the corporation made its first offering of stock to the public, selling the shares at $18 each. The share prices moved higher or lower throughout every trading day as buyers and sellers made their own decisions about the value of the stock and its future prospects. Some made a profit, others lost money. By late 2007, the shares hit a high of $164 as investors sought to participate in the solar industry. By the close of business on April 28, 2011, the stock was selling at $16.12 per share. On that day, Total, a global oil, gas, and chemical company based in France, offered to buy 60 percent of the shares from existing shareholders for $23.25 per share. Anyone owning shares on that date could receive a 44 percent "premium" by selling to Total. Total, by acquiring the shares, earned the right to participate in future profits of SunPower. Since Total would own and therefore vote 60 percent of SunPower shares, it will be able to affect the selection of board directors and other strategic issues. SunPower Corporation will most likely benefit from this alliance with Total's business connections in 130 countries. Total's strong finances will allow SunPower Corporation to borrow money for expansion at a lower interest rate than it could negotiate on its own.

Transactions such as this, in which a large corporation buys all or a majority of a small or midsize corporation, are part of the competitive discipline enforced by consumers. If SunPower is to provide competitive products and pricing, it must operate efficiently and hold its own costs, including the cost of debt, to a minimum. The need for larger manufacturing plants, international sales and distribution networks, and continuing research and development persuade owners of many growing companies to sell to larger firms. Large corporations need new products to meet changing customer demands. By acquiring a corporation with patents for proven technologies, the larger corporation (the buyer) avoids the expense and risk of doing its own research and development. In this case, Total expanded its product line by acquiring SunPower. While small businesses are vital to technology development and job growth, big corporations are vital to propelling these technologies to their full potential. Acquisitions are one path to the goal that all businesses share: satisfying the customer.

Another competitor in the solar energy industry is First Solar, Inc., which was founded in 1999 and conducted research and development until early 2002, when it undertook commercial operations designing and manufacturing solar modules. The company did not become profitable until 2006 and did not become a public company until November of that year. The corporate office is in California. Manufacturing plants are located in Ohio, Germany, and Malaysia. First Solar uses a thin-cell technology and cadmium telluride rather than the crystalline silicon used by most other solar panel manufacturers. First Solar faces all the challenges of any corporation trying to grow its sales and profits, as well as the special challenges of ramping up production while continuously improving the energy efficiency of its solar panels.

All of the alternative energy companies face the challenges inherent in growth. The skills required for leading a large high-technology manufacturing business with thousands of employees differ from those required to lead a research and development firm with a laboratory and a few employees. Many entrepreneurial founders seek experienced executives from larger corporations to manage that growth. Combining small-company innovation with big-company experience can help grow a business, thus creating more jobs and serving more customers.

All solar manufacturers face the challenge to reduce the cost of producing a kilowatt of electricity from current levels if solar is to become a significant part of the world's energy. At present, no solar technology is cost-effective compared to electricity from conventional power plants. Many of the customers who install solar panels currently rely on subsidies or tax credits from their respective federal or state government to reduce the cost of a solar installation.[62] Germany has been especially generous with subsidies to its citizens, but the country is now reducing the amount of such assistance. These companies are all trying to reach "grid parity"—a status in which the cost to generate a given amount of electricity from solar power will be equal to the cost of generating the same amount of electricity on the commercial electric grid. At that point, of course, government subsidies would be unnecessary and sales of solar panels should increase dramatically. Sales and profits would skyrocket for whichever company is first to achieve "grid parity."

Those potential rewards—profits—have attracted substantial investment into these corporations. That invested capital has funded the research and experimentation needed to develop a saleable panel and to continue improving the

---

62 Government subsidies are generally paid for installation of any system that meets certain minimum standards of energy production. This approach rewards the mediocre as well as the superior technology and is hardly an incentive to put more money into research and development.

panels. Every year, the cost per kilowatt drops as competitors race toward grid parity. Investment has also allowed the building of factories to produce solar cells and panels for sale to customers who want them now, even if the "payback" in lower utility bills will take many years.

———

Rentech, Inc., was incorporated in 1981. The company's patented technology converts biomass, including lawn clippings and shrubs, into synthetic gas for electric power generation. The process also allows fossil-based fuels, including coal, to be upgraded into ultra-clean diesel and jet fuel. The process has been proven in commercial jets. For many years, commercial airlines based in South Africa have used a fifty/fifty mixture of conventional oil-based jet fuel and coal-based ultra-clean jet fuel. Every gallon of ultra-clean fuel eliminates a gallon of oil-based fuel. More recently, the United States Air Force has certified the mixture for use in its military jets. The "cradle to grave" emissions of nitrogen oxide, sulfur oxide, and particulate matter are lower for this fuel than for other liquid fuels. The fuels produced by the Rentech process can be used without modification in existing diesel and jet engines.

The largest portion of America's energy usage is transportation, and most of that is personally owned automobiles. We cannot address our dependence on foreign oil or make major reductions in environmental damage unless we find fuels that reduce our oil-derived gasoline, diesel fuel, and jet fuel.

But there is another reason for enthusiasm about these innovations. New employment opportunities are heavily dependent on innovation. Electric lighting became available in the late 1800s. Thomas Edison's first municipal generating station produced its first electric power, supplying street lights, in 1882. The White House was wired for electric lighting in 1891. Workmen from other trades and young men seeking their first jobs learned how to install wiring and fixtures. They became the first electricians. At first, only the wealthy could afford to replace the gas fixtures in their homes or build new homes with electric lighting. As the technology became more widely accepted, more electricians were needed. The transition was gradual, but it brought new employment opportunities. By 1900, the *Statistical Abstract of the United States*, published by the Bureau of the Census, reported fifty thousand electricians working in the United States—a job category that had not been recorded in 1890.

Rentech is planning a commercial-scale plant for converting biomass into jet fuel and diesel, to be built in Adams County, Mississippi. Construction will employ twenty-one hundred people directly and generate another thirty-four hundred jobs indirectly. Once built, the plant will employ four hundred people on site and most likely support an additional thirty-two hundred jobs. As additional plants are built, the number of jobs created by this new technology will grow. Job growth depends on innovation.

As the table at the beginning of the chapter shows, these companies have short histories as public companies, and most have not established consistent profit records. In any of these, an investor takes on quite a bit more risk than would be involved in, for example, drilling for oil. One or more of these companies may not survive, especially if their particular technology proves incapable of reaching grid parity. Even today, newer private companies, not yet publicly traded, are developing new solar technologies or improving existing methods. Check out Xunlight Corporation, founded as a technology spin-off from the University of Toledo.[63]

The potential for large profits, and thus higher share prices, draws investment into these high-risk businesses. One or more companies may develop and manufacture alternative energy systems that will be important to the world's population and welcomed by the world's consumers. One or more may fail completely, and its investors will sustain real financial loss. Can you pick the winners and losers? Would you put your own money at risk by investing in these innovations?

Investors and the analysts who follow these companies after they become publicly traded corporations impose discipline upon the business. They seek out the most promising technology and the best management teams and monitor ongoing performance, thereby ensuring that each company works diligently and smartly toward the goal—in this case, clean energy systems for customers worldwide. Investors seek technology that customers will recognize as providing real value; that is the path to profits. Technology that fails to draw customers is abandoned, and the remaining capital, if any, moves to more promising places.

That same process of allocating investment capital sorted out the technologies that were competing in the race to provide energy for factories and homes more than one hundred years ago. That is why electric light bulbs beat out gas lights as the successor to kerosene lamps. Alternating current was selected over direct current, and central power generation plants were built instead of small generating units in every customer's home or business. Potbellied wood stoves and hand-stoked coal furnaces gave way to automatic heating systems using gas

---

63   Xunlight Corporation's website: www.xunlight.com

or oil and, more recently, geothermal energy. There were winners and losers in those investments also. Constantly allocating and reallocating capital to technologies based on the value they will have for customers seems a rough and tumble game. Some people get rich, or at least find stable employment and attractive compensation, while others suffer lost investment dollars or plant closings and unemployment.

Since the public financial history of the alternative energy companies does not give us multiyear ROE figures for 2002–2006 to compare with other corporations, we'll move on to some other industry groups and look at corporations in each of them as we try to determine a "normal" ROE. The alternative energy business is just one example of how the quest for profits brings people to risk their savings in development of new products. Research and development (R&D) is a substantial expense in the pharmaceutical business, which we'll explore next.

Chapter Five

"Big Pharma"

	Sales 2006 (Billions)	Net Profit 2006 (Billions)	Shareholder Equity on 12/31/05 (Billions)	ROE 2006 %	Average Annual Profit 2002–2006 (Billions)	Average Shareholder Equity 2002–2006 (Billions)	5-Year Avge ROE 2002–2006
Pfizer	$48.4	$15	$65.6	21	$2.6	$11.7	22.5
Glaxo SmithKline	$42.9	$10.1	$13	55.3	$7.9	$13.5	58.8
Merck	$22.6	$5.5	$17.9	31.4	$6.1	$17.3	35

Pfizer[64] is the largest pharmaceutical company in the world, based on sales and on shareholder equity. Its brand-name prescription medications include Lipitor, Celebrex, Zoloft, and Norvasc. Pfizer's home office is in New York, but almost 50 percent of total sales are outside the U.S. Pfizer also manufactures popular over-the-counter products such as Listerine, Benadryl, Rolaids, Visine, and Purell. Pfizer employs approximately ninety-eight thousand people.

Pfizer traces its history back to 1849, when it was founded by Charles Pfizer and his cousin, Charles Erhart, using $2,500 borrowed from Pfizer's father. In 1928 Alexander Fleming discovered the antibiotic properties of penicillin mold while working as a researcher at St. Mary's Hospital in London. That event made medical history, but failed to significantly change medical practice because the

---

64   Much of the following information is from Pfizer's website, www.pfizer.com.

antibiotic could not be reliably and economically produced. Penicillin research was taken up again in 1939 by Oxford University researchers Ernst Chain and Howard Florey.[65] The production process remained impractical until Pfizer adopted its deep-tank fermentation process, originally developed for citric acid production, to penicillin. During World War II, the company invested millions of dollars of shareholder money into equipment and facilities for this new method of mass-producing penicillin, the "miracle drug" in the fight against bacterial infection.[66] By many measures, Pfizer is a great company.

But investors are looking for profits that reward their investment. Pfizer's one-year and five-year ROE lag far behind its nearest (in shareholder equity) competitor, GlaxoSmithKline, and are much weaker than the ROEs produced by the much smaller Merck. Will the major difference in ROE persuade some investors to sell their Pfizer shares and buy GlaxoSmithKline or Merck shares? How does Pfizer's board of directors react to this key measure of their stewardship of investors' funds? In 2007, the board appointed Jeffrey Kindler as the new CEO for the company. Kindler has embarked on a number of initiatives to reinvigorate Pfizer's profits and ROE. As one of these initiatives, Pfizer is taking the novel step of investing, as a venture capitalist,[67] in a variety of small medical research companies that have new drugs in the early stages of clinical testing. Not every one of these investments will lead to a new successful medicine. A successful venture capital investment usually takes about eight years to produce any profit, either by sale of the company or by finally launching a new, approved medicine. Meanwhile, the research company uses the venture capital funds to pay salaries and other operating expenses during the years of research and testing that must precede any sale of the medication.

---

65   Fleming, Chain and Florey received the Nobel Prize in Medicine in 1945 for their work with penicillin.

66   Pfizer corporate history available at http://www.pfizer.com

67   Venture capitalists are individuals or groups of individuals, or companies, who provide money to young companies ("startups") that own promising technology patents or research data in exchange for an equity share of the company. The companies seeking venture capital are often too small, or too new, to issue stock to the public, and they need long-term investor commitments, usually for eight to ten years, to fund ongoing research and product development until the product is eventually ready to manufacture and sell. Since many new products, including new medicines, eventually prove unsuccessful, venture capitalism in the pharmaceutical industry is considered high-risk investing. The investors are hoping that with careful selection, perhaps one in twenty of their startups will eventually produce a profitable product.

Will Pfizer's new strategy work? Fortunately, investors are willing to take the risk that the strategy will boost profits in the future. And society will benefit from the new medicines.

Manufacturers in all industries devote part of their sales revenue to research and development (R&D) to improve current products or develop new ones. Pharmaceutical and medical device (e.g., pacemakers, stents, artificial joints, etc.) manufacturers have the highest R&D expenses as a percentage of sales. In 2003, major pharmaceutical firms channeled 13 percent to 19 percent of sales into R&D. For medical device makers, the reinvestment into R&D was typically 10 percent to 16 percent of sales. This huge reinvestment funds a steady search for new remedies for human ailments.

Most of the major contributions of pharmaceutical research have occurred during the last century. Access to health care is often affected by household income, insurance coverage, and geographic location. But when the President of the United States or his immediate family is ill or injured, the finest medical care is immediately available. That has been true since the early days of our republic. Tracking the medical care of our First Families provides a dramatic review of the progress in the best available medical and pharmaceutical science.

President William McKinley was shot at close range while shaking hands with well-wishers visiting the Pan-American Exposition at Buffalo, New York, on September 6, 1901. One chest wound proved superficial; that bullet fell out as he was being moved. The second .32 caliber bullet entered his abdomen. Within ten minutes, he was at the Exposition's emergency hospital and attended to by no less than six physicians. Surgery began one hour and twenty minutes after the shooting, led by Dr. Matthew Mann, professor of obstetrics, and assisted by Dr. Herman Mynter, professor of operative surgery at the University of Buffalo. The White House physician, Dr. Presley Rixey, who would later become surgeon-general of the U.S. Navy, was also present. Ether was administered as the anesthetic. Ether is highly flammable and it precluded the use of the gas lights in the room. During the surgery, strychnine and later brandy were given hypodermically to regulate the pulse. At the conclusion of the operation, morphine was given for pain.

The patient was then transferred by ambulance to the home of John Milburn, president of the Exposition. The physicians periodically issued bulletins on McKinley's condition, reporting that the patient was progressing well. Occasionally, digitalis or strychnine was administered as needed to regulate the pulse. As days passed, the physicians were particularly relieved there were no signs of peritonitis. During the first six days after surgery, he was given three to six enemas per day. By then the president was taking beef juice for nourishment, and he was in good spirits. The following day, he had some toast and coffee in the morning, but by afternoon he was complaining of nausea and headache, and his skin was noted as moist and cold. Around midnight, oxygen inhalation was started and salt solution administered subcutaneously. The president was still able to take whiskey and water, as well as clam broth and chicken broth by mouth, but no solid food. Hypodermics of camphorated oil were given, in addition to hypodermic strychnine, adrenaline, and brandy to regulate the pulse. At 5 p.m. on the eighth day post-op, the bulletin described the president's condition as grave. Oxygen was resumed. From this point, his condition deteriorated, and at 2:15 a.m. on the ninth day after the shooting he died.[68]

At autopsy, the cause of death was determined to be primarily the damage to tissues caused by the bullet, which led to gangrene involving the stomach, pancreas, and kidney, along with degenerated condition of the muscle tissue of the heart.[69]

Two cases emphasize dramatically the impact of antibiotics. In 1924, Calvin Coolidge Jr., the sixteen-year-old son of the president of the United States, developed a blister on his toe while playing tennis. He put some iodine on it and went about his normal activities. Two days later, he felt weak and complained of pain in his leg, and the White House physician examined him. Antiseptic dressings were applied and the teen was confined to bed for rest. Blood samples examined microscopically revealed *Streptococcus pyogenes*, a bacterial pathogen that is especially dangerous if it enters the bloodstream, as in this case. The boy was taken to Walter Reed Hospital, and every available medical expert on blood infections was consulted.

Physicians were powerless once this bacterium had entered the bloodstream. In *Handbook of Therapy—Seventh Edition*, written in June 1923 by Oliver T. Osborne, MD, professor of therapeutics at Yale University, and Morris Fishbein, MD, assistant to the editor, *Journal of the American Medical Association*, and published by the AMA, there are no antibiotics in the list of useful drugs. For infections such as this or pneumonia, the treatment consisted of cooling the fever, regulating the pulse with digitalis, strophanthin or possibly strychnine, and using epinephrine or caffeine to support blood pressure. But the blood infection,

---

68   *Medical and Surgical Report of the Case of President McKinley, by Presley M. Rixey, Medical Inspector, U.S. Navy,* reprinted in *U.S. Navy Medicine,* vol. 59, March 1972, p. 45–53.

69   *Notes on the Autopsy on President McKinley, September 14, 1901, by Presley M. Rixey, Medical Inspector, U.S. Navy,* reprinted in *U.S. Navy Medicine,* vol. 59, March 1972, p. 53–56.

known as septicemia, would take its own course. Young Coolidge passed away seven days after getting the blister.[70]

In 1936, Franklin D. Roosevelt Jr., son of the president, had every reason to look forward to life. He was healthy, a senior at Harvard, recently engaged to Ethel du Pont and well liked in her family of chemical company magnates. One day before Thanksgiving, a sinus infection became serious enough to warrant admission to Massachusetts General Hospital. Physicians at first expected the infection to resolve itself after a few days of rest. But the patient's recovery was unsteady and slow. Eleanor Roosevelt, called from Washington as her son's condition worsened, arranged for the best specialist in the area to take charge of the case. He examined Franklin and became concerned about an abscess under the patient's cheek. Lab tests confirmed that a severe strep infection had affected the sinuses and throat and might spread to the bloodstream. The patient's fever was persistent. The specialist, Dr. George Loring Tobey Jr., was aware of a new drug named Prontosil and obtained a supply from the U.S. subsidiary of the German pharmaceutical firm Bayer. The drug had been developed after years of experimentation by several European scientists, all looking for some treatment effective against infections that had entered the body. Sulfa, the active ingredient in Prontosil, had been identified in the lab as effective against strep, and only recently a study involving a large number of patients had confirmed its effectiveness in humans suffering strep infections. The drug was administered, and within twenty-four hours, the fever had dropped, the swelling subsided, and the patient was more energetic. While several weeks of rest were still needed to fully recover from the sinus infection, the strep had been defeated. When the press learned that a new drug had saved the life of the president's son, the new wonder drug was publicized to the world. The headlines described a dramatic discovery that had taken place just a few days before Christmas in 1932. The long years of trial and error leading to the discovery were not mentioned.[71]

President Eisenhower awoke in the middle of the night of September 23–24, 1955, with severe chest pain. Just short of his sixty-sixth birthday, he was in Denver, Colorado, in the midst of a working vacation. His wife called the White House physician, Dr. Harold Snyder, who arrived at 3 a.m. Immediately suspecting a coronary thrombosis, he had the president sniff an amyl nitrite capsule and gave injections of papaverine, a vasodilator, and morphine to relieve pain and anxiety. The president's blood pressure, pulse, and respirations were carefully monitored. Once the pain subsided, he was able to sleep until 1 p.m. and then an

---

70   Thomas Hager, *The Demon Under the Microscope,* 100-102.
71   Thomas Hager, *The Demon Under the Microscope,* 186-191.

electrocardiogram was taken to investigate the extent of heart muscle damage. At that point, the president was driven to the hospital at a nearby military base. Papaverine and morphine were administered regularly over the next few days. On the third day, phenobarbital was substituted for morphine and continued for several weeks. Coumadin, a blood thinner, was given by mouth on the first day. Then heparin, another blood thinner, was administered intravenously several times during the second day. Coumadin was resumed on the fourth day and continued through the first week after the attack. For the first week, an oxygen tent was draped over the president's bed. Quinidine, an antiarrhythmic drug, was also administered on the second through the fifth days.[72]

The Secret Service report of the president's hospitalization gives additional details of treatment. The president's breakfast on September 28, just five days after the attack, consisted of sausage, eggs, toast, and milk. Lunch consisted of broiled steak, baked potato, buttered asparagus, and a slice of bread, fresh fruit, and buttermilk. Dinner was vegetable soup, cold roast beef, cold ham, sliced tomatoes, one half slice of whole wheat bread, butter, pineapple chunks, and buttermilk.[73] The role of cholesterol in heart disease was unknown.

President Eisenhower recovered steadily and resumed running Cabinet meetings and attending to his other duties by Christmas.

––––

ExxonMobil's profit far exceeded any of the major drug companies. In fact, ExxonMobil's profits for 2006 were more than the total of the three largest drug companies. But when we consider the dollars of shareholder equity involved to produce the profits and compare the return on equity, ExxonMobil's 2006 ROE is far below that of GlaxoSmithKline, and the five-year average return for Exxon Mobil is not much higher than Pfizer's, and it's lower than the five-year returns of Merck and GlaxoSmithKline.

Are big oil companies and big pharmaceutical companies somehow taking advantage of the public and taking profit dollars and high ROE because of the unique positions these industries have in society? What's a *normal* ROE, where there isn't the pressure of "I have to buy it, no matter the cost"?

---

72   Letter from Dr. Harold Snyder to William E. Robinson, October 5, 1955. Courtesy of the Eisenhower Presidential Library, Abilene, Kansas.
73   Report of Special Agent in Charge James Howley to Secret Service Chief, dated September 29, 1955. Courtesy of the Eisenhower Presidential Library, Abilene, Kansas.

Chapter Six

Consumer Staples

	Sales 2006 (Billions)	Net Profit 2006 (Billions)	Shareholder Equity on 12/31/05 (Billions)	ROE 2006 %	Average Annual Profit 2002-06 (Billions)	Average Shareholder Equity 2002-06 (Billions)	5-Year Avge ROE 2002-2006
Anheuser-Busch	$15.7	$1.966	$3.3	49.8	$2.02	$3.1	64
Kellogg	$10.9	$1.0	$2.28	48.5	$.874	$1.79	48
General Mills	$11.6	$1.1	$5.7	18.9	$.973	$4.89	20
Heinz	$9.0	$.792	$2.05	43.0	$.772	$1.9	40
Altria	$101.4	$12.0	$35.7	30.3	$10.14	$30.1	33.7

Anheuser-Busch is the world's largest brewer, operator of several large theme parks in the U.S., and the world's largest recycler of aluminum beverage cans. Budweiser, Michelob, and O'Doul's are some of its best-known brands, and this corporation owns a 27 percent equity stake in Tsingtao (China) and 100 percent of Harbin (China). Anheuser-Busch is the exclusive U.S. importer of Stella Artois, Beck's, Bass Pale Ale, and several other foreign-made brands. Anheuser-Busch's beers are popular—they represent 50 percent market share in the U.S. and 9 percent of all the beer consumed in the world. What a happy balance of affairs: thirty thousand employees have gainful employment, the world has the beer that it wants, and shareholders enjoy a five-year average ROE of 64 percent—more than twice the five-year average ROE of ExxonMobil.[74]

Kellogg presents a similar intriguing story. Kellogg is the world's largest manufacturer of ready-to-eat cereals. Whether you prefer Frosted Flakes, Rice Krispies, Special K, Froot Loops, Frosted Mini-Wheats, Pop-Tarts, All Bran, or Nutri-Grain, Kellogg made it for you. Of course, you can select from a competitor's products. General Mills makes the popular Cheerios—America's best-selling cereal—and Wheaties, Total, and Trix. There's plenty of competition in the grocery aisles.

General Mills sales in 2006 were about 7 percent higher than Kellogg's, but General Mills had about 10 percent more employees. The average employee at Kellogg is producing almost 3 percent more dollars of food sales than his or her counterpart at General Mills. Is this because of better training, better equipment, or some other factor? How does management at General Mills account for the much lower ROE and less efficient deployment of people? These are big, multiyear differences in ROE. Shareholders do see a difference.

––––

America's food supply has changed dramatically since the early 1900s. Consumer pressure, government regulation, and the quest to grow profits have brought about an industry in which small and large businesses offer a wide assortment of foods, beverages, meats, fish, poultry, and ever more detail in product labels. There are products for consumers with particular dietary concerns, such as celiac disease, lactose intolerance, or diabetes. A century ago, all foods were organic. Antibiotics had not been discovered. There were no artificial colors, flavors, or preservatives. Today, organic foods are becoming more available as a growing number of consumers decide that chemical-free food is worth the higher price. Convenience stores, pizza shops, frozen ready-to-eat meals, and fast food restaurants compete with mom's home cooking as more consumers decide to outsource their food preparation work.

America's diet today is also the result of a century of research into disease etiology and nutrition. In 1900, city dwellers were sometimes victims of food that had been deliberately adulterated to conceal spoilage. Raw milk was sold, unpasteurized, direct from the farm. A few people thought that cows infected

––––

74   In 2008, Anheuser-Busch merged with InBev to form Anheuser-Busch InBev N.V. The corporate headquarters are in Belgium.

with tuberculosis might be spreading that disease, but no formal research had confirmed that. Dairy farmers drank the raw milk, as did their families. Surely that attested to the safety of the product. There were dietary problems in rural areas also. Rickets had long been recognized as a disease that caused softening of the bones, especially noticeable in children. Hookworm was another affliction, much more common in southern climates. The causes and cures of these ailments were not well understood. In the first years of the new century, a new and more frightening disease was spreading.

In 1902, a doctor in Georgia reported symptoms matching those of pellagra in a patient who had sought treatment for ankylostomiasis (hookworm).[75] Pellagra had been documented as a specific condition by a Spanish physician as early as 1735. Pellagra had always been thought to be confined to southern Europe, and many American physicians knew nothing of the disease. But their European colleagues knew it as a scourge. Symptoms progressed in a matter of months from dermatitis and diarrhea to dementia and, in many cases, death. There was no cure.

A doctor in Alabama found an outbreak of pellagra among black patients at the Mount Vernon Insane Hospital in the summer of 1906. Eighty-eight patients were diagnosed. Sixty-four percent of those patients died that summer. When the Medical Association of Alabama published the report, physicians across the state took notice. The *Journal of the American Medical Association* also published the report. The staggering death rate alerted physicians across the country to a new and frightening ailment.[76]

The early reports of pellagra in America were tentative in their diagnoses, since respected medical writers considered pellagra to be a European disease, not present in America. *Pediatrics,* a comprehensive review published in 1901 by Thomas Morgan Rotch, professor of diseases of children at Harvard University, is more than seven hundred pages long. It discusses numerous skin and digestive disorders, but it does not mention pellagra. *Principles and Practice of Medicine,* by Sir William Osler, was perhaps the most respected single medical resource of the era. Osler discusses pellagra as a nutritional disturbance due to altered maize, occurring extensively in parts of Italy, in the south of France, and in Spain, but

75   H. F. Harris, *A Case of Ankylostomaisis Presenting the Symptoms of Pellagra.* Transactions: Medical Association of Georgia (1902), 220–227. Courtesy of the Medical Association of Georgia.
76   G. H. Searcy, *"An Epidemic of Acute Pellagra,"* Transactions, Medical Association State of Alabama, 387–392, 1907.

states that the disease is not found in America.[77] Some local physicians were reluctant to contradict these authorities.

In 1908, the *American Journal of Insanity* published a report on pellagra cases in the South Carolina State Hospital for the Insane, prepared by the hospital's medical staff.[78] One of the authors, Harvard-trained Dr. James Woods Babcock, visited Italy that year to observe pellagra patients there and confer with their physicians. Babcock's trip to Italy strengthened his conviction that the disease he confronted in America was pellagra. After the trip, he persuaded the South Carolina Board of Health to hold a conference on pellagra in Columbia, in December 1908. A second conference was held the following year, drawing hundreds of physicians from around the country and abroad. They reported numerous outbreaks of the disease, mainly in orphanages, mental hospitals, and prisons.[79]

By 1909, pellagra cases were documented in twenty-two states, including New York, Pennsylvania, Massachusetts, and Illinois. The U.S. Public Health Service sent postcards to physicians and state health authorities, requesting information on any cases they had treated. An investigation of pellagra cases at the Illinois Hospital for the Insane concluded that impure water was responsible for the outbreak, while stating that corn and other starchy foods may have contributed by affecting the intestines.[80]

The New York Academy of Medicine invited Dr. Babcock and Dr. J. J. Watson, also of South Carolina, to present their findings. In the preceding year, 12 percent of the patients admitted to the South Carolina State Asylum had pellagra. Babcock and Watson reported that moldy or spoiled corn had not been proven to cause pellagra, but that evidence tended to support the theory. Dr. Watson described the mental depression found in serious cases as "varying from one of the blues to acute melancholia, always accompanied by hallucinations and delusions, the sufferer imagining that even his nearest relatives have turned against him."[81]

---

77   William Osler, *Principles and Practice of Medicine*, Fourth Edition (1901), 395.

78   *What Are Pellagra and Pellagrous Insanity? Does Such a Disease Exist in South Carolina, and What Are Its Causes?* vol. 64 (4):703. (1908).

79   William S. Hall, *Psychiatrist, Humanitarian, and Scholar: James Woods Babcock, M.D.* Journal of the South Carolina Medical Association, October 1970. Courtesy of the South Carolina Medical Association.

80   *"More Causes of Pellagra,"* New York Times, October 9, 1909.

81   *"Pellagra Victim Shown to Doctors,"* New York Times, December 17, 1909.

People were frightened. This "new" disease turned healthy adults into disoriented, helpless victims. Many died within months. It was spreading rapidly, and no one knew why. Physicians were at a loss to explain the disease, although there was no lack of theories. Perhaps Italian immigrants had brought it to this country. Maybe some poison was affecting the food supply. The *Southern Medical Journal* published a paper in July 1911 listing six different theories of causation, followed by the assessment that, "These various and conflicting ideas of etiology permit, as yet, no precise conclusions." While noting that mortality statistics were meager, especially regarding cases treated at home, these physician-authors reported, "A death rate of 35 to 65 percent noted in asylum cases is, we believe, none too low for the cases treated at home throughout the southern states."[82] The Public Health Service opened a special ward for pellagra research in Savannah, Georgia.

As early as 1905, Dr. Louis W. Sambon of the London School of Tropical Medicine had offered a theory that pellagra was spread by a blood-sucking insect acting as an intermediate host. That had been demonstrated as the method of spreading malaria just a few years earlier, bringing the 1902 Nobel Prize in Medicine to Dr. Ronald Ross. Pellagra, like malaria, was far more prevalent in warmer climates. Also, Sambon had seen pellagra patients in England and Scotland and in several other European areas where people did not eat corn. In 1910, Sambon studied pellagra in Italy and wrote that the responsible insect might be the buffalo fly. Meanwhile, Dr. Babcock had been steadily mobilizing his community and state against this disease.

A two-year study was launched in 1912 in Spartanburg County, South Carolina. Two wealthy merchants, Col. Robert M. Thompson of New York City and J. H. McFadden of Philadelphia, donated $15,000 to finance the project. With this assurance of ample funding, the commission considered the full spectrum of theories about the disease. The research team was led by Dr. Joseph Siler of the U.S. Army Medical Corps. Siler had worked with Sambon in Italy. Two entomologists were brought along, since insects were considered possible carriers. Local physicians referred 284 patients to the team, and a detailed lifestyle questionnaire was completed for each. Working through the spring and summer, when pellagra symptoms typically appeared, the commission conducted the most intensive and systematic research on pellagra to date.

---

82 Gilman J. Winthrop and H. P. Cole, *"The Etiology and Treatment of Pellagra,"* *Southern Medical Journal,* July 1911, Volume 4, Issue 6, p. 484–487.

The commission carefully investigated climate, sanitation, water supplies, dwelling conditions, economic and financial circumstances, occupation, individual and family medical history, distribution of cases by age, sex and race, presence of various insects, and the seasonality of cases. There were laboratory studies of blood, urine, feces, and stomach contents. Intestinal bacteria from a larger group of patients were studied.

The Commission's 148-page report on its first season of work contains numerous charts and tables of data. Some of the findings were startling. In the general population of the county, women contracted pellagra at three times the rate of men, and in the age group twenty to forty-four, women showed a rate of infection nine times greater than the male rate. There were two whites in Spartanburg County for every black, but whites with pellagra outnumbered blacks by ten to one.

The researchers concluded that ingestion of good or spoiled maize as the essential cause of pellagra was not supported by the study, that pellagra was probably an infectious disease communicable from person to person by means unknown. The researchers also discounted the buffalo fly as responsible, but proposed that if a blood-sucking insect were involved, then the *Stomoxys calcitrans* (stable fly) would be the most probable carrier. Then came the final conclusion: "No specific cause of pellagra has been recognized."[83]

Leading citizens in Spartanburg proposed to open a new charity hospital for the study and treatment of pellagra. Presidents of three large cotton mills in the area pledged $7,000 to launch the fundraising effort. Merchants, other mill owners, and the public were also asked to contribute.[84] A building was made available for the hospital and lab at nominal rent. Similar efforts were underway in Georgia and Illinois.

The Public Health Service continued to gather data and conduct field investigations of outbreaks where requested by state authorities. Cases were reported from forty states and the District of Columbia. The death rate among reported cases in Texas was 47 percent. In Oklahoma and Virginia, the death rate exceeded 50 percent.[85]

---

83   J. F. Siler, P. E. Garrison, and W. J. MacNeal, *First Progress Report of the Thompson-McFadden Pellagra Commission of the New York Post-Graduate Medical School and Hospital.*

84   "Put Pellagra Cases in South at 50,000," *New York Times,* December 3, 1912.

85   Annual Report of the Surgeon General, 1913, p. 253–54. NARA II.

In 1913, the Thompson-McFadden Commission resumed its studies in Spartanburg, with the new hospital and laboratory at its disposal. The entire county was surveyed again to build on the data collected in the first year. A total of 847 cases of pellagra were found, three times more than in the prior year. The researchers also completed a more intense house-to-house study of six mill villages in Spartanburg County where pellagra cases seemed to be concentrated. Researchers recorded the sex, age, race, occupation, and details of the food habits of each family. The database covered more than five thousand people, including 115 suffering from pellagra. Local physicians again cooperated in the work, and this year, specialists from other areas of the country and abroad brought their expertise. Physicians analyzed the data to determine whether heredity was a factor and evaluated the possibility of pellagra being caused by dietary deficiency, similar to beriberi and scurvy.

At the end of the commission's second summer of inquiry, Dr. Sambon visited the Spartanburg facility. He praised the work being done in America on this disease of international importance. A few days earlier, Dr. Sambon had declared in New York City that food had absolutely nothing to do with the spread of pellagra and that the theory of the disease being caused through eating corn was "exploded."[86] Sambon's visit was well received. The citizens and medical professionals of Spartanburg had been relentlessly working toward a cure. Now one of the world's leading experts was joining in and recognizing their efforts.

Not everyone was happy with the attention. The South Carolina legislature convened an investigation accusing Dr. Babcock of, among other things, causing injury to the progress and reputation of South Carolina by calling attention to the prevalence of pellagra. The Legislative Committee fully exonerated Dr. Babcock, but the bitterness of the entire affair led him to resign his position as superintendent of the state-run institution. He devoted the remainder of his career to a private mental health facility.[87]

The Second Progress Report summarized the commission's conclusions. Children under the age of two, adolescents for about five years following puberty, and adult males in the active period of life were least frequently affected. The commission found no definite connection between occupation and pellagra. The high frequency of cases in women and children pointed to home as the place

---

86   "Prof. Louis Sambon Here," *New York Times*, September 1, 1913.

87   William S. Hall, *Psychiatrist, Humanitarian, and Scholar: James Woods Babcock, M.D., Journal of the South Carolina Medical Association*, October 1970. Today, Dr. Babcock is recognized for his leadership in work on pellagra and for his decades of leadership in building South Carolina's mental health care system.

where the disease is contracted. Pellagra spread most rapidly in districts where unsanitary methods of sewage disposal were used. A house-to-house canvass of the homes of more than five thousand people failed to disclose any definite relation of the disease to any dietary element. Buffalo flies were exonerated, since the disease was found where no buffalo flies existed.

————

Early in 1914, the U.S. Public Health Service assigned Dr. Joseph Goldberger to lead its work on pellagra. Twelve years had passed since the first American case had been published, seven years since the Alabama report of an "epidemic of acute pellagra" with a 64 percent fatality rate. Two years of well-funded studies of the Thompson-McFadden Commission had generated a great deal of data, and still too many theories competed for attention.[88] The number of competent researchers was limited. More importantly, delays in finding the cause and a cure added to the number of sick, and many of the sick were dying. There had to be a way to focus resources and alleviate suffering.

Goldberger proposed a new strategy. The four-page plan he submitted in a letter to the U.S. Surgeon General emphasized clinical experiments to prove or disprove each of the current theories. Work would stop on any theory discredited by results. That would free resources for work in other areas. Goldberger's leadership would become evident on many occasions in coming years. But this first action, outlining a strategy for efficient use of available resources, was the key to making progress.[89]

Goldberger had been working with communicable diseases for several years. His observations in the first weeks on the new job persuaded him that pellagra was likely not contagious. Several hundred patients at the Georgia State Sanitarium in Milledgeville, Georgia, had pellagra, but none of the staff was affected in spite of frequent close contact with patients. Also, attempts to infect monkeys with the disease by injecting serum from human pellagra victims had failed. The first step would be carefully documented experiments to prove or disprove the contagious disease theory. Meanwhile, psychiatrists would continue to explore

---

88   The commission's third and final report, released in 1917, was a collection of eleven separate reports addressing separate theses about the disease. There was no attempt to synthesize these findings.

89   Letter from Joseph Goldberger to Surgeon General, March 2, 1914. Record Group 90, Central File Public Health Service 1897-1923. Box 149, file 1648. NARA II.

the relationship of pellagra to the dementia observed in patients, since there were obvious cognitive impacts of the disease. Epidemiology studies would continue at institutions that had large numbers of pellagrins. The prior efforts at gathering data from the general population would have to be improved. There were gaps in the data since most states still did not require reporting of cases to their own health authorities. Goldberger was unsure whether the growing number of reported cases reflected actual spread of the disease or simply increased awareness on the part of physicians and the public.

The strategy also called for experiments to determine the effect of diet, including changes in diet. Even in the summary of its first progress report, read at the Pellagra Meeting in Spartanburg in September 1913, the Thompson-McFadden Commission researchers commented, "The foods rich in animal protein, namely meat, milk, and eggs, although used in abundance by a few individual pellagrins in our series, are, nonetheless, conspicuous by their deficiency in many of the cases."[90] The summary of the Commission's Second Progress Report, published in January 1914, had included:

> Those...who used milk rarely or never did seem to be somewhat more subject to the disease, but the correlation was far from complete...Our attempt to discover in this way the essential pellagra-producing food or the essential pellagra-preventing food...suggests to us, at any rate, that neither of them exists within the dietary of the population which we have studied.

But later in the same summary, in a list of findings, is a final note, "The immediate results of hygienic and dietetic treatment in adults have been good, but after returning to former conditions of environment, most of the cases have recurred."[91] Whether these reports impressed Goldberger is unknown. But

---

90 J. F. Siler, P. E. Garrison, W. J. MacNeal, *Pellagra: A Summary of the First Progress Report of the Thompson-McFadden Pellagra Commission.* In a separate, earlier report Siler and Garrison had observed that in 85 percent of the cases, economic circumstances were poor and the disease was most prevalent among people of insufficient means.

91 J. F. Siler, P. E. Garrison, W. J. MacNeal, *Further Studies of the Thompson-McFadden Pellagra Commission: A Summary of the Second Progress Report.* Published in the *Journal of the American Medical Association,* vol. LXII, pp. 8–12. January 3, 1914. Most of the individual research papers were published in various journals during 1914, and the commission's complete Second Report and the research papers were printed in the *Archives of Internal Medicine* in September

embarking on his new assignment just one month later, and trying to develop a strategy for scientific work, he would certainly have reviewed the available research on the disease.

Goldberger and a few of his Public Health Service colleagues were struck by the monotonous food served at several of the institutions where PHS physicians had been invited to assist. Corn meal, biscuits, hominy, and syrup made from corn or sugar cane were served at almost every meal. That was not unusual. Cornmeal, molasses, and salt pork or fatback were staples of the Southern diet. But fresh meat, milk, and other high-protein foods that he and his colleagues considered vital to good health were rarely served. Goldberger proposed practical experiments to pursue this diet theory to a conclusion.

At the sanitarium in Milledgeville, Goldberger suggested a special diet for the sickest pellagra patients. He also wanted closer supervision of the dining area after seeing healthy patients take food from the plates of more passive patients. Each patient was fed a half-pound of fresh beef, several eggs, green vegetables, and milk each day. Those who could not eat solid food were given cod liver oil three times each day.

Within four weeks, there were improvements in seventeen of the acute patients who received this treatment. At first, mental and nervous symptoms abated. "That is, where these patients had been more or less completely disoriented, confused and apprehensive, with both visual and auditory hallucinations, practically no retentive powers and as a consequence very defective memory, they became clear, realized their surroundings, oriented themselves, their apprehension subsided, and their ability to retain impressions was unimpaired." Later, their skin improved. Some of the patients gained weight. When the experiment concluded, seven patients had died, thirteen had improved, and four were considered cured.[92]

During the same summer of 1914, sixty-eight of the 211 children (32 percent of the population) at the Methodist Orphanage in Jackson, Mississippi, were diagnosed with pellagra. But among those less than six years old, only 10

1914.
92 W. F. Lorenz, *The Treatment of Pellagra, Public Health Report 29* (September 11, 1914) and J. Goldberger, C. H. Waring, and D. G. Willets, *The Prevention of Pellagra, Public Health Report 30* (October 22, 1915). To assure that data gathered was not influenced by Goldberger's opinions, the treatment he prescribed at each facility was conducted and reported by other physicians. Separate physicians periodically examined the patients to provide their evaluations.

percent were affected. Of the sixty-six children over twelve years old, only one had pellagra. For some reason, children between six and twelve were suffering disproportionately from the disease. All of the children lived in similar quarters, with the same sanitary conditions and water supply, and were exposed to the same environmental conditions.

> But in the diet of those suffering from pellagra, there was noted a disproportionately small amount of meat or other animal protein food, and consequently the vegetable component, in which corn and syrup were prominent and legumes relatively inconspicuous elements, form a disproportionately large part of the ration. Although other than this gross defect no fault in the diet is appreciable, the evidence clearly incriminates it as the cause of pellagra at these institutions.[93]

Goldberger increased the amount of fresh animal and leguminous protein foods in the orphans' diet. Each child was given seven ounces of milk twice daily, for those between six and twelve years old, or three times daily for those under six. The meat ration was increased to three or four servings per week. Each child ate one egg in the morning. Beans and peas, formerly served only in summer and fall, were continued year-round. Beans provided especially high protein content at lower cost than fresh meat. Corn was not excluded from the diet, but the amount was reduced as the high-protein foods were increased. The orphanage could not afford the improved diet, so federal funds were used to purchase the supplemental food.

One year later, sixty-seven of the children who had pellagra in 1914, including nine who had suffered two seasons of pellagra, were still at the orphanage. None exhibited any recurrence. Nor was there any evidence of pellagra in the children and adults who had been pellagra-free in 1914.[94] No other change had occurred at the orphanage. The year-long dietary intervention had prevented recurrence.[95]

---

93 J. Goldberger, *Cause and Prevention of Pellagra,* Public Health Report 29 (September 11, 1914), 2354–2357.

94 J. Goldberger, C. H. Waring, and D. G. Willets, *The Prevention of Pellagra,* Public Health Report 30, 3119–3124. October 22, 1915.

95 Thompson-McFadden researchers had noted recurrence rates of 40 to 70 percent in the years 1912–1914 among those who survived an initial attack, although their reports on this were not published until August and September 1916.

The same dietary experiment was conducted at the Baptist Orphanage in Jackson, Mississippi, administered by a different Public Health Service physician. Results duplicated the Methodist Orphanage success.[96] The precise cause of pellagra remained a mystery, but the experiments confirmed that a protein-rich diet prevented suffering.

Next, Goldberger set an experiment to show that reducing the protein in the diet of a healthy person led to pellagra. Gov. Brewer of Mississippi agreed to pardon twelve prisoners in exchange for their voluntary participation in the experiment. Mississippi had been especially hard hit by pellagra. A solution was needed, and Goldberger's studies offered hope. The state penitentiary was chosen because there was no history of pellagra at that institution. If a change in diet produced pellagra symptoms in a pellagra-free environment, the case for dietary causation would be strong indeed.

From February to April 1915, the prisoner volunteers continued their normal prison diet. No symptoms appeared. Then a high-carbohydrate, low-protein diet was introduced for the volunteers. Their breakfast was biscuits, fried mush, grits and brown gravy, syrup, and coffee with sugar. Lunch consisted of corn bread, cabbage or collards, sweet potatoes, and grits and syrup. Supper was fried mush, biscuits, rice and gravy, cane syrup, coffee, and sugar. All other prisoners continued their normal diet and activities, thus constituting a control group. In mid-July, one volunteer was released, suffering from prostatitis. That left eleven participants, ages twenty-four to fifty. To assure the validity of the findings, other physicians participated in their general care, diagnoses, and in excluding other dermatoses. Six volunteers developed the dermatitis symptomatic of pellagra. The experiment was ended October 31. No prisoner in the control group had developed any symptoms of pellagra, but six of the eleven volunteers on the restricted diet had. To Goldberger and his associates, the restricted diet had produced the pellagra.[97] The volunteers were pardoned as promised. Once again, the importance of diet had been demonstrated. Adequate protein could alleviate one of the nation's major health problems.

In the summer of 1915, the Public Health Service reported:

The striking results following the feeding experiments of Dr. Goldberger and his associates...seem to justify the conclusions (1) that pellagra is

---

96   Ibid, 3121.
97   J. Goldberger J and G. A. Wheeler, "Experimental pellagra in the human subject brought about by a restricted diet," *Public Health Reporter*, 1915, 30:3336–3339. NARA II.

not a communicable (neither infectious nor contagious) disease, but that it is essentially of dietary origin; (2) that it is dependent on some yet undetermined fault in a diet in which the animal or leguminous protein component is disproportionately small and the nonleguminous vegetable component disproportionately large; and (3) that no pellagra develops in those who consume a mixed, well-balanced, and varied diet.[98]

Goldberger's theory of dietary causation had been scientifically validated. Here was a way to prevent and alleviate suffering. But it was not politically correct. Some elected officials and appointees at government-run institutions rejected the suggestion that patients in many protective institutions were not being properly fed. God-fearing caregivers in charitable institutions were providing less than excellent care for their charges. The notion that so many people, especially in the South, were suffering terrible illnesses because they were too poor or too uninformed to make healthy diet choices was an insult. Many rejected the reports of experiments proving diet causation and ignored the available preventive and curative diet treatments.[99]

In April 1918, Goldberger summarized an effective method of safeguarding the public welfare:

A properly-selected or well-balanced diet is one that includes in sufficient quantities...besides the cereals, starches, sweets, and fats, a sufficient quantity of milk or some lean meat and an abundance of green vegetables and fruit...Milk is the most important single food in balancing a diet and preventing or curing pellagra.

This report received editorial praise in the *Southern Medical Journal*, which admonished physicians:

Those of the profession of a retrogressive tendency must no longer sin by acts of omission, but should readily embrace the findings of scientists, and despite the fact that their patient may have as much to eat as any doctor's patient, they should bear in mind that there is a differ-

---

98   Annual Report of the Surgeon General, 1915, 28. NARA II.
99   J. Goldberger, C. H. Waring, and W. F. Tanner, "Pellagra Prevention by Diet Among Institutional Inmates," *Public Health Reporter*, 1923, 38:2364–2365.

ence in having things to eat and the actual, bona fide partaking of such edibles.[100]

Nonetheless, some physicians continued to oppose the diet theory. Some claimed it was too simple an explanation for such an obviously complex disease. Others were sure that a proper treatment must involve medication, not just diet. In 1918, the Pellagra Commission of the National Medical Association reported that, "Pellagra is a communicable and therefore preventable disease."[101]

Pellagra cases dwindled for several years, and Goldberger's staff was considerably reduced. Early summer 1921 brought a resurgence of pellagra throughout the cotton belt. The recession of 1920–21 had caused a severe drop in demand for cotton. A pound of cotton brought farmers thirty-four cents in 1920, but just fourteen cents in 1921.[102] Much of the crop could not be sold at all. Anyone relying on cotton for a living, whether land owner or tenant farmer, was short of cash and had nothing to borrow against. The number of cases tripled over the previous year. Pellagra, the disease long associated with poor economic circumstances, was flourishing again.

Goldberger alerted the U.S. Surgeon General of the new outbreak. President Harding called the Red Cross into action.[103] Emergency aid was provided. The recession soon ended, and cotton prices in 1922 rebounded to twenty cents per pound, higher than they had been in any year prior to World War I. Resurgence of the disease revived the old theories, six years after Goldberger and his Public Health Service colleagues had confirmed that a varied diet and adequate protein could prevent and cure the disease.

The *New York Times* published an article by Dr. Van Buren Thorne noting that experts were divided between two main theories of causation: poor nutrition (Goldberger et al) and infection arising from poor sewage disposal (Thompson-McFadden Commission). The corn theory had not completely disappeared

---

100 *Southern Medical Journal*, 11(8): 593, August 1918.
101 H. M. Green, "Report of the Pellagra Commission of the N.M.A.," *Journal of the National Medical Association*, 1918, 164. The National Medical Association was the professional organization of black physicians, who were not accepted for membership in the American Medical Association in that era. At some conferences, including those of the National Conference on Pellagra in South Carolina, black physicians were permitted to sit in the gallery.
102 *Statistical Abstract of the United States, 1924,* Table 296.
103 "Plague Threatens 100,000 Victims in the Cotton Belt," *New York Times,* July 25, 1921. "Orders Relief for Pellagra Victims," *New York Times,* July 26, 1921.

either.[104] In their 1923 edition of *Handbook of Therapy*, Dr. Oliver Osbourne of Yale University Medical School and Dr. Morris Fishbein, associate editor of the *Journal of the American Medical Association*, commented that some were still trying to connect pellagra to some factor related to corn in the diet. Osbourne and Fishbein also noted the continuing hypothesis that pellagra was contagious. Quite a few practitioners were holding to discredited theories, rejecting the data from experiments that showed how to avoid suffering.

Goldberger was never able to point to a specific cause of pellagra. He died in 1929. His essential contribution was discovering how to prevent and cure the disease. Within a few years, some food processing companies started adding vitamin B to their cereal products, proclaiming its value as a "growth promoting vitamin."[105] Research continued at a number of universities to identify the responsible dietary element.

In 1937, the cause of pellagra was finally proven to be a deficiency of the B vitamin niacin (nicotinic acid). Two years later, the American Medical Association gave its support to "fortifying" staple foods such as milk and bread. Nutritive standards known as minimum daily requirements were developed, and by early 1943 most of the nation's major flour mills and bakeries were adding niacin and thiamine to their products. The federal government used its wartime powers to order that vitamins be to all white bread. That order expired when the war ended. South Carolina, which had taken an early lead in the fight against pellagra, was the first state to require by law the enrichment of white bread and cornmeal.[106]

A more modern challenge for food producers is the growing evidence that artificial colors and other synthetic additives, such as preservatives, may trigger behavioral responses in children and contribute to the growing numbers diagnosed with Attention Deficit/Hyperactivity Disorder (ADHD). The detrimental effect of artificial colors and additives on children's behavior was first proposed in the 1970s by Dr. Benjamin Feingold, chief of allergy at Kaiser Permanente Medical Group in San Francisco and board certified in pediatrics and pediatric allergy. Dr. Feingold reported his clinical observations and dietary recommendations

104 Van Buren Thorne, "Puzzling Pellagra," *New York Times*, July 31, 1921.
105 Ralston Purina Company advertisement, *Time*, December 7, 1931. p. 39.
106 Etheridge, Elizabeth W. *The Butterfly Castle: A Social History of Pellagra in the South."* P. 208-217.

in *Why Your Child Is Hyperactive*. The American Medical Association arranged press conferences around the country, and the diet received significant media attention. In recent decades, small-scale studies in the United States seemed inconclusive. Without carefully controlled clinical studies of large numbers of children using the diet, compared to a control group of other children with similar symptoms on a different diet, there was considerable skepticism. But a larger study at University of Southampton has led the United Kingdom's Food Standards Agency to revise its advice on certain artificial colors and the preservative sodium benzoate.[107]

The study involved children in each of two age groups—three years old and eight to nine years old, from varied socioeconomic backgrounds—from September 2004 to March 2007. Informed parental consent was obtained for each participating child prior to the study. The artificial colors used in the study are common in beverages and prepared foods sold in the United Kingdom and the United States, including tartrazine (Yellow 5 in the U.S., E102 in Europe and the U.K.). The preservative sodium benzoate is also common in the U.S. and the U.K.

The researchers acknowledge that hyperactivity in children, characterized by inattention, impulsivity, and overactivity, has been attributed to nongenetic effects including premature birth, institutionalized rearing, and maternal smoking during pregnancy. There is also a substantial body of evidence including numerous studies of twins indicating that genetic factors are a major contributor to individual differences in hyperactivity. Taking all of that into account, the authors report in the main results of their study:

> The importance of these findings is that they confirm that the adverse effect of certain artificial food colour that has been implicated in children with hyperactive syndromes can also be demonstrated in two samples taken from the general population.

The Food Standards Agency's independent Committee on Toxicity issued a statement after reviewing the study findings:

---

107 The report is under project title "Chronic and acute effects of artificial colourings and preservatives on children's behavior." Project code: T07040. School of Psychology, University of Southampton (UK), Principal Investigator Prof. Jim Stevenson, Co-Principal Investigators Prof. Edmund Sonuga-Barke, Prof. John Warner. Available as pdf at http://www.food.gov.uk/multimedia/pdfs/additivesbehaviourfinrep.pdf.

We consider that this study has provided supporting evidence suggesting that certain mixtures of artificial food colours together with the preservative sodium benzoate are associated with an increase in hyperactivity in children from the general population. If causal, this observation may be of significance for some individual children across the range of hyperactive behaviors, but could be of more relevance for children towards the more hyperactive end of the scales.[108]

The report was published in the British medical journal *Lancet* and forwarded to the European Food Safety Authority.

The report has significant implications for many Americans. According to the Centers for Disease Control, 4.4 million children aged four to seventeen years have a history of ADHD diagnosis—almost 8 percent of the total population in that age group. Of those who were diagnosed, about 2.5 million are taking medication for the disorder. Ritalin and Adderall are among the prescribed medications. The concept of a link between artificial colors and preservatives in food and hyperactivity has been viewed with skepticism in mainstream American medical practice. But in February 2008, an editorial in the American Academy of Pediatrics *AAP Grand Rounds* publication indicated that the Southampton Study, as it is becoming known, warrants revisiting the issue.

Will this become our next environmental concern? Some artificial colors are coal- or petroleum-based. They are produced by the same high-temperature, high-pressure refining process used to make gasoline and diesel fuel. Have you eaten your petrochemicals today?

There was important interaction between a nonprofit organization and food companies during the thirty-year interval from Dr. Feingold's clinical observations to the Southampton Study. In 1976, a group consisting mainly of parents of hyperactive children who had heard of the Feingold Diet formed the Feingold Association of the United States, "dedicated to helping children and adults apply proven dietary techniques for better behavior, learning, and health." The group published materials that explained the diet. Annual conferences were held, with presentations by physicians familiar with the diet. Perhaps the most important contribution of the association has been extensive consultation by association staff with food processing companies. The association publishes and updates lists of products that are free of additives and preservatives. That information

---

108 The Food Standards Agency news release can be seen at: http://food.gov. uk/news/pressreleases/2007/sep/colours.

enables parents to modify the family diet to eliminate items suspected of provoking hyperactive behavior. To meet growing consumer interest, some manufacturers now label the products that contain no artificial colors or flavors. Consumers, a nonprofit group, and food processing companies are improving the quality and labeling of food in areas far beyond the scope of government regulation.

Thirty-five years later, a small "home office" staff (never more than five people) and a network of part-time and volunteer workers across the country still gather and share the vital information. The Southampton Study provided that long-awaited statistical study. Hopefully, additional work will further refine our understanding. But the lives of thousands of children have been improved by a small organization working with cooperative manufacturers.[109]

———

Making breakfast cereal or ketchup in a competitive world has its challenges, but it must be easier than drilling for oil in Equatorial Guinea or Angola. Yet shareholders of Kellogg's and Heinz get a better reward for their invested money than ExxonMobil shareholders. Profits make headlines, but return on equity is the heart of the story.

---

109 Feingold® Association of the United States. Information at www.feingold.org.

Chapter Seven

Health Insurance Companies

	Sales 2006 (Billions)	Net Profit 2006 (Billions)	Shareholder Equity on 12/31/05 (Billions)	ROE 2006 %	Average Annual Profit 2002-06 (Billions)	Average Shareholder Equity 2002-06 (Billion)	5-Yr.Avge ROE 2002-2006 %
United Health	$71.5	$4.16	$17.7	21.5	$2.6	$11.8	22.5
WellPoint	$56.95	$3.06	$24.99	12.5	$1.57	$16.1	9.8
Aetna	$25.1	$1.6	$10.1	17.5	$1.09	$8.6	12.7
Cigna	$13.6	$5.5	$17.9	31.4	$6.13	$17.3	35.0

The winner in this business category, for highest five-year average ROE, is Cigna Corporation. But Cigna's ROE is lower than that of Anheuser-Busch, Kellogg, or Heinz.

Companies in this arena compete to provide employee health insurance programs to major corporations, as well as small- and midsize businesses. These corporate customers demand not just competitive premiums and broad coverage, but also efficient claims administration services, accessible networks of physicians, and employee wellness programs such as informational brochures and Web-based information centers on a wide variety of health topics. Some businesses conduct periodic surveys of their employees to measure satisfaction with the health insurer's services. To make sure they are getting the best value for their premium dollars, many businesses hire professional consultants or insurance brokers to independently analyze proposals and assist in determining which insurer is offering the best combination of price and service quality. Corporations are tough customers. They use their purchasing power to get the best health and wellness program for their employees at the best available price. Employer-provided health insurance is a very competitive business.

Behind the scenes, health insurers perform a number of major tasks to better serve their customers' employees. The major insurers negotiate with hospitals, physicians, laboratories, pharmaceutical companies, and other health care providers to get fee discounts in exchange for listing the providers in the insurer's network of preferred providers. In most employer programs, employees can visit "out of network" providers, but they must pay higher fees. The discounts allow health insurers to charge lower premiums, saving employees and employers money. Insurers also maintain libraries of treatment protocols and update them frequently to reflect the latest clinical experience with diseases and injuries. This allows the insurer's physicians and nurses to confer with the primary care physicians or specialists to ensure that the most appropriate treatment plan is made available to a patient—the plan that is most likely to deliver the best medical outcome for the patient. This long-term trend toward evidence-based medicine is not easy. Patients may see it as unjust denial of benefits when coverage for a particular procedure or medication is denied based on lack of statistically-validated effectiveness in similar cases. Inevitably, tensions mount when the intellectual desire to focus available health-care dollars into proven remedies conflicts with the heartfelt desire to "do something" for a gravely ill family member.

Much of WellPoint's business is in providing services to citizens on Medicare. Is this a good business strategy? WellPoint's ROE is significantly lower than those of its competitors. Will shareholders start to press for better results or simply sell the stock and move their money into a more promising company?

———

What factors are driving up medical costs and health insurance premiums? Life expectancy in the U.S. increased steadily during the twentieth century and continues to increase. As a result, a growing proportion of medical care is devoted to managing chronic diseases over multiyear periods. The life expectancy numbers in the chart below are from "Health, United States, 2007," which draws from sources including the Centers for Disease Control and Prevention and the National Center for Health Statistics.

Life Expectancy in the U.S. All Races, Both Sexes								
	1900	1950	1960	1970	1980	1990	2000	2005
At Birth	47.3	68.2	69.7	70.8	73.7	75.4	77.0	77.8
At age 65	n/a	13.9	14.3	15.2	16.4	17.2	18.0	18.7
At age 75	n/a	n/a	n/a	n/a	10.4	10.9	11.4	12.0

The advance in life expectancy is one of the factors contributing to the growth of health care expenses. More people are living longer. When the Medicare law was enacted in 1965, a typical sixty-five-year-old could anticipate living another fourteen to fifteen years. Today, a sixty-five-year-old can reasonably look forward to living almost twenty more years. As the Henry J. Kaiser Family Foundation reports, "The U.S. population is aging, and because older people use more health care than younger people, population aging will have a small but persistent impact on cost growth in the years to come."

Many diseases that were once deadly within days or weeks are now manageable chronic conditions that patients survive for many years. These therapies cost money.

One example, which directly affects Medicare, is the growing number of Americans living with end stage renal disease (ESRD). Until the 1960s, loss of 80 percent to 90 percent of kidney function would have been fatal within days or weeks. Today, with modern dialysis treatments, many ESRD patients survive for years. Each of these patients needs a kidney transplant as soon as a compatible organ becomes available. Until an organ transplant is performed, dialysis treatments are needed, usually three times each week. By law, Medicare covers much of the treatment costs, regardless of patient's age. At the end of 2005, 485,012 Americans required regular dialysis treatments; 106,912 were new beneficiaries of the treatment that year.[110] The number of patients requiring dialysis has been increasing by about 5 percent annually. Kidney dialysis, a therapy that did not exist in the early 1960s, is now a significant Medicare expense. A total of 17,249 kidney transplants were performed in 2005, up from about 14,600 the prior year. In 1980, there were fewer than 3,800.[111] In 1960, there were none.

Recent rapid increases in child obesity, coupled with the presence of diabetes—a potential precursor of kidney disease—in 8 percent of the U.S.

110 National Institutes of Health (NIH), U.S. Dept. of Health and Human Services. Available at www.usrds.org.
111 Kidney transplant data from National Kidney and Urologic Diseases Clearinghouse (NKUDIC); http://kidney.niddk.nih.gov/kudiseases/pubs/kustats/index.htm.

population, could lead to a more rapid increase in the number of dialysis patients in the years ahead. Adding urgency to the diabetes discussion is the prevalence of impaired fasting glucose (IFG), which is a form of prediabetes and raises the risk of developing type 2 diabetes, heart disease, and stroke. In 2003–2006, 25.9 percent of U.S. adults aged twenty years or older had IFG. That's fifty-seven million adult prediabetics facing debilitating disease.[112] This portends explosive medical costs ahead.

In 2004, the total health care expenditures in the U.S. were $1.6 trillion.[113] Every year, as we live longer and benefit from new treatments, we spend more dollars on health care. If our economy grew at the same pace, that would not be a problem. But in the U.S., total health care spending has grown much faster than our economy, at an average annual rate of 7 percent since 1991.[114] As a result of that disparity, health care expenditures for our country have swollen from 5.1 percent of the gross domestic product in 1960 to 15.3 percent today. If, from time to time, you wonder "Where does all the money go?" this is part of the answer. In 1960, 94.9 percent of our national income was available, after medical costs, for other costs like housing, food, transportation and leisure, and savings. Today, less than 85 percent remains for those other items.[115] Anyone who pays for health care, either directly or through insurance premiums, is feeling squeezed. In 2011, the first Baby Boomers will reach sixty-five years old, and for twenty years after that a geriatric bubble, with its higher medical costs, will move through the economy.

Whether the bills for these drugs, medical devices, and related professional services are channeled through health insurers or through tax-supported government programs, or some mix of these, is a political question for voters to decide. But the fundamental question—how to afford these rapidly rising costs—is an economic one.

The affordability crisis is clear: in 2011, the average premium for an employer-based health insurance plan for a single person reached $5,429; for a family, the premium in an employer-based plan was $15,073. Sales at most mature companies are growing at 3 percent to 10 percent per year. Our gross domestic product grows, on average, about 3 percent per year. But growth in medical expenditures, and therefore health insurance costs, have averaged about

---

112 Centers for Disease Control, National Diabetes Fact Sheet, 2007.
113 Kaiser Family Foundation. Amount excludes insurance program administration, research, and construction. $1.6 trillion dollars is $1,600,000,000,000.
114 Kaiser Family Foundation
115 "Health, United States" 2007. http://www.cdc.gov/nchs/hus.htm.

6 percent annually from 2005 to 2011.[116] The question for our society is how to pay for an expense that is growing faster than our collective ability to pay.

Some businesses require employees to share the cost by paying a larger share of the premium or pay a larger deductible or co-pay. Other employers simply drop the coverage. Elected officials, or those who want to be elected, offer programs to move more of the cost to "the government," which means taxpayers, either individual, corporate, or both. Other politicians want business to bear more of the burden. These actions may shift the cost burden, but they do not address the fundamental problem of rapidly growing costs arising from our longer lives and improved ability to treat chronic conditions and respond to acute situations.

———

In March 2010, President Obama signed the Patient Protection and Affordable Care Act. The new law mandates reforms in health insurance coverage, promotes preventive and early detection measures, and requires employers with more than fifty employees to offer a health insurance plan or pay a fine. The law also requires virtually all Americans to obtain health insurance. The president announced, in promoting and signing the bill, that its provisions would slow the rate of increase in health care costs for the nation. Even after enactment, the law was controversial. Attorneys general of some states filed suits asking courts to find the law, or certain sections of it, unconstitutional. Some members of Congress called for complete repeal.

Over time, voters will determine the fate of the law. The president's signature sets in motion one more experiment in the quest to improve the general welfare, to achieve a level of social justice. In coming years, results can be tracked against expectations. Will hospital emergency departments be less crowded as more people have access to primary physicians? Will prescription coverage lead more patients to take the proper dosage at prescribed intervals? Will parents take their children for periodic vision, hearing, and dental exams? Will controls on payments for prescription drugs and medical devices slow the pace of research, discovery, and innovation? Will new systems for medical records improve patient outcomes? Will the health of the nation's citizens improve

---

116 Kaiser Family Foundation. Premiums shown include employer and employee share. http://kaiserhealthnews.org/Stories/2011/September/27/Employer-Health-Coverage-Survey-Shows-Employer-Spending-Spike.aspx.

in measurable terms? What unanticipated results will occur in future years? We have much to learn as this new experiment progresses.

———

For our next discussion, let's explore a business that is less complex than health insurance. How about retail sales? Just open a store, buy inventory, add a profit margin, and watch the money roll in, right?

Chapter Eight

Retailers

	Sales 2006 (Billions)	Net Profit 2006 (Billions)	Shareholder Equity on1/31/05	ROE 2006 %	Average Annual Profit 2002-06 (Billions)	Average Shareholder Equity2002-06 (Billions)	5-Year Average ROE 2002-2006 %
Walmart[117]	$345	$12.2	$53.2	22.0	$10.0	$44.1	22.6
Tiffany[118]	$2.6	$0.254	$1.831	14.1	$.223	$1.449	15.4
Sears	$53.0	$1.4	$11.611	6.2	N/A	N/A	N/A
Target	$59.5	$2.8	$14.2	17.8	$2.1	$11.1	18.9
JCPenny	$19.9	$1.1	$4.0	26.4	$.699	$5.4	12.9
Costco	$60.2	$1.1	$8.9	12.1	$.879	$5.1	17.2

Two-thirds of America's gross domestic product is consumer-driven. Retail stores, whether small shops serving local communities, multinational merchandisers with "big-box" operations, or mail-order powerhouses, are the intermediaries

---

117 Walmart's fiscal year runs from February 1 to January 31. Thus, the 2006 numbers shown in the table are for the period February 1, 2005, to January 31, 2006. All of the above retailers close their fiscal years in late January, so the time periods shown above are consistent.

118 Sears Holdings Corp., the corporation shown here, was formed in 2005, following the merger of Kmart and Sears, Roebuck and Co. Thus, there is no meaningful multiyear record. Some potential investors will see that as riskier than a retailer with a visible performance record. Others may see it as an emerging opportunity.

who get the product from manufacturer to customer. The fates of the country's great mercantile chains have been tied to the country's history, and the rise and fall of great fortunes have depended upon their leaders' ability to meet the constantly changing needs of the customer.

The American colonies depended almost entirely on imports for manufactured goods, with almost the entire domestic economy tied to agriculture. Long-distance shipping was by ship or barge, using rivers and lakes, and local shipping was accomplished by wagon. After the Revolutionary War, small-scale manufacturers arose, but sellers of goods were mainly taking in products from local farmers and artisans and selling to the local population. With the establishment of canals in the 1820s to 1830s, and the railroads during the following decades, trading over larger areas became possible. Merchants could serve larger populations from a single point. As steam engines replaced water-driven wheels, factories became far more efficient. With increased efficiency and output, the prices of manufactured goods fell.

By the outbreak of the Civil War in 1861, manufacturing was a major part of the economy of the North. But retailing remained a very local, fragmented business, dominated by proprietor-owned and operated stores. Wholesale "jobbers" connected these far-flung, local stores to manufacturers in distant cities. The wholesalers often provided services like staying in touch with manufacturers and selecting the goods that would go into the stores. Into this world, in the second half of the nineteenth century, came two men who would make major changes to how Americans shopped: Marshall Field and Montgomery Ward.

Field is best known for the retail stores that bore his name until late in the twentieth century, with a world-renowned flagship store in downtown Chicago.[119] But his main contribution to retailing was to offer an efficient distribution system to the independently owned "general stores" that sold products of every kind to Americans in an era when more than 90 percent of the population lived on farms. Field provided a trusted supply channel that saved time and money for the shopkeepers. He recommended quality goods for their stores and allowed them to consolidate their purchases. At the same time, the success of the huge retail store was helped by the growth of Chicago's population, from fifty thousand in 1860 to two million in 1900. In the same decades, America's middle class—people with money to spend on home furnishings, manufactured clothing, and decorative items—was growing rapidly.

---

119 The Marshall Field store in Chicago is the second-largest retail store in the world. Only Macy's in New York City is larger, by only a few square feet.

Field was a conservative businessman. He did not borrow money, even for mortgages on buildings. Cash flow from his business was used to buy new inventory or expand operations. In the aftermath of the 1871 fire, when his store was underinsured, his cash savings allowed rebuilding to proceed.[120]

In 1872, Montgomery Ward, who had worked briefly for Marshall Field's company, started a mail-order business dedicated to "furnishing farmers and mechanics throughout the Northwest with all kinds of merchandise at wholesale prices." By 1886, Ward's catalogue included over ten thousand items. Obviously, a lot of people liked buying by mail and felt secure with Ward's money-back guarantee. The business thrived.

The growth and obvious success of both Field and Ward attracted others to compete in the retail business. By 1893, a small mail order company that had specialized in watches and expanded into jewelry and silverware was adding clothing, bicycles, sewing machines, and other items to its catalogue. Sears, Roebuck and Company was an entrepreneurial success, but not particularly well managed. Richard Sears was a born salesman and advertising genius. His partner, Alvah Roebuck, was a skilled watch repairman. As the orders came in by mail, their order-tracking system was overwhelmed, and their finances became precarious. Alvah, who appreciated the precision of a good watch, could not take the stress, and he sold his share of the business to Sears. Fortunately, one of Sears's suppliers, Julius Rosenwald, was interested. In 1895, he, along with his brother-in-law Aaron Nussbaum, became partners in Sears, Roebuck and Company.

This dynamic, well-organized team was immensely successful. By 1900, sales at Sears, Roebuck and Company reached $10 million per year and surpassed Montgomery Ward. In 1901, Nussbaum left the firm and sold his interest to Rosenwald for a handsome profit. The business continued to grow rapidly. New systems were needed for receiving goods from suppliers and preparing orders for shipment to customers. A new building, almost three million square feet in area, was built. It was highly mechanized, with rail tracks, conveyors, gravity chutes, moving sidewalks, and elevators for moving freight and sorting merchandise. It was also very expensive. By early 1906, Rosenwald believed that the company needed more working capital (cash for ongoing operations) and wanted to pay off some of the high-interest bank loans that had financed the new building. He needed reliable capital for the long-term health of the business.

---

120 Information on Marshall Field's career is from numerous articles in the *New York Times,* including a lengthy obituary published January 17, 1906.

Investment bankers at Goldman Sachs and Lehman Brothers explained that a more efficient way to accomplish Rosenwald's goals would be to have the company issue stock and "go public"—to sell stock to people who wanted to invest in the corporation. The American economy had been expanding for more than a decade; people had money to spend or to save, and some of the savers wanted to invest. Working with the investment bankers, Sears raised $30 million in an offering of common stock and an additional $10 million by issuing preferred stock.[121] For the first time, Sears, Roebuck and Company was owned by people who were not executives of the firm. But the shift from private ownership by a limited number of shareholders to "public ownership," in which shares traded on the stock exchanges open to the public, produced the desired capital. By 1907, sales reached $50 million.[122] By 1920, sales reached $235 million. Sears would remain the country's largest retailer until after World War II.

In 1916, the company established the Profit Sharing and Pension Program of Sears, Roebuck Employees. Every employee was eligible to participate after one year of service by contributing 5 percent of their salary or wages, up to a specified maximum. Each year, the company contributed 5 percent of its profits, dividing that among the participants' accounts, to boost the number of shares in each account. The program merged the interests of the employees with those of other shareholders. It sent a clear message to supervisors and middle managers that the board of directors and senior executives valued employees at all levels of the organization. Some long-term workers eventually drew out of the program more than they had earned in salary during their entire working lives. By 1954,

---

121 Owners of common stock own a fractional share of the corporation. For example, if a person owns one hundred shares of the common stock of a corporation that has issued one hundred thousand shares, then the person owns $1/1,000^{th}$ of the corporation. Common shareholders often receive dividends as a sharing in the corporation's profits. The board of directors determines the timing and amount of dividend payments for common stock. There is no guarantee of a common stock dividend, and some corporations do not pay dividends on common stock. Preferred stock is actually a way for a corporation to borrow money. Those who purchase the preferred shares are assured that their dividend will be paid out before any dividend to common shareholders (thus the term "preferred"). The yield (payout) on preferred shares is established when the shares are issued and does not change. Thus you may hear a preferred stock described as "Sears, Roebuck and Company, 5 percent preferred." But preferred shares normally carry none of the voting rights that come with common stock.

122 Information on the early years of Sears, Roebuck and Company is from *Shaping an American Institution* by James C. Worthy, and from company history available at: http://www.searsarchives.com.

the employees owned 25 percent of the common stock of the company. At the end of the 1960s, Sears was still the world's largest retailer—nearly twice the size of Montgomery Ward, the second largest. Through the stock market on Wall Street employees owned a major part of this corporation that served customers on Main Street.

Enlightened attitudes toward customers and employees did not assure continuous success. In the spring of 1920, the nation's largest retailer saw its sales drop 33 percent, from $245 million in 1920 to $164 million in 1921, and the company fell from a profit of $11.7 million to a loss of $16.4 million in the same period. The company reduced employment by 15 percent between 1919 and 1920, and by another 16 percent between 1920 and 1921. Julius Rosenwald, president of the company, reinvested $20 million of his own savings into the company and abolished his own salary for three years to save the company from defaulting on loan covenants. Montgomery Ward also sustained a 33 percent drop in sales and lost money in both 1920 and 1921. Many retailers closed permanently. Sears's sales volume did not return to the 1920 level until 1925. By then, Rosenwald was sixty-two years old and ready to retire. The board hired Charles M. Kittle, a railroad executive with no retail experience. Kittle brought some improvements, mainly to internal processes, but he died suddenly in January 1928. He was succeeded by General Robert Wood, a West Point graduate (class of 1900) who had been tremendously successful at Montgomery Ward. Wood had joined Sears as a vice president when Kittle was hired, and he seemed the natural successor.

Wood's tenure spanned the Great Depression, World War II, the post-war recovery and the Korean War. The company made many changes reflecting other developments in American society. The traditional "target market" for Sears had been farmers. But the farmers were moving into cities. Workers had more discretionary income and more leisure time, as well as larger and more comfortable homes. Wood had for years studied the annual *Statistical Abstract of the United States*, which showed the remarkable demographic changes in the country. To keep the company up to date on the changing American consumer, Wood established marketing as a professional discipline within Sears management. As Wood defined it, marketing is the "study of needs and wants of the customer, and the fulfilling of those needs and wants with a superior product or service at the very lowest possible prices."[123]

Years later, Peter Drucker, one of America's foremost writers on management of large firms, commented on the approach that Wood established: "True marketing starts out...with the customer, his demographics, his realities, his needs, his values. It does not ask, 'What do we want to sell?' It asks, 'What does the customer

---

123 James C. Worthy, "*Shaping An American Institution*", 60.

want to buy?'"[124] Wood recognized that Sears, like any other business, was at the mercy of its customers. They decide whether the company succeeds or fails.

Anybody who read the quarterly statements to shareholders or read the financial press knew about the strong profits at Sears. Those profits attracted competitors. New retail chains located their stores out in the suburbs, often in shopping malls that were now drawing customers away from the cities and near-suburbs where Sears had invested heavily. Sam Walton opened his first Walmart stores in rural areas of the South and Southwest. The new organizations were lean and energetic. The Sears organization had become comfortable with success and overstaffed. Sears's market share was slipping, and internal costs were increasing. In 1975, ROE was 9.8 percent, compared to 16.1 percent in 1955, the year after Woods retired.

By the 1980s, Sears management concluded that traditional retailing was a dead business. They adopted a new strategy that might have been called "financial services while you shop." Sales counters for Allstate Insurance were placed in the stores. Sears purchased the securities firm Dean Witter Reynolds and Coldwell Banker, the nation's largest real estate firm. The strategy sounded exciting at the time, but it proved unsuccessful. While Sears, Roebuck and Company management was bemoaning the imminent demise of traditional retailing, Walmart saw a big opportunity—in traditional retailing.

———

The Walmart strategy emphasized efficient distribution from the manufacturer to the customer in the aisle. Today, Walmart Stores is the world's largest retailer, with stores throughout the U.S., Latin America, Asia, and Europe. Walmart sells $345 billion of items that customers find meet their needs. Its motto is "Always Low Prices." The corporate mission, printed in the Annual Report and known throughout the company, is "We save people money so they can live better." Walmart must be doing something right. In a typical week, 137 million Americans—roughly 45 percent of the U.S. population—visit a Walmart store. Worldwide, there are more than 175 million customers weekly.[125]

To get additional capital to pay for more stores and distribution centers, Walmart offered three hundred thousand shares of stock to the public in 1970 at $16.50 per share. Employees were among the early buyers. The stock has split

---

124 Peter Drucker, *"Management Tasks, Responsibilities, Practices"*, 64.
125 Store traffic numbers are from Walmart's website.

many times.[126] For anyone who bought the stock in 1972, when it first traded on the New York Stock Exchange, and held it continuously, each share is today worth almost one thousand times its original cost. That is an average annual increase of 26 percent in the share price, disregarding the dividends paid over the years. Since 2000, the stock price has actually fallen, after quadrupling between 1997 and 2000.

There are several lessons in this. First, joining the employee stock plan or the 401(k) plan can be a very good thing. If company profits grow, the stock price will very likely rise over the long term. The participating employee benefits from the dividends and from the rise in the stock price. In many plans, the employer matches a percentage of the employee's savings, in effect giving the employee a pay raise. The second lesson is that no stock moves continuously upward in price. Third, the price of any stock can fall. Sometimes the fall is dramatic and occurs with no warning. The preceding lessons should convince anyone never to put all their savings into the stock of any one corporation, no matter how successful it has been in the past.

Today, employee stock plans and 401(k) plans offer a variety of stocks and mutual funds, to allow spread of investment risk, and one or more money market funds, to allow some portion of the account to remain free of the ups and downs of stock prices. In addition, 401(k) plans have tremendous income tax advantages for every participating employee. These "tax shelter" characteristics were enacted by Congress specifically to provide workers in all income levels a major opportunity to accumulate savings and investment funds.

The store traffic and sales figures make it clear that Walmart meets the needs of millions of customers. But Walmart also arouses controversy. Some object to its employment practices; others are saddened by the closing of small retailers when a Walmart opens nearby. Still others dislike the "big box" architecture and fear traffic congestion and other nuisances.

Economists have documented several ways in which Walmart effects the population generally and low-income families in particular. One of the more

---

126 A "stock split," as the term implies, occurs when a corporation's board of directors declares that, at a certain date, each share of stock will be "split" into (usually) two shares. If a share of stock is selling on the split date at $100 per share, and a two-for-one split is completed, each share of stock will be worth $50. Each shareholder who held, for example, twenty-five shares of stock, automatically owns fifty shares when the split is completed. Bottom line: before the split, the shareholder owned twenty-five shares, each worth $100, for a total of $2,500; after the split, the shareholder owns fifty shares, each worth $50, for a total of $2,500. The only purpose of a split is to make the price of each share more affordable to individuals who want to buy shares.

recent studies is a working paper published by the National Bureau of Economic Research (NBER) in December 2005.[127] The authors are Jerry Hausman, of the Department of Economics at Massachusetts Institute of Technology, and Ephraim Leibtag, of the U.S. Department of Agriculture. Their work is based on "panel data" assembled from thousands of households, specifically to learn how consumers respond when Walmart Supercenters open and compete with traditional supermarkets (e.g., Albertsons, Kroger, Acme, etc.). Each household used a barcode scanner to record all food purchases over a forty-eight-month period. Most households shopped at supercenters and traditional supermarkets, as well as convenience stores. Walmart began selling food in 1988 and in 2002 became the largest grocery chain in the U.S.

It will come as no surprise that Walmart's prices for most food items are lower than the prices charged for the same item by traditional supermarkets—15 percent to 25 percent lower. Also, when Walmart opens a food store, the traditional supermarkets in the area reduce their prices to avoid losing customers. The authors calculate this reduction to be about 4.8 percent. So even if you never shop at Walmart, you pay less for your groceries or other purchases because prices have been lowered in response to competition from Walmart. The average effect totals about 25 percent of a family's food expenditure. That is significant in any household's budget. Consumers clearly benefit from the presence of supercenters.

The authors found, and quantified, where the major benefit (the authors use the term "compensating variation") flows. The largest reduction in food cost, 29 percent, went to the households with annual income less than $10,000. The percent reduction fell as income rose, but even households with annual incomes of $100,000 saved 20 percent. Most likely, lower income households were doing a larger portion of their total food purchases at the supercenter to maximize their savings. The authors' conclusion was straightforward: "Lower household income has a significant effect on estimated household compensating variation. Minorities also gain a significantly higher amount of consumer surplus. The spread of supercenters has the greatest impact on poorer households and minority households."

Walmart has followed in the footsteps of Field, Ward, and Sears, Roebuck and Company—building its business by best meeting customers' needs, and in doing so earning a profit for its shareholders. Walmart delivers savings especially to low-income households while achieving industry-leading ROE. The success will last as long as millions of customers, each for their own reasons, walk through the front doors of those stores.

---

127 Available at nber.org; Working Paper w11809.

Chapter Nine

Automobiles

	Sales 2006 (Billions)	Net Profit 2006 (Billions)	Shareholder Equity on 12/31/05 (Billions)	ROE 2006 %	Average Annual Profit 2002-2006 (Billions)	Average Shareholder Equity 2002-2006 (Billions)	5-Year Average ROE 2002-2006 %
General Motors[128]	$207.3	$2.0	$14.6	15	($.9)	$18.8	N/M
Toyota	$189.3	$15.5	$89.8	17	$11.1	$80.1	13.9
Honda	$94.0	$5.0	$35.1	13.2	$4.5	$30.6	14.8
Ford[129]	$160.1	($12.6)	$12.9	Neg.	$5.0	N/M	N/M

Imagine, for a moment, how much money you could make if you knew how to build a car that got twice the fuel economy of an equivalent car—same size, same seating capacity, same comfort features and accessories. People who drive, say, a Lincoln Town Car limousine could get twice as many miles per gallon as they get with today's Lincoln Town Car limousine. People who drive a Toyota Camry

---

128 In accounting, the parentheses surrounding a number signifies a negative number. In 2006, General Motors (GM) lost $1.978 billion; in 2005, GM lost $10.4 billion; these losses exceeded the profits earned in 2002, 2003, and 2004. While it is beyond the scope of our study here, GM lost $38.7 billion in 2007. N/M indicates "not meaningful."

129 In 2006, Ford Motor Company lost $12.6 billion. The loss of $12.6 billion in 2006 was greater than the total profits of the prior four years and eliminated all shareholder equity.

would get twice as many miles per gallon as they get driving today's Toyota Camry. How much money could you make if you had the secret to that technology and could build cars and trucks that delivered that kind of fuel economy, especially in today's world when gasoline prices have exceeded $4 per gallon in some places?

Some people started thinking about that forty years ago. They have spent a lot of money developing the technology—actually, multiple technologies that all contribute to the goal. Some of those people worked for car companies in Japan. Some of them worked for chemical companies. Some who worked on these projects in the early days have already retired, and handed over their work to younger employees. Think of all the money that has been invested over the years, for engineers and researchers, experimental prototypes, testing, and test facilities.

The automobile industry serves a worldwide population. There are six hundred million cars, trucks, and motorcycles distributed among a world population of 6.4 billion, an average of one vehicle for every ten people. If the fuel-saving technologies work, the reward could be generous indeed for those who risked all that money—*if* the customers buy those vehicles.

The General Motors that produced the financial results above passed through a complete restructuring in 2009, with massive investment by the federal government. The shareholders lost their investment. The difficulties that led to the demise of General Motors and Chrysler are well publicized, as is the growth of Toyota and Honda. The table shows how much the corporate results differed. GM, Chrysler, and Ford pointed out that their production costs were higher because they had higher costs for pensions and retiree health care than Toyota and Honda. That alone left GM, Chrysler, and Ford less profitable than their competitors.

But to be fair, Toyota and Honda have been very successful marketers by offering American buyers a variety of vehicles with higher fuel efficiency and excellent quality at attractive prices. Starting in the 1970s with very small market share and selling compact cars, Toyota and Honda continued to refine their designs and expand their models, watching and listening to what customers wanted to buy. Hundreds of thousands of consumers decided to buy these cars. Their manufacturing and assembly processes, which underwent continuing improvement, were transferred to America,[130] and American companies were

---

130 Toyota's strategy for many years has included manufacturing, or at least assembling, cars in the countries where they will be sold.

sought out to supply parts. While GM and Ford were laying off workers, offering early retirement plans, and closing factories, Toyota and Honda were building new plants in the U.S. and hiring employees. As a result, the total number of Americans employed in the automobile industry has remained stable, at about two million, over the past decade.

All of these automobile companies are now being challenged by Hyundai, which is based in Korea. Cars made in China will soon be coming to America. It's a competitive world, and consumers will decide who wins every time they visit the showroom. Even buying a used car from a friend indirectly affects the manufacturer, since the resale or trade-in value of used cars influences buyers of new cars, and thus the potential profits of manufacturers.

———

In August 1902, Henry Ford, who would become the nation's preeminent "car guy," and Alex Malcomson, a successful coal merchant, formalized a partnership in which Ford gave Malcomson 50 percent interest in his patents, tools, models, and drawings, plus one race car still to be built and a commitment to develop a passenger car. Malcomson's contribution was cash. But that cash quickly ran out. Ford and Malcomson looked for new money.

At its incorporation in 1903, Ford Motor Company issued one thousand shares of common stock. Henry Ford and his partner Alex Malcomson accepted 255 shares each in exchange for the machinery, patents, and designs that the two had developed and brought with them into the new firm. With 51 percent of the total shares, Ford and Malcomson could dominate any key decisions as long as they voted their shares together. The Dodge brothers, John and Horace, whose company manufactured the main components of Ford's automobiles, received fifty shares each. They paid for the shares with parts and materials. John Gray, a banker who had loaned the cash-strapped Ford-Malcomson partnership $10,500, received 105 shares as repayment. Gray also became the first president of Ford Motor Company, which gave the new company some credibility with the shareholders. Then there was Albert Strelow, who owned the building that Ford and Malcomson had been using to assemble the cars (fifty shares); Vernon Fry, a cousin of Malcomson (fifty shares); attorneys John Anderson and Horace Rockham (fifty shares each); Charles Woodall, a bookkeeper (10 ten shares); Charles Bennett, a local manufacturer looking for an investment (fifty shares); and James Couzens, whom Henry Ford had enlisted at the insistence of the new shareholders to bring sorely needed administrative organization and financial discipline to the business.

Couzens wanted to purchase twenty-five shares but needed just a bit more cash to do that. He approached his sister, a schoolteacher. Rosetta Couzens took $100 from her own savings, with which James was to purchase one share for her. James purchased the twenty-four shares he could afford and the single share for his sister. These were the original shareholders of the Ford Motor Company. This original subscription brought only $28,000 in cash into the corporation, but it also cemented some important relationships and talent to the organization.[131]

The new organization quickly showed its merit. The new company was so profitable that by the end of the first year of business, the shareholders had received back in dividends almost their entire original investment.[132] Ford would have continued his past practice of holding up sales of any cars until he had included every one of his innovations. But since his innovations never ended, there would have been no sales. Under the discipline imposed by James Couzens, who was serving as de facto financial officer, cars were built to the specifications that existed when they were ordered, then shipped. New innovations were built into new models in a carefully managed process. The multidisciplined management team was doing what the entrepreneur partners could not. Where Henry Ford's prior ventures had failed, the new Ford Motor Company thrived.

By early 1906, disagreements on business strategy led Malcomson, Fry, Bennett, and Woodall to the sell their stock, and Albert Strelow decided to sell his shares to join a gold rush in Canada. Under the terms of the original stock issue, the shares could only be sold to an existing shareholder. Henry Ford bought the shares. That increased his total shares to 585, giving him 58.5 percent of the votes in any shareholder decision—a clear majority. At the same time, James Couzens increased his holdings to 109 shares. The other original investors, including Rosetta Couzens, held onto their shares.[133]

Ford was now free to pursue his vision. He would focus the company on building a simple, high-volume, low-price car. First came the Model N in 1907, which produced the company's first year in which profit exceeded one million dollars. Then came the car that rocked the world—the Ford Model T, first presented in 1908 after nearly two years of design and experimentation. The Model T was not the lowest priced automobile on the market, but it was immediately accepted as the best value for the price. The advertised price of $850 for a five-passenger, twenty-horsepower touring car drew plenty of prospective custom-

---

131 Robert Lacey, *Ford: The Men and the Machine,* 72.
132 Ibid, 75.
133 Robert Lacey, *Ford—The Men and the Machine,* 82.

ers, most of whom decided for optional additional features such as headlights, top, speedometer, and windshield, which brought the price up to $985.[134] No other manufacturer was offering comparable power, sturdiness, and reliability, which were key attributes in a country with few paved roads and a population living mainly on farms and in small villages.

The price was beyond the reach of factory workers, many of whom earned less than $800 per year. Rosetta Couzens could not afford a car on her teaching salary of about $850. There were no installment plans. Customers paid cash when they placed their order. But for a typical university professor bringing home $2,500 per year, and for many merchants, physicians, and quite a few farmers, the Model T was affordable. Within six months, the company had received firm orders for all the vehicles that could be produced in a year and suspended taking orders. In the first twelve months of the Model T, ending September 30, 1909, Ford Motor Company sales increased 60 percent compared to the prior year![135]

In fiscal year 1909–1910,[136] sales doubled, and they doubled again in the following year, with the company employing sixty-nine hundred workers. The Model T was a marketing success. Its design and reliability were winning customers.

Growth in sales demanded growth in production capacity. Building automobiles involved a relatively small number of skilled workers making the parts. Then semiskilled workers, each at his own bench, assembled the parts into components, which were passed on to workers assembling cars in small batches as the chasses moved on wooden cradles from station to station within the plant. A few components were added at each station.

In 1913, Ford starting using a tabletop assembly line to assemble magnetos. Formerly, one worker assembled one magneto at a time, putting together all thirty-five to forty pieces, and passed the completed magnetos to the station where they were placed on the car chassis. An experienced worker could produce one magneto in fifteen minutes. In the new process, the magneto being assembled passed along a waist-high shelf, along which employees were lined up side by side. Each employee performed just one or two of the steps needed—place one magnet, or tighten one screw—then passed the unit along to the next employee, who performed just one more step, then passed it along.

---

134 Douglas Brinkley, *Wheels for the World*, 111.
135 Robert Lacey, *Ford: The Men and the Machine*, 94.
136 In the early years, Ford Motor Company observed a fiscal year October 1 to September 30, rather than the calendar year. The period from October 1, 1909, to September 30, 1910, would be referred to as fiscal year 1910, or FY 1910.

Assembly time: thirteen minutes and ten seconds. With the addition of a motorized belt, and adjustments to the tasks assigned each worker, assembly time dropped quickly to five minutes per magneto.[137] Each worker's productivity had tripled.

The assembly line process was applied to other components and to the overall chassis assembly through a series of experiments, measurements, and constant adjustments. Results were dramatic. In less than a year, the average time needed to build a complete Model T was reduced from twelve and a half man-hours per car to ninety-three minutes. If the goal had been simple cost-cutting, Ford could set his selling price slightly lower than his competition and keep most of the reduction in assembly cost as profit. But Henry Ford saw a bigger opportunity. He aimed to grow his business by growing the available customer base. He could now assemble almost ten times as many vehicles with the same number of workers. That would allow a much lower sales price, which made the Model T affordable to even more customers and produced more cash flow that could be reinvested into still more efficiency to drop prices further. Profit per car would fall, but the total profit to Ford Motor Company would grow in the long term as more and more people purchased the Model T.

But the semiskilled bench workers who took pride in building complete magnetos or engine blocks, etc., received very little satisfaction or sense of achievement in mindlessly turning the same nut on the same part for nine hours every day. That same change in job description affected virtually every job in the plant. By December 1913, with the plant conversion barely completed, and with a 13 percent pay raise already in their pay envelopes, workers were leaving faster than new ones could be hired. There were more than a dozen automobile companies and plenty of other manufacturers looking for workers and still running their plants the old fashioned way. Employee turnover at Ford Motor Company soared to 380 percent.[138] Ford saw the danger. Hiring and training fifty-three thousand new people each year just to maintain a staff of fourteen thousand workers was unsustainable. If the company could not attract and retain workers, the growth plans would collapse.

Henry Ford became a passionate proponent of human resources within the Ford Motor Company. In January 1914, the board of directors approved the proposal for a profit-sharing bonus that would in effect raise the worker's wages from $2.34 to $5 per day.[139] In addition, the workday was cut from nine hours to eight. This would allow for a third shift, and four thousand new employees

---

137 Robert Lacey, *Ford: The Men and the Machine,* 108–109.
138 Douglas Brinkley, *Wheels for the World,* 159.
139 The concept of the $5 day is attributed to James Couzens in an unpublished manuscript by Ida Tarbell (Brinkley, 166.)

were hired so the Highland Park plant could operate around the clock. The news was immediately heralded throughout the country. Most newspapers included editorials praising this landmark action, which would lift many workers from out of the drudgery of subsistence living into the ranks of those with discretionary income—a few extra dollars to save or spend. Quite a few business leaders criticized the plan, convinced that the Five Dollar Day would surely lead to the downfall of Ford Motor Company, very likely to the collapse of many businesses, and possibly to the ruin of the nation.[140]

But they did not know what Henry knew. The productivity increases achieved in just a few months by establishing the assembly line process throughout the Highland Park plant were not yet known or even imagined outside of Ford Motor Company. Ford's strategy of offering a singe, basic model with ever-lower selling prices to win new customers depended on continuously lowering the per-unit cost of producing cars. The productivity improvement from the new assembly process was the key to Ford's continuing sales growth, increased profits, and thus the higher pay scale.

His concept for improving the lifestyle of Ford employees went beyond money. To participate in the bonus pay, and thus the $5 per day wage, an employee had to have completed six months of employment and had to qualify in one of three classifications: (1) married men living with and taking care of their families; (2) single men over twenty-two years of age who are of proved thrifty habits; (3) young men under twenty-two years of age or women who are the sole support of some next of kin.[141]

Many workers had poor reading and writing skills, or they spoke little English. Less than one third of Ford's workers were American-born. Classes were established at Ford plants to provide on-site English language training. Attendance was mandatory for those who were foreign-born and wanted to receive the bonus pay that would get them to the $5 per day pay level. Workers gained not just higher pay but greater literacy, which no doubt raised their quality of life. Pamphlets were distributed promoting good housekeeping, healthy diet, and frequent bathing as important to good health. The new Sociological Department sent investigators, accompanied by translators, to workers' homes to be sure the higher compensation was being used to create a better life, as evidenced by better housing, savings, life insurance, and similar "permanent" improvements. A worker who squandered his[142] pay, especially in the numerous bars, opium dens,

---

140 Robert Lacey, *Ford: The Men and the Machine*, 118–120.
141 Henry Ford, *My Life and Work*, 96.
142 In the early years of the program, female workers did not receive bonus

and houses of prostitution that accompanied Detroit's economic miracle, risked losing the profit-share incentive and falling back to the $2.34 basic wage.[143] At the end of one year, 87 percent of the workers were receiving the bonus pay. Eighteen months after the plan started, more than 99 percent of workers were receiving it. The work force stabilized.[144]

All of this was accomplished while the sale price of the Model T was being periodically reduced. The car's original price in 1908, $850 without the extras, was reduced to $490 in 1914 and $360 by 1916, and most of the extras had become standard equipment. Ford's market strategy was, "Instead of giving attention to competitors or to demand, our prices are based on an estimate of what the largest number of people will want to pay, or can pay, for what we have to sell."[145] Each price reduction attracted more customers, which increased total demand, making the assembly line efficiencies even more valuable. In 1909, General Motors had about 10 percent market share to Ford Motor Company's 10 percent. By 1912, Ford had overtaken GM, and it continued to widen its lead in the fast-growing market until 1921, at which point Ford Motor Company was selling six out of every ten new cars in America—a market dominance that neither GM nor Ford would ever achieve again.[146]

———

In 1916, Henry Ford wanted to build another, much larger plant. This would be far more than an assembly plant. Ford's vision now was to establish an industrial complex that would supply all the raw materials to make all the components needed for automobiles. Ford Motor Company would become self-sufficient. The intent was not primarily to gather the suppliers' current profit margins on Ford business. That could have been accomplished by buying the suppliers. Ford's intent was to make the entire supply chain more efficient. New methods

---

pay. Ford's expectation, consistent with sentiment of most business leaders, was that women should work only until their weddings, and then they should devote themselves to family and household, relying on the husband as breadwinner for the family.

143 This involvement in workers' home life seems intrusive today. But early in the twentieth century, public sentiment supported social controls on individual behavior. By 1919, Prohibition was the law of the land.

144 Henry Ford, *My Life and Work*, 97–98.

145 Ibid, 110.

146 Arthur J. Kuhn, *GM Passes Ford, 1918-1938.* Credited to General Motors Corporation, *The Automobile Industry: A Case Study of Competition.*

would be brought into the processes of steelmaking, paint manufacture, and virtually every other process connected with producing automobiles.

The new plant along the Rouge River would be an industrial colossus devoted entirely to manufacturing Ford automobiles. The cost of construction would be huge. The board of directors recognized that profits would actually decline in the first few years after construction, until demand and production came close to the much larger capacity of the new plant. The board, at Henry Ford's urging, decided the funds for construction would be raised by reducing cash dividends and investing the retained profits into construction of the new plant.

Some of the Ford shareholders disagreed, preferring that the large dividend payments continue. They saw the company, with its huge sales and profits, as a cash cow. Why invest so heavily in the future when today is so lucrative? They filed suit, asking the court to force distribution of at least 75 percent of cash surplus as dividends and to prohibit development of the Rouge plant.

The Michigan court decided that the board of directors of a corporation has very liberal discretion as to conduct of the business and the disposition of the corporation's profits. The court found that building the plant was a commercial decision within the board's discretion, but it found the cut-off of dividends to be arbitrary since the corporation's books showed enough cash on hand to build the new plant, pay dividends, and still have $30 million in cash reserves. The company's business plan projected ample positive cash flow going forward. "A business corporation is organized and carried on primarily for the stockholders," wrote the judge, ordering that the dividends sought by the shareholders be paid.[147]

Ford Motor Company paid the dividends as ordered, and Henry Ford set out to buy all the shares held by others. By this time, all of them were wealthy just from the dividends they had received over the years. Most settled for $12,500 per share. James Couzens, negotiating for himself and his sister, obtained $13,000 per share. The $100 investment that Rosetta Couzens, a schoolteacher, had made in 1903 produced a buyout of $262,036, in addition to the $95,000 she had received in dividends over the sixteen years of her share ownership. By 1919, Henry Ford owned the Ford Motor Company, as the saying goes, lock, stock, and barrel. He redistributed the shares, keeping 55 percent himself, 3 percent to his wife Clara, and 42 percent to his son Edsel, who by that time had been named president. All of the earning power of Ford Motor Company, and all decisions regarding dividends, investment in new plants, and every other issue of corporate

---

147 Dodge v. Ford, 204 Michigan 505.

governance, were now the province of these three people. There would henceforth be no confusion about what was in the interest of stockholders.

———

The rapid expansion of Ford Motor Company had an impact on life throughout southeastern Michigan. The medical needs of so many workers and their families were overwhelming the hospitals of Detroit and the surrounding area. Henry Ford, as a prominent citizen and industrial leader, was asked to lead the committee to raise donations. Henry, however, had little patience with committees. He offered to build the hospital at his own expense, as long as the entire planning process was left to him. He set out to build the finest hospital in the world.

The building differed from hospitals of the day. Each patient had a private room with a window for sunshine and its own bathroom with hot and cold water. There were separate departments for medicine, surgery, obstetrics, pediatrics, laboratory, and x-ray. Most of the first staff physicians were drawn from Johns Hopkins, the pre-eminent medical school in America at the time. Every new patient was examined by a senior physician, then by at least two other physicians. Blood tests were part of the basic diagnostic process. Each examining physician sent his written report and diagnosis to the head of the hospital. The intent was to ensure that each patient received a thorough evaluation as the foundation of an appropriate therapeutic plan. It was a significant departure from the practice at many hospitals, where the patient's sole physician would establish a diagnosis, and professional courtesy at the time prevented any other physician from disagreeing.

The nurses were all graduate nurses. Meals were served by separate attendants, so nurses could focus on professional care of their assigned patients. Physicians and nurses were full-time employees of the hospital, and they had to agree to have no outside practices. Physician salaries were equal to the earnings of a physician in private practice. The nurses earned six dollars per eight-hour day.

The hospital also differed from many others in its focus on high-quality care at prices affordable to the working man. Most hospitals of the day were either charity institutions providing free care to the poor or profit-making ventures providing comfortable accommodations for the well-to-do. Ford believed that a worker should have access to good care, while preserving his pride and independence by paying a fee for service. The daily charge for a room, including nursing service and meals, was $8. For the initial medical exam, the fee was $15.

The first patient was admitted in 1919, and the Henry Ford Hospital today, still at the original Grand Boulevard site, continues to be one of the finest hospi-

tals in the country, with a Level 1 trauma center, multiorgan transplant capabilities, and 903 beds.

———

A serious economic recession in 1920–1921 had a long-term impact on
both Ford Motor Company and rival General Motors.[148] The Federal Reserve
Board's Index of Industrial Production dropped 38 percent between February
1920 and March 1921, before conditions started to improve. At U.S. Steel, sales
fell 44 percent, profits fell 66 percent, and employment was reduced by 28
percent before business picked up again. As noted earlier, sales at the nation's
two leading retailers fell 33 percent. Sears, Roebuck and Company reduced its
employment by 29 percent. General Motors was also in distress, with too little
cash and too much unsold inventory.

Before the recession, Ford was by far the largest automobile manufacturer,
with about 40 percent market share. But Ford sales also dropped sharply in the
summer months of 1920. The recession was not part of the company's business
plan. When sales dropped sharply in the summer of 1920, a cash flow crisis became imminent.

Henry Ford went into action. He laid off hundreds of white-collar workers,
offering many of them work in the plant, and he stretched his payments to suppliers from sixty days to ninety days. To convert the parts inventory to cash in the
midst of falling sales, Ford increased car production by 25 percent, slashed prices, and insisted that his dealers take much larger deliveries of new cars and spare
parts onto their lots—and pay for them upon delivery—or risk losing their Ford
franchise. Few dealers wanted to lose the franchise to sell the best-selling car
in America, so they paid. Ford avoided the cash shortage that could have forced
him to sell shares to others or default on existing debt, either of which would
have cost him the absolute control of the company. Ford's 25 percent increase in

---

148 The recession of 1920–1921 is sometimes referred to, and was at the
time, as a depression. There is some conjecture that it resulted from very high
income tax rates passed during the war, a cyclical unwinding after the high-
production, inflationary war years, or too-rapid expansion of civilian production capacity. But few, if any, attempts have been made to study this period,
unlike the Great Depression of the 1930s. The seriousness of the 1920–1921
recession is hard to gauge since there were no federal unemployment statistics
as we know them today, but the major layoffs at U.S. Steel and Sears, Roebuck
and Company show a deep, year-long disruption.

sales in 1921, when GM sales were slowed by the economy, boosted Ford's market share to an all-time high of 60 percent and pushed GM's share down to 14 percent. But Ford's success, contrasted with General Motors' difficulties, scared General Motors management into a multiyear, multidiscipline self-improvement program that would reshape GM into an efficient, formidable competitor.

During and after the 1920–1921 recession, Ford held to its strategy. Offering a basic car for reliable transportation at an ever-lower price allowed sales to grow as the car became more affordable to more people. In 1921, the price difference between the Model T and a comparably equipped Chevrolet was 25 percent.[149] General Motors made plans to challenge Ford's dominance of the low-price basic market, but this would take years to execute. In the same year, there were 9.5 million automobiles registered in the U.S. By 1924, the number reached 15.5 million. The largest number of these were Fords.

But by the mid-1920s, the sale of used cars offered an option to customers looking for low priced, basic transportation—Ford's target customer. Why not purchase a slightly used car from a neighbor or from a dealer, for less money than the Ford Motor Company price for a new Model T? And the owner selling his Model T might well be looking for something new, with a little more comfort or just a different look. The Model T changed very little from year to year, except for invisible under-the-hood mechanical improvements. Anyone looking to trade up to a better ride would look at a different brand, perhaps Chevrolet, Buick, or maybe a Maxwell, or something from Willys-Overland. There were plenty of car companies vying for business. Ford dominated the low-price market segment, where most first-time buyers were found. But Ford had no appeal to the trade-up market and thus little assurance of repeat customers. General Motors' strategy of offering a variety of brands and annual model changes became a competitive advantage by mid-decade.

Henry Ford's drive to own all of the company stock within his own family and assume total control had also led to the departure of some talented executives who had helped build the company. James Couzens had brought financial discipline to the company in its early days and established a network of sales agencies throughout the U.S. and Europe. By 1906, he had become virtually Henry Ford's partner in managing the business, as well as the second-largest shareholder. Couzens resigned his management position in 1915 after several major disagreements, although he retained his seat on the board of directors and his 11 percent share of the company stock until 1919. The chief engineer

---

149 Alfred Sloan, *My Years With General Motors*, 69.

from the early days of the company, C. Harold Wills, left in 1919. In 1922, Ford Motor Company bought Lincoln Motor Company at a bankruptcy auction and thereby acquired the services of both Henry Leland,[150] one of Detroit's most revered car executives, and his capable son Wilfred. Within a year, Henry Ford forced both of them out. By early in the 1920s, almost every executive of independent stature had resigned from the Ford Motor Company. In 1923, Henry Ford wrote, "And so the Ford factories and enterprises have no organization, no specific duties attaching to any position, no lines of succession or of authority, very few titles, and no conferences…we have no elaborate records of any kind, and consequently no red tape."[151]

———

Management at General Motors Company was very different. The company had been organized in 1908 when William C. Durant used shares of stock in his successful Buick Motor Company[152] to purchase several other car companies. Durant was a capable entrepreneur. Both he and Ford visualized a growing market for the automobile. But Durant believed that a successful car company would need to offer a number of different models at different price points to attract buyers with different interests—a concept accepted today by every significant car company. Until 1920, General Motors had increased its sales by acquiring numerous rival car companies through a series of mergers and acquisitions. This strategy of growth by acquisition allowed GM to offer a variety of designs at different price points to attract a variety of customers. Durant lacked the organizing skills needed to consolidate his growing company into a successful organization.

Durant was also distracted by his own efforts to enhance his personal fortune by short-term trading in General Motors stock. During 1920, without the knowledge of his business associates, he had been speculating in General Motors stock, both borrowing money to buy shares and lending out shares for speculation

---

150 In 1902, Leland had worked briefly with Henry Ford in the Henry Ford Company. But Leland left and established Cadillac, a high-priced car for upper-income customers, while Ford focused on lower-priced segment of the market. Leland had established Lincoln in 1920. The strain of new production costs and the collapse of sales during the recession brought Lincoln Motor Company to bankruptcy.
151 *My Life and Work: An Autobiography of Henry Ford,* 70.
152 In 1908, Buick actually built more cars than any other car manufacturer: 8,487 compared to Ford's 6,181.

by others. This was an extremely risky strategy, but if the share price rose, even slightly, the profits could be huge. In November 1920, the price of GM shares fell in the recession, and Durant's luck ran out. He could not meet his margin obligations to his stockbroker.

Two years earlier, a $25 million purchase of General Motors stock by the E. I. DuPont de Nemours Company had given the chemical firm a 23.8 percent ownership of General Motors. That participation was subsequently increased to 28.7 percent. When Durant's investment strategies became obviously imperiled, an investment banker at Morgan and Company alerted Pierre S. du Pont, who was GM's chairman. If Durant's shares were liquidated in a forced sale to meet his margin debts, the market price of GM shares would drop sharply. That would produce a significant loss in value for every shareholder and leave prolonged anxiety regarding the company's stability. Morgan & Company was brought in to gather investors with a total of $60 million, over one weekend, to prevent the debacle to GM's stock price. Morgan & Company accomplished the large bailout, and GM continued to operate without disruption.[153]

Appalled at Durant's speculative scheme, the GM board of directors bid him adieu, and Pierre du Pont was appointed president in addition to his duties as chairman. At that point, the corporation desperately needed a person of stature and credibility to restore confidence among shareholders, suppliers, employees, and the public. Pierre du Pont was the perfect choice. Durant's departure brought management change to GM that would propel it to new levels of performance. In 1923, du Pont resigned as president of General Motors, and the board of directors appointed a man who would become one of America's greatest corporate leaders of the twentieth century, Alfred P. Sloan, Jr.

Sloan was an electrical engineer by training and a brilliant man. He had graduated from Massachusetts Institute of Technology, class of 1895. With a concentration and energy that would be displayed throughout his business career, he had completed the prescribed four-year course of study in three years. In 1899, at Sloan's urging, his father and an associate had purchased the failing Hyatt Roller Bearing Company. Sloan, just twenty-three years old, was put in charge, and over time he acquired a large equity stake in the business.

Sloan grew the business mainly through a "consultative selling" strategy. He met with his customers' engineers and worked with them to design axles and other components that incorporated Hyatt roller bearings. As he helped his customers solve their design problems, he was boosting his own sales. Hyatt Roller

---

153 Alfred P. Sloan, Jr., *My Years with General Motors*, 14, 34–39.

Bearing Company was soon a principal supplier to Ford Motor Company, which bought almost 50 percent of Hyatt's production, General Motors, and more than a dozen other automobile companies. In 1916, William Durant offered to buy Hyatt Roller Bearing Company to be the core of a new parts division to be called United Motors. Sloan and the other shareholders accepted a total price of $13.5 million. Sloan's share was just over $5 million, mainly in shares of United Motor stock. Durant retained Sloan as head of the new GM parts division and as a member of the executive committee of General Motors.

William Knudsen had started up the Rouge Plant and then set up a network of Ford assembly plants around the country. Knudsen left Ford in February 1921 and joined General Motors, where he took charge of Chevrolet. Ford himself described Knudsen as the best car production man in the United States. Knudsen eventually became president of General Motors and guided that company through the Great Depression, when it surpassed Ford Motor Company in market share. During World War II, Knudsen was appointed to oversee all U.S. war production.

The du Pont investment brought new discipline to the ways in which General Motors handled its money. Even in this vast and growing corporation, cash was not unlimited, but ideas for spending were. As the du Ponts exerted their influence, potential investments in new plants, technologies, and materials were rigorously compared. The corporation's capital would be committed where the carefully estimated return on investment was highest. Earlier, less formal methods had left the company cash-short and in jeopardy on several occasions. Compensation and incentive plans at every level of the company were carefully refined to get manager and employee performance aligned with shareholder interest in efficient use of capital. The man responsible for this financial overhaul was John Jacob Raskob, the du Pont-appointed chairman of General Motors finance committee.

Raskob had been working for Pierre S. du Pont since 1900. He had started as personal secretary but quickly impressed his boss with his competence and financial acumen. Raskob's responsibilities were increased, and his boss presented opportunities for Raskob to invest in du Pont ventures. From his own savings, and at times with loans from banks or his boss, Raskob made investments in his early years that became the basis of a substantial fortune. Durant's departure made Raskob's position even more prominent.[154]

---

154 John J. Raskob Papers at Hagley Museum and Library.

The 1920s witnessed the growth of two car companies with very different managements and strategies. Ford Motor Company, with Edsel Ford as president but Henry always the dominant shareholder and decision-maker, was plagued by resignations of key lieutenants who had contributed so much to the phenomenal success of the company. Ford relied on continuous growth in the market for basic transportation and one product—the Model T. All variations to it were personally approved by Henry Ford. The manufacture of parts and the entire assembly process were vertically integrated to impose control and ensure low-cost production.

Meanwhile, at General Motors, a group of seasoned automobile executives became increasingly well-organized and efficient. In 1919, while Durant was still president, Alfred Sloan had submitted a detailed plan for a more formal organization of General Motors and its various brands. After the debacle of 1920, Pierre du Pont gave Sloan's plan considerable attention and implemented much of it. The loose confederation of car companies competing against each other for customers was formed into a corporate structure in which each brand-name division focused on a specific customer segment. Financial controls and investment decisions were centralized. Market research and production planning were elevated to the corporate level. To ensure that the entire management team adhered to the strategy, compensation plans included incentives in the form of common stock shares.

Sloan became president in 1923. He continued to refine the organizational structure and the relationship between the brand executives and corporate management. The organization became even more focused on market segmentation by assigning price points to each brand, avoiding the overlaps and outright competition that had existed previously. Each brand could experiment with specific changes for its own models, within the price ranges assigned by the corporation, but broader engineering issues or pure experimentation were to be conducted at corporate labs. Soon General Motors was updating each model every year. Great attention was paid to body style. In 1925, Chevrolet introduced the Model K to compete directly with the Model T in price and quality.

The growing business required a constantly growing talent pool. The General Motors Institute was established in 1926 to provide training and professional development, and thereby advancement opportunity, to managers and line workers. There were full-time programs in cooperative engineering, technical trades, and automobile servicing. Part-time studies involved semiskilled trades, accounting, foremanship and courses in practically every aspect of the automobile industry. GMI offered an avenue for plant workers with little formal education to train for promotion to higher positions. GMI programs were available to "young men of promise already employed in the GM industries and…

young men of the right type coming out of high school." The course offerings provide insight into GM management's views of what constituted sound training of managers. In addition to engineering and technical courses, there were courses on psychology, labor problems and incentives, economics, accounting, costs and cost controls, salesmanship, business law, statistics, and business cycles. Over time, GMI prepared many of General Motors' senior executives.[155]

There was one other important difference between these two companies—their ownership. With all the shares of Ford Motor Company in the hands of Henry, Clara, and Edsel Ford, all the risks, and all the rewards, resided in this one family. Profits could be distributed as dividends among these three shareholders, or kept within the company as undistributed profits—essentially a company savings account—for future use or distribution, in whatever way these three shareholders deemed appropriate. In reality, that meant Henry Ford would decide. Of course, if things went badly, the losses would be their problem also. General Motors, however, was owned by shareholders, many of whom bought and sold their shares on the public market. E. I. DuPont Company owned approximately 25 percent of the shares from 1920 until 1957, when the Supreme Court ordered DuPont and GM to separate, but through it all there were thousands of shareholders: managers, employees, investors, and speculators. Some were wealthy. Others had just a few spare dollars to invest. But all these shareholders benefited from the flow of dividends and at times from rising share prices. A direct sharing in the success—profits—or failure of General Motors was available to the public.

To add to the excitement, Walter P. Chrysler launched a new model that hit $50 million in sales in its first year. He pulled together the Chrysler Corporation in 1925. The "Big Three," along with several others, would now compete for the patronage of American and foreign customers.

By the mid-1920s, Ford Motor Company, relying on its Model T, was losing market share to GM, whose Chevrolet sales jumped 220 percent between 1922 and 1925. By 1926, Ford's market share was down to 34 percent. People were trading in their Model T and buying new Chevrolets, Essexes, or Buicks. The Model T had not lost any of its reliability. It had changed very little in style. Customers just wanted something new, with a quieter engine that would maintain the higher speeds allowed by paved highways, and a more user-friendly transmission. Pressured by the competitive challenge, Henry Ford had some decisions to make.

---

155 Arthur J. Kuhn, *GM Passes Ford, 1918—1938,* 23, 169–70.

Henry turned sixty in 1923. In 1924, and again in 1927, an investment banking firm offered one billion dollars for the Ford Motor Company.[156] At that valuation, Henry Ford's 55 percent ownership holding made him one of the wealthiest men in America, without considering the shares held by his wife (3 percent) and son Edsel (42 percent). He could retire. He was in good health. He was interested in politics. He had backed Wilson's reelection in 1916. Ford counted Wilson as a soul mate who shared his commitment to world peace, prohibition, and women's suffrage. Ford had run for the United States Senate in 1918 and almost won. There had been talk of a possible run for president in 1924. Or he and Clara could travel the world. But Henry Ford did not back away from competition in the car business. He finally allowed a new model.

The Model T was a worthy successor to the Model T. It was also a major investment for the Ford Motor Company. The Model T facility at Highland Park was closed in May 1927 and a new assembly plant was established at Rouge. In 1927 and 1928, the company lost $250 million while making the transition, establishing the new plant, retooling equipment, and launching a new advertising program.[157]

The Model A had all the modern conveniences, including balloon tires, electric starter, and ample insulation to give it a much quieter ride than the Model T. The four-cylinder engine could out-accelerate most six- and eight-cylinder cars. The rounded body style was a welcome departure from the boxy predecessor. The $495 average price tag was $100 lower than the comparable Chevrolet and put Ford back in competition for the first-time buyer, the working man or farmer who had always been the target of Ford's efforts. The first Model A rolled off the assembly line late in 1927. Getting the assembly line up to full production capacity took another year.[158] In 1929, more than 1.5 million Model As were sold, giving Ford Motor Company a 34 percent share of the automobile market, compared to Chevrolet's 20 percent. Ford Motor Company earned $90 million in profits. Ford Motor Company was recapturing its former glory. Then came the Great Depression. In 1930, Ford profits fell to $40 million. In 1931, the company lost more than $37 million.[159]

---

156 *New York Times*, February 3, 1927.
157 Allan Nevins and Frank Hill, *Ford: Expansion and Challenge, 1915-1933*, 458.
158 Charles E. Sorensen, *My Forty Years with Ford*, 225.
159 Allan Nevins and Frank Hill, *Ford: Expansion and Challenge, 1915-1933*, 573.

General Motors' Chevrolet division had launched a new model with a six-cylinder engine in 1929, directly competing with Ford's Model A. General Motors management noticed declining sales during the spring and summer of 1929. Fewer customers were buying cars. Reacting quickly, GM trimmed production so that inventories were sold off faster than new cars were made. Cash from sales was saved rather than reinvested in new vehicles. By 1932, car and truck production for all manufacturers in the U.S. and Canada had declined 75 percent, from 5.6 million units to 1.4 million. The low-price models were the hardest hit.

The very different corporate strategies of General Motors and Ford produced two different results. General Motors had brands and models for every price bracket, so General Motors' sales fell less, by 71 percent, from $1.5 billion in 1929 to $432 million in 1932. Sales of the higher-priced brands allowed the company to remain profitable every year through the 1930s. Ford Motor Company relied almost entirely on the Model A, and as its sales fell, profits disappeared. Between 1931 and 1937, Ford Company lost $132 million.[160] General Motors' market share passed Ford's, and GM remained the largest automobile manufacturer in the world throughout the twentieth century.[161]

———

Today, as more customers consider fuel efficiency in making their purchase decisions, more car manufacturers are converting their assembly lines from pickup trucks and SUVs to smaller, fuel-efficient models. Toyota and Honda enjoy the "first mover" advantage. Their technology has improved over many years, and their assembly plants are specifically designed for fuel-efficient vehicles. As they produce larger numbers of these vehicles, their cost per unit falls and profits rise. Their strategic investment over the past decades, based on the belief that many customers—not just a few—will eventually value fuel efficiency, will likely be rewarded with profits. As other manufacturers catch up, customers will have more choices.

Is there any way for Ford, General Motors, or Chrysler to catch up? In 2006, Ford hired a new president and CEO, Alan Mulally, from Boeing. Mulally's experience as president of Boeing's commercial airplane division certainly gives him experience leading a large manufacturing operation. But the Ford Motor Company Board of Directors may have seen another important qualification in Mulally's

---

160 Arthur J. Kuhn, *GM Passes Ford, 1918-1938,* 317.
161 Alfred P. Sloan, Jr., *My Years with General Motors,* 199.

resume. At Boeing, he had been deeply involved in planning and production of Boeing's newest passenger jetliner, the 787. That aircraft was the first to be constructed using carbon-fiber materials, instead of the traditional aluminum-and-steel airframe and body. The result was not just a bigger airliner. The result was an airplane that uses 20 percent less fuel than the same plane built using traditional body technology. The plane also requires fewer parts and is much more resistant to corrosion, which is a major concern in airplane maintenance and safety.

Ford makes the hood of its Mustang Shelby GT500KR from carbon fiber. This is a first step in manufacturing larger sections of production (mass market) cars from this incredibly light but very strong material. Consider the fuel savings if every car or truck, of whatever size, can be made of carbon fiber.[162] As vehicle body parts become lighter, the steering, brakes, suspension system, and other components can also be made smaller and lighter. Now think about the fuel savings if these lighter cars were equipped with hybrid engines, using technology that Ford already uses in some of its vehicles.

The powerful role of consumer decisions in the life and death of corporations is clear in the troubles of Chrysler and General Motors in 2008 and 2009. Their market share had been declining gradually for decades. When gasoline prices surged to $4 per gallon in the summer of 2008, both companies were caught with too much inventory in trucks and SUVs and too few fuel-efficient models. As customers purchased fuel-efficient models from other manufacturers, cash flow weakened. With the financial crisis that struck in the fall of 2008, auto sales plummeted for all manufacturers. The surge in gasoline prices may be seen as the immediate cause of the Chrysler and GM problems, but the root cause was failure to meet changing consumer preferences. Chrysler and GM had repeated the mistake of Henry Ford in the mid-1920s.

Our scan of seven industries reveals an important pattern. In each industry, one or a few companies stand out by delivering considerably better ROE than competitors in the same industry, while dealing with all the same challenges. Corporations with higher ROEs tend to thrive, while competitors search for new CEOs or new strategies and sometimes disappear entirely, with share-

---

162 For a dramatic presentation on the potential of carbon fiber, visit the website of Rocky Mountain Institute, www.rmi.org. Look for the Stanford Energy Lectures and watch the video on transportation. While you are there, watch the other two Stanford Energy Lecture videos.

holders losing all their equity. Any vision of big oil companies, health insurers or competitors in any other industry somehow marching in unison fall apart when we compare the individual corporations, the customer niches they pursue, market strategies and financial performance. Customers making their purchase decisions enforce this rough-and-tumble competition among corporations. Corporations with the highest ROE for shareholders have often been the best employers, with the highest safety records and best environmental practices in their industries. Broad pronouncements that open with "all those oil companies" or "all those big corporations" fail to acknowledge the vastly different merits and accomplishments of firms within an industry.

A corporation's profit is the amount of money remaining after all the expenses of the business—parts, office supplies, depreciation[163] on buildings and equipment, utilities, compensation for employees, management and executives, and interest paid on loans, taxes, etc.—are subtracted from revenue. For most businesses, sale of products or services are the major source of revenue, although for some, such as insurance companies, interest and dividends from investments may be an important component of revenue.

There are only four things that can happen to corporate profits once they are earned. Many sovereign governments, including the U.S., collect income taxes on corporate profits to finance the government's programs. In the U.S., many individual states also collect income tax on corporate profits. The applicable tax rate for the jurisdiction is multiplied by the gross profits. The tax due is then paid as a company expense. Whatever is left, referred to as "net" or "after-tax" profits, can then be used either to pay cash dividends to shareholders or to buy shares of stock back from shareholders who want to sell. Any after-tax profits not used for dividends and share buy-backs are retained in the company. These retained earnings can be used by the company like a savings account—to provide funds for a future investment or contingency. The corporation's board of directors, which represents the shareholders, makes the decision about the amount of money to be distributed in dividends, used for buying back shares, or retained by the company. Of course, if there is no after-tax profit, there is nothing for the board to divide. When investors, corporate officers, or business reporters talk of profits,

---

163 Depreciation expense is the recognition that some property used in business, such as a building, truck, or major piece of machinery, has a useful life that continues long after the year in which it is put into service and will gradually lose value due to age, wear and tear, and obsolescence. Accountants use a depreciation expense each year, over the life of the property, to fairly present the gradual loss of value of such property during the year.

they use net profits, since those are the only profits available to the corporation for its future use or for return to the shareholders.

As we follow the money to determine just who benefits from these corporate profits, we can illustrate where ExxonMobil's 2006 profits went:

Where Do All the Profits Go—Who Gets the Money?

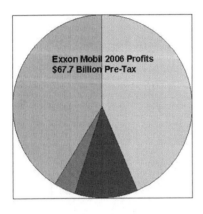

The pie chart shows the portion of corporate profits that go to the government, presumably for the benefit of society at large, compared to the portion that goes to the benefit of the shareholders—the people who took the risk that produced the profit. The profit number shown most often in the media is the "after-tax" profit— the portion of the company's profits that shareholders get as their reward for risk-taking. The share of profits that goes directly to the government in income tax is rarely recognized. When ExxonMobil reported its 2006 profits, the number most frequently in headlines, or even in detailed articles, was $39.5 billion.

But that is the after-tax number. The fact that ExxonMobil paid $27.9 billion in income taxes was unacknowledged.[164] The reporting is correct, since income taxes are an expense and profit is calculated by subtracting all expenses from all revenue.

To understand the role of profits and wealth in our society, we need to understand how government regulation and tax arrangements affect business. For the full story, we'll look at some interesting history.

---

164 Clifford Kraus, *New York Times,* February 1, 2007; other articles by Associated Press, *Chicago Tribune.*

VOTERS

Chapter Ten

"The Unexpected Death of Laissez Faire"

We the people of the United States, in order to form a more perfect Union, establish Justice, insure domestic Tranquility, provide for the common defense, promote the general Welfare, and secure the Blessings of Liberty to ourselves and our Posterity, do ordain and establish this Constitution for the United States of America.
—Preamble to the Constitution of the United States of America

The bosses never intended Theodore Roosevelt to become president of the United States in 1901. But Garret A. Hobart, vice president during President William McKinley's first term, died in November 1899. Seven months later, McKinley was the Republican convention's unanimous nominee for a second term as president. Roosevelt's nomination to the vice presidency was the result of a deal to get him out of New York politics, where he had been an irrepressible reformer as an assemblyman, police commissioner of New York City, and current governor of New York. A number of Roosevelt's initiatives irritated the local and state political bosses. Roosevelt had enacted a tax on corporations that had been granted utility or transit monopolies, several acts affecting hours of employment, and a strong Civil Service Act, which limited the patronage powers of the political machines. The bosses concluded that the State of New York, and the nation as well, would be better served by relegating Theodore

Roosevelt to the quiet backwater of the vice presidency, in the shadow of the popular and dependable President William McKinley.

The McKinley-Roosevelt ticket won comfortably in the 1900 election. Yet President McKinley was assassinated just six months after the inauguration, and Roosevelt became president early in the morning of September 14, 1901. Mark Hanna, senator from Ohio and chairman of the Republican National Committee, remarked privately on the train taking McKinley's body and the new president to Washington, "Now look, that damned cowboy is president of the United States."[165]

In his reelection campaign of 1900, President McKinley had spoken little about business or economic issues, except to remind his countrymen that their circumstances had improved dramatically in the years since his inauguration, which had happily coincided with the end of a serious recession. Neither he nor his predecessor Grover Cleveland had done anything to alleviate the suffering of the unemployed or to stimulate recovery. Nor was that expected. Employment and wages were private arrangements between employer and worker; relief for the unemployed was a matter for local government or charity. The major issue of the 1896 election, in the midst of a serious recession, had been whether to adopt silver as a legal backing for paper dollars. McKinley's victory affirmed the nation's preference for "sound money" backed by gold, but Congress did not pass legislation restoring the gold standard until March 1901. Perhaps the election of McKinley had calmed some professional investors and industrialists, but beyond that, the economy was left to cure itself.

By 1900, the nation's economy was in its fourth year of strong expansion. Net national product had been rising an average of 6 percent per year, and per capita output was growing at nearly 4.5 percent per year.[166] Steel production—an economic bellwether in that era—had more than doubled since 1896. New mills were opening as investors hoped to get in on the profits of this growing industry. Coal production was also at a record high. Cotton was the mainstay of the agricultural economy of southern states. Cotton production had set new records in 1897 and 1898, and the 1899 crop was only slightly lower in weight but higher in sale price.[167] The national unemployment rate averaged 5 percent that year, but few would have known that number, since this was not a federal

---

165 H. H. Kohlsaat, *From McKinley to Harding—Personal Reflections of Our Presidents*, 101.

166 Milton Friedman and Anna Jacobson Schwartz, *A Monetary History of the United States, 1867-1960*, 1963, National Bureau of Economic Research.

167 Steel, coal and cotton production from *Statistical Abstract of the United States, 1900*, Tables 86, 81, 94.

issue. Long forgotten were the worries of 1896–1897, when more than 14 percent of working-age adults were unable to find work.[168] Americans were feeling
flush and spending money on the niceties of middle class life. Sales from the
catalogues of Sears, Roebuck and Company had jumped from $1.7 million in
1896 to $10.6 million in 1900.[169] Montgomery Ward's mail order business was
also doing well. Marshall Field was one of the nation's wealthiest men, catering
to the consumers of Chicago and the Midwest.

The war against Spain in 1898 had been swift and successful. Four months
of hostilities, with a total of 298 American dead, had given America dominion
over Cuba, Puerto Rico, and the Philippines.[170] The war expenses had increased
the national debt by 20 percent, to just over one billion dollars, but the Treasury
was able to issue bonds paying just 2 percent annual interest.

McKinley's war record and the strong economy appealed to the white male
demographic. There were no other significant voter demographics,[171] so he won
reelection. Americans assumed that the twentieth century would see a continua-
tion of the laissez-faire (except for high tariffs) policies that had marked the closing years of the nineteenth century.[172] But McKinley's assassination six months
into his second term put Theodore Roosevelt in the White House. By winning
an additional term, Roosevelt extended his presidency across much of the first
decade of the twentieth century. He, and every president since, left an imprint
on government/business relations. The bullet that ended McKinley's life ended
the era of laissez-faire government/business relations in America.

America in 1901 was a nation of seventy-six million souls, ten million of
whom were foreign born, and many of these spoke little English. The flag that

---

168 *Historical Statistics of the United States, Colonial Times to 1970,* U.S. Department of Commerce, Series 85–86.
169 Boris Emmet and John H. Jeuck, *Catalogues and Counters,* 117.
170 Annual Message to Congress, December 5, 1898.
171 Women in most states would not be eligible to vote until the Nineteenth
Amendment was ratified in 1920. Black men in southern states were typically
kept from voting by brute intimidation or by local requirements such as poll
taxes, which were finally prohibited by the Twenty-fourth Amendment in 1964.
172 "Laissez faire" literally, in French "allow to do" or "allow to make," refers
to a policy of allowing owners and operators to conduct business without any
regulation or involvement by government. In the purest sense, this differs from a
pro-business policy. The tariff laws of the late nineteenth century were intended
to favor domestic businesses and workers over competition from foreign businesses and their workers. In every other respect, government policy (especially at
the federal level) toward business fit the laissez-faire model of noninvolvement.

draped McKinley's casket had forty-five stars. New York, Pennsylvania, Illinois, and Ohio were the most populous states. These four were home to almost a third of the nation's total population. California was the twenty-first most populous state, ranking just behind Mississippi.

Some industrial workers were unionized, but workplace conditions, hours, and wages were largely unregulated. Management made the rules and set the wages in ways that reflected either a desire for continuity of operations or ambivalence to strikes. A worker disabled on the job was dependent on charity for his medical expenses and to support his family. Ten- and twelve-hour shifts and six-day weeks were the norm in factories, as they had been for eons on farms and ranches.

Children worked as soon as they could perform useful tasks. A few years of school were enough to master reading, writing, and arithmetic. Less than 10 percent of the population aged fourteen to eighteen went beyond eighth grade. About 3 percent of those aged eighteen to twenty-two attended college or professional schools.[173]

Some states had passed laws establishing standards of minimum pay or requirements for overtime pay. A few states had prohibited judges from issuing injunctions against picket lines, in which workers publicly displaying their grievances might intimidate replacement workers trying to enter the plant. But in a series of decisions, the United States Supreme Court held that these "anti-injunction" laws interfered with the employer's constitutional right to "liberty of contract" or constituted a confiscation of property without due process of law and voided the state laws.

Theodore Roosevelt became president just months after the formation of the largest corporation in American history. A group of investors represented by J. P. Morgan purchased various companies in the steel and related industries. The largest acquisition was Carnegie Steel. The resulting United States Steel Corporation was the first American corporation to have a market value of more than one billion dollars. In spite of its size, and whatever may have been the objectives of Morgan and his investors, United States Steel Corporation continued to face competition as new investors sought their share of the profits from surging demand for steel.

The Sherman Antitrust Act of 1890 had been part of a legislative compromise that included passage of a tariff (named for Congressman and future President

---

173 *Statistical Abstract of the United States, 1900,* Table 121, and U.S. Census Bureau, decennial census of population, 1900.

William McKinley) that would allow many businesses to operate without much fear of foreign competition. The protective tariff was intended to shield American companies and jobs from foreign competitors paying lower wages abroad. Some members of Congress were concerned that without foreign competition American producers would boost prices. They would vote for the tariff only if competition inside the U.S. was assured by law, and the Antitrust Act was their assurance. [174]

The Sherman Act declared illegal "every contract, combination in the form of trust or otherwise, or conspiracy, in restraint of trade among the several states, or with foreign nations." Further, "Every person who shall monopolize, or attempt to monopolize, or combine or conspire with any other person or persons, to monopolize any part of the trade or commerce among the several states, or with foreign nations, shall be guilty of a misdemeanor..." A person found guilty of violating the law could be fined up to $5,000 or imprisoned for up to one year, or both. In addition, property owned by the guilty party, and being transported across state lines could be seized by the federal government. Anyone whose business or property was injured by actions prohibited in the Act could sue for triple damages.

But the 1890s saw a surge of mergers and acquisitions, trusts, and other combinations, in spite of a number of antitrust cases filed by both Republican and Democratic administrations. Several cases reached the United States Supreme Court, with mixed results. In *United States v. E.C. Knight Company* the Supreme Court pointed out that manufacture alone did not constitute commerce. The Court also pointed out that monopolizing the manufacture of a product within a single state did not constitute restraint or monopoly of "interstate commerce," which was the only commerce the federal government was authorized to regulate under the Constitution. The states retained the right to regulate intrastate business under their own powers. [175] The Sherman Act had seemed so simple and uncomplicated—just two handwritten pages of text—but questions of interstate commerce would be the subject of much legislative and judicial work in the twentieth century.

Philander Knox, the attorney general who had served McKinley and now served Roosevelt, had been reviewing trusts but found none ripe for antitrust

---

174 A trust is a legal entity into which people can deposit shares of corporations (or other property) for care. The trustees (managers of the trust) receive the dividends and cast the shareholder votes for the deposited shares. The depositors of the shares receive a trust certificate, defining their share in the trust, and receive payments from the trust (funded by the corporation dividends) and appoint the trustees. During the 1880s, trusts had become a convenient way to concentrate the power of multiple corporations in the same or related industries.

175 *United States v. E.C. Knight and Company,* 156 U.S. 1 (1895).

prosecution. Roosevelt ordered a new review and Knox came across a holding company, Northern Securities Company, which held most of the shares of two interstate railroads.[176] The merged railroads owned substantially parallel lines running from the Great Lakes and the Mississippi River to the Pacific Ocean at Puget Sound. On February 19, 1902, Roosevelt ordered Knox to file an anti-trust suit against Northern Securities.

A few months later, Roosevelt was searching for a candidate to replace a Supreme Court justice who was retiring. Roosevelt hoped for a justice who would support a more vigorous application of the antitrust law. Henry Cabot Lodge, senator from Massachusetts and dean of one of New England's most patrician families, recommended a man with a record of two decades serving on the Supreme Judicial Court of Massachusetts, including three years as its chief justice. Oliver Wendell Holmes Jr. met with the president in July.

The president no doubt admired the combat record of the thrice-wounded Civil War veteran and his degrees from Harvard College and Harvard Law School, as well as the doctor of laws degree from Yale University. Holmes was descended from early New England families. His established judicial philosophy acknowledged the legislative and executive branches as the elected representatives of the people, and therefore they were entitled to great deference in law-making. That would ease the mind of a president dedicated to vigorous enforcement of the Antitrust Act.

Their conversation must have been satisfactory. Within days, Roosevelt nominated Holmes to the Supreme Court, and Holmes took his seat in December 1902.

———

By October 1902, a strike of coal miners in anthracite regions of Pennsylvania had lingered five months without resolution. Coal was the almost-universal heating fuel, especially in cities where its relative ease of transport and delivery made it preferable to wood. Coal also fueled the locomotives that moved the country's raw materials, manufactured goods, and food. A winter without coal in millions of homes, schools, and hospitals would threaten public health. A rail traffic stoppage would cause an economic collapse. All of that coal was mined by companies effectively controlled by one group of owners. Their power was ab-

---

176 Northern Securities Company, according to court documents, owned more than 90 percent of the shares of Northern Pacific Railroad and more than 75 percent of the shares of Great Northern Railroad.

solute at the moment, but the competitive threat of different energy sources—bituminous coal and kerosene—toughened their resolve to hold wages low and avoid any other concessions.[177]

Union leaders had counseled their workers that a strike was not likely to be successful, even if sustained through the whole summer. Thousands of nonunion miners were willing to take their places. Substitution of kerosene or bituminous coal for anthracite in an emergency would make ghost towns of the anthracite regions and throw thousands permanently out of work. But the union miners focused on the wealth of the mining companies. Their objectives were clear: for the 40 percent of miners who were paid by the ton, a 10 percent increase in their pay per ton; for those paid on a per diem basis, a nine hour workday instead of ten, with no change in the daily rate, but since the mines would likely operate 10 percent more days per year (220 instead of 200), these miners would also earn 10 percent more per year. This was a compromise from their original demand of 20 percent increases. Management would not meet with the union leaders or negotiate. The miners had started their strike on May 12. Now, after a summer of no work and no pay, their resolve was still solid. No resolution was in sight.[178]

The federal government had no legal basis for intervention. Pennsylvania's governor had contained the early violence by sending state militia troops into the region.[179] But Roosevelt summoned the presidents of the major mining companies and John Mitchell, president of the United Mine Workers, to Washington. The president made clear his intent not to lobby for a pro-union or pro-management solution, but to "represent the people," the families that would suffer in a winter without coal. Roosevelt pressed the two sides to consider the public interest and settle the strike. The mine owners were furious that the president of the United States expected them to deal with a labor leader whose followers, from their viewpoint, represented a conspiracy to restrain trade and had damaged their property and brought civil strife to an entire region. Both sides offered to allow a third party to settle the dispute. But the owners wanted a federal court to decide, and the union leaders insisted on an arbitration panel appointed by the president. The

177 For separate confirmation that kerosene was less expensive than coal for domestic heating and cooking purposes, see *The Battle with the Slum,* by Jacob Riis, p. 39.

178 *Bulletin of the Department of Labor, No. 43—November, 1902.* Report to the President on Anthracite Coal Strike.

179 The term militia was used prior to 1916 when an Act of Congress established the term National Guard. However, the function of the units under command of the governor of each state did not change and is preserved under the Constitution.

meeting adjourned with no resolution. The situation was now so tense that Roosevelt ordered ten thousand regular army troops to be placed on alert, and he quietly advised his Cabinet members that if any further violence occurred, he would seize the mines under eminent domain and operate them as government entities.

Roosevelt's Secretary of War, Elihu Root, took a leave of absence. With Roosevelt's knowledge, Root approached J. P. Morgan, who had personal and financial ties to the mine owners. No doubt Morgan recognized the dire financial consequences for the nation and himself if the strike continued. Companies without sales could not produce profits, and every customer who changed to an alternative fuel would be lost forever. Root and Morgan, working quietly as private citizens, constructed a framework acceptable to the mine operators and the labor leaders. The mines would reopen immediately, and President Roosevelt would appoint a commission, with individuals acceptable to both sides, to investigate and issue a report on the coal mine situation. Two weeks after the unproductive meeting in Washington, the groups agreed to go back to work and to cooperate with a Coal Strike Commission appointed by the president. The winter passed without incident. The report of the Commission helped the miners win a 10 percent wage increase and a nine-hour day.[180] Roosevelt's careful advocacy of the "public interest" rather than pro-management or pro-labor proposals was a political success. Early in 1903, the Department of Commerce and Labor was established.

––––––

The Supreme Court announced its decision in the Northern Securities case on March 14, 1904. The original Circuit Court decision had barred Northern Securities Company from voting the stock of the railroad corporations or exercising any control over their actions, and enjoined the railroad corporations from paying any dividends to Northern Securities. The Supreme Court upheld the Circuit Court decision by a 5-4 majority. The administration had its victory. The Sherman Act was still viable. Then Justice Holmes delivered a surprise. His opinion in dissent from the majority pointed to many deficiencies in both the text of the Sherman Antitrust Act and the majority opinion in this case. Acknowledging the intense public interest in this case, Holmes wrote:

---

180 Report to the President on the Anthracite Coal Strike of May-October, 1902, by the Anthracite Coal Strike Commission. Available at http://darrow. law.umn.edu/documents/Report%20Anthracite%20Comm.pdf.

Great cases, like hard cases, make bad law. For great cases are called great not by reason of their real importance in shaping the law of the future, but because of some accident of immediate overwhelming interest which appeals to the feelings and distorts the judgment. These immediate interests exercise a kind of hydraulic pressure which makes what previously was clear seem doubtful, and before which even well settled principles of law will bend. What we must do in this case is find the meaning of some not very difficult words.

Holmes continued: "Judges...when their task is to interpret and apply the words of a statute, their function is merely academic to begin with—to read English intelligently—and a consideration of the consequences comes into play only when the meaning of the words is open to reasonable doubt."

The Sherman Act was a criminal statute, Holmes wrote, because its purpose, and its plain wording, was to make certain acts a crime:

The words cannot be read one way in a suit which is to end in fine and imprisonment another way in one which seeks an injunction...before a statute is to be taken to punish that which always has been lawful, it must express its intent in clear words. So I say we must read the words before us as if the question were whether two small exporting grocers should go to jail.

Holmes continued:

The statute is of a very sweeping and general character. It hits every contract or combination of the prohibited sort, great or small, and every person who shall monopolize, or attempt to monopolize...any part of the trade or commerce among the several states. There is a natural inclination to assume that it was directed against certain great combinations, and to read it in that light. It does not say so.

His other concerns in this particular case:

This act is construed by the Government to affect the purchasers of shares in two railroad companies because the effect it may have, or, if you like, is certain to have, upon the competition of these roads. If such remote result of the exercise of the ordinary incident of property and personal freedom is enough to make that exercise unlawful, there is hardly any transaction concerning commerce between the States that may not be made a crime by the finding of a jury or a court.

The Act, as written, might send the members of a partnership of two trading corporations to prison, or perhaps it forbids a man from purchasing as much stock as he likes in these two corporations. A single railroad down a narrow valley or through a mountain gorge monopolizes all the railroad transportation through that valley or gorge. Indeed, every railroad monopolizes, in a popular sense, the trade of some area. The Act attacks small monopolies as well as the great, and the words of the Act make such a distinction impossible. Congress would not have wanted society to disintegrate into single men, each at war with all the rest, nor would Congress have intended to prevent all combinations for a common end. But the law sets no clear boundaries. Three other Justices concurred with Holmes's dissent.[181]

Justice Holmes became known, over time, as the Great Dissenter. On several issues, his dissenting opinions eventually found their way into majority decisions. Oliver Wendell Holmes Jr. became one of the great justices of the twentieth century and a major arbiter of business-government interaction.

———

Theodore Roosevelt won reelection in 1904 with almost 57 percent of the popular vote. Corporations contributed almost three fourths of the Republican National Committee's campaign fund. J. P. Morgan, the financier, and George Jay Gould, railroad magnate, along with other corporate leaders, were also major contributors.[182] The business leaders might have had an early wish for Senator Mark Hanna to get the Republican nomination instead of Roosevelt, but Hanna had died of typhoid fever in February. Roosevelt was pressing progressive ideas, but there was some logic and consistency in his administration's policies. After all, Justice Holmes, a Roosevelt appointee, upheld the need for clarity in legislation. The coal strike had been well handled. The Democratic candidate, in contrast, seemed inept and uninterested in his own campaign.

---

181 *Northern Securities Company v. United States*, Appeal from the Circuit Court of the United States for the District of Minnesota. 193 U.S. 197.
182 *New York Times*, October 3, 4, 5 and 19, 1912, reporting testimony before the Senate Campaign Fund Committee.

Roosevelt was passionate in his drive for honest and efficient service by public officials. His interest in regulation of business and corporations reflected a commitment that everyone was entitled to a "square deal." But TR was no socialist. Upton Sinclair sent the president a copy of *The Jungle* shortly after its release in 1906. Roosevelt read the novel about conditions in the meat-packing industry, and wrote to Sinclair:

> Personally I think that one of the chief early effects of such attempt to put socialism of the kind there preached into practice, would be the elimination by starvation, and the diseases, moral and physical, attendant upon starvation, of the same portion of the community on whose behalf socialism would be invoked.[183]

In the same letter TR acknowledged the difficulties faced by workers who are crippled by accident, become too old to work, or struggle with the expenses of a large family. He continues:

> There are many, many men who lack any intelligence or character and who therefore cannot thus raise themselves. But while I agree with you that energetic, and, as I believe, in the long run, radical action must be taken to do away with the effects of arrogant and selfish greed on the part of the capitalist, yet I am more than ever convinced that the real factor in the elevation of any man or any mass of men must be the development within his or their hearts and heads of the qualities which can alone make either the individual, the class or the nation permanently useful to themselves and to others.

Roosevelt perceived that not all business was bad, and not all trusts or large corporations were evil. The deeds of the entity should be judged, not its size. His annual message to Congress in December 1905 opened with a recognition that, "The people of this country continue to enjoy a great prosperity." He went on, just a few paragraphs later:

> The fortunes amassed through corporate organization are now so large, and vest such power in those that wield them, as to make it a matter of

---

183 Letter, TR to Upton Sinclair, March 15, 1906. Upton Sinclair, *My Lifetime in Letters*, 11–14.

necessity to give to the sovereign—that is, to the Government, which represents the people as a whole—some effective power of supervision over the corporate use...I am in no sense hostile to corporations. This is an age of combination, and any effort to prevent all combination will be not only useless, but in the end vicious, because of the contempt for law which the failure to enforce law inevitably produces. We should, moreover, recognize in cordial and ample fashion the immense good effected by corporate agencies in a country such as ours, and the wealth of intellect, energy, and fidelity devoted to the service of the public, by their officers and directors. The corporation has come to stay, just as the trade union has come to stay. Each can do and has done great good. Each should be favored so long as it does good. But each should be sharply checked where it acts against law and justice.[184]

———

On April 18, 1906, San Franciscans were awakened at 5:12 a.m. by the shaking of a major earthquake and the roar of collapsing buildings. The immediate damage to brick and wood-frame buildings was catastrophic. People were trapped in the wreckage. Streets were blocked by debris and water mains were broken. Within minutes, fires broke out in several areas of the city. When the last fire had been extinguished two days later, America's ninth largest city and major Pacific port was in ruins.

Towns to the north and south were also heavily damaged. In Palo Alto, almost every commercial building was damaged. Most of the buildings of Leland Stanford Junior University were damaged or completely destroyed. Santa Clara, Sunnyvale, Mountain View, Menlo Park, Redwood City, San Mateo, Half Moon Bay—all had suffered significant damage.

President Roosevelt telegraphed his concern and dispatched Dr. Edward Devine, a well-known social work leader from New York City, as his personal representative. The two had become well acquainted during Roosevelt's days

184 John T. Woolley and Gerhard Peters, *The American Presidency Project (online)*, Santa Barbara, California. Available at: http://www.presidency.ucsb.edu/ws/?pid=29546.
Years later, in his autobiography, Roosevelt again maintained that bigness was not in itself an evil and that large, well-run corporations were necessary to American competitiveness and to promote abundance by continuously bringing down the cost of living. See *Theodore Roosevelt: An Autobiography*, Appendices A and B.

as police commissioner in New York City and as governor of New York. Army troops from the Presidio assisted police in maintaining order. But before any federal aid had arrived, Mayor Schmidt had assembled a Citizens' Committee of the city's business leaders to lead the recovery.

Ten days after the event, Secretary of Commerce and Labor Metcalf telegraphed his report of the situation to the president. The death toll was approximately three hundred, and about one thousand were injured. In a city of five hundred thousand, almost 60 percent were homeless. Almost every municipal building was destroyed. Most places of business were damaged, many beyond repair. The city was peaceful—no looting, arson, or mayhem. The telegraph, telephone, railroad, and cable car systems were not functioning. There was enough water for drinking, hardly enough for sanitation, and no supply adequate for firefighting. Army quartermasters distributed tents, blankets, and other relief supplies as they arrived; about 250,000 people were being fed at emergency kitchens. Red Cross workers would soon take over these tasks. The relief operations had come together with the combined leadership of the governor, the mayor, the chairman of the Citizens' Committee, Gen. Funston, and Dr. Devine, who was the agent of the National Red Cross as well as the President Roosevelt's representative.

The cooperation was real. On the same day that Metcalf sent his report to the president, Gen. Greely (Funston's superior) sent a report to the War Department in Washington, and Dr. Devine sent a separate report to the National Red Cross Association office. While each focused on his own area of responsibility and expertise, their evaluations are consistent, and each reports the same distribution of authority and responsibility. Initiative and cooperative effort had been evident from the first moments of the emergency. When Greely's report was received at the War Department, the Secretary of War conveyed to Governor Pardee a "suggestion from the President that in order to avoid any possible legal complications the Governor should call upon the President formally for the use of United States troops in San Francisco."

The efforts were effective. Seven months later, the number requiring shelter in the camps was seventeen thousand. Six thousand five hundred small cottages would be built to house them. The city's businesses and homeowners were busy rebuilding.[185] Fire insurance policies paid for much of the damage, including buildings that had been dynamited to stop the flames spreading through the city.

---

185 *New York Times,* April 20, 23, 27, 28 and November 21, 1906.

As he had forcefully expressed during the coal strike in 1902, Roosevelt believed that the general public, as well as workers and investors, had an interest in the proper conduct of business. In June 1906, he signed the Pure Food and Drug Act authorizing federal inspectors to gather samples and analyze foods, drugs, and liquors in interstate or international commerce. Actions that constituted unlawful adulteration or misbranding were listed, as were basic requirements for labeling. The Agriculture Department's Bureau of Chemistry was to certify the results of sample tests and refer any discovered violations to the federal district attorney for prosecution. The Act was a first assertion of a federal role in safeguarding the nation's food supply and a pharmaceutical industry that was already changing from thousands of wandering "snake oil salesmen" into science-based pharmaceutical firms.

Theodore Roosevelt again conveyed his thoughts about the interactions of investors, employees, voters, and government officials in his Annual Message to Congress in December 1907:

> The relations of the capitalist and the wage-worker to one another, and of each to the general public, are not always easy to adjust; and to put them and keep them on a satisfactory basis is one of the most important and one of the most delicate tasks before our whole civilization. Much of the work of the accomplishment of this end must be done by the individuals concerned themselves, whether singly or in combination; and the one fundamental fact that must never be lost track of is that the character of the average man, whether he be a man of means or a man who works with his hands, is the most important factor in solving the problem aright. But it is almost equally important to remember that without good laws it is almost impossible to reach the solution.[186]

———

In the election of 1908, William Taft was elected to succeed Theodore Roosevelt, who had pledged after his 1904 election victory not to run for another term. Taft had been hand picked by TR as his successor, and that endorsement alone assured victory. Taft's administration adhered to the Roosevelt policies,

186 John T. Woolley & Gerhard Peters, The American Presidency Project [online]. Santa Barbara, California. Available at http://www.presidency.ucsb.edu/ws/?pid=29548.

but lacked the energy. Roosevelt was so frustrated watching from the sidelines that he challenged Taft's nomination for a second term. When the Republican Party nominated Taft, Roosevelt launched a third-party campaign.

Woodrow Wilson won the election of 1912 largely because Theodore Roosevelt's third-party candidacy took votes that otherwise would have gone to the Republican Taft.

In his inaugural address, Wilson reflected on the state of the economy and the nation:

> We see that in many things that life is very great. It is incomparably great in its material aspects, in its body of wealth, in the diversity and sweep of its energy, in the industries which have been built up by the genius of individual men and the limitless enterprise of groups of men. It is great, also, very great, in its moral force. We have built up, moreover, a great system of government, which has stood through a long age as in many respects a model for those who set to seek liberty...
>
> But the evil has come with the good, and much fine gold has been corroded. With riches has come inexcusable waste. We have squandered a great part of what we might have used, and have not stopped to conserve the exceeding bounty of nature, without which our genius for enterprise would have been worthless and impotent, scorning to be careful, shamefully prodigal as well as admirably efficient. We have been proud of our industrial achievements, but we have not hitherto stopped thoughtfully enough to count the human cost, the cost of lives snuffed out, of energies overtaxed and broken, the fearful physical and spiritual cost to the men and women and children upon whom the dead weight and burden of it all has fallen pitilessly the years through. The groans and agony of it all had not yet reached our ears, the solemn, moving undertone of our life, coming out of the mines and factories and out of every home where the struggle had its intimate and familiar seat. With the great government went many deep secret things which we too long delayed to look into and scrutinize with candid, fearless eyes. The great Government we loved has too often been made use of for private and selfish purposes, and those who used it had forgotten the people.

Wilson listed tariff reform as the first priority in his economic agenda, which also included modernizing the banking and credit system to avoid panics such as had occurred in 1907, improving labor conditions, bringing the benefits of science and improved capital flows to agriculture, and assuring the replenishment of natural resources.[187]

One month after the inauguration, Wilson addressed a joint session of Congress for the specific purpose of changing the nation's tariff. High tariffs had been a major source of federal revenue since the Civil War, and for the previous twenty years tariffs at even higher rates had protected American manufacturers from foreign competition. On average, manufactured goods imported from foreign countries were subject to duties of 45 percent. This protection from foreign competition allowed prices that protected the profit margins of domestic manufacturers. Wilson explained his position:

> I have called the Congress together in extraordinary session because a duty was laid upon the party now in power at the recent elections which it ought to perform promptly, in order that the burden carried by the people under existing law may be lightened as soon as possible, and in order, also, that the business interests of the country may not be kept too long in suspense as to what the fiscal changes are to be to which they will be required to adjust themselves.
>
> We must put our business men and producers under the stimulation of a constant necessity to be efficient, economical, and enterprising, masters of competitive supremacy, better workers and merchants than any in the world. Aside from the duties laid upon articles which we do not, and probably can not, produce, therefore, and the duties laid upon luxuries for the sake of the revenues they yield, the object of the tariff duties henceforth laid must be effective competition, the whetting of American wits by contest with the wits of the rest of the world.[188]

Wilson believed that American businesses should be able to compete in a world marketplace or suffer the consequences. He recognized that businesses would "adjust themselves" to the changes. Some workers would lose jobs under those adjustments. Companies unable or unwilling to adjust would go out of

---

187 Inaugural Address, March 4, 1913. John T. Woolley and Gerhard Peters, The American Presidency Project, Santa Barbara, California. Available at http://www.presidency.ucsb.edu/ws/?pid=25831.

188 *Address to A Joint Session of Congress on Tariff Reform, April 8, 1913.* John T. Woolley and Gerhard Peters, The American Presidency Project [online]. Santa Barbara, California. Available at http://www.presidency.uscb.edu/ws/?pid=65638.

business. But high tariffs, he believed, were hurting American consumers and workers. Manufacturers were able to charge higher prices than might be available in a marketplace open to foreign-made goods. Wilson also believed that artificially high prices kept American goods from foreign buyers, which held down employment. The Underwood Tariff Act of 1913 made major reductions in the tariff rates for most imports—the first significant cuts since the Civil War. The average tariff fell from 45 percent to 28 percent.

The Underwood Act also established an income tax on individuals and businesses. A flat tax of 1 percent applied to all personal income in excess of $3,000 per year ($4,000 for married couples), plus a surtax ranging from 1 percent to 6 percent on higher incomes. This provision of a basic income amount that was exempt (tax-free) regardless of total income, with progressively higher tax rates applied to upper income brackets, has remained a core feature of American tax income tax law.[189] From such humble beginnings, the federal income tax has become a major source of government revenue.

With the tariff reform enacted, Wilson pointed the attention of Congress to his second priority—strengthening the nation's antitrust laws. Roosevelt's administration had achieved some major antitrust victories, including Northern Securities and the breakup of Standard Oil.[190] Taft's administration had filed no less than eighty suits, with mixed results. But no one was satisfied with the current situation. Lack of clarity, not lack of effort, had been a major hindrance to enforcing the Sherman Act. Juries often found defendants not guilty, perhaps concluding that prosecutors had failed to prove intent to "restrain trade." The Supreme Court had offered a confusing array of decisions in cases brought under the Sherman Act. Business leaders complained that the legal uncertainties were causing hesitation and delay even in the most innocent affairs.

In its Standard Oil decision in 1911, the Supreme Court had declared that:

The Anti-Trust Act of July 2, 1890...should be construed in the light of reason; and, so construed, it prohibits all contracts and combinations

189 The application of the progressive feature is misunderstood by many who assume that the marginal tax rate that applies to their highest income bracket also applies to every dollar of their income. In fact, all taxpayers enjoy the exemption for the lowest income bracket, and the higher rates apply only to their respective brackets of income. A taxpayer's marginal (highest) tax rate is applied only to income in that uppermost bracket, not to any lower bracket.
190 The case against Standard Oil was initiated in Roosevelt's term. The appeal was argued (and reargued) before the Supreme Court and decided during Taft's administration.

which amount to an unreasonable or undo restraint of trade or inter-state commerce. The combination of the defendants in this case is an unreasonable and undo restraint of trade in petroleum and its products moving in interstate commerce, and falls within the prohibitions of the act so construed.[191]

Here, almost ten years after Holme's dissent in the Northern Securities case, the majority of the Justices decided that the Act prohibited:

Classes of acts, those classes being broad enough to embrace every conceivable contract or combination which could be made concerning trade or commerce or the subjects of such commerce, and thus caused any act done by any of the enumerated methods anywhere in the whole field of human activity to be illegal if in restraint of trade, it inevitably falls to reason that the provision necessarily called for the exercise of judgment...it follows that it was intended that the standard of reason... was intended to be the measure used for determining whether, in a given case, a particular act had or had not brought about the wrong against which the statute provided.[192]

There was one dissent in this case. Justice Harlan concurred with the main decision that Standard Oil Company of New Jersey and its subsidiary companies constituted a conspiracy in restraint of trade in violation of the Anti-Trust Act of 1890 and must be dissolved. But he challenged the decision of his colleagues on the Court by which they determined that Congress had intended the Sherman Act to prohibit only "undo" or "unreasonable" restraint of trade. In effect, the Supreme Court added words to an act of Congress.

Harlan pointed to uncertainties that would arise from such tampering:

It is now, with much amplification of argument, that the statute...does not mean what the language used therein plainly imports, but that it only means to declare illegal any such contract which is in unreasonable restraint of trade, while leaving others unaffected by the provisions of the act; that the common law meaning of the term "contract in restraint of trade" includes only such contracts as are in unreasonable restraint

---

191 *Standard Oil Co. of New Jersey v. United States,* 221 U.S. 1 (1911)
192 Ibid, 221, U.S. 60.

of trade. And, when the term is used in the Federal statute, it is not intended to include all contracts in restraint of trade, but only those which are in unreasonable restraint thereof.

In other words, we are asked to read into the act by way of judicial legislation an exception that is to be done upon the theory that the im-policy of such legislation is so clear that it cannot be supposed Congress intended the natural import of the language it used. This we cannot do.[193]

The Supreme Court had thus determined that the Sherman Act—a federal criminal statute—could not be taken at its plain language, and that some con-spiracies, corporations, and combinations in restraint of trade may be legal while others were unreasonable and thus illegal. This new decision was especially sur-prising since the Supreme Court had stated in at least three prior cases that the Sherman Act prohibited, by its plain language, "every contract, combination in the form of trust or otherwise, or conspiracy, in restraint of trade among the several states," and any distinction between reasonable or unreasonable, or large and small, was therefore moot.[194] The Court had also acknowledged that only Congress had authority to change the text of the law if it intended some other meaning. The Senate had formally reviewed the Act in 1909, with full awareness of the Court's interpretation, and concluded that no change was needed in the law. Now the justices had suddenly declared a new meaning of the Act, insisting that a "rule of reason" must be applied in each case.

How was any businessperson or investor, or his legal counsel, to know what was legal or illegal? Since an agreement or contract to commit a crime might be declared void and unenforceable, how might one proceed with confidence? How could anyone predict which mergers, partnerships, agreements, contracts, or other arrangements would result in criminal charges and conviction? Whose judgment, or sense of reason, should be applied to determine the legality of each of the many transactions occurring in the world of commerce?

Wilson recognized the problem for businesses of all sizes. There was also a need to clarify that unions, which were combinations of individuals conspir-ing to actions, including strikes, which would restrain interstate trade, were not illegal. The result was the Clayton Act of 1914. The Clayton Act did not

---

193 Ibid, 221 U.S. 88.
194 *U.S. v. Trans-Missouri Freight Ass'n*, 166 U.S. 290 (1897); *U.S. v. Joint Traf-fic Ass'n*, 171 U.S. 505 (1898); *Shawnee Compress Co. v. Anderson*, 209 U.S. 423 (1908).

repeal or amend the Sherman Act. However, it declared certain actions illegal, including price discrimination in selling commodities (price differences based on grade or quality of the commodity, or difference in shipping costs, were permitted), and rebates or discounts that were tied to an agreement between buyer and seller to avoid dealing with competitors of the seller. The Clayton Act also declared that nonprofit labor and agricultural organizations were not prohibited by the antitrust laws. Corporations could establish subsidiary corporations to carry out their business. Shareholders could own stock in multiple corporations, as long as they did not vote their shares in a manner to restrain trade. Finally, directors and employees of large banks (defined as having in excess of $5 million in deposits, capital, surplus, and undivided profits) were prohibited from serving as an employee or director of any other bank. In towns with population less than two hundred thousand, an employee, officer, or director of one bank could not serve any other bank in the same location. Specific regulations were established for common carriers. The Clayton Act provided welcome clarity.

Then attention turned to reform of financial markets. Shortages of credit were not uncommon and created one more hurdle to the stability of business. Some were the result of bank managers making poor lending decisions. Other shortages were predictable in timing if not in extent, particularly in the fall when farmers had to pay their seasonal help, and in January when many corporations paid dividends to their shareholders. The Federal Reserve Act was signed two days before Christmas.

By the end of his first year in office, Wilson had accomplished his program for business and economic reform. But presidents do not always control their own agenda.

———

On April 20, 1914, a long-festering labor dispute in the mining regions of Colorado turned into deadly combat between armed groups of miners and Colorado militia troops. Seven months earlier, at a convention in Trinidad, Colorado, miners told their individual stories. Some described fatal or crippling accidents caused by inept supervision and work conditions that violated Colorado's mine safety code. Others complained of company scales that short-weighted their day's production, cheating them of pay. Then there were the guards, who used violence with impunity to discourage union activity. Some miners felt pressure to use the company store, even when the same goods could be found elsewhere for less. When the last worker had told his story, a list of demands was drafted. Miners wanted these issues addressed, and they wanted more money. They also demanded recognition of the United Mineworkers' Union as their bargaining agent. The miners at the conference voted to strike.

Within a week, miners walked out of the facilities of nineteen companies across southern Colorado. Of these, Colorado Fuel and Iron was the largest. CF&I was the largest producer of coal and steel in the West at the time and one of the largest employers in southern Colorado.

Many of the mine employees lived in company-owned houses in company-owned towns and shopped in company-owned stores. These were not the sooty, crowded company towns of an earlier generation, but airy manifestations of a new "business of benevolence" taking hold in many industries around the turn of the century. The single family homes, with windows on all sides and open porches, were neatly spaced along wide streets. Electric streetlights and sanitary water supplies, schools with kindergartens, hospitals, and social clubs provided the comforts of middle-class life to workers' families. Colorado Fuel and Iron had established a Sociological Department more than a decade before Ford Motor Company. The sanitary and attractive worker settlements attracted workers from the crowded coal fields of the eastern U.S. and even from mining towns in Wales and Eastern Europe.[195] All of this was the result of two decades in which strikes and lockouts alternated with periods of harmony. But workers found conditions underground intolerable and many resented the companies' influence on life outside the mines.

Not all miners were union members, and none of the employers recognized any union as a bargaining agent, so the mines continued to operate with workers who decided to stay and new workers who took jobs vacated by strikers.

Strikers who lived in company-owned houses were required to vacate. Thousands moved into tent settlements organized by the union. Many of the tents were shipped from West Virginia, where a miners' strike had just been settled. Each new town developed its own culture and spirit. The settlement at Ludlow seemed especially militant. Several shooting incidents took place. Late in October, the governor ordered the Colorado militia to "obtain a speedy return of law and order in the disturbed districts," and he summoned leaders of labor and management to a conference.

---

195 Thomas G. Andrews, *Killing for Coal: America's Deadliest Labor War,* 198–199.

Mine owners had already agreed to every one of the miners' demands except recognition of the union. The workers' representatives explained that they considered a union vital to their safety. They had seen too many accidents caused by supervisors' negligence and new workers with insufficient training. The meeting ended with no resolution of the union issue. The miners had lost whatever political leverage they had assumed their pro-labor governor would provide. As new workers took up the positions vacated by strikers, the miners lost their economic leverage. Winter took hold of the tent cities. Frustration mounted.

On April 20, one of the numerous violent incidents that had plagued the area escalated into a prolonged exchange of gunfire between miners and militiamen. Several tents caught fire, and several women and children hiding in them were killed. Governor Ammons appealed to President Wilson for federal troops.

The arrival of U.S. Army troops stopped the violence but did not resolve the dispute. The United Mine Workers leaders backed away from their demand for a union, but the executives of mine-owning companies adamantly refused any negotiations. They pointed out that ten thousand miners were still working and that a relative minority of troublemakers were responsible for the violence.[196] Wilson had considered seizing the mines until resolution was achieved, then returning the mines to the owners, but his attorney general advised there was no legal basis for such action. In November, seeking a way to allow removal of the troops, Wilson appointed a three-man commission to resolve any issues the parties might voluntarily bring to it.[197] The miners realized that Wilson's commission was their only hope for additional progress. To continue the strike was pointless. At a conference in Pueblo they voted to end the strike.

———

Wilson believed that competition was the best way to force businesses to serve the public. This was not just a matter of domestic policy. He saw open, competitive trade among nations as important to maintaining peace. Europe was engulfed in war. American businesses were searching for new customers, and Wilson saw trade as one method of persuading other nations to remain neutral. In an address at the Pan-American Financial Conference in May 1915, he told the delegates from eighteen nations of North and South America:

---

196 "Refuse to Settle Strike," *New York Times*, May 1, 1914.
197 "Wilson Names Strike Board for Colorado," *New York Times*, November 30, 1914.

The way to peace for us, at any rate, is manifest...It is the knowledge that men can be of the greatest service to one another, and nations of the greatest service to one another, when the jealousy between them is merely a jealousy of excellence, and when the basis of their intercourse is friendship...I am perfectly certain that this is the only basis for the friendship of nations—this handsome rivalry, this rivalry in which there is no dislike, this rivalry in which there is nothing but the hope of a common elevation in great enterprises which we can undertake in common.

Encouragement of international trade was a constant theme of Wilson's speeches even after his key legislation had passed.

Eighteen months later, Secretary of Commerce William Redfield rebutted in detail the Republican charge that dropping the tariff had resulted in foreign-made goods swamping the American market to the detriment of domestic manufacturers and the loss of jobs for American workers. In fact, domestic manufacture had increased every year, far more rapidly than the growth of foreign-made imports. [198]

Wilson won reelection, mainly because "he kept us out of war," while Europe had suffered the devastation of World War I since 1914. The American economy had been robust almost continuously since 1896, righting itself from several recessions and the Panic of 1907. Wages had advanced more quickly than living expenses. Many workers were now covered by workers compensation insurance, which paid their medical expenses and a portion of their wages in the event of on-the-job injury.

Just two months before the election, Wilson signed the Keating-Owen Child Labor Act. The law prohibited the interstate shipment of product from any mine or quarry that employed children under the age of sixteen, or the product or articles of any factory, mill, cannery, workshop, or manufacturing facility that employed children under the age of fourteen, or where children between fourteen and sixteen worked for more than eight hours in a day, or before six o'clock in the morning or after seven o'clock at night, nor for more than six days in a week. The Secretary of Labor was authorized to enter and inspect all such facilities for purposes of enforcing the Act. Violators, including anyone who hindered entry or inspection authorized by the Act, were subject to fines and/or imprisonment upon conviction. The Keating-Owen Act helped keep children out of the most

---

198 *New York Times,* October 1, 1916.

dangerous occupations and had the indirect result of keeping more children in school for a few more years, since they could not so easily be employed.

————

When American entry into the war became likely, higher defense costs were paid by higher taxes—a surcharge on high incomes—and by selling bonds. The Emergency Revenue Act in 1916 increased the tax rate on all corporate profits from 1 percent to 2 percent. Personal incomes up to $3,000 per year ($4,000 for a married couple) remained exempt from tax, but the rate on incomes from the exemption level up to $20,000 increased from 1 percent to 2 percent, and the rate on all incomes in excess of $20,000 increased from 7 percent to 15 percent. Six months later, the Special Preparedness Fund Act raised corporate tax rates to 6 percent. The personal tax exemption was reduced to $1,000 ($2,000 for married couples) and a tax rate of 67 percent applied to all income in excess of $2,000. In 1918, the top personal rate, charged against all income in excess of $4,000, was raised to 77 percent.

Throughout the war, the exemption amount excused most married wage-earners from paying any federal income tax. Those with taxable income less than the exemption amount did not have to file a return. Many single wage-earners, including the Five Dollar Day workers at Ford Motor Company plants earning $1,300 per year, would pay income tax only on the small amount of income beyond the exemption level. Unskilled workers in many plants earned less. The average schoolteacher salary of $871 in 1920 was also less than the exemption. Nevertheless, the number of personal returns increased from 337,000 in 1915 to 3.5 million in 1917 and peaked at 7.7 million in 1923. In 1915, federal revenue from income taxes totaled $80 million; in 1918, $2.9 billion; and in 1920, revenue peaked at $4 billion.

The United States Treasury also borrowed to raise money for war expenses. The first Liberty Loan bonds issued in April 1917 raised $5 billion for the government. Bonds paid 3.5 percent interest annually. Six months later, the Second Liberty Loan raised $3 billion, paying 4 percent interest, with a twenty-five-year term. Subsequent issues raised $3 billion at 4.5 percent and another $6 billion at 4.25 percent issued six weeks before the end of hostilities.[199] The final effort was a Victory Loan issue in April and May 1919. All the bonds were backed by the full faith and credit of the United States, so payment was never in question. To

———

199 Unless otherwise noted, all interest rates herein are annual rates.

protect the buyer against inflation, the option of collecting interest and principal in gold, rather than paper dollars, was printed on each bond. Popular advertising and appeals to patriotism encouraged individuals of all income levels to participate. Individuals with a few extra dollars and wealthy investors looking for stable income with very little risk bought most of the debt. Commercial banks invested in approximately 20 percent of the total issue of the loans.[200] The funds were used to supply and pay American forces and to lend to Allies, who had already spent their own resources in the years of warfare prior to America's entry.

Wilson had continuously insisted on American neutrality after Europe erupted in war in July, 1914. But a series of submarine attacks on neutral ships took American civilian lives. There were diplomatic protests. When Germany declared that its submarines would attack and sink without warning all vessels, including passenger vessels of neutral countries, that approached the coasts of Great Britain or Ireland, or the western coast of Europe or the Mediterranean coast of any country, Congress declared war. The resolution, dated April 6, 1917, declaring war on Germany passed both the House and Senate with only one vote against it.

This would be no short campaign or easy victory. The carnage in Europe made that clear. The Selective Draft Act was passed, requiring all males between the ages of twenty-one and thirty to register for military service. In his proclamation establishing the draft process, Wilson noted:

In the sense in which we have been wont to think of armies, there are no armies in this struggle, there are entire nations armed. Thus, the men who remain to till the soil and man the factories are no less a part of the army that is in France than the men beneath the battle flags. It must be so with us. It is not an army that we must shape and train for war; it is a nation.

Congress had debated relying on a volunteer army, at least initially, but acceded to Wilson's proposal for a universal draft. There would be no paid substitutes, as had been permitted in the Civil War. There would be no bands of volunteers raised and commanded by private citizens, trained for a few weeks and shipped to the front, as had fought the Spanish-American War twenty years earlier. This would be a force trained and disciplined not only in weapons and tactics, but also to avoid, as far as possible, the diseases that had ravaged previous armies.

---

200 The Seeley G. Mudd Manuscript Library at Princeton University includes a large collection of information on the Liberty Loans.

A nation needs all men; but it needs each man, not in the field that will most please him, but in the endeavor that will best serve the common good. Thus, though a sharpshooter pleases to operate a trip-hammer for the forging of great guns and an expert machinist desires to march with the flag, the nation is being served only when the sharpshooter marches and the machinist remains at his levers…each man shall be classified for service in the place to which it shall best serve the general good to call him. The significance of this cannot be overstated. It is a new thing in our history and a landmark in our progress.[201]

Neither wealth nor fame nor power bought exemption from military service. Grover Cleveland Bergdoll, son of a wealthy brewing family in a suburb of Philadelphia, applied for conscientious objector status, which the draft board refused. He evaded the draft authorities, but was arrested in 1920, court-martialed, and sentenced to five years in prison. He escaped and fled to Germany. The federal government seized his $800,000 fortune and arrested him again when he returned to the United States under a false name in 1939. He was sentenced to three additional years in prison for the escape and finally released in 1944. Eighty percent of his confiscated fortune was eventually returned to him.[202] The war dead included Quentin Roosevelt, youngest son of the former president, killed in aerial combat, and the poet Joyce Kilmer, shot during a reconnaissance patrol. Kilmer was thirty-one years old and left a widow and four young children.[203] Two other sons of Theodore Roosevelt were seriously wounded.

America's industrial capacity shifted to arms production. Ford Motor Company's plant at Rouge River built wooden-hulled Eagle boats for minesweeping. DuPont's mills turned out gunpowder and explosives at unprecedented rates. In December 1917, the railroads were placed under federal government direction. All railroad operations and facilities were placed under a director general of railroads appointed by the president. Wilson's proclamation made clear that railroad corporate officials had cooperated fully in the war effort, but that federal direction would best align the nation's transport facilities with its war priorities. A new depot might be needed where civilian production would not justify the investment; the urgency for one type of military supply might take precedence

201 Proclamation of the Selective Draft Act, May 18, 1917.
202 "Bergdoll Returns, Is Seized by Army," *New York Times*, May 26, 1939, and "Bergdoll Leaves Federal Prison," February 4, 1944.
203 *New York Times*, August 18, 1918, August 22, 1918.

over another. The director general and his staff would sort that out. Ownership of the railroad property remained with the corporations, which remained the property of the shareholders. Each railroad corporation would be assured of profits equal to the average annual profits of the preceding three years. The president noted the importance of maintaining the profitability of these companies and the flow of dividends to the many banks, local governments, pensioners, and others who depended on those payments.

After the armistice in 1918, the nation returned to peacetime endeavors, which would require investment of capital. The nation also faced repayment of the huge wartime debts. The interest on all those Liberty Bonds was payable semi-annually, and eventually the principal, $21 billion, would come due. Beginning in 1919, Congress reduced the income tax rates by legislation almost every year over the next ten years[204] and continued to pay down the war debt with revenues that exceeded peacetime expenditures.[205] Repayment of the war loans made to allies was also anticipated as a source of funds.

Warren Harding succeeded Wilson, after winning the election with 60 percent of the popular vote. No presidential candidate had ever amassed such a large popular majority. His administration is most remembered for the Tea Pot Dome scandal, in which members of the Interior Department accepted bribes to obtain favorable oil drilling rights. Harding died of a heart attack while in San Francisco in August 1923. Vice President Calvin Coolidge became president.

In 1924, Treasury Secretary Andrew Mellon, who served Presidents Harding, Coolidge, and Hoover, wrote in his book, *Taxation: The People's Business*:

> The problem of the government is to fix rates which will bring in a maximum amount of revenue to the Treasury and at the same time bear not too heavily on the tax payer or on business enterprises. A sound tax policy must take into consideration three factors. It must produce sufficient revenue for the government; it must lessen, so far as possible, the burden of taxation on those least able to bear it; and it must also remove those influences which might retard the continued steady development

---

204 Internal Revenue Service, Statistics of Income Bulletins, Fall 2003 (corporate taxes) and September 22, 2004, Table A (personal taxes).
205 *Statistical Abstract of the United States, 1929,* Table No. 216.

of business and industry on which, in the last analysis, so much of our prosperity depends.

The history of taxation shows that taxes which are inherently excessive are not paid. The high rates inevitably put pressure upon the taxpayer to withdraw his capital from productive business and invest it in tax-exempt securities or to find other lawful methods of avoiding the realization of taxable income. The result is that the sources of taxation are drying up…and capital is being diverted into channels which yield neither revenue to the government nor profit to the people.[206]

Mellon was one of the wealthiest men in the country. Here he describes the decision-making process used by investors considering the various investment options for their savings. The son of a prominent Pittsburgh banker, he had built his fortune slowly, over decades, making equity investments in many of the start-up companies that came to his bank looking for loans. Many of them needed far more capital than any bank or group of banks would prudently lend unless there were also shareholders with equity risk in the business. They were typically businesses that required large up-front investment in plants and manufacturing equipment and several years of building sales before a profit might be expected. Mellon chose carefully and skillfully. His talent was identifying talented business-people who had a great business idea or new technology, but needed long-term investment—patient money—to move ahead. Mellon took no management role in the operation of the businesses, but he served on the board of directors. He had spent decades fostering new corporations in new industries. Here is one of the nation's most active investors pointing out that high tax rates cause investors to avoid the risks of investing in business, including innovative technologies.[207] That link between high tax rates and reduced investment in innovation would become well documented in later years.

––––––

206 Andrew W. Mellon, *Taxation: The People's Business*, 9, 13.
207 Mellon mentions "other lawful means of avoiding the realization of taxable income." This "tax avoidance" is distinct from "tax evasion," which is the use of illegal means to avoid taxation. Example: a blind person who claims the extra deduction allowed on the income tax return form uses tax avoidance. A sighted person who claims that deduction practices "tax evasion," also known as tax fraud.

Herbert Hoover had never held elective office before his election as president in 1928. But his role as Secretary of Commerce in the Coolidge administration let voters associate Hoover with the country's booming prosperity. The big issue in the 1928 campaign was Prohibition. In 1919, citizens had hoped that ratification of the Eighteenth Amendment and passage of the National Prohibition Act over President Wilson's veto would solve some of the country's social ills. By 1928, many voters were skeptical but still hopeful. Surely more efficient law enforcement would produce the desired benefits. Hoover's "dry" platform drew many voters who could not abide the thought of repeal. There was also the other issue: Al Smith, the Democratic candidate, was Catholic. Smith's nomination "set off the most vicious anti-Catholic, anti-Jewish, anti-Negro movement that we have ever had during any political campaign."[208]

Concern about possible repeal of Prohibition and that Al Smith's policies as president would be dictated by the Pope in Rome gave Hoover victories in Southern states that had rarely voted Republican since the Civil War, including Tennessee, Florida, North Carolina, Virginia, and Texas. Hoover won handily, with 58 percent of the popular vote and 84 percent of the Electoral College votes.

———

The business recession that became the Great Depression actually started quietly. For anyone watching the numbers, the first sign of trouble was a decline in construction, especially home building, early in the summer of 1929. Banks and some large corporations were lending money to individuals who speculated in the stock market, rather than to builders for construction loans, homebuyers for mortgages, or to cities for municipal projects. The stock speculator willingly paid higher interest rates, sometimes as high as 18 percent, to finance his "sure thing" in the stock market. Anyone seeking money for a more traditional purpose, such as a home mortgage, would not pay more than 5 percent or 6 percent interest. As a result, many construction projects had been postponed. The speculators believed there were endless profits to be made by trading stocks, especially with borrowed money. The lenders collected their interest and felt secure because the loans were collateralized by stocks, the value of which seemed only to go up. The lenders also felt secure because they could demand payback of these "call loans" at any time, simply by phoning the stockbroker. Everyone

---

208 Harry S. Truman, *Memoirs: Years of Trial and Hope, 1946-1952*, 203.

involved believed this to be the perfect financial arrangement—low risk, high reward—that would last forever. It ended badly. The stock market crash in October 1929 is the highly visible and well-publicized event that many identify as the start of the Great Depression.

The collapse of the stock market directly affected a very small percentage of the population. From a population of 120 million people (approximately thirty million families), there were 1,548,707 customers (less than 5 percent of the country's households) with accounts on the various exchanges. The vast majority of these (1,371,920) were accounts at member firms of the New York Stock Exchange.[209] The most widely owned stock was United States Steel, with about 560,000 shareholders. Employment and economic activity remained strong enough after the crash that Christmas sales in 1929 exceeded those of 1928, which had been a very good year. As the stock speculation cooled, corporations returned to their core businesses, most banks returned to more stable investments, and wealthy individuals who had avoided the crash for the most part remained invested in Treasury bonds. The widespread misery of the Depression was unemployment, not stock market losses, although losses in the stock and bond markets did have serious indirect consequences even on the poor and unemployed who never owned securities.

The slowing economy and wobbly stock market had concerned government officials throughout the summer, but the dramatic headlines of the stock market crash called for immediate action. The Federal Reserve lowered its discount rate a full point, to 5 percent, and continued to lower the rate in steps, to 2 percent by mid-1930. The lower interest rates were meant to encourage banks to make more loans. The incentive of potential profit from borrowing from the Federal Reserve at 2 percent and lending that money to a credit-worthy homebuyer or business at 5 or 6 percent motivated the banks to lend. President Hoover signed a construction stimulus law in mid-November and a personal and corporate income tax reduction in December. In 1929, most wage-earners were exempt from income taxes. For those in the lowest income bracket (wages above $4,000 up to $8,000), the reduction of tax rate from 3 percent to 2 percent meant a 33 percent reduction in income tax for 1929. The lower rate for the next bracket (above $8,000 up to $10,000) provided a 20 percent reduction in taxes payable on that income. The tax reductions immediately boosted the amount of money available to consumers, since taxes were payable quarterly. The size of the rate

---

209 John Kenneth Galbraith, *The Great Crash, 1929,* 78.

reductions meant that most taxpayers would not owe any payment for the fourth quarter of 1929.

Hoover summoned corporate presidents to Washington and urged them to continue construction and investment.[210] Union leaders and business executives were pressed to voluntarily hold wages and employment steady and avoid strikes and lockouts. Hoover lobbied governors and mayors to move forward with public works projects to boost local employment. He also ordered that more detailed employment information be gathered during the census of 1930. Hoover's calls for voluntary actions were effective initially. Henry Ford responded by increasing the wages for his unskilled workers from $5 per day to $7 per day.[211] Westinghouse, a major producer of electrical appliances and equipment with fifty thousand employees, reduced the total number of employees by 12 percent over the next year, but increased the average annual pay per employee almost 6 percent.[212]

By January 1, 1930, the Dow Jones Industrial Average was up 25 percent from its November low, and by April, it was up 48 percent, to close at 294. That would prove to be the highest closing average of the entire decade. Construction activity and employment rose in the first half of 1930 from a low point in December 1929 and January 1930.[213] There were still signs of business investment activity. John Raskob, former chairman of General Motors' Finance Committee, built the Empire State Building as a real estate investment, breaking ground in January 1930 and officially opening on May 1, 1931, as the tallest building in the world. In Pittsburgh, the Gulf Corporation, a large oil company largely owned by the Mellon family, started work on a new forty-four-story high-rise office building in February 1930 and finished in 1932. The pace of bank failures in the first six months of 1930 was no higher than the average failure rate in the 1920s, and no major banks or industrial companies closed. Home construction was still noticeably lagging because builders were still having trouble borrowing, but many believed the worst was over. Airlines in the U.S. carried four times as many passengers in the first six months of 1930 as they had in the same months of 1929.

---

210 The corporate president of the 1920s was the equivalent of today's CEO, and he sometimes also served as chairman of the Board of Directors—a dual role that appears in many corporations today.

211 Robert Lacey, *Ford: The Men and the Machine*, 305.

212 Ronald W. Schatz, *The Electrical Workers*, 61.

213 Hoover's address to Chamber of Commerce, May 1, 1930. President's Organization for Unemployment Relief, Chrono Files of Edward Eyre Hunt, January 1928–Sept. 1930, Record Group 30, Box 1. NARA II.

On June 30, the federal government's fiscal year ended with a surplus of $184 million,[214] in spite of a shortfall in customs duties. Recovery was underway.

In the same month, Hoover signed the Smoot-Hawley Tariff Act into law.[215] The tariff was intended to raise the price of foreign-made goods and thus provide advantage to goods produced by American workers and protect their jobs. The new rates applied mainly to agricultural products, and two-thirds of all goods remained duty-free. But the tariff on some manufactured goods raised the price Americans would pay on many imported goods. Politicians were fiercely divided in their opinions about the tariff. It passed only after long debate in Congress that started before the stock market crash and by only a slim margin in the Senate.

The response from other countries was immediate and powerful. Other democracies have their own politicians who answer to their own voters. Canada was the largest market for U.S. exports, and Smoot-Hawley became a key issue in the Canadian election in July 1930. Canada raised its own tariff rates in retaliation.[216] Great Britain quickly prioritized trade relationships within the British Commonwealth nations, colonies, and protectorates that included Canada, many Caribbean islands, Guyana, Australia, New Zealand, India (which included modern Pakistan, Bangladesh, and Sri Lanka), South Africa, Burma (now Myanmar), Singapore, the Malayan peninsula, Palestine, Hong Kong, Sierra Leone, Ghana, Nigeria, Rhodesia (now Zimbabwe) and Kenya, Aden, Egypt, Iraq, Kuwait, several of the modern Arab Emirates, Papua New Guinea, and other lands. The tariff war also gave foreign investors an opportunity to build their own plants to manufacture goods previously imported from America, since they could sell at high prices protected from American competition. Americans bought fewer foreign-made goods. As foreign countries enacted their own tariffs, their citizens bought fewer American goods. Exports of American merchandise fell from $4.6 billion in 1930 (just before the tariff was signed) to $3.1 billion in 1931 (a drop of 34 percent) and to $1.9 billion in 1932 (an additional 37 percent drop).[217] With the loss of foreign customers, unemployment in America rose. The tariff intended to protect

---

214 *Statistical Abstract of the United States, 1930,* U.S. Department of Commerce. Table 182.

215 The Smoot-Hawley Tariff was formally known as the U.S. Tariff Act of 1930 and sometimes known as the Hawley-Smoot Tariff.

216 National City Bank of New York, monthly report of economic conditions, governmental finances and United States securities, September 1930. President's Organization for Unemployment Relief, Chrono Files of Edward Eyre Hunt, RG 73. NARA II.

217 *Statistical Abstract of the United States, 1933,* Table 459.

American jobs was destroying them, but that view was not widely accepted at the time. Unemployment one year after the crash did not exceed 9 percent.

The tariff became a major issue in the 1932 presidential election. Roosevelt pointed to the tariff as a major contributor to the economic depression. Hoover defended the tariff during the election season, and even in 1952 when he wrote his memoirs.[218] Today, politicians still point to it as a poster child for all that is good or evil, depending on one's political orientation about government interference with free trade among nations, whether by tariffs, quotas, or buy American clauses.

Professional economists had their own view of the Smoot-Hawley Tariff and its impact. Before its passage, more than one thousand economists signed a letter to Hoover opposing the tariff, advising that other countries would pass retaliatory tariffs.[219]

Modern economists still study the tariff's role in the Depression. Mario Crucini and James Kahn, staff economists at the Federal Reserve Bank of New York, concluded that the tariff was responsible for about 10 percent of the overall output decline during the Depression. Using a model they had devised in 1996, and taking into account work done subsequently by other economists, Crucini and Kahn estimated in 2003 that had the tariff been passed in more robust economic circumstances, it might have caused a modest recession. Passing the tariff during a worldwide economic slump aggravated existing problems and contributed to the serious declines in production and unemployment.[220]

This reduction of imports further damaged the American economy. Many European governments had been repaying war debts to the United States. Foreign banks also owed millions to banks in the U.S. Those debts were payable in U.S. dollars. Foreign companies earned dollars by selling products to American customers. As long as Americans bought foreign-made goods, the foreign banks and countries could repay their debts. But the Smoot-Hawley Tariff duties made foreign-made goods less competitive in America. When the flow of dollars to foreign manufacturers slowed drastically, foreign banks and treasuries could not repay their debts. Within two years, every European country except Finland defaulted on its debts to the U.S. government. More ominously, many foreign banks defaulted on payments to U.S. banks and investors. When foreign

---

218 Herbert Hoover, *Memoirs: The Great Depression, 1929—1941,* 287–301.
219 "1,028 Economists Ask Hoover to Veto Pending Tariff Bill," *New York Times,* May 5, 1930, verbatim text of letter and list of signers.
220 Federal Reserve Bank of New York "Tariffs and the Great Depression," Staff Report no. 172, September 2003, Mario J. Crucini and James Kahn.

banks failed to pay the interest on their loans, American banks could not pay their depositors, and investors lost their income. In December 1930, the Bank of United States—one of the largest in the country—failed. Its four hundred thousand depositors, mostly in New York City, were suddenly unable to access their savings.[221] Even the economists who had urged a veto of the tariff probably underestimated the impact these defaults would have on Americans.

––––––

In the same month in which the Smoot-Hawley Tariff was enacted, General Electric, the largest manufacturer of consumer and capital electrical equipment in the world, established an unemployment insurance pool covering all of its employees. The pool was funded by deducting 1 percent from the earnings of every employee of the corporation, including the president, and combining this with a matching contribution by the corporation. An employee who was laid off would collect one-half of his or her earnings, up to $20 per week, for as long as twelve weeks. The same plan had been offered five years earlier. General Electric employees, enjoying the full employment that had blessed most of the 1920s, had rejected it. In 1930, the employees voted overwhelmingly in favor, and the board of directors approved its implementation.[222] At the time, no state had an unemployment insurance system, nor was there any federal plan.[223]

Three months later, in September 1930, Gerald Swope, president of General Electric, was gravely concerned about the decline in manufacturing activity and sales and rising unemployment. He visited the White House to encourage Hoover to commit up to two billion dollars in stimulus spending for public works such as new hospitals, prisons, highways, and public housing projects.[224] This was a staggering sum in a year when the entire federal budget was $3.4 billion. No doubt all that new work would have provided great sales opportunities

221 The depositors were eventually able to recover about 84 percent of the money due them, as the bank's assets were liquidated and money doled out over the following two years. How many small businesses and individual depositors went bankrupt while waiting for their money is unknown, but this was a major concern of the New York Fed governor as he urged other banks to merge with, or lend money to, the Bank of United States. His efforts were unsuccessful, and several branches were already sustaining runs by depositors, so he ordered the bank closed and liquidated.

222 Ronald W. Schatz, *The Electrical Workers*, 59.

223 Lester V. Chandler, *America's Greatest Depression, 1929-1941*, 31.

224 Ronald W. Schatz, *The Electrical Workers*, 53.

for General Electric. It also would have created jobs. But Hoover was already presiding over a federal budget that called for a deficit of one billion dollars, the first annual deficit since 1919.[225] He believed that such works, if not carefully planned, would involve wasteful spending and create a permanent group of workers who would forever depend on public employment. Hoover also believed that conditions would improve in about six months, far sooner than major infrastructure projects could be planned and designed. Hoover probably also pointed to the construction underway at the Federal Triangle, just one-half mile from the White House, where new buildings were being built to accommodate the Departments of Commerce, Labor, and Justice, the Post Office, the Internal Revenue Service, and the National Archives. It was the largest single building project ever undertaken by the federal government and certainly stimulated the economy in the Washington area. But outside of the District, in the fall of 1930, the recovery was stalling.

In January 1931, Hoover boosted spending for Federal construction and maintenance projects. Fiscal year 1931 spending in these categories totaled $739 million—three times the expenditures of 1929. A few symptoms of an improving economy appeared in the early months of 1931, but as the year progressed, conditions became dire. Prices were falling sharply because of weak demand. Factory unemployment was rising dramatically. In New York City, eighty-five thousand meals per day were being served at scores of bread lines funded by private donations. The Hearst newspaper chain funded two truck-mounted kitchens that served bread and soup to those in need.[226] Those rendered homeless by eviction or foreclosure were settling in Hoovervilles, the shabby tent cities that sprang up throughout the country. People sold their cars to raise cash, if they could find a buyer. The number of automobiles registered by the states had fallen almost 3 percent between 1929 and 1931.[227] Veterans of World War I marched in Washington, DC, seeking early payment of the bonus they were scheduled to

---

225 The federal budget for fiscal year (FY) 1931 covered the period July 1, 1930 to June 30, 1931. References to the budget for a particular year are for July 1 of the prior year, to June 30 of the year mentioned. Similarly, FY 1932 refers to July 1, 1931 to June 30, 1932.
226 Edward Robb Ellis, *A Nation in Torment*, 129–30.
227 *Statistical Abstract of the U.S., 1933*, Table 372.

receive in 1945. Congress passed legislation to pay the bonus, but Hoover vetoed it in July, as Roosevelt would do again in 1935 and 1936.[228]

In June 1931, newspaper magnate William Randolph Hearst used a nationwide radio broadcast to recommend that government immediately launch a $5 billion public works project to create jobs for the unemployed. Hearst newspapers followed the radio address with a series of editorials and articles promoting the plan. Hoover and his administration ignored Hearst. Weeks later, Hearst newspapers launched an editorial campaign criticizing Hoover and his failure to provide more aggressive public spending. Millions of readers saw the editorials and satirical cartoons.

In September, Gerard Swope of General Electric publicly called for a revision of antitrust laws. He urged that national trade associations promote collaboration by corporations within each industry to match production schedules to consumer demand. The objective of this economic planning was to stabilize employment. These trade associations would fix prices, quality standards, and other factors as needed to stabilize the economy. The associations would operate under the supervision of a federal regulatory body, either in the Department of Commerce or some new agency. Short-term unemployment insurance would protect any employees who were laid off whenever production and demand were temporarily out of balance. Swope's speech to the National Association of Electrical Manufacturers' Association was reported at length in the *New York Times* and much discussed in the business community.[229] One month later, the American Institute of Steel Construction endorsed Swope's plan. In December, the president of the United States Chamber of Commerce visited Hoover, advising him that the members of the Chamber had voted favorably on this concept of economic planning and urging him to take up the matter with Congress. Hoover

---

228 In their veto messages, both presidents cited the high total cost of the early payments, the concentration of the proposed special benefit on a small group within the population, and the major change from the carefully designed veterans' benefit programs established after World War I. In 1931, the cost would have been $3.4 billion, about equal to the entire federal budget that year. However, veterans were permitted under a 1931 law to borrow advances of up to 50 percent of their eventual award. They borrowed almost $800 million under that plan in early 1931. By May 1935, three million vets had borrowed $1.7 billion under that program. The bill that Roosevelt vetoed in 1935 would have cost $2.2 billion in immediate cash outlays, adding to the annual deficit that was already budgeted at $4 billion.

229 "Swope Offers Plan to Unify Industries," *New York Times*, September 17, 1931.

replied that such a plan would obviously lead to the return of monopolies, thus protecting inferior managements and ultimately hurting consumers. Hoover's attorney general wrote that such a plan would be unconstitutional.[230]

These business leaders were so alarmed by financial trends that they were now seeking a dramatic change in the regulatory environment. Hearst's advertising revenue, the lifeblood of the newspaper industry, had declined by 15 percent in 1930 and then fell 24 percent in 1931—a 35 percent drop in the two-year period.[231] Sales at Sears, Roebuck and Company had fallen 23 percent from 1929 to 1931. At Montgomery Ward, sales were off 25 percent in the same period.[232] In turn, hundreds of suppliers to these retailers saw their own revenues fall as orders shrank. Westinghouse, a rival of General Electric, saw sales drop 46 percent between 1929 and 1931.[233] At United States Steel, sales dropped 50 percent in the same two years.[234] The number of telephones in service in the U.S. dropped by 1.8 percent between 1929 and 1931 after growing steadily every year since 1895.[235]

The presidents and board members of these companies were not just concerned about lower sales and profits, or the financial implications of idle plants and machinery. Their larger concern was the loss of human capital. With so little money coming into the cash registers, there was less work to be done and fewer dollars for payroll. As skilled workers and salespeople were laid off, corporate cultures built over more than two decades with employee stock plans, profit-sharing, and extensive training and promotion programs were melting before their eyes. Work-sharing plans were used to keep as many workers as possible employed by reducing each worker's hours per week. These were less efficient for business operations and less rewarding for employees. Many were now working only a few hours each week, which could hardly support their families. As executives looked up from the grim financial reports of their own companies, they saw similar gloom in the national economy. Antitrust laws prohibited any specific collaboration with others in the same industry, and these men had vivid memories of the government's antitrust campaign two decades earlier. They had

---

230 Herbert Hoover, *Memoirs: The Great Depression, 1929-1941*, 334–335.
231 David Nasaw, *The Chief—The Life of William Randolph Hearst*, 426.
232 Boris Emmet and John E. Jeuck, *Catalogues and Counters*, 664.
233 Ronald W. Schatz, *The Electrical Workers*, 60.
234 Douglas A. Fisher, *Steel Serves the Nation—The Fifty Year History of United States Steel, 1901—1951*, 224–225.
235 *Statistical Abstract of the United States, 1934*, Table 345, citing American Telephone & Telegraph Co.

also experienced firsthand the recession of the early 1920s. Yet their proposals to Hoover and his cabinet officers were rebuffed.

By October 1931, 624,000 people were unemployed in Chicago—40 percent of the labor force.[236] People and businesses were buying so little that, by December 1931, the price index of all items purchased in thirty-two large cities by wage-earners and lower-salaried workers, mainly food, clothing, and rent, had fallen to price levels from 1917–1918. They remained at that level until the end of the decade.[237]

———

The misery was felt in every job category. Those with little or no skills were the first to be laid off and the last hired. Chronic, long-term unemployment was widespread. The chairman of a California Labor Camp Committee stated in January 1932:

> Many of them were laborers, but there were also businessmen and trades- men. There were many professional men and many high school and college graduates. In one camp we had eighteen college graduates and thirty-three high school graduates, which is a very high percentage. We have graduates of some of the largest colleges in the United States. As I say, we have quite a number of small tradesmen and businessmen who have gone broke. We have a doctor and a dentist... We have men who had been bankers and brokers. They listed themselves as clerks, and after that they came in to get a job, many of them giving a false name, as a matter of pride.[238]

Also in January 1932—two and a half years into the recession and twenty- eight months after the stock market crash—Hoover signed the Reconstruction Finance Corporation (RFC) Act, authorizing government loans to banks, building and loan societies, insurance companies, and similar financial institutions. Rail- roads were also eligible for RFC loans. The railroads were deemed too big to fail because they employed so many, their operations were vital to the flow of com- merce, and because so many banks, insurance companies, and individuals relied upon income from railroad bonds. If the railroads defaulted on bond payments,

---

236 Lester V. Chandler, *America's Greatest Depression, 1929-1941*, 45.
237 *Statistical Abstract of the United States, 1939*, U.S. Department of Commerce, Table 360.
238 Lester V. Chandler, *America's Greatest Depression, 1929-1941*, 47.

the asset value and lending capacity of the banks and insurers would be reduced, and individuals relying on the interest payments would lose spending power. The RFC was authorized to accept as collateral various securities that the banks found unmarketable. Congress authorized five hundred million dollars for immediate use, plus $1.5 billion to be used if needed. The borrowing banks paid interest to the government at 5.5 percent per year.

The prime objective of the RFC Act was to enable the banks and financial firms to make loans to businesses and individuals, a process that had stalled as banks worried about keeping cash on hand to meet withdrawal demands from concerned depositors. In July, new legislation broadened the RFC's charter and authorized federal loans to states that needed funds for relief payments to citizens or for major infrastructure projects. By August, the RFC had paid out $866 million and authorized an additional $224 million. Although a similar agency had been established during World War I, the RFC was a major change in peacetime federal government activity.[239] With occasional legislative changes, it was maintained throughout the New Deal period and finally abolished in 1954.

The RFC approach to restoring bank liquidity by massive loans reappeared as the government's response to the financial crisis that developed late in 2008, particularly the Capital Purchase Program of TARP, in which banks issued preferred stock to the Treasury Department. These loans required the banks to make dividend payments to the Treasury at 5 percent for each of the first three years, then rising to 9 percent if not repaid.

In March, the Senate Banking Committee, with Hoover's encouragement, authorized an investigation into various suspected abuses of the stock market, including conspiracies to drive particular stock prices up and down. But the committee and its appointed investigating counsel were not up to the task. The president of the New York Stock Exchange, Richard Whitney, appeared three times before the committee and submitted extensive data on short-selling as the committee had demanded. Records of ten brokerage firms were subpoenaed. By early summer, there were a few admissions of stock pooling—nothing beyond what had

---

239 Warren Harding was inaugurated March 4, 1921, in the midst of recession and high unemployment, but his inaugural speech focused on foreign policy. He made little mention of the weak economy, unemployment, or relief activity. These were not considered Federal issues. The Index of Industrial Production turned upward one month later. There was another recession in 1924, brief and shallow. The entire decade became known as the Roaring Twenties.

long been suspected and was not illegal at the time. The committee did not lack financial sophistication. One of its members was Senator James Couzens, representing Michigan. He had been Ford Motor Company's chief financial and administrative officer and second largest shareholder before resigning to enter public life in 1915. But neither the senators in attendance nor the committee's legal counsel, assisted by one secretary and one financial advisor, were able to draw any information useful for drafting new laws, nor did they discover any admissions of criminal activity.[240] When Congress adjourned in July, the Banking Committee hearings were suspended. They did not resume until February 1933.

In March 1932, the U.S. Department of Labor surveyed sixty-five hundred companies in all branches of industry. Less than 26 percent of firms were operating full-time. Of all workers counted as employed, 56 percent were only part-time, working on average 59 percent of normal full-time schedules.[241]

The following statement was given to a congressional committee early in 1932 by the executive director of the Welfare Council of New York City:

> When the breadwinner is out of a job, he usually exhausts his savings if he has any. Then, if he has an insurance policy, he probably borrows to the limit of its cash value. He borrows from his friends and from his relatives until they can stand the burden no longer. He gets credit from the local grocery store and the butcher shop, and the landlord forgoes collecting the rent until interest and taxes have to be paid and something has to be done. All of these resources are finally exhausted over a period of time, and it becomes necessary for these people, who have never before been in want, to ask for assistance.[242]

With profits reduced or nonexistent at so many companies, dividends reduced or suspended, and so many unemployed, the federal government's revenue from personal and corporate income taxes fell from $2.3 billion in the fiscal year that ended June 30, 1929, to $1.1 billion in fiscal year 1932. The federal government moved from a $734 million surplus in 1929 to a $181 million surplus in 1930 and a $462 million deficit in 1931.[243]

---

240 Constantly frustrated by an inability to obtain useful information, the Committee actually employed a series of three attorneys during this period.
241 Lester V. Chandler, *America's Greatest Depression, 1929-1941*, 35.
242 Lester V. Chandler, *America's Greatest Depression, 1929-1941*, 41.
243 For government entities and nonprofit organizations, a surplus exists in any period in which revenue exceeds expenses. A deficit exists when expenses exceed revenue. The term profit is used only in reference to businesses.

On June 30, 1932, the fiscal year closed with a deficit of $2.5 billion. The presidential election was just four months away.

———

Labor Force, Employment, and Unemployment in the United States 1929 to 1939[244]											
Year	1929	'30	'31	'32	'33	'34	'35	'36	'37	'38	'39
Labor force (millions)	49.2	49.8	50.4	51.0	51.6	52.2	52.9	53.4	54.0	54.6	55.2
Employed (millions)	47.6	45.5	42.4	38.9	38.8	40.9	42.3	44.4	46.3	44.2	45.8
Unemployed (millions)	1.6	4.3	8.0	12.1	12.8	11.3	10.6	9.0	7.7	10.4	9.5
Unemployment rate (%)	3.2	8.7	15.9	23.6	24.9	21.7	20.1	16.9	14.3	19.0	17.2

This depression, and the unemployment that accompanied it, lasted much longer than any before or since. The unemployment persisted in spite of the largest government job and welfare programs that have ever been seen in this country[245]—designed to both provide useful employment and to jump-start the economy by encouraging consumer spending and thus boost demand for products.

Robert S. McElvaine is a social historian who has written extensively about the Great Depression. He points out, as is visible in so many photographs taken during the Great Depression years: "Gradually, those over forty, though fit physically, began to *feel* old and *look* and *act* poor. Keeping up the appearance necessary to secure employment, particularly of the white-collar variety, became increasingly difficult…With shabby suits, frayed collars, worn shoes and perhaps a couple of front teeth gone, men *looked* like bums."

---

244 *Historical Statistics of the United States, Colonial Times to 1970, Part 1.* U.S. Department of Commerce. Series D. There have been many estimates of unemployment for the years 1900–1939 prepared by such agencies as the National Industrial Conference Board and by various authors. In these, unemployment was calculated as a residual, first estimating the civilian labor force, then estimating employment, and taking the difference as the unemployment figure. Since 1940, more direct figures have been obtained and published in the U.S. Bureau of Census Current Population Survey and by the Department of Labor. The series used here uses estimates of unemployment on as close as possible to current labor force concepts. Thus the series seems to offer figures most useful for comparisons on a consistent basis over the century.
245 James T. Patterson, *America's Struggle Against Poverty in the Twentieth Century*, 58.

"We do not dare to use even a little soap," wrote a jobless Oregonian, "when it will pay for an extra egg or a few more carrots for our children."[246]

Many research economists now concur with the contemporaneous assessment of John Maynard Keynes that the business slowdown in the first few years of the Depression reflected the effects of high interest rates set by the Federal Reserve (Bernanke 1995 and Hamilton 1987).[247] The Federal Reserve lowered rates rapidly in the months following the crash, and more slowly during 1930 and 1931. But by mid-1930, the Fed's Open Market Policy Conference (OMPC), apparently concerned about risk of inflation even while prices were falling, became more conservative. When urged to increase its purchases of Treasury bonds as a means of lowering commercial loan and mortgage rates, the OMPC declined.

In October 1931, the Federal Reserve raised its discount rate a full percentage point, making it more expensive for banks, which were already shaky, to borrow from the Fed or each other. Consequently, any loans to businesses became more expensive, increasing one more burden on businesses that were already staggering.

———

Throughout the late 1920s, just over four million federal income tax returns were filed annually by individuals or married couples. Married couples earning less than $3,500 were exempt, as were singles earning less than $1,500. Thus on the eve of the Depression the adult, married stockman at the Sears, Roebuck and Company mail-order facility in Philadelphia, earning $28 per week,[248] was exempt, as was the Ford Motor Company assembly line worker, even at the 1930 rate of $7 per day, five days per week, fifty-two weeks each year, including one week of paid vacation. The average unmarried schoolteacher in Pennsylvania earned $1,538 and so paid tax on just $38 of income. The entire salary of the same teacher, if married, was exempt. Teachers in New York earning $1,978 per year and in Delaware ($1,451), Illinois ($1,634), Colorado ($1,450), and California ($2,175) did the same calculations.[249] A junior professor at Harvard University that year earned $1,375. The highest salary for a full professor there was $12,000.[250]

246 Robert S. McElvaine, *The Great Depression—America, 1929-1941*, 172.
247 "The Great Depression and the Friedman-Schwartz Hypothesis," *Journal of Money, Credit and Banking*, December 1, 2003.
248 Boris Emmet and John E. Jeuck, *Catalogues and Counters*, 286.
249 *Statistical Abstract of the United States, 1931*, Table 110.
250 Thomas K. McCraw, *Prophet of Innovation—Joseph Schumpeter and Creative*

With the 1932 presidential elections approaching, both major political parties pointed to the federal deficit and pledged to raise taxes and balance the federal budget. In June 1932, Congress and President Hoover raised federal income tax rates in an attempt to increase tax revenues that had been falling dramatically as corporate profits and personal incomes fell.

This Revenue Act of 1932 was the largest percentage increase in taxes in American peacetime history. For most taxpayers, the law applied to income for the full calendar year 1932. For businesses that used a fiscal year, the new law applied to the entire fiscal year that ended during calendar year 1932. The new law also lowered the exemption levels. The exemption for single taxpayers was lowered to $1,000 and the basic tax rate increased from 1.125 percent to 4 percent; for married couples the exemption dropped to $2,500. Proponents in both parties preached that a more inclusive tax would promote the working man's interest in his government and raise much-needed revenue as well. Those with incomes above $1,000,000 per year saw their marginal tax rate increase from 25 percent to 63 percent. Corporations lost their exemption of the first $3,000 of income, which had sheltered many small companies from any income tax. The tax rate of 12 percent that had applied to corporate profit in excess of $3,000 was replaced with a tax rate of 13.75 percent against every dollar of profits.[251]

The plan was simple and logical: higher tax rates and reduced exemptions should produce more tax revenue. This Revenue Act was intended to increase federal revenues by $1.1 billion. The plan failed. Income tax revenues for FY 1933 sank to $746 million, compared to the $1.1 billion collected in FY 1932. Total federal revenue in fiscal year 1933 (July 1, 1932, to June 30, 1933), with the new tax law in effect, were only $2 billion, consisting mainly of income taxes, excise taxes, and customs fees, compared to $4.2 billion in 1930. The federal deficit was $1.8 billion, compared to a $900 million surplus in 1930.[252] Higher income tax rates were producing less income tax revenue.

There were other effects of the new tax law. Individuals, families, and corporations paying higher taxes had less cash available for spending or paying debts. Motor vehicle production fell to a level not seen since the war-constrained 1918 level, with 1.4 million vehicles compared to 5.6 million in 1929. By the end

---

Destruction, 210.
251 Public Law No. 154 (47 Stat. 169).
252 U.S. Treasury Fact Sheet, available at www.treas.gov/education/fact-sheets. Also, "Republican Roots of New Deal Tax Policy," 2003, Tax Analysts, available at www.taxhistory.org.

of 1932, there were 9 percent fewer vehicles registered than in 1929.[253] Sales at Sears, Roebuck and Company fell 14 percent, from $320 million in 1931 to $275 million in 1932.[254]

As sales activity fell, fewer employees were needed. Annual payroll at Sears was reduced by $17 million between 1929 and 1932. Lower retail sales meant less demand at manufacturing plants, and more layoffs rippled through the economy. When businesses closed their books on 1932, six months after the tax hike, many had no after-tax profit.

————

In September, two months before the presidential election, the president of the United States Chamber of Commerce, Henry I. Harriman, urged Hoover to press Congress for legislation to implement Gerard Swope's plan for industry associations that would coordinate and manage production, prices, and other aspects of manufacture. He pointed out that Franklin Roosevelt had recently agreed to support it. If Hoover would not, then business leaders would throw their support to Roosevelt. Hoover declined.[255]

Business leaders took action. Joseph Kennedy, father of the future president, had been gathering contributions from business leaders and forwarding them to the Roosevelt campaign. When Kennedy was not meeting with wealthy contributors, he was a frequent passenger on Roosevelt's campaign train as it crisscrossed the country. Three weeks before the election, a major contribution arrived from William Randolph Hearst, who also used his editorial pages and weekly movie-theater newsreels during the summer and fall to support Roosevelt's candidacy.[256] Pierre du Pont, scion of the chemical company, backed Roosevelt.[257] So did J. I. Straus, president of the retail firm R. H. Macy & Co., and William Woodin, president of American Car and Foundry Company and chairman of the board of American Locomotive Company.[258] Alfred Sloan of General Motors had long believed that corporate executives should remain neutral in politics and remained silent. But John J. Raskob, who had earned a fortune as treasurer of the DuPont

---

253 *Statistical Abstract of the United States, 1933,* Table 372.

254 Boris Emmet and John E. Jueck, *Catalogues and Counters,* 650.

255 Herbert Hoover, *Memoirs: The Great Depression, 1929-1941,* 335.

256 David Nasaw, *The Chief: The Life of William Randolph Hearst,* 458.

257 "Pierre du Pont's Vote Will Go to Roosevelt," *New York Times,* November 5, 1932.

258 *New York Times,* March 21, August 29, October 21, November 3, 1932.

Company and at General Motors before retiring in 1927, backed Roosevelt. Charles Marsh, co-owner of the Marsh-Fentress newspaper chain, influenced the newspapers to favor Roosevelt.[259] Robert Wood, president of Sears, Roebuck & Company, had been a life-long Republican but supported Roosevelt.[260] Henry Ford was a notable exception. He publicly endorsed Hoover with a huge pro-Hoover banner displayed in the main assembly plant.[261]

The business executives who contributed to Roosevelt's victory acted out of self-interest, not altruism. During the 1920s, large corporations had centralized their own management structures and formalized their planning processes. They had grown their sales and profits and paid higher wages to their employees. They believed that the federal government could promote business recovery by sponsoring a broader, centralized planning of the economy. This, they were sure, would restore profits and reemployment at the corporations for which they were responsible. Swope and others were well aware that their businesses depended directly on providing employment, stopping the decline of prices and wages, and reviving the economy. They believed that government policy should change to allow and support the coordinated planning.

In November 1932, Franklin Delano Roosevelt was elected thirty-second president of the United States. He carried forty-two of the forty-eight states and won 57 percent of the popular vote. Democrats took control of the House of Representatives, with 313 seats compared to the Republicans 117. In the Senate, Democrats now held fifty-nine seats to the Republicans thirty-six.

———

Then came the interregnum—four long, leaderless months between the election and inauguration. Voters had clearly repudiated Hoover and his policies. Congress and the people now looked to Hyde Park instead of the White House for policy signals. Roosevelt, secure in his victory and watching the continued economic deterioration, was reluctant to commit to any specific policy, least of all any policy attributable even in part to Hoover's administration. While Roosevelt quietly bided his time, there were many voices from the desert proclaiming policies for the coming savior. Some were inspired by their recent visits to Communist Russia. Others had massive schemes for measuring and planning

---

259 Philip Kopper, *Anonymous Giver—A Life of Charles E. Marsh*, 55.
260 Boris Emmet and John E. Jeuck, *Counters and Catalogues*, 616.
261 Arthur M. Schlesinger Jr., *The Crisis of the Old Order, 1919-1933*, 432.

every task of production and assuring every inhabitant of the land an income adequate to support consumption of all the products of the land. Most insisted on a balanced federal budget while also insisting on federal support of extended unemployment insurance, old-age insurance, and minimum wages.

Roosevelt waited, even deferring selection of his first Cabinet members until mid-February.[262] Throughout the waiting period, it seemed that every visitor offering advice to the president-elect came away convinced that his plan would be adopted. Even John Nance Garner, Speaker of the House and new vice president elect, was confused. In December, he indicated support for Hoover's proposed national sales tax intended to balance the budget, only to withdraw support after consulting Roosevelt.[263] Four long winter months passed, while the nation waited and wondered.

Business conditions worsened. In December, the financial officer of Hearst's media empire advised his boss that bankruptcy was imminent. Hearst Consolidated, the parent corporation of Hearst's empire, had financed the numerous acquisitions of other companies by borrowing heavily. Now there was too little cash coming in and no cash reserves to meet mortgage payments, interest payments on loans, payroll, newsprint from Canadian mills, and other operational costs. The banks and suppliers would not renegotiate or advance new loans especially to a firm with dwindling sales. The only way to avoid shutting down all the operations and going out of business would be a sharp cut in payroll. Choosing between two bitter alternatives, Hearst agreed to pay cuts of 39 percent across the board.[264] For Hearst and many other business leaders, including avid Roosevelt supporters, the reality of falling revenue trumped best intentions.

For many of the largest corporations, 1932 was the worst year of the Great Depression, with regard to profits. Sears, Roebuck and Company lost $2.5 million that year,[265] and U.S. Steel lost a staggering $71 million.[266] General Motors made a profit,[267] but Ford and Chrysler lost money. American Telephone & Telegraph Co. profits had fallen 36 percent from $217 million in 1929 to $139 mil-

---

262 Raymond Moley, *After Seven Years*, 109–137.

263 Arthur M. Schlesinger Jr., *The Age of Roosevelt: Crisis of the Old Order, 1919-1933*, 449.

264 David Nasaw, *The Chief*, 462.

265 Boris Emmet and John E. Jeuck, *Catalogues and Counters*, 332.

266 Douglas A. Fisher, *Steel Serves the Nation—The Fifty Year History of United States Steel*, 224–225.

267 Arthur J. Kuhn, *GM Passes Ford, 1919-1938*, 317.

lion in 1932.[268] Total corporate pretax profits fell from $9.6 billion in 1929 to a loss of $3 billion in 1932. Corporations spent the savings accumulated in prior years to pay out more in wages and expenses than they were collecting in sales. The first quarter of 1933 was looking no better.

Small-business proprietors and professionals were devastated. Many small stores and manufacturing businesses, some informally referred to as "mom and pop operations," were in this category. The owners often mixed their own wages and business profits in the same cash drawer, and the term "proprietor's income" recognized that concept. By 1932, their total income had fallen to 36 percent of 1929 levels—a 64 percent pay cut. Rental income for landlords, many of whom were individuals or families with an apartment or house to rent out, had fallen to 50 percent of 1929 levels.[269]

During January 1933, two plumbers installing a bathtub in Philadelphia penciled a note on the side of the tub before sliding it against the wall:

This work kept two men from starving during the depression.[270]

In the weeks leading up to the March 4 inauguration a number of banks failed, and just days before the inauguration, many governors ordered all of the banks in their states to close. The largest failure, Guardian Bank in Detroit, shocked the entire Midwestern part of the country. In total, more than five thousand banks had suspended operations since the October 1929 market crash. The new wave of anxiety strengthened Roosevelt's already-powerful mandate.[271]

---

268 *Statistical Abstract of the United States, 1933*, Fifty-fifth Number, U.S. Department of Commerce, Table 345, citing American Telephone & Telegraph Co.
269 Lester V. Chandler, *America's Greatest Depression, 1929-1941*, 26.
270 The note on the tub was signed by Louis J. Volpe on January 9, 1933. It remained hidden until July 2010 when the tub was removed during renovations. My thanks to Donald Smith, executive director of Neighborhood House at Christ Church, for sharing the discovery.
271 The Twentieth Amendment to the Constitution shifted the inauguration date to January 4. Although ratified in January 1933, the Amendment by its own language did not take effect until the first October following the ratification.

Chapter Eleven

"…the only thing we have to fear is…"

On March 4, 1933, Franklin Delano Roosevelt took the oath of office. The opening paragraph of his inauguration speech included some of the most memorable words of his long tenure as president. "So, first of all, let me assert my firm belief that the only thing we have to fear is fear itself—nameless, unreasoning, unjustified terror which paralyzes needed efforts to convert retreat into advance."

The nation was surely paralyzed. Most banks were closed. Depositors could not get their money, payrolls could not be met, and bills went unpaid. Governors had ordered the closings to avoid runs that could turn violent. Almost thirteen million Americans were completely out of work. The national unemployment rate, which had averaged 3.2 percent in 1929, was 24.9 percent. Many who had jobs worked only a few hours a week.

Roosevelt pledged "action, and action now" in his inauguration speech. Two days later, he called the Congress into emergency session. During the first 104 days of his administration, Roosevelt made ten speeches and sent messages to Congress sponsoring fifteen pieces of major legislation—legislation that made sweeping changes in the relationships between government, businesses, and nonprofit agencies. His legislative accomplishments still represent one of the busiest presidential agendas in history.

Restoring confidence in the banks was the essential first step. Without banks, there could be no working economy. Congress passed an Emergency Banking Act before most members had read the text in an effort to get the banks reopened. The new law permitted banks that were audited and deemed sound to reopen, and it permitted use of Federal Reserve notes to meet future runs.

Jobs were another urgent need. The Civilian Conservation Corps was established within weeks of the inauguration. Single men between the ages of eighteen and twenty-six were eligible to join the CCC. Most were city-dwellers and soon found themselves assigned to camps in rural areas, working mainly on reforestation and soil conservation projects. Pay was $30 per month, of which $25 was required to be sent home to the recruit's family. The $1 per day was equal to the pay of unskilled farm workers. The men also received work clothes, housing, food, and medical care. Young men long idle and lacking job prospects were grateful for the cash and perhaps more grateful for the escape from unending idleness. Within three months, the CCC had signed 275,000 young men, exceeding the number of officers and enlisted men in the regular army. At its peak in 1935, the CCC employed about five hundred thousand in twenty-six hundred camps throughout the country.[272]

Congress, sharing Roosevelt's concern about budget deficits, authorized him to cut government salaries and veterans' pensions under the new Economy Act. The cuts were logical in view of the drop in the prices of goods and services throughout the economy in the prior two years.

Roosevelt listened to advisors of many backgrounds, but his "brain trust" consisted of academics. Raymond Moley and Rexford Tugwell were the most influential. Moley, a professor of political science and law at Columbia University, had been a senior policy advisor and speechwriter for Roosevelt during the campaign. He became assistant secretary of state, but he spent much of his time as a close advisor to the new president on a variety of issues. Rexford Tugwell, chairman of the Economics Department of Columbia University, advised the campaign on economic matters, especially farm policy, and became assistant secretary of agriculture after the inauguration. Presidents of leading corporations also provided advice.

The National Industrial Recovery Act (NIRA), introduced in May, established a national planning process to get the economy back to productive, job-

---

272 *Statistical Abstract of the United States, 1937,* Tables 145, 378.

creating activity. The Act required industries to form associations and establish codes for the purpose of coordinating production with demand for products, thereby stabilizing employment. Initially, a general blanket code was approved and distributed. Based on its principles, each industry prepared its own code, which would take effect upon approval by the president of the United States. The industry codes established prices, and the president was authorized to suspend existing antitrust laws if he determined it necessary. The new National Recovery Administration (NRA) was charged with managing the code-writing process and enforcing compliance with the Act. A licensing scheme was enacted, and the president could withhold a license from any business that failed to comply with the industry code. The NRA model of economic planning was very much the system that Swope, Harriman, and other business leaders had been recommending since 1931.

There was one last-minute surprise. Section 7(A) of the Act gave workers the right to organize and bargain collectively through representatives of their own choosing, and it prohibited employers from "interference, restraint, or coercion" against workers exercising these rights.

NIRA was a fundamental change in the customer/business/government relationship. Centralized economic and industrial planning replaced competition and market-based pricing and production, with the goal of increasing and stabilizing employment. The finest minds in business, government, and labor were now empowered, and required, to plan in detail the production, prices, quality, work conditions, hours and wages, and trade practices of every industry. Within a year, more than six hundred industry codes had been established and approved.

For the many who believed that cooperative planning and strong centralized control would promote business recovery and secure a better employment environment, the National Recovery Administration (NRA), and its twin for agriculture, the Agriculture Adjustment Administration (AAA), offered high promise. The summer of 1933 was marked by parades celebrating these New Deal programs and the quiet work of industry associations coming together to begin drafting codes. As codes were approved, and businesses pledged allegiance to their provisions, Blue Eagle signs with the legend "We do our part" appeared on store windows and factory gates and on the front pages of newspapers operating under their own industry code. In his July 24, 1933, fireside chat Roosevelt explained the workings of the NRA to his radio audience:

If all employers in each competitive group agree to pay their workers the same wages—reasonable wages—and require the same hours—reasonable hours—then higher wages and shorter hours will hurt no employer. Moreover, such action is better for the employer than unemployment and low wages, because it makes more buyers for his product. That is the simple idea which is the very heart of the National Recovery Act. On the basis of this simple principle of everybody doing things together, we are starting out on this nationwide attack on unemployment.

Already all the great, basic industries have come forward willingly with proposed codes, and in these codes they accept the principles leading to mass reemployment. But, as important as is this heartening demonstration, the richest field for results is among the small employers, those whose contribution will be to give new work for from one to ten people. These smaller employers are indeed a vital part of the backbone of the country, and the success of our plan is largely in their hands.[273]

The nation was coming together, from the three boards appointed by the president to advise him in this—representing the leaders in labor, industry, and social service—to governors whose resolutions at their annual conference approved the plan, to large and small companies that were already implementing the required actions. Volunteers canvassed small towns and large cities to recruit twenty million consumers pledged to buy only where the Blue Eagle was displayed.[274]

The difficulties were minor in view of the scale of the change being made in the fundamental operation of the economy. Steel company executives walked out of one early meeting with the secretary of labor when they were told that the president of the American Federation of Labor would sit as the labor representative on the steel industry council, although none of the companies' workers were represented by the A. F. of L.[275] But the issue was resolved and the iron and steel industry code was completed in November.

The highest accolade from the business and investment community was a radio broadcast by John J. Rockefeller Jr., son of the oil magnate, on August 27. Rockefeller commended the NRA as a worthwhile experiment intended to get millions of men back to work, thus boosting national morale and enabling the

---

273 Speech Files, Container 15, #643, Franklin D. Roosevelt Library, Hyde Park, NY.
274 "NRA Opens Drive to Line Up Nation," *New York Times*, August 29, 1933.
275 "Steel Men Leave Meeting," *New York Times*, August 16, 1933.

average man to resume normal purchasing. Rockefeller promoted the minimum wage rates and maximum hour regulations in the codes as needed to assure that a few employers could not keep prices low by sweating their labor. He went on to recognize the importance of workers being represented at the bargaining table, and he urged peaceful cooperation between representatives of labor and management. Rockefeller concluded his endorsement of the NRA with warm words praising President Roosevelt:

> For more than three years we as a people have been in the deadly grip of fear. There is but one antidote for fear, and that is faith. Faith in our fellow men, faith in our institutions, faith in our neighbors, national and international, and underneath and above all in that eternal spirit of truth, justice, goodness and love, faith in which alone makes life most worth while. It is for us, my friends, of whatever race or creed, to banish fear, to re-establish faith and to go forward with a united front under the leadership of the man whose humility and open-mindedness testify to his greatness, President Roosevelt.[276]

Rockefeller's endorsement was genuine. He needed no favor from the president or anyone else. In 1933, John D. Rockefeller Jr. was one of the wealthiest men in America and in the world.

Henry Ford was another of the world's wealthiest men. His prescription for industrial recovery was the opposite of both Hoover's approach, which encouraged companies to voluntarily keep wages and prices high, and Roosevelt's approach embodied in the NIRA, whereby industries collaborated to put a legally enforceable floor under prices and wages. In running his own company, Ford believed that market forces outweighed optimism and elaborate plans. He had long ago published the strategy he had used in dealing with the 1920 recession:

> Therefore in September [1920] we cut the price of the touring car from $575 to $440. We cut the price far below the cost of production, for we were still making from stock bought at boom prices. It was said that we were disturbing conditions. That is exactly what we were trying to do. We wanted to do our part in bringing prices down from an artificial to a natural level. I am firmly of the opinion that if at this time or earlier

---

276 "John D. Rockefeller Jr.'s Plea for Support of the NRA," *New York Times*, August 27, 1933.

manufacturers and distributors had all made drastic cuts in their prices and had put through thorough house-cleanings we should not have had so long a business depression. Hanging on in the hope of getting higher prices simply delayed adjustment. Nobody got the higher prices they hoped for, and if the losses had been taken all at once, not only would the productive and buying powers of the country have become harmonized, but we should have been saved this long period of general idleness.[277]

There was much speculation about whether Ford Motor Company would sign the automobile industry code or raise some legal challenge, and the speculation continued until September, when the company quietly signed. At the end of October, William Randolph Hearst published a front-page editorial against the NRA, condemning it as "opposed to every fundamental conception of democracy and every principle of individual liberty on which democracy was based."[278]

Large corporations, already familiar with planning their own activities, separation of tasks, and a certain amount of bureaucracy, adapted to the National Recovery Administration. But small business owners soon became distraught. In some cases, the prices established in the codes were too low for them to cover their costs. Codes established a minimum number of employees per firm, based upon average weekly sales volume, and set a maximum number of work-hours per week per employee. All of this posed numerous problems for businesses where family members worked long hours, workers and managers handled multiple tasks, and prices changed frequently to attract customers. Government enforcement agents were quick to threaten fines or imprisonment for infractions—the law provided penalties of up to $500, six months imprisonment, or both. Equally distressed were consumers, who noticed their sudden lack of bargaining power as merchants pointed to the Blue Eagle. Roosevelt himself criticized as "chiselers" those who sold at below-code prices, assuming they were also paying below-code wages.[279]

The universal applause that greeted the introduction of industry codes under NIRA in the summer of 1933 had faded by early 1934. The protests from all sides were strong enough that Roosevelt appointed a special review board to investigate complaints and recommend changes. On the first anniversary of the Act, General Hugh Johnson, Administrator of the NRA, acknowledged

---

277 Henry Ford, *My Life and Work,* 130–131.
278 *New York American,* October 31, 1933.
279 "Roosevelt Orders Fines, Jail Terms for NRA Violators," *New York Times,* October 18, 1933.

the complaints that "Big Business" was enjoying monopoly status and that small businesses were being oppressed, consumers being gouged, and labor being disregarded, but Johnson stated that these complaints, while widespread, were mistaken.[280] In July 1934, in just one of many incidents, seventy small print shops in the Bronx returned their Blue Eagle emblems to the government, protesting the wage scales.[281] The leaders of large corporations were becoming more dissatisfied as time progressed. Hundreds of lawsuits opposing various provisions of the NIRA were making their way through the courts. One of the cases originated when several members of the Schechter family in Brooklyn were convicted of criminal violations of the Act. The conviction was appealed all the way to the Supreme Court.

Title II of the NIRA funded the Public Works Administration (PWA) to pursue large public works projects intended to "prime the pump" of business activity. The projects were to be "self-liquidating," so the project would cost the government little or nothing over the long term. Hydroelectric dams would sell their electricity; bridges would collect tolls. Roosevelt expected the NRA to produce a sustainable rise in business employment and viewed the Public Works Administration projects as an important but temporary stimulus measure. These infrastructure projects would require engineers, skilled tradesmen, equipment operators, and laborers. The projects would also boost demand for steel, concrete, and other basic materials.

Some of the first PWA projects to be authorized had been planned years earlier by cities and counties, but deferred when local tax revenues fell in the first years of the Depression. Numerous highway projects were approved less than two months after the PWA was established. Funding for the Triborough Bridge[282] and for the Lincoln Tunnel in New York were approved in August, as was money for the Grand Coulee Dam in Washington state and numerous irrigation and flood control projects in western states. To complete the Naval Hospital in Philadelphia, $2.25 million was authorized. In September, construction funds for the Bonneville Dam in Oregon were approved. Employers were to pay "prevailing wages" and in no case less than the minimum regional wage established by the Cabinet Advisory Board. Each employee was limited to thirty hours per week, to spread the available work. As months passed, funds were authorized for construction of post offices, hospitals, canals, and new urban housing for

---

280 "NRA Chief Points to Achievements," *New York Times,* June 17, 1934.
281 "Seventy Bronx Printers Return Blue Eagle," *New York Times,* July 26, 1934.
282 Recently renamed the Robert F. Kennedy Memorial Bridge.

low-income families. By April 1934, actual payments had exceeded $1 billion of the $3.3 billion total authorized for the program, and the money kept flowing into 1935, when additional sums were authorized by Congress. The spending created jobs, and many of the projects built with PWA funds are still in use today.

———

During the Hoover-Roosevelt interregnum, the Senate Banking Committee had hired new counsel to continue the investigation of stock market activities leading to the crash of October 1929. Ferdinand Pecora, a fifty-one-year-old attorney with twelve years of experience as the chief assistant district attorney for New York County, brought new vigor to the task as lead counsel for the committee. Pecora assembled a team to assist in preparing for the hearings, including several colleagues from the district attorney's office and a number of accountants. Supplementing this paid staff were two professionals with in-depth knowledge of the stock market and corporate finances. Max Lowenthal had already made a fortune as an attorney handling stockholder lawsuits against corporations. John T. Flynn was a freelance writer on economics. Lowenthal and Flynn volunteered their services and provided important guidance and interpretive skills to the team. After reviewing the information obtained in earlier stages of the investigation, Pecora established a strategy for going forward.

The investigators focused on one bank or financial institution at a time and subpoenaed records, including the income tax records of the company officers. The staff sifted through cartons of files, often working at the corporate offices. Copies were made of important documents. Charts were prepared to demonstrate the flow of money in suspicious transactions. Lists of potential questions were prepared, with references back to the documents. When Pecora questioned each witness, he already had the answer in the papers at his table in the hearing room.

Pecora's first target was National City Bank, one of the country's largest commercial banks, and its related investment company, National City Company. Pecora had earlier subpoenaed all records and minutes of meetings for the five-year period prior to October 1929. Charles E. Mitchell, president of the bank, was the first witness called. Surprised by Pecora's detailed questions and obvious knowledge of the bank's operations, Mitchell admitted in his first day of testimony that he had sold shares of stock to his wife to create a $2.8 million loss for tax purposes, thereby avoiding income tax for 1929. There were admissions of money transfers between the bank and investment company without disclosure to shareholders and loans with inadequate collateral to bank officers trying to cover their own stock market losses. The press reported all of this in great detail. On February 27, Mitchell resigned as chairman of the bank. The New York district attorney filed suit against Mitchell for tax evasion. On March 2, as people from around the country came to Washington, DC for the inauguration, Mitchell left the city, alone and carrying his own luggage.[283] The reference in Roosevelt's inaugural address to the "money changers driven from the temple" was obvious.

Pecora's investigators turned next to Morgan & Company, the largest private investment bank in the country. Pecora invited J.P. Morgan Jr. for a courtesy meeting. Morgan arrived with his attorney, John W. Davis, who had been the Democratic Party candidate for president in 1924. After their meeting, Pecora presented subpoenas for twenty-three specific types of records from the bank. His staff spent all of April and most of May reviewing the documents and preparing for Morgan's testimony. On his second day of testimony, the banker revealed that during the late 1920s Morgan & Company had favored certain wealthy individuals to purchase shares at steep discounts from the price at which the same shares were to be sold soon after in the public market. This provided a guaranteed profit for the favored few. The "preferred list" included quite a few of the best-known people in America.

The list of participants was bipartisan: former president Calvin Coolidge; Charles O. Hilles, chairman of the Republican National Committee; Charles Adams, who had been Hoover's secretary of the navy; and William McAdoo, who was Treasury secretary under Woodrow Wilson. This was an especially delicate situation since Senator McAdoo was a member of the Senate Banking Committee conducting the investigation. The favored list also included John J. Raskob, chairman of the Democratic National Committee, and William H. Woodin, a former president of American Car and Foundry Company who was, on the day of this particular revelation, serving as Roosevelt's secretary of the treasury. Then there were the corporate chieftains who had received such favors: Owen Young, chairman of General Electric, Walter Gifford of AT&T, Myron Taylor of United States Steel, and Walter Teagle of Standard Oil of New Jersey, to name a few. Bankers on the list included Albert Wiggin of Chase, George F. Baker of First National, Bernard Baruch, and Richard Whitney, president of the New York Stock Exchange. Assorted national heroes such as General John Pershing and the

---

283 Donald A. Ritchie, *Congress Investigates, 1792-1974,* "The Pecora Wall Street Expose."

aviator Charles Lindberg, as well as members of some of America's most distinguished families, were listed as recipients of such favored treatment.[284]

While Morgan was testifying, Congress passed the Glass-Steagall Act, which required the separation of investment banking from commercial banks. Insurance companies were also required to stand apart from banking and securities underwriting. Private banks such as Morgan & Company would have to split into two independent companies to separate investment functions from banking activities. Glass-Steagall remained in effect until its repeal in 1999.

In subsequent months, Pecora investigated the investment firms Kuhn, Loeb & Company, which was the second most prominent private bank in the U.S.; Dillon, Read & Company; and Chase National Bank, which was then the largest commercial bank in the world. The Senate committee, and therefore Pecora's investigation, shifted its attention to the New York Stock Exchange and subpoenaed records of the most active floor traders, and then sent detailed questionnaires to the 1,375 members of the exchange. By January 1934, the investigation turned to the bank failures of early 1933 in Detroit and Cleveland.

As a direct result of information developed by these hearings, several bank executives paid back income taxes, with interest and penalties. In total, several million dollars were collected. There were no criminal charges or civil proceedings for those on the "favored" list. At the time, no law prohibited such arrangements.

The purpose of a Congressional investigation is the development of information needed for drafting effective legislation. This investigation led directly to many provisions of the Securities and Exchange Act of 1934, which Roosevelt signed on June 7. Updated periodically over the decades since, the Act remains a major part of the regulatory environment of the stock markets. Its provisions are a part of the training of stockbrokers and financial advisers and a major topic in their licensing exams. Ferdinand Pecora was invited to the signing ceremony at the White House and received one of the seven pens used by the president. When Roosevelt asked Pecora if the new law would be good or bad, he responded, "It will be a good bill or a bad bill, Mr. President, depending upon the men who administer it."[285]

The months of detailed revelations of price manipulation and favoritism added dark clouds of disgust to a landscape dreary with widespread unemployment and hardship. The stories that came out of the hearings convinced many

---

284 Ron Chernow, *House of Morgan*, 370–374.
285 Donald A. Ritchie, *Congress Investigates, 1792-1974*, 243.

that the market was not a place of fair dealing where honest people should place their trust.

———

Roosevelt's actions in the first hundred days were popular. The CCC jobs program offered some immediate financial relief and boosted morale and moved hundreds of thousands of frustrated, unemployed young men out of the cities. In radio broadcasts he referred to as fireside chats, the president explained that the steps he was taking were based on simple truths. In March, he explained the actions being taken to reopen the banks and assure that funds would be adequate to meet all necessary withdrawals. In May, he told his audience of the plan to bring electric power into the Tennessee River Valley, new legislation aimed at easing mortgage distress, of plans to grant a half billion dollars to state and local government relief efforts, and briefly mentioned plans for a major public works program and measures to improve industrial wages by reducing competition and controlling production. In July, the recently passed National Industrial Recovery Act and Agricultural Adjustment Act were explained. In October, he reported on progress made: of the rehiring of four million of the ten million he estimated had been involuntarily without work in March, of the completion of NRA codes by all the large industries of the country, intended to get industry and workers back into production and increase purchasing power through higher wages, of public works already authorized to proceed, and ongoing work by the Reconstruction Finance Corporation. On every occasion, the voice was confident and reassuring, the language simple and nontechnical.

To help people deal with the approaching winter, the Civil Works Administration was established on November 8, 1933. This agency's goal was to provide immediate, temporary white-collar and blue-collar jobs. To finance this winter of work, Roosevelt shifted $400 million from the Public Works Administration. To administer the program, he appointed Harry Hopkins.

Hopkins proved himself uniquely talented in distributing government funds quickly. On the day after Roosevelt signed the executive order launching the CWA, Hopkins telegraphed governors to select the work to be done, hire the people, and start work. Unlike the PWA projects, the CWA work required no federal review or approval. On that first day in his new job, Hopkins dispensed $5 million to local governments.[286]

---

286 Robert E. Sherwood, *Roosevelt and Hopkins*, 44–45.

There was no longer any attempt to channel government relief for the unemployed through private charities or the Red Cross. Hopkins hired a few former social workers as his aides. All of them traveled throughout the country to get firsthand assessments of needs and progress, but there was little bureaucracy or formality. The money was federal, but the program administration was local. Within weeks, four million people moved from the relief rolls to CWA employment. They taught classes, organized files, and completed small construction and repair projects. The first paychecks arrived in time to brighten the holiday season. The CWA was closed in the spring of 1934, in the expectation that PWA projects and reemployment in private industry would by then provide ample jobs.

———

But millions were still jobless, without money, and terribly frustrated. They listened to Roosevelt, but they also heard other voices speaking to them about social justice. Father Charles Coughlin, a Catholic priest based in Royal Oak, Michigan, drew large radio audiences. He praised Roosevelt's policies during the first year of the New Deal, but he turned fiercely against Roosevelt early in 1934. Coughlin railed against the leading bankers and proclaimed a need to use silver as the precious metal backing the dollar, in place of gold. The shift to silver, he believed, would allow America to build its trade with countries that used silver-backed currencies, including India and China, thus boosting employment in American factories. Coughlin had the full support of his bishop. He quoted frequently, if selectively, from the official writings of several Popes. Coughlin spoke against "cancerous capitalism which poured wealth into the laps of the wealthy, which obstructed its just distribution, which perverted the leisure to be gained by the people into the bondage of forced idleness."[287] In letters to his followers, he urged them: "This is your battle—the battle between the common people and the entrenched powers of wealth."[288]

At about the same time, Senator Huey Long of Louisiana promoted a complete redistribution of wealth. Under his Share Our Wealth program, each household would receive:

---

287 Charles E. Coughlin, *The New Deal in Money,* 117.
288 Letter from Rev. Charles E. Coughlin to Marie Krenz, January 1934.

A guarantee of family wealth of $5,000; enough for a home, an auto-mobile, a radio, and the ordinary conveniences, and the opportunity to educate their children; a fair share of the income of this land thereafter to that family so that there will be no such thing as merely the select to have those things, and so there will be no such thing as a family living in poverty and distress.

There would be periodic redistributions, perhaps every seven years, to assure perpetuation of the new egalitarian order. People over sixty years old would receive a pension of $30 per month to encourage them to stop work-ing and allow younger workers to take their place. Veterans would receive a bonus, and any sick or disabled veteran would receive health care, whether the infirmity was service-related or not. To pay for this plan, a combination of in-come and inheritance taxes, and an annual capital levy, would remove assets and income from the wealthy. Long insisted in his speeches and pamphlets that this redistribution would still leave as much as $10 million to $15 million in many wealthy families. Long's broadcast went on to criticize the various New Deal re-lief programs. "You can have the NRA and PWA and CWA…You can wait until doomsday and see twenty-five more alphabets, but that is not going to solve this proposition."[289]

The most recent government assessment of national wealth had been com-pleted in 1922 and was still being reported in the *Statistical Abstract of the United States* in the 1934 and 1935 editions. That tally showed a total wealth of $321 billion, or $2,918 per capita. This wealth figure included illiquid items such as irrigation systems and shipping canals, railroad cars, electric generating stations, and $1.4 billion in ships belonging to the United States Navy. Long did not explain what would happen when the real estate and stock certificates taken from the wealthy were sold to accomplish the spreading of wealth or how navy ships were to be divided into personal shares. Many dreams dissolve when con-fronted by mathematics, but millions of dispossessed Americans were ready to embrace any plan that offered relief. The plan sounded so simple and effective when proclaimed by the flamboyant senator. Long's popularity grew far beyond Louisiana.[290]

---

289 Long described his plan in a national radio broadcast on Sunday evening, February 23, 1934, entitled "Every Man a King." Reprinted in the Congressio-nal Record, 73d Congress, 2d session, p. 3450–53.
290 T. Harry Williams, *Huey Long;* Frank Freidel, *Franklin D. Roosevelt—A Rendezvous with Destiny;* and Robert S. McElvaine, *The Great Depression—America,*

In August 1934, Upton Sinclair, an avowed Socialist since the turn of the century, won the Democratic Party nomination to run for governor of California. Sinclair quickly obtained support from several Democrats closely associated with Roosevelt, and a well-publicized invitation to the president's home at Hyde Park.[291] Sinclair lost the race for governor. But even businessmen of liberal political beliefs had to wonder about the future direction of national policy.

The president's State of the Union speech of January 4, 1935, and his budget message to Congress proposed no new taxes for fiscal year 1936. FDR wanted a budget in which expenditures exceeded revenue only by the amount spent on work relief for the unemployed. The sense of emergency prevailing in 1933 had subsided. Two billion dollars in federal funds had been spent on relief to the destitute and aid to homeowners, administered by local agencies. The CCC and PWA were in full operation. But unemployment remained high—five million still unemployed and on relief. Roosevelt rejected Huey Long's plan:

> We do not destroy ambition, nor do we seek to divide our wealth into equal shares on stated occasions. We continue to recognize the greater ability of some to earn than others. But we do assert that the ambition of the individual to obtain for him and his proper security, a reasonable leisure, and a decent living throughout life, is an ambition to be preferred to the appetite for great wealth and great power.[292]

By the spring of 1935, Long was receiving as many as thirty thousand letters every day he made his anti-Roosevelt, anti-rich speeches. His local Share Our Wealth clubs claimed eight million members. Long was a serious political force with the ability to influence the 1936 presidential election.[293]

———

Two years after his inauguration, and four and a half years since the stock market crash of 1929, Roosevelt wanted additional resources to revive employment. Congress responded with the Emergency Relief Appropriation Act of 1935, providing $4.9 billion—the largest peace-time appropriation in

---

1929-1941.
291 Raymond Moley, *After Seven Years,* 298.
292 Speech Files, Carton 20, #759, Franklin D. Roosevelt Library, Hyde Park, New York.
293 *The Secret Diary of Harold L. Ickes: The First Thousand Days, 1933-1936,* 462.

history—and granting the president wide discretion in how to use the funds. The president could establish, by executive order, any new agencies and programs he deemed appropriate to combat unemployment and provide relief. He could appoint workers and administrators outside of the Civil Service law, set their compensation, and determine wage rates and hours of work for all projects except construction of permanent buildings to be used by the federal government. There were very few restrictions. The funds had to be used within the United States, its territories, and possessions. Military equipment and munitions could not be purchased with these funds, but buildings could be built or renovated on military posts. The Federal Emergency Relief Administration and the Public Works Administration were renewed, but the president could modify their roles as he deemed appropriate. The new law was the first of several that collectively became known as the Second New Deal.

Roosevelt signed the Act on April 8. The Public Works Administration (PWA), established in 1933, was continued, maintaining its focus on self-liquidating infrastructure projects, with construction costs split between federal and state or local government. On April 30, the president established the Resettlement Administration to resettle destitute or low-income families from rural and urban areas to other communities, deal with soil erosion, reforestation, and flood control projects, and to make loans to farmers for purchase of land and equipment. On May 6, he established the Works Progress Administration (WPA), authorized to use federal funds to pay for projects recommended by local or state governments. Jobs that required manual labor and little planning were the primary focus of the WPA, with workers to be hired mainly from the unemployment relief rolls. On May 11, the Rural Electrification Administration (REA) was established to extend electric utility service into rural areas.

The president appointed Harry Hopkins as administrator of the new Works Progress Administration. The president's executive orders prescribed an elaborate approval process, but those formalities were usually waived. Hopkins quickly became the de facto top executive in charge of this new effort. In meetings attended by the president, Hopkins obtained approval for lists of hundreds of projects on the basis of nothing more than a project name and location.

Hopkins had worked with the president to craft the program, and he shared the president's goal of moving all "employables" from relief rolls into employment. Government-funded and -organized employment was to be created for all who were able to work but unable to find private-sector jobs. Relief for the remaining unemployed—those who were physically or mentally unable to work—would become once again the responsibility of the state governments. Hopkins committed to the president that all the employables would be hired by July 1. There were, at that point, 3.5 million employables out of work. Fortunately that commitment was not made public. By mid-May, Hopkins predicted full employment by November 1.[294]

By June, thousands of new WPA projects had been approved. Hopkins had excellent connections to mayors, local councilmen, and governors. The availability of federal funds drew applications from every corner. Communities that were able to contribute to the project cost, or able to sell bonds to pay some of the cost, were expected to do so, but for the many that had no access to capital, the federal government would pay all of the costs. Projects ranged from building construction to road and highway projects and municipal airports. In many small towns, sewer and water systems were modernized or extended.

The WPA marked an important change in Roosevelt's strategy for job stimulus and relief for the unemployed. Earlier PWA requirements that the projects be of a permanent and self-liquidating nature (with the cost of construction recouped through tolls, etc.) were not applied to WPA work. Finally, the PWA strategy of funding major projects to provide direct employment for skilled and unskilled workers and indirect employment for miners, steel workers, and other suppliers of materials and equipment soon became secondary to WPA's labor-intensive projects requiring little or no training. The federal funds would go directly to these wage-earners, who would spend the money. This was the new approach to "priming the pump" of the economy.

Not all WPA jobs required hard physical labor. The Federal Writers' Project employed people to write guidebooks for tourists, organize archives, and document interviews with interesting local characters. Unemployed artists found work in the Federal Arts Project painting murals in public buildings and creating sculptures. The Federal Theater Project paid actors to tour the country and present plays in towns and rural areas.

Most WPA workers were paid $850 per year—not much more than the subsistence income that would have provided only the basics in 1910 and far less than the $1,300 per year average teacher salary in the U.S. in the 1930s. But the regular pay was security, if not comfort, for those who could find no other work.

———

294 *The Secret Diary of Harold L. Ickes: The First Thousand Days, 1933-1936.* Entries dated May 3, 1935, (p. 358) and May 21, 1935 (p. 366, 409–410).

On the evening of May 8, 1935, three men joined the president for a quiet discussion of economic and tax policy. The meeting does not appear on the president's appointment diary. The White House Usher's Diary shows the assembly of Vincent Astor, who had inherited the Astor real estate fortune, Raymond Moley, who had been a Roosevelt brain trust member since the 1932 campaign, and Edmond Coblentz, publisher of the *New York American* and personal emissary of William Randolph Hearst.[295] The evening started amiably enough, with caviar supplied by the American ambassador to Russia and cocktails in the Oval Office. Their discussion covered FDR's policies, including tariffs, taxes, and fighting communism, which Hearst regarded as a major threat to America.

Roosevelt spoke of negotiating reciprocal tariff and trade agreements with individual countries under a June 1934 law giving him that authority. He had campaigned on the premise that international competition was important to limit the profits that any domestic manufacturer could earn. He also recognized that foreign countries were unlikely to buy our goods if America did not buy from them.

Roosevelt also told the visitors of his commitment to extending the National Industrial Recovery Act (NIRA). The original Act would expire in a few months, and Roosevelt wanted a new, improved law. He described a policy of decentralization of industry, using General Electric as an example. Assuming that General Electric has a plant making spark plugs in Schenectady employing five hundred people, the government might order General Electric to relocate the plant and its employees to a rural area, such as Duchess County. Each family would have its own small farm to fall back on if the spark plug business became slack or suffered seasonal variations.

Then came the discussion of taxes. The president explained that he was fighting not just communism, but Huey Longism, Coughlinism, and several other forms of radicalism. Roosevelt declared that he was trying to save the capitalist system, but he needed to acknowledge the current thinking about wealth and large incomes. Then Roosevelt came to specifics: "It may even be necessary to throw the forty-six men who have incomes in excess of $1,000,000 per year to the wolves. In other words, limit incomes through taxation to $1,000,000... Further, it may be necessary to see to it that vast estates bequeathed to one person are limited in size." Vincent Astor at one point interjected that these taxes

295 The White House Usher's Diary daily page is available online at http://daybyday.parelorentzcenter.org/archive/05-08-1935-2.pdf; also at Pare Lorentz Center at the Franklin D. Roosevelt Presidential Library & Museum. © Pare Lorentz Film Center.

would render the Astor estate bankrupt when he died. The president's reaction was, "Well, that's just too bad." Taxes were going to be increased, not reduced, although the president did not indicate whether higher income tax rates or other taxes were planned. Roosevelt stated that it was not the communists to be feared in the current situation, but young men, thinking men who were disciples of this new idea of fairer distribution of wealth. As the discussion continued, the president searched for a word other than communism to describe this policy. Coblenz suggested that this plan for fighting communism might be called "neocommunism." The president laughed. The meeting did not break up until 1:10 a.m.[296]

Most likely, no one slept well that night. Moley had been counseling the president for several months against any further changes in taxation, and he was surprised by the president's comments. The president, apparently also disturbed by the course the meeting had taken, quickly sent an emissary to Hearst at his California estate to put a gentler spin on the meeting than Coblenz's written account would convey. That, for the moment, pacified Hearst. One week later, he telegraphed his editors to take a balanced view of the administration's policies. "We can find some things to commend while finding others to criticize and I think an attitude of more or less obvious fairness and impartiality would be helpful."[297]

Two weeks after the White House meeting, in an address to Congress explaining his veto of the veterans' bonus bill, Roosevelt listed as one of his objections the fact that Congress had adopted a budget for 1936 with no new taxes and therefore no revenue to pay for the bonus. He said nothing about any intention to ask for new taxes.

———

On May 27, 1935, the Supreme Court announced its decision on the Schechter case, which had come to it on appeal after the Brooklyn-based poultry firm was convicted of violating the National Industrial Recovery Act. The Court found that the defendants' chicken wholesaling business did not constitute interstate commerce. Since the federal government had no authority under the

296 Letter and report, E. D. Coblentz to William Randolph Hearst, May 9, 1935, and report addendum, May 13, 1935, Edmond D. Coblentz Papers, Bancroft Library.
297 Telegram, William Randolph Hearst to E. D. Coblentz, May 15, 1935, Edmond D. Coblentz Papers, Bancroft Library.

Constitution to regulate intrastate business, the Court's decision also rendered all 750 industry codes void. The justices held the National Industrial Recovery Act to be unconstitutional since Congress, by delegating power to make "codes of fair competition," had improperly delegated its constitutional power to make laws to the president and to associations drafting the codes.[298] The decision was unanimous. America's experiment with national economic planning by industry associations came to an end.

The NRA, with all its detailed industry plans and enforcement actions, had failed to solve the unemployment or underemployment problems. Industry codes had boosted hourly wage rates for skilled tradesmen and unskilled laborers. The average wage for unskilled labor in manufacturing industries jumped from 30.5 cents per hour to 40.7 cents—the same rate that had been paid in 1929. In construction work, the hourly wage rose to pre-crash levels in 1935, at forty-eight cents per hour.[299]

But in 1934, there were 10 percent fewer firms in business, and that number was not much improved in 1935.[300] Total payrolls of manufacturing industries in 1935 were only 66 percent of the 1929 total, and manufacturers employed 15 percent fewer employees than in 1929.[301] Construction employment, which was intended to get a major boost from the NRA's public works projects, was down 42 percent compared to 1929 and 5 percent below the depressed level of 1932, the last full year before the NRA programs were launched. Mining and quarrying were also supposed to benefit from the stimulus of public works spending, but they recovered only to about their 1931 employment levels.[302]

While private employment and payrolls were shrinking, government employment and payrolls were expanding. Government employment had doubled between 1929 and 1935. Work relief programs at federal, state, and local levels employed 3.1 million people in jobs that had not previously existed.[303] In 1929, one in every ten American workers was directly employed by government; by

---

298 A. L. A. Schechter Poultry Corp v. United States, 295 U.S. 495 (1935).
299 *Statistical Abstract of the United States, 1940,* Table 377.
300 *Statistical Abstract of the United States, 1940,* Table 345.
301 *Statistical Abstract of the United States, 1938,* Table 367.
302 *National Income and Product Account Tables,* Bureau of Economic Analysis, U.S. Department of Commerce, Tables 6.4A, 6.5A, 6.8A.
303 Ibid, Table 6.4A. The number of people in military service and public education had changed very little, but the number employed in federal, state, and local civilian nonschool administrative positions not involved with relief work had increased 21 percent between 1929 and 1935.

1935, that ratio had become one in five. With all of that, in 1935, one person of every five in the work force was completely unemployed.[304]

In mid-June, Roosevelt sent Congress his revenue proposal for the coming fiscal year. The "no new taxes" message to Congress six months earlier, which was left unchanged in the bonus bill veto message, was now set aside. The new message was stark. The president spoke of a difference between inherited wealth, which he considered to be static wealth, and dynamic wealth that makes for a healthy diffusion of economic good. He proposed a new tax on inheritances and gifts to reduce the concentrations of inherited economic power. Roosevelt's tax policies were beginning to sound like Huey Long's.

Further, to prevent the effects that come from great accumulations of wealth, higher tax rates should be imposed on the profits of larger corporations and on the highest household incomes in the country. He advised the Congress that "the duty rests upon the Government to restrict such incomes by very high taxes." Roosevelt asked for a Constitutional Amendment to allow the federal taxation of interest paid by states and municipalities on bonds they issued and to allow states to tax the interest paid by the federal government on its bonds. He urged upon Congress "the very sound public policy of encouraging a wider distribution of wealth."[305]

The Revenue Act of 1935 raised the marginal rates on all personal incomes above $50,000 per year. The highest tax rate rose to 79 percent (4 percent basic tax plus 75 percent surtax) on income in excess of $5,000,000. For corporate incomes, this Act introduced graduated tax rates that replaced the flat 13.75 percent rate of the 1932 Act. The new marginal rates for corporate income above $15,000 started at 14 percent and rose to a maximum 15.75 percent. In addition, there was an excess profits tax, which was a tax on high return on equity. Capital-efficient companies paid higher tax on the same profit than their less efficient competitors, effectively penalizing efficient stewardship of capital. Tax deductions for corporate gifts to charity were limited to 5 percent of profits. Congress passed the Revenue Act of 1935, but only after a summer of fierce debate. Roosevelt signed the new tax law on August 30, 1935.

Two weeks earlier, he had signed one of the most famous and most enduring programs of the New Deal, the Social Security Act. Both employers and employees would pay the new tax, each paying 1 percent of wages into a new federal

---

304 *Historical Statistics of the United States, Colonial Times to 1970, Part 1.* U.S. Department of Commerce. Series D.
305 Speech Files, Carton 22, #786, Franklin D. Roosevelt Library, Hyde Park, New York.

trust fund. The trust would accumulate funds until 1940, when the first federal old age pensions would become payable. Agricultural workers, household employees, those in nonprofit organizations, and self-employed people were exempt from the program. This new tax pulled $252 million out of the economy in the first year, from workers who might have spent it and employers who might have invested it or distributed it as dividends.[306]

In his statement on signing the Act, Roosevelt provided his vision of the societal benefits:

> This law, too, represents a cornerstone in a structure which is being built but is by no means complete—a structure intended to lessen the force of possible future depressions, to act as a protection to future Administrations against the necessity of going deeply into debt to furnish relief to the needy—a law to flatten out the peaks and valleys of deflation and of inflation—in other words, a law that will take care of human needs and at the same time provide for the United States an economic structure of vastly greater soundness.[307]

In the same summer of 1935, the National Labor Relations Act was signed, restoring workers' right to elect unions as their bargaining agents in contract negotiations, a right that had been lost when the Supreme Court found the NIRA unconstitutional.

———

Even before the Social Security Act was signed, fear had spread through the business community. Roy Howard, chairman of Scripps-Howard Newspapers, was a supporter of Roosevelt and the objectives of the New Deal. He had been the president's luncheon guest at the White House several times, and as recently as April, his editorials had defended the administration against its opponents. On July 18, he wrote to Roosevelt, asking for a meeting to talk things over.

> Frankly, I am not altogether happy about things as they stand, and at least on the basis of such information as I have, I find myself less completely

---

306 *Statistical Abstract of the United States, 1940, Sixty-Second Number,* Table 178.
307 Speech Files, Carton 22, #791, Franklin D. Roosevelt Library, Hyde Park, New York.

in sympathy with some of the technique recently employed in Washington, even though my enthusiasm for the basic principles at stake has in no wise lessened.

Meantime, hoping the heat—no one of the various kinds being administered in Washington these days—is not bothering you unduly, I am, with kindest personal regards,

Faithfully yours,

Roy[308]

The meeting could not be scheduled before Howard was due to leave on a trip to Asia, so Howard wrote a longer letter explaining his concerns. Even as head of a major newspaper chain, Howard still considered himself first and foremost a reporter—an observer of people and events who chose his words carefully. His letter of July 30 was candid:

My dear Mr. President:

As an editor still wholeheartedly sold on the objectives of the New Deal, I have been seeking reasons for the swing away from the program of liberal minded business men, many of whom, former advocates, are changing to skeptics, critics, and outright opponents—all at a time when there is no apparent corresponding abandonment of the idea by others of the electorate.

I do not accept it as a fact that the interests of what we broadly term business, necessarily are in conflict with mass interests. We are not a political minded people. The chief concern of the average American is business, not politics.

As a non-partisan editor I expect to continue in support of your stated interpretation of American liberalism—not withstanding my dissent and disagreement as to some details, some theories, and quite a few theorists. Therefore, it is in a friendly and I hope constructive spirit that I attempt a few reportorial observations, a few editorial opinions, and ask a few questions which I believe timely and pertinent.

That business has been growing steadily more hostile to your administration is a fact too obvious to be classed as news. So long as this

---

308 Letter, Roy Howard to FDR, July 18, 1935; PPF 68, Franklin D. Roosevelt Library.

hostility emanated from financial racketeers, public exploiters, and the sinister forces spawned by special privilege, it was of slight importance. No crook loves a cop. But any experienced reporter will tell you that across the nation business men who once gave you sincere support are now not merely hostile, they are frightened stiff. Many of these men whose patriotism and sense of public service will compare with that of any men in public life, have become convinced and sincerely believe:

That you are out to wreck even legitimate business, regardless of what it has contributed to higher standards of living, if it can be convicted of a crime of "bigness;"

That you are fathering a tax bill that aims at revenge rather than revenue—revenge on business, which having been saved from complete collapse by your bold experimentation, has now cooled in its one time enthusiasm for your reforms;

That from consideration of next year's election the administration has side-stepped broadening the tax base to the extent necessary to even approximate the needs of the situation;

That you are still putting reform ahead of recovery, even though it has become obvious that the fruits of reform may easily be lost unless recovery can be expedited;

That though avoiding a frontal attack, you are out to destroy the profit system, through forcing the government more and more into business through projects competing with private business;

That in the case of such private businesses as may be left you are planning a standard of size and bigness to be established by political and economic theorists—for the most part men without actual experience with such annoying but inescapable problems as to how to meet a payroll, or a bill for raw materials;

That there can be no real recovery until the fears of business have been allayed through the granting of a breathing spell to industry, and a recess from further experimentation until the country can consolidate its gains;

That under guise of logical correctives against those evils in business which contributed so largely to the depression, your subordinates have indulged in indiscriminate "head-hunting," and in blunderbuss indictments of whole groups and entire industries, instead of naming individuals and making indictments personal and specific;

That until there is some personal re-assurance that the White House does not class all successful business men as public enemies, per se, business will not co-operate, but will oppose you by taking its case directly to the people to show that the New Deal is not an orderly modernization of our national economy, but an attempt to inflict upon the country a modified dictatorship, collectivism, and regimentation;

Naturally, I dissent from most of the above opinions and while I know that the jitters with which business is affected are very real, I believe them to be for the most part without justification. Nevertheless, I believe that recovery will never be effected by government alone. It must come from intelligent and patriotic co-operation between government and business—of the type we witnessed for a brief moment in the summer of 1933. So long as business is shaking with fear—fear that is genuine, even if unwarranted; as long as business regards every move by the administration as an attempt at its destruction; as long as government continues in a punishing mood, the road to recovery will remain hopelessly blocked. Therefore, I make bold to offer a simple and friendly suggestion:

Make one more demand of your patience and your tolerance. Repeat once more just where you stand on the attitude of the administration toward business—all business.

I know that you have repeatedly stated your position on sections of the nation's problems, but as an editor I know also the necessity for repetition and re-iteration in getting facts over to the public. Spell out as you have to me and to others in private conversation, your real objectives and your concept of the future of business in America. There is need to undo the damage that has been done by mis-interpreters of the New Deal.

I know that you feel as I do—that with all its faults, and the abuse it has developed, our system has in the past enabled us to achieve greater mass progress than has been attained by any other system on earth. Smoke out the sinister forces seeking to delude the public into believing that the orderly modernization of a system we want to preserve, is revolution in disguise.

Cordially and sincerely yours,

Roy H. Howard[309]

---

309 Letter, Roy Howard to FDR, July 30, 1935; PPF 68, Franklin D. Roosevelt Library.

Howard trusted Roosevelt completely. A cover note to Howard's letter invited the president to make any changes in phrasing that the president might wish, but not the tone of the letter, and then to write a response so that both letters could be published together. Howard wanted dialogue and clarity. He obviously believed the president's objectives to be consistent with the public welfare, but he saw the fear that was paralyzing the business community.[310] More than a month later, the two letters were released by the White House for publication on Friday afternoon, September 6.

Howard's letter to the president appeared with minor changes to the original text, but dated August 26.[311] The president's reply was dated September 2. Given the mental state of the business community at that moment, one week after an income tax hike and three weeks after signing of the new Social Security tax, many business owners and executives probably read both letters more than once.

My dear Mr. Howard:

I appreciate the tone and purpose of your letter, and fairness impels me to note with no little sympathy and understanding the facts which you record, based on your observations as a reporter of opinion throughout the United States. I can well realize, moreover, that the many legislative details and processes incident to the long and arduous session of the Congress should have had the unavoidable effect of promoting some confusion in many people's minds.

I think we can safely disregard the skeptics of whom you speak. Skeptics were present when Noah said it was going to rain and they refused to go into the ark. We can also disregard those who are actuated by a spirit of political partisanship or by a willingness to gain or retain personal profit at the expense of, and detriment to, their neighbors.

---

310 William Randolph Hearst's reaction to the summer's events was different. His earlier fears had been revived by the new tax law, which directly affected his income as well as his business interests. In August, at Hearst's instruction, Coblentz sent a memo to all Hearst editors instructing them that henceforth the words "Raw Deal" were to replace "New Deal," and "Soak the Successful" would replace "Soak the Thrifty," which had earlier replaced "Soak the Rich" in Hearst publications.

311 The letter as submitted by Howard, dated July 30, is in the president's files as noted above, as is a note from Steven Early, the president's press secretary, dated August 9, acknowledging the letter.

Then there were those who told us to "do nothing." We had heard of the do-nothing policy before and from the same sources and in many cases from the same individuals. We heard it when Theodore Roosevelt and Woodrow Wilson proposed reforms. The country has learned how to measure that kind of opposition. But there are critics who are honest and non-partisan and who are willing to discuss and to learn. I believe we owe, therefore, a positive duty to clarify our purposes, to describe our methods and to reiterate our ideals. Such clarification is greatly aided by the efforts of those public-spirited newspapers which serve the public well by a true portrayal of the facts and an unbiased printing of the news.

However, experience is the best teacher and results the best evidence. As the essential outline of what has been done rises into view, I am confident that doubts and misapprehension will vanish. I am confident further that business as a whole will agree with you and with me that the interests of what we broadly term business are not in conflict with, but wholly in harmony with, mass interests.

I note what you say about hostility emanating from "financial racketeers, public exploiters and sinister forces." Such criticism it is an honor to bear. A car with many cylinders can keep running in spite of plenty of carbon—but it knocks. When it is overhauled an important part of the job is the removal of the carbon.

In the large, the depression was the culmination of unhealthy, however innocent, arrangements in agriculture, in business and in finance. Our legislation was remedial, and as such, it would serve no purpose to make a doctrinaire effort to distinguish between that which was addressed to recovery and that which was addressed to reform. The two, in an effort toward sound and fundamental recovery, are inseparable. Our actions were in conformity with the basic economic purposes which were set forth three years ago.

As spokesman for those purposes I pointed out that it was necessary to seek a wise balance in American economic life, to restore our banking system to public confidence, to protect investors in the security market, to give labor freedom to organize and protection from exploitation, to safeguard and develop our national resources, to set up protection against the vicissitudes of old age and unemployment, to relieve investors and consumers from the burden of unnecessary corporate machinery. I do not believe that any responsible political party in the country will dare to go before the public in opposition to any of these major objectives.

The tax program of which you speak is based upon a broad and just social and economic purpose. Such a purpose, it goes without saying, is not to destroy wealth, but to create broader range of opportunity, to restrain the growth of unwholesome and sterile accumulations and to lay the burdens of government where they can best be carried. This law affects only those individual people who have incomes over $50,000 a year, and individual estates of decedents who leave over $40,000.

Moreover, it gives recognition to the generally accepted fact that larger corporations enjoying the advantages of size over smaller corporations possess relatively greater capacity to pay. Consequently the act changes the rate of tax on net earnings from a flat 13.75 percent to a differential ranging from 12.5 percent to 15 percent. No reasonable person thinks that this is going to destroy competent corporations or impair business as a whole. Taxes on 95 percent of our corporations are actually reduced by the new tax law. A small excess profits tax is also provided as well as an intercorporate dividend tax which will have the wholesome effect of encouraging the simplification of overly complicated and wasteful intercorporate relationships.

Congress declined to broaden the tax base because it was recognized that the tax base had already been broadened to a very considerable extent during the past five years. I am aware of the sound arguments advanced in favor of making every citizen pay an income tax, however small his income. England is cited as an example. But it should be recalled that despite complaints about higher taxes our interest payments on public debts, including local governments, require only 3 percent of our national income as compared with 7 percent in England.

The broadening of our tax base in the past few years has been very real. What is known as consumers' taxes, namely the invisible taxes paid by people in every walk of life, fall relatively much more heavily upon the poor man than on the rich man. In 1929, consumers' taxes represented only 30 percent of the national revenue. Today they are 60 percent, and even with the passage of the recent tax bill the proportion of these consumers' taxes will drop only 5 percent.

This Administration came into power pledged to a very considerable legislative program. It found the condition of the country such as to require drastic and far-reaching action. Duty and necessity required us to move on a broad front for more than two years. It seemed to the Congress and to me better to achieve these objectives as expeditiously as possible in order that not only business but the public generally might know those modifications in the conditions and rules of economic enterprise which were involved in our program. This basic program, however, has now reached substantial completion and the "breathing spell" of which you speak is here—very decidedly so.

It is a source of great satisfaction that at this moment conditions are such as to offer further substantial and widespread recovery. Unemployment is still with us but it is steadily diminishing and our efforts to meet its problems are unflagging. I do not claim the magician's wand. I do not claim that Government alone is responsible for these definitely better circumstances. But we all know the very great effect of the saving of banks, of farms, of homes, the building of public works, the providing of relief for the destitute, and many other direct government acts for the betterment of conditions. And we do claim that we have helped to restore the public confidence which now offers so substantial a foundation for our recovery. I take it that we are all not merely seeking but getting the recovery of confidence, not merely the confidence of a small group, but that basic confidence on the part of the mass of our population, in the soundness of our economic life and in the honesty and justice of the purposes of its economic rule and methods.

I like the last sentence of your letter and I repeat it—"With all its faults and with the abuses it has developed, our system has in the past enabled us to achieve greater progress than has been attained by any other system on earth. Smoke out the sinister forces seeking to delude the public into believing that an ordinary modernization of a system we want to preserve is revolution in disguise."

Very sincerely yours,

Franklin D. Roosevelt

This revelation that a breathing spell was at hand caused a massive sigh of relief to the business owners and executives who read it on the homebound trains or heard of it on the evening newscasts.

Their fear reflected more than just higher income tax rates and the new Social Security tax. The business community was also following the plight of Andrew Mellon, who had been Hoover's secretary of the treasury. Mellon was one of the country's wealthiest men. His personal fortune included large holdings in Gulf Oil Company, Aluminum Company of America, and other large corporations. Soon after Roosevelt's inauguration, Attorney General Homer Cummins announced an investigation into Mellon's 1930 and 1931 income tax returns. This was a departure from well-established practice, and from federal law, which gave the Treasury Department's Internal Revenue Service jurisdiction for investigation and prosecution of violations of income tax law. The IRS reviewed the tax returns and found in September 1933 that Mellon was entitled to a refund of $7.5 million for the 1931 tax year. In October, the Justice Department nonetheless sent three investigators to Pittsburgh to review Mellon's tax records. After three weeks, they found nothing amiss.

Undeterred, Cummings announced in March 1934 the convening of a grand jury in Federal District Court in Pittsburgh to consider a criminal charge of filing a fraudulent tax return. The grand jury heard the government's presentation of five witnesses. Consistent with established grand jury practice, there were no defense witnesses. In May, the grand jury voted that the government's case did not provide sufficient basis for an indictment. Walter Lippmann, a widely syndicated newspaper columnist, published his own evaluation of the entire process as "a most discreditable performance...low and inept political maneuver...one of those stunts that politicians stoop to every now and then, thinking that they can gain some advantage by it for their party."[312]

Most workers, and certainly most of the unemployed, took little note of Mellon's situation. But for owners of businesses large and small, this raised fearful questions. If the full investigative and prosecutorial powers of the federal government could be used to harass a former treasury secretary, even after no evidence of wrongdoing was found, what safety did the average businessman have? Mellon could afford to pay the accountants and lawyers for his own defense. A man of lesser means in the same situation would face public humiliation, financial ruin, and possibly a prison term. The administration's apparent embrace of Upton Sinclair was equally appalling. The pursuit of Mellon, the president's embrace of an avowed socialist, and the legislation passed in the summer of 1935 had their effect.

---

312 *New York Tribune*, May 13, 1934; *Pittsburgh Post Gazette*, May 12, 1934.

Publication of the letters between Roy Howard and the president, and the pledge of a "breathing spell," was indeed a relief for the business community. Some accepted it at face value: not a change in direction, but at least a quiet time during which the accumulated results of so many experiments might be measured. Others perhaps prayed that a pause and reflection might eventually lead to reversal of some of the more onerous policies. A business community candidly described as "frightened stiff" would be slow to hire, slow to invest, and slow to innovate. Roosevelt's outreach to the business community was not the only news of the weekend.

On Sunday, September 8, Huey Long was shot while leaving the Louisiana Capitol building. Although serving as a United States Senator, Long often returned to Baton Rouge to control the state legislature's deliberations. By 1935, almost every state or local-level position in Louisiana was filled with Long's political supporters. He died two days later from internal bleeding after surgery. His bodyguards killed the assassin, a young man retaliating for Long's attempts to remove the man's father-in-law from a judgeship.

———

On November 15, 1935, Canada and the United States signed a reciprocal trade agreement finally lowering the tariff rates between the two countries. The Canadian prime minister had visited Roosevelt in April 1933. Their joint statement after that meeting expressed hopes for a new trade agreement between the countries. Eleven months later, Roosevelt asked Congress for authority to negotiate such agreements and Congress had granted the authority in June 1934. On at least four occasions during 1934, Canadian officials had contacted the United States State Department to start discussions, but the Americans delayed. Finally, in late December, Secretary of State Cordell Hull wrote that "this Government holds itself in readiness to begin immediate preparations for trade agreement negotiations." Finally, three years after Roosevelt's election on a platform that severely criticized the Smoot-Hawley Tariff, America mended relations with its largest trading partner. [313]

---

313 *Foreign Relations of the United States.* United States Department of State, 1934, Volume I, p. 845–875, and 1935, p. 30–33. NARA II. Secretary Hull was a lifelong, committed free-trader. The president, under terms of the Smoot-Hawley Tariff, had authority to lower rates as much as 50 percent. The long delays in dealing with Canada had to be at Roosevelt's direction.

The "breathing spell" lasted just four months, slightly more than one quarter in business time. In January 1936, Roosevelt's State of the Union speech included harsh comments on business. He had directed his writers to prepare a "fighting speech."[314] Raymond Moley, one of the original brain trust and Roosevelt's key policy aide and speechwriter since the 1932 campaign, noticed the sharp change in tone and content. Roosevelt spoke for several minutes about the growing international tensions and emphasized America's neutrality. Then came the discussion of business. As the stenographer's notations in parentheses attest, many in Congress listened appreciatively:

> Within democratic Nations the chief concern of the people is to prevent the continuation or the rise of autocrats that beget slavery at home and aggression abroad. [Applause] Within our borders, as in the world at large, popular opinion is at war with a power-seeking minority.
>
> In these later years we have witnessed the domination of government by financial and industrial groups, numerically small but politically dominant in the twelve years that succeeded the World War. The present group of which I speak is indeed numerically small and, while it exercises a large influence and has much to say in the world of business, it does not, I am confident, speak the true sentiments of the less articulate but more important elements that constitute real American business. [Applause, cheers]
>
> We have returned the control of the Federal Government to the City of Washington. [Prolonged applause] To be sure, in so doing, we have invited battle. We have earned the hatred of entrenched greed… They seek—let me put it this way, they seek the restoration of their selfish power.
>
> They seek—this minority in business and industry—to control and often do control and use for their own purposes legitimate and highly honored business associations; they engage in vast propaganda to spread discord among the people—they would "gang up" against the people's liberties. [Applause, laughter, cheers]
>
> The principle that they would instill into government if they succeed in taking power is well shown by the principles which many of

314 Raymond Moley, *After Seven Years*, 330.

them have instilled into their own affairs: autocracy toward labor, toward stockholders, toward consumers, toward public sentiment. Autocrats in smaller things, they seek autocracy in bigger things. "By their fruits ye shall know them." [Applause]

But such fear as they instill today is not a natural fear, a normal fear; it is a synthetic, manufactured, poisonous fear that is being spread subtly, expensively and cleverly by the same people who cried in those other days, "Save us, save us, else we perish." [Applause, cheers, stamping of feet]

The speech included a brief comment on taxes:

National income increases: tax receipts, based on that income, increase without the levying of new taxes. That is why I am able to say to this, the second session of the Seventy-fourth Congress, that based on existing laws it is my belief that no new taxes, over and above the present taxes, are advisable or necessary. [Applause, cheers][315]

Two months later, Roosevelt sent a supplemental budget message to Congress, proposing a new tax on undistributed corporate surplus.[316] Profits not paid out in dividends would be subject to the undistributed surplus tax. The objective was to force companies to pay out the major part of their annual profits as dividends. Then the dividends would be taxable again as personal income to the shareholder, since the 1936 Act eliminated the exemption of dividends (already taxed as profits on the corporation's tax return) from the personal income tax.[317] This was the inauguration of the practice that is still in effect today, known today as "double taxation" of dividends. Under the 1936 law, any profit earned by a corporation would be taxed at corporate income tax rates as high as 15 percent. Then whatever part of that profit was paid as a dividend to shareholders would be taxed again on the shareholder's income tax return.

An additional surtax, starting at 15 percent of the year's earnings, would apply if a corporation were found to be accumulating profits beyond the "reason-

---

315 Speech Files, Carton 24, #834, Franklin D. Roosevelt Library, Hyde Park, New York.
316 Speech Files, Carton 24, #850, Franklin D. Roosevelt Library, Hyde Park, New York.
317 "Equity Theory as Myth in the Origins of the Corporate Income Tax," Steven A. Banks, *William and Mary Law Review*, December 1, 2001, §460.

able needs of the business." The tax would apply to the "net income [profits] of every corporation…availed of for the purpose of preventing the imposition of the surtax upon its shareholders…through the medium of permitting earnings or profits to accumulate instead of being distributed." Interest on bonds or notes issued by the federal government also became taxable income under the 1936 Act.

The 1936 Act also contained an ominous Section 102 (b), in text similar to that of Section 104 (b) of the Revenue Act of 1932: "The fact…that the earnings or profits are allowed to accumulate beyond the reasonable needs of the business, shall be prima facie evidence of a purpose to avoid surtax upon shareholders." This was a powerful threat. No formulas or other criteria for calculating "reasonable needs" were established in the Act. If IRS officials determined, on their own, that profits were accumulating beyond the reasonable needs of the business, the corporation would have to prove the reasonableness of the accumulation. Large businesses, equipped with accountants and lawyers, saw the obvious effort to tax at whim. For smaller businesses, just the expense of defending against the IRS and its prima facie claim would be crippling, even if the court upheld the company's position.

———

From mid-1935 on, Roosevelt had used the broad discretion given him in an effort to achieve full employment and stimulate the economy. Hopkins continuously spent more than the funds that the president allocated to him, and Roosevelt shifted money from the PWA and other government agencies to make the most of the WPA employment.[318]

In the fiscal year that ended June 30, 1936, just four months before the presidential election, almost eight million families (27 percent of all that had income that year) earned $750 or less; sixteen million families (55 percent of the total) earned $1,250 or less. For homeowners, those earnings included a hypothetical amount calculated to represent the value of the use of the home.[319] Their actual wages were something less. Almost seven years after the stock market crash, and three and a half years into the New Deal, almost a third of all families had incomes less than the "minimum living wage" that social workers had calculated

---

318 *The Secret Diary of Howard L. Ickes, The First Thousand Days, 1933-1936*, 436-437.
319 *Statistical Abstract of the United States, 1939*, Table 352.

as necessary to a basic standard of living in the early years of the century. The unemployed received even less in relief payments. Many who had once enjoyed the prosperity of the middle class now struggled for the basics.

As voters went to the polls for the 1936 elections, the CCC, PWA, and WPA programs employed 3.3 million people. Eighty percent of these were WPA employees. An additional 971,000 families and 435,000 individuals were still on unemployment relief.[320] Harry Hopkins's quiet prediction of full employment by the fall of 1935 was unfulfilled.

But a majority of voters approved Roosevelt's programs—the millions of "work-relief" jobs funded by tax revenues, the assurance of Social Security pensions, tax rate increases on higher incomes—and his speeches describing some small minority of unnamed individuals who would "gang up against the people's liberties." They approved of his railing against accumulation of corporate profits "beyond the reasonable needs of the business." Roosevelt won his second term by a landslide: more than twenty-seven million votes for FDR, less than seventeen million for Alf Landon. The voters reelected Roosevelt by the largest popular vote majority in history, 61 percent. The Electoral College tally was 523 to 8. Roosevelt won every state except Maine and Vermont. Democrats added seven Senate seats and twenty-one House seats.

————

The Depression continued in America. The unemployment rate remained high. Government work projects simply could not compensate for the loss of private-sector jobs or create new jobs as the working-age population grew 1.4 percent each year.

————

320 *Statistical Abstract of the United States, 1937,* Tables 374, 375 and 376.

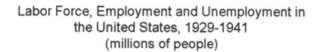

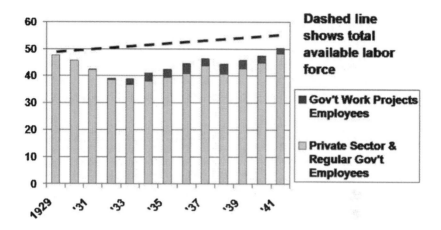

A report by Dr. Simon Kuznets of the National Bureau of Economic Research in 1937 pointed to a major factor in the lingering unemployment. From 1919 to 1929, expenditures for producers' durable goods (equipment and machinery) and privately financed construction had averaged $19 billion per year on a fairly stable basis except for the recession years 1921 and 1922, when the expenditures fell to $15 billion per year. But from 1932 to 1935, the figure averaged $4.7 billion per year. Those business leaders whom Roy Howard described as "frightened stiff" were not investing in new equipment. The dramatic fall in capital investment had contributed to the ongoing economic problems.

The stimulus of stepped-up public works was intended to maintain employment and raise demand for basic materials, which would boost employment. That would create consumer demand, promoting investment in producer durable goods and buildings for business. But the tariff curtailed demand for exports. Higher taxes reduced the money available for spending and private investment. Higher taxes also reduced the after-tax reward for any successful investment. That loss of producer confidence was a heavy weight holding down capital spending and related employment.[321] By 1938, private consumption had barely recovered to 1929 levels, and residential construction was at 55 percent of 1929 levels.[322]

---

321 *National Income and Capital Formation, 1919-1935,* by Simon Kuznets, published by NBER, 1937. http://www.nber.org/books/kuzn37-1.
322 Lester V. Chandler, *America's Greatest Depression, 1929-1941,* 132, Table 8-3.

Economic life did not stop completely. General Motors offered new automobile models every year. Boeing Aircraft Company worked on several experimental models and by 1935 had built the first multiengine bomber, which would become the B-17 Flying Fortress of World War II fame.[323] Some large corporations continued to invest in plants and equipment throughout the Depression. E. I. DuPont de Nemours, the chemical manufacturer, spent more than $160 million from 1930 to 1936 and increased its total workforce by sixty-five hundred. Ongoing research in the new field of organic chemistry yielded the miracle fiber nylon in 1938.[324] United States Steel spent $600 million on an expansion program started in 1928, closing obsolete plants while modernizing others and building new ones.[325] Throughout the decade, Sears, Roebuck and Company added to its number of retail stores every year except 1932. Merrill Lynch completed a new high-rise office building in New York City in 1933. Even when unemployment was at its peak in the winter of 1932–1933, 40 percent of the workforce had full-time employment. In March, 1933, a 1932 graduate of Eureka College named Ronald Reagan landed a job as radio announcer at a local station in Davenport, Iowa. His starting salary was $100 per month.[326] But these were faint heartbeats in a very weak economy.

America's economic pulse had been weak since 1931. The lifeblood of the economy lacked the pumping action of investment and innovation: people inventing new products and growing new industries to replace old ones, thousands of large and small businesses using new plants and equipment to boost efficiency, working in new ways, and hiring more people.

The 1936 tax act made after-tax profits even less likely. By mid-1937, the economy was slipping back again, and unemployment rose. By the fall of 1937, the "recession within a depression" had deepened. Unemployment worsened. By March 1938, the number of unemployed had increased by 2.5 million compared to one year earlier.[327]

The pain was felt most acutely by workers—white collar and blue collar—and their families. Lester Chandler points out the following from a "Survey of

---

323 Edward Jablonski, *Flying Fortress: Illustrated Biography of the B-17s and the Men Who Flew Them.*

324 William S. Dutton, *Du Pont: One Hundred and Forty Years,* 359.

325 Douglas A. Fisher, *The Fifty Year Story of United States Steel, 1901-1951,* 41, 49.

326 Ronald Reagan, *An American Life: The Autobiography,* 69.

327 This unemployment figure is from Frank Freidel, *FDR: Rendezvous With Destiny,* 225.

Employment Service Information" by the U.S. Government Employment Service, 1938:

Of the unemployed registering with the U.S. Unemployment Service in the period July 1936-March 1937, 9.5 percent had been unemployed more than four years, 15.7 percent more than two years, and 22.6 percent more than a year."[328]

———

In November, the weekly magazine *Life* reported a "Main Street Revolt" that had Congressmen worried about their reelection prospects for 1938. *Life* reported widespread agreement that the undistributed profits tax was "Devil Tax Number 1," and the second most unpopular tax was the capital gains tax. The article included a letter from Walter C. Uline, owner of a small furniture company in Nappanee, Indiana (population 2,950), to his Congressman. Uline had voted for Roosevelt in 1932 and 1936. Uline's letter emphasized the need to "modify legislation that has proven to be detrimental to our progress...What I am interested is the legislation which has adversely affected small business." He also told the reporter of his fear that the newly formed union would wreck his business. Uline apparently thought that large and small businesses had different needs.[329]

One month later, Gerard Swope of General Electric issued a statement on the business outlook for the coming year. Swope wrote that the lack of confidence on the part of business and lack of faith in the future is "undoubtedly due to the restrictive taxation on business and private enterprise." Swope particularly hoped for revisions of the tax on undistributed profits, to help small businesses particularly, and of the capital gains tax, which "now interferes with the natural economic flow."[330]

In January 1938, the Senate Committee on Unemployment held hearings to assess the business situation. Unemployment had been rising in preceding months. The Social Security Board supplied statistics showing dramatic increases in the number of employable people applying for unemployment relief. Applications had increased 68 percent in December over the previous month in Fort

---

328 Lester V. Chandler, *America's Greatest Depression, 1929-1941*, 42.
329 *Life*, November 29, 1937.
330 "Swope Sees Lack of Faith in Future," *New York Times*, December 31, 1937.

Wayne, Indiana. Applications were up 70 percent in Toledo, Ohio, and 35 percent in Portland, Oregon.

Lammot duPont, president of E. I. DuPont de Nemours and Co., Inc., testified that sales at the chemical giant had been falling since the previous April, and they fell off more rapidly in December. The firm employed 55,500 people in December, 1937, up 32 percent from the number employed in 1929. Hourly wages were 56 percent higher than they had been in early 1933. But he noted that the company had laid off forty-three hundred people between September and December—about 7 percent of the total—as sales had fallen and were forecast to fall another 23 percent in the coming six months. He was still committed to $38 million in new construction during 1938, but he added a note of concern.

Lammot duPont explained that the company's ability to increase sales, expand its operations, and hire more people depended on its ability to continuously develop new products for better living. To justify the risk of investing in the development of these new products, there must be some likelihood of adequate profit. He testified that a "fog of uncertainty" affected business decision-making, and he described its components:

> The amount or type of taxes, fear of higher prices due to steadily increasing public debt, the uncertainty as to the future value of money, the unprecedented number of strikes last year, the multiplication of legal rules under which business must operate.
>
> The capital gains tax undoubtedly has the effect of determining capital investment. If an investment proves successful, most of the profit goes to the government. If unsuccessful, the individual bears all the loss; the investor hesitates to venture several to one on a venture attended with a risk.
>
> The undistributed profits tax inhibits the reinvestment of earnings of a corporation. If it turns in its need for capital to the investor public, it encounters today a lack of venture money. It cannot prudently use bank loans, which are short term money, for venture purposes that require long term patient money.
>
> Change of law with respect to these and certain other taxes, together with simplification of the tax structure, would relieve management of some of the present worries and give greater confidence for the future.[331]

---

331 *New York Times,* January 11, 1938.

Congress had its answer. The president of one of America's largest corporations had described the connection between taxes and regulation on profits, business confidence, long-term investment in new products, and employment—the key issue under investigation. After years of growing during the Depression, the company was now laying off workers and reluctant to invest in new products. He had just told the Senators how to remedy the nation's problem of falling employment. Both Swope and du Pont had pointed to the same issues that Walter Uline, owner of a middle-America main street business, had written about—including taxes. The concerns of large and small business were remarkably similar.

But no action was taken, except to repeal the tax on undistributed profits. Roosevelt stepped up the Justice Department's antitrust activities. He appointed Thurman Arnold as assistant attorney general for antitrust matters and increased the number of lawyers assigned to the antitrust unit from a few dozen to more than two hundred. Arnold had just published his views on business in *The Folklore of Capitalism*. For business leaders, the message was clear enough.

By 1939, business investment remained 59 percent below the 1929 level. The total number of people employed in private and government jobs remained 13 percent below the 1929 number. Total hours worked in 1939 were 21 percent below the level of 1929. Private hours (not including government workers) had fallen more than 25 percent. Manufacturing work hours, where wages tended to be higher, in 1939 were 29 percent fewer than in 1929.[332] The massive public works of PWA, the make-work projects of WPA, and the ongoing federal support of relief efforts—all aimed at boosting purchasing power and restoring the economy—were inadequate substitutes for the missing stimulus of private investment and innovation.

On a Sunday evening in May 1939, at supper in the White House, the president was bemoaning the business community's persistent lack of confidence in the economy. The president's wife, Eleanor, the most perceptive and straightforward social commentator of the era, spoke up: "They are afraid of you."[333]

---

332 "A Second Look at the U.S. Great Depression from a Neoclassical Perspective," Harold H. Cole and Lee E. Ohanian, Federal Reserve Bank of Minneapolis Research Department Staff Report.
333 Jerre Mangione, *An Ethnic at Large,* 247. The dinner and guest list appear on the White House Usher's Diary page for May 14, 1939, available at Pare Lorentz Center at the Franklin D. Roosevelt Presidential Library & Museum. © Pare Lorentz Film Center.

As late as 1940, the unemployment rate in the U.S. was 14.6 percent.[334]

————

Fear sat not only on the hearts of the wealthy or those in business. All the new social safety nets, including unemployment insurance and old age pensions and the federally funded jobs for millions of people, were intended to put aside fear itself and restore confidence. But fear about the future remained. Throughout the decade of the thirties, Americans withheld that fundamental investment in the future, that vote of confidence that "things will be OK." The primal instinct to have children was deferred to such an extent that for the first time in history Americans were not reproducing enough to replace those who died.

By 1934, Congress took note and held hearings on the birth control issue. Judging from the "intrinsic rate of natural increase in the population," as reported in the *Statistical Abstract of the United States*, the Depression in America lasted until 1940. Then, in spite of growing concerns about war, the fertility rate actually increased. Even with the movement of millions of men to foreign lands starting in 1942, the fertility rate did not slip back to Depression levels. Was the improving fertility rate a result of economic certainty—more jobs and virtually guaranteed profits, however thin, for investment in war materials production? The fertility rate dropped to Depression levels again in the late 1960s, but the intrinsic rate of natural increase in the population would never again drop to negative numbers until 1972–1979.

————

There are numerous views on when the Depression ended in America. According to Lester Chandler, it lasted until at least 1941. Some other economists, such as Robert Higgs, set the end of the Depression much later.[335] Some historians mark December 7, 1941, the date of the Pearl Harbor attack, as the end of the Depression.[336] But if unemployment was the major cause of pain for the general population during the Depression, then we should look to the unemployment rate to mark its end. The average unemployment rate did not return

334 U.S. Department of Labor, Bureau of Labor Statistics.
335 Robert Higgs, "Regime Uncertainty: Why the Great Depression lasted so long and Why Prosperity resumed after the War," *Independent Review*, March 22, 1997.
336 Robert S. McElvaine, *The Great Depression—America, 1929-1941*, 321.

to 1929 levels until 1943, when the population of civilian "employables" was reduced by nine million men and women serving in the armed forces, and factories were booming with war production.[337]

Other industrialized nations took market-oriented actions earlier and recovered more quickly.[338] As early as 1934, the United States was falling noticeably behind other industrial nations. In steel production—a key economic barometer in the pre-plastics era—America fell from 47.5 percent of world production in 1929 to 32 percent in 1934. In the same period, the U.S. share of global automobile production slipped from 39 percent to 24 percent.[339] Other nations recovered much more quickly than the U.S.[340]

Britain offers the most striking contrast. As presented by R. K. Webb, a Columbia University historian:

> In general, the thirties were a period of gradual but steady recovery. As Britain had not fallen so deeply into depression as other industrial countries, her recovery was easier…the decade was marked by a rise in real wages and living standards.[341]

Great Britain's policy for dealing with the Depression was different. Britain's empire comprised a huge, multifaceted economy. Those nations, denied access to the American market, traded more within their own ranks. The heart of the strategy was affirmed by the people voting in a coalition government of Labour-Socialists, Conservatives, and Liberals under Prime Minister Ramsey MacDonald. The government's policy, as described by Winston Churchill, was one of "severe austerity and sacrifice. It was an earlier version of 'Blood, sweat, toil, and tears'…The sternest economy must be practiced. Everyone would have his wages, salary, or income reduced. The mass of the people were asked to vote for a regime of self-denial…the government abandoned the gold standard… confidence and credit were restored."[342]

---

337 *Statistical Abstract of the United States, 1946,* Table 238.
338 Several economists have concluded that the New Deal fiscal policy (taxes and spending policies) were, at best, not very constructive or worse. See especially E. Carey Brown, "Fiscal Policy in the Thirties—A Reappraisal," *American Economic Review,* December 1956, 46, 857–79.
339 National Bureau of Economic Research, Bulletin 58, November 15, 1935.
340 Harold E. Cole and Lee E. Ohanian, *A Second Look at the U.S. Great Depression from a Neoclassical Perspective,* 9.
341 R. K. Webb, *Modern England: From the 18th Century to Present.*
342 Winston Churchill, *The Gathering Storm,* 37.

———

The U.S. entry into World War II changed the economy. The immediate need for ships, planes, tanks, ammunition, and supplies was obvious. All available factories would be needed, and more would have to be built quickly. Some civilian products, such as automobiles, became completely unavailable as manufacturing plants were converted to build military products. Gasoline and many food items were rationed. Hundreds of thousands (eventually, eleven million Americans would be in uniform) joined the military, and there were more jobs for the remaining civilians. [343]

Some war production plants were built by the government, using money raised by the Treasury Department selling war bonds. After the war, these plants were sold at auction. Corporate dollars also flowed easily into new plant and equipment for the war effort. Even a thin after-tax profit (there were elaborate price controls in effect, just in case someone tried to profiteer) was adequate when there was no risk—the sale of all goods produced was guaranteed by government contracts. So, even a low after-tax ROE was acceptable. But the motivation was more primal: losing this war was not an option.

———

Later chapters will examine more of the long-term, wide-ranging consequences of tax legislation enacted during the Depression, beyond the devastating effect that these taxes had on employment.

---

343 *Statistical Abstract of the United States, 1946,* Table 238.

Chapter Twelve

The Dark Age of American Innovation

As the war ended, reconstruction of Europe became a major concern. There would be no repetition of the post–World War I reparation schemes that had bankrupted Germany and set the stage for Nazism. The Marshall Plan[344] and U.S. corporate tax policy encouraged U.S. corporations to do business and establish plants in Europe. The domestic economy was boosted during President Truman's tenure, 1945 to 1953, by millions of soldiers returning from war. They took up civilian jobs, married, and became consumers of housing and all the necessities of family life.

President Truman explicitly renewed the nation's commitment to FDR's economic policies. Truman specifically rejected Congressional calls for lower income tax rates, based on his conviction that the high rates were needed to generate large revenues for paying down the national debt. Congress enacted a modest tax reduction by overriding Truman's veto.[345] Truman, on business, said, "I would risk my reputation and my fortune with a professional politician sooner

---

344 Under the Marshall Plan, devised by Secretary of State George Marshall, the United States spent $13.6 billion assisting Europe's economic rehabilitation.
345 Harry S Truman, *Memoirs: Years of Trial and Hope 1946-1952*, 37.

than I would with the banker or the businessman or the publisher of a daily newspaper! More young men and young women should fit themselves for politics and government."[346]

President Eisenhower refused tax cuts, except for a modest increase in deductions. A balanced federal budget was central to his economic thinking.[347] He equated high tax rates with high revenues. Eisenhower also initiated construction of the interstate highway system, inspired by the German autobahns. The benefits of efficient roads to commerce were obvious. Eisenhower also saw this major program as an employment stabilizer. The pace of highway construction could be stepped up during recessions and eased in periods of full employment. Eisenhower's public works spending exceeded even Roosevelt's.[348]

By the late 1950s, the limitations of an economy based on housing, highways, and high taxes were becoming painfully apparent. Growth of the labor pool was constrained by the low birth rates during the 1930s and the loss of 405,000 who had died in service during World War II and 36,000 in the Korean War,[349] yet a recession in the winter of 1957–1958 sent unemployment to 7 percent. Reduced economic activity was producing less-than-budget tax revenues while expenses were exceeding budget.[350] Eisenhower was increasingly concerned but saw few opportunities for improvement.[351]

President Kennedy's inauguration, in January 1961, took place in the midst of another recession, the fourth since the end of the war. The United States was suffering the highest unemployment rates since the Depression, still at 7 percent. Meanwhile, Europe was enjoying strong corporate profits, virtually full employment, and modern industrial technology built in the post-war recovery. On March 24, 1961, President Kennedy signed a law extending unemployment relief benefits for more than three million workers whose state benefits were exhausted or would soon run out. In April, Kennedy called upon Congress to enact an investment tax credit for businesses, noting that,

346 Robert H. Ferrell (ed.), *The Autobiography of Harry S. Truman*, 116.
347 Dwight Eisenhower, *The White House Years, Waging Peace, 1956-1961*, 463.
348 Stephen A. Ambrose, *Eisenhower: Soldier and President*, 387, 545.
349 Congressional Research Service Report for Congress, July 13, 2005. Available at http://www.history.navy.mil/library/online.
350 Ibid, 213, 687.
351 Dwight Eisenhower, *The White House Years, Waging Peace, 1956-1961*, 604.

To meet the needs of a growing population and labor force, and to achieve a rising per capita income and employment level, we need a high and rising level of both private and public capital formation.[352]

He also planned to eliminate some tax code provisions that had strongly favored overseas investment by American corporations and thereby discouraged investment in the U.S. This had been part of America's effort to rebuild Europe and Japan after World War II. As a result of that effort, Europe had the most modern and efficient manufacturing plants in the world in just about every industry. Kennedy's objective was to quickly level the playing field, from a tax perspective, for investment in machinery and equipment in the U.S. In the same message, he encouraged Congress to make major changes in the tax code, to close loopholes, broaden the number of people paying taxes, and lower both the corporate and individual tax rates, which were still near the high rates enacted to finance World War II.

The investment tax credit was enacted, but Congress was slow to reduce tax rates. By January 1963, after twenty-two months of economic recovery, unemployment had remained stubbornly high. For five years, the unemployment rate had been at or above 5 percent. The first Baby Boomers would graduate from high school in 1964. Some would go to college, but many would be seeking jobs. Again Kennedy presented the case for lower tax rates:

If we are to prevail in the long run, we must expand the long run strength of our economy. We must move along the path to a higher rate of growth and full employment.

To achieve these greater gains, one step, above all, is essential—the enactment this year of a substantial reduction and revision in Federal income taxes.

It is increasingly clear...that our obsolete tax system exerts too heavy a drag on private purchasing power, profits, and employment... It discourages extra effort and risk. It distorts the use of resources. It invites recurrent recessions, depresses our Federal revenues, and causes chronic deficits.[353]

---

352 Special Message to Congress on Taxation, April 20, 1961. John T. Woolley and Gerhard Peters, *The American Presidency Project* (online), Santa Barbara, California. Available from: http://www.presidency.ucsb.edu/ws/?pid=8074.
353 Annual State of the Union Message, January 14, 1963. Ibid, http://www.presidency.ucsb.edu/ws/?pid=9138.

Kennedy's statements explicitly countered the beliefs that had guided Franklin Roosevelt, Harry Truman, and Dwight Eisenhower that high tax rates on corporations and high-income individuals would maximize federal tax revenues.

Kennedy's tax-reduction proposals were passed after his death. Corporate tax rates were reduced only slightly, but two successive tax cuts reduced the top marginal personal income tax rate—the same rate applied to dividends earned by wealthy investors—from 91 percent in 1963 to 77 percent in 1964 and then to 70 percent in 1965.[354] Those in the highest income tax brackets (all taxable income over $200,000 in 1965 and later) were still watching more than two-thirds of their top-bracket income go to the government. But in the three years following the 1965 tax-rate cuts, federal government income tax revenue increased by 10.4 percent annually. In the three years prior to the tax cut, federal income tax revenue had increased at an average annual rate of just 5.3 percent.[355] Lower tax rates were producing more total income tax revenue for the government.

———

Kennedy may have noted one other problem. The products that advance our standard of living begin as experiments in workshops or garages, in laboratories or test kitchens. The inventors may be engineers with advanced degrees, eminent medical researchers, or teenagers working with scrap parts or tinkers soldering at a basement workbench. When the experiments have produced a viable object ready for the world of commerce, the inventor files a patent application to register the new product as his own intellectual property. We can measure the pulse of creativity in the economy—the source of tomorrow's new products and better living standards—by tracing the number of patent applications.

The U.S. Patent and Trademark Office started counting the applications for patents of inventions in 1840. The count in that first year was 735. For the next ninety years, the number of applications increased, on average, about 1.4 percent per year. The chart below shows the years of growth and years of declines in the number of applications. Wars are obviously disruptive,

---

354 Tax rates from Statistics of Income Bulletin, September 22, 2004.
355 *Statistical Abstract of the United States, 1965,* Table 533; *1966,* Table 540; *1970,* Table 564.

indicated by the sharp drops in 1898 for the Spanish-American War and 1918 during the U.S. involvement in World War I. Possibly the diversion of so many young people into military duty is a factor. These war-related quiet periods were followed by dramatic surges in applications as soon as hostilities ended. Applications also fell when recessions occurred, clearly visible in the early 1870s, in the 1893–1896 period and during the serious recession of 1920–1921.

U.S. Patent Applications for Inventions (thousands)

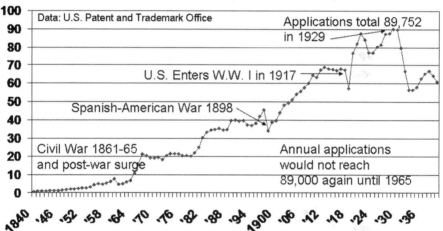

But the most dramatic disruption started with 1930 applications essentially being flat with 1929's record high number of 89,752. Earlier setbacks had lasted a few years. The longest no-growth period had been 1867 to 1879, when the applications hovered around twenty thousand per year. But the application drought that became obvious in 1931 was of unprecedented magnitude and duration. The nation would not see eighty-nine thousand applications again in a single year until 1965—twenty years after the end of World War II. The average annual rate of growth in applications for the period 1930 to 1965 was less than zero. In 1960, the year President Kennedy was elected, 79,590 applications were filed—11 percent fewer than in 1930. During the years 1956–1960 applications had averaged 76,956 per year—14 percent fewer than in 1930. Something more permanent than war or recession was damping the creative fire of America's Greatest Generation, and of many born later.

U.S. Patent Applications
for Inventions (thousands)

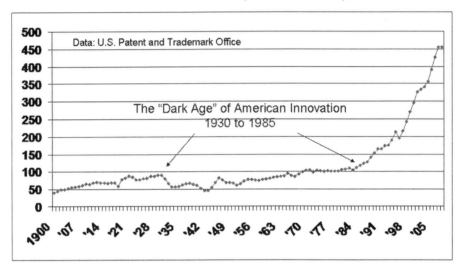

The income tax reductions of the mid-1960s were accompanied by increasing numbers of patent applications. From 1965 until 1980, the number of applications grew, but only at an average annual rate of less than 1 percent. The negative growth trend of 1930–1965 had finally been broken in spite of the damping effect of the Vietnam War and war-related tax surcharges that boosted the top marginal rate for high incomes during 1968, 1969, and 1970. But the Kennedy tax cuts, the massive space programs that led to the first moon landing in 1969 and the first space shuttle mission in 1981, and the intensive quest for energy efficiency prompted by the oil embargo of 1973 did not restore the rate of growth in average annual applications to pre-1930 levels. Something mysterious and pernicious was still stifling the growth rate in patent applications.

————

In 1981, another experiment produced more positive results. Ronald Reagan had been elected on a platform of lower taxes and less government interference with business. The tax rate for every personal income bracket and on most corporate income tax brackets was lowered during his first one hundred days in office. For personal taxes, the rate on taxable income in excess of $3,400 up to $5,500 was cut from 14 percent to 12 percent—allowing all workers to keep 14 percent more of their income in that bracket. The rates for all higher income brackets were similarly reduced. Married couples had previously paid tax rates of 49 percent and higher on income above $45,800. Under the new law, the threshold for 49 percent and higher tax rates increased to $60,000. The top personal marginal income tax bracket for a married couple filing jointly was lowered from 70 percent on all taxable income over $215,400 to 50 percent on all taxable income over $85,600.

For corporate taxes, there were modest reductions in rates for most income brackets. The rate charged on the first $25,000 of profit fell from 17 percent to 16 percent in 1982 and then to 15 percent. The rate on the top corporate income bracket was reduced from 48 percent to 46 percent.

For the first time in almost fifty years, those in the highest income tax bracket would get to keep half of their taxable income, although the double taxation of dividends still reduced each dollar of pre-tax corporate profit to twenty-seven cents that a high-income investor could keep as discretionary income. The combined impacts of the corporate and personal tax systems still gave the federal government almost three quarters of every dollar of pre-tax profit earned by an investor. The lower corporate and personal tax rates made business investment more attractive to people at all income levels.

This reduction in tax rates was accompanied by a higher growth rate in patent applications. From 1981 to 1985, applications rose at an average annual rate of 2.4 percent, more than double the rate of 1965–1980. Something was re-awakening the slumbering giant of American innovation. Inventors and investors were coming together. Federal personal income tax receipts grew 4.1 percent annually between 1982 and 1985. Corporate income tax receipts grew 8.2 percent annually. Total federal receipts from all sources grew 6.3 percent annually. Reagan's thesis that lower tax rates would produce more tax revenue through economic growth was proven. However, total federal spending grew 9 percent annually in the same period, largely consisting of increased defense spending (up 15.8 percent annually) and human resources spending (up 7.9 percent annually) in the same period. As spending grew faster than receipts, deficits soared.[356]

In November 1984, voters elected Ronald Reagan to a second term as president, with 59 percent of the popular vote, just short of Franklin Roosevelt's record 61 percent. Reagan carried every state except Minnesota, the home state

---

356 *Statistical Abstract of the United States, 1990,* Tables No. 497, 498, 499 provide detailed accounts of federal revenues (including corporate and personal income taxes) and outlays for each year 1980-1989.

of his opponent, Walter Mondale. Forty-eight years earlier, voters had elected Franklin D. Roosevelt to a second term for his soak-the-rich, anti-business, government-centered work relief and security programs. The children and grandchildren of those 1936 voters gave Ronald Reagan a sweeping second-term victory, embracing his less-government, lower taxes, private initiative-based agenda. The middle ground of America had shifted. That middle-class, middle-of-the-road voter who determines, with his or her ballot, the nation's strategy for promoting the general welfare had adopted a new strategy. With the voters' mandate clearly stated, the president and Congress launched a more significant experiment.

The Tax Reform Act of 1986 established permanent reductions to be phased in during 1987 and 1988. These reduced the top marginal rate for the highest personal income bracket from 50 percent to an attention-getting 28 percent. The top corporate income tax rate dropped from 46 percent, which had prevailed from 1981 to 1986, to 34 percent. The 1986 Act also changed the income brackets and the tax rates applied to the lower income brackets of corporate income, which would most likely apply to a company just starting to earn a profit, perhaps after several years of start-up sales that did not yet cover expenses. Again, tax rates were lowered for workers and investors at all income levels.[357] The double taxation of corporate dividends was preserved. But under the new tax rates an investor in the top income tax bracket could now retain as discretionary income 47 cents of every dollar of pre-tax corporate profit. Those in lower brackets kept more.

This was radical change, not the minor tinkering with deductions, exemptions or a few points of tax rate that many congressmen and presidents offer as tax reform. Taxpayers at every income level kept more of their wages and investment profits. The potential after-tax rewards for going to work, or investing in business, were much more enticing. People noticed the change, and acted on it.

A new era of innovation was launched. Applications surged into the patent office. From 1986 to 1991, the number of applications grew 6.8 percent per year on average, in spite of a stock market crash in October 1987 and a slight setback in 1991, perhaps attributable to Operation Desert Storm, the first Iraq war. While the top marginal tax rate has fluctuated in years since, it has not exceeded 40 percent, and patent applications have soared at an average annual rate of 12 percent over the period 1987–2008.

---

357 Corporate tax rate and bracket data from IRS Statistics of Income Bulletin, Fall 2003, Publication 1136. (Rev. 12-03).

A profound change had propelled the patent application rate to dramatic new growth after fifty-six years of anemic performance. The Dark Age of American Innovation, measured in patent applications, had finally ended. A lingering vestige of the Great Depression was finally gone.[358]

The lower tax rates produced more total income tax revenue, not less. From 1986 to 1992, with the lower rates, the federal government revenue from personal income taxes grew at an average annual rate of 3.5 percent, and corporate income taxes grew on average 9.8 percent annually, reflecting the growth in corporate profits. Investors and inventors formed more new ventures. The economy grew. Once again, lower tax rates produced higher revenues for the government![359]

———

People in every income bracket make decisions with one eye on the tax code. They need to. For many middle- and upper-income families, taxes (primarily on income and real property) are the largest single item in their household budget.[360] Economists refer to this sensitivity to taxes as the principle of elasticity of taxable income (ETI)—the role of tax rates and structures as incentives or disincentives for individual financial activity. In one of the more promi-

---

358 During President Clinton's administration, tax changes effective in 1993 raised the top personal tax rate to 39.6 percent, applicable to taxable income in excess of $250,000. This still allowed top-bracket investors to keep 39 cents of each dollar of pre-tax corporate profits. Many households saw little or no change from the Reagan-era tax rates. There was little impact on patent application rates.

359 *Statistical Abstract of the United States, 1993,* Tables 509, 510, 512. In the same years, total federal receipts grew 7 percent annually and federal spending increased 6.2 percent annually, on average, consisting of human resources spending (up 10 percent per year) and defense (up 1.5 percent per year). The size of annual deficits was reduced considerably until 1989 when Medicare started to rise 13 percent annually and other health outlays rose 28 percent annually.

360 For an interesting exercise, add your federal income tax (Form 1040, Line 60) + state and local wage and income taxes (Schedule A, Line 5) + Medicare wage tax (Form W-2) + Social Security wage tax (W-2) + local real property tax (Schedule A, line 6), and compare that total to any of your other expenses for the same year.

nent studies, Martin Feldstein, professor of economics at Harvard University, used federal income tax returns of four thousand married couples.[361]

Feldstein's purpose was to estimate the sensitivity of reported taxable income to changes in tax rates. The Tax Reform Act of 1986 had made substantial changes in marginal tax rates, creating a useful natural experiment for studying taxpayer reactions to changes in marginal tax rates. He compared data of *the same couples* from their 1985 and 1988 income tax filings. The couples included middle, high, and very high earners. The 1986 Act exempted many low-income households from paying any income tax and entitled some to a new "earned income credit," therefore low-income households were not studied. His conclusion:

> There is a very substantial response of taxable income to variations in marginal tax rates. The estimated sensitivity of taxable income to variations in marginal income tax rates implies that a change in income tax rates has substantially less impact on tax revenue than would be true if there were no behavioral response to marginal tax rates. This sensitivity of taxable income also implies that high marginal tax rates create significant deadweight losses by inducing taxpayers to act differently than they otherwise would. Both implications are relevant to the design of appropriate tax policies and to choices about the desirable level of government spending.

One of the more recent and comprehensive studies is by Emmanuel Saez, professor of economics at University of California, Berkley, and Joel Slemrod, University of Michigan Business School, and Seth H. Giertz of the University of Nebraska. Their report, "The Elasticity of Taxable Income with Respect to Marginal Tax Rates: A Critical Review"[362] was written for submission to the *Journal of Economic Literature*. These authors conclude:

> Nonetheless, the essential insight underlying the ETI remains valid: that income tax rates cause taxpayers to respond on a wide range of margins and, under some conditions, all of these responses reflect inefficiency,

---

361 Martin Feldstein. 1995. "The Effect of Marginal Tax Rates on Taxable Income: A Panel Study of the 1986 Tax Reform Act." *Journal of Political Economy* 103(3): 551-572, 2.

362 The entire paper is available at http://www.nber.org/papers/w15012; copyright by Emmanuel Saez, Joel B. Slemrod, and Seth H. Giertz.

because they would not have been undertaken absent the tax rates. This is especially true of high-income, financially savvy taxpayers who in most countries have access to sophisticated tax avoidance techniques... Given this finding, it is especially critical to understand the mechanisms and efficiency consequences of any given tax change—legal structure, taxpayer information, and so on.

All these economists concluded that income tax rates and structures applied to corporations and individuals have consequences (what the economists call inefficiencies or deadweight losses) that are felt throughout society—by working people, midlevel managers, inventors, executives, and owners of small businesses—not just shareholders of corporations. Feldstein's comment that this "is relevant to the design of appropriate tax policies and to choices about the desirable level of government spending" emphasizes the important connection between tax policy, economic activity, and total revenue for the government, which at some point affects how much the government can spend. Tax policies that discourage profitable business activity constrain tax revenue and thus limit government spending or force deficits.

The data on patent applications strongly suggests that such policies also hinder innovation and thus slow job creation and advances in the quality of life for everyone. Innovation clearly slowed during the high-tax, anti-business policies established in the 1930s, recovered slightly with the mid-1960s tax cuts, and surged ahead with the more dramatic tax reductions of the 1980s. Government-led highway programs, energy projects, and moon shots have not driven innovation as powerfully as allowing employees to keep more of their wages and investors to keep more of their profits. Millions of people, each making their own independent decisions, determine the pace of innovation, apparently with one eye focused on the tax code and the potential for after-tax profits.

One ethicist writing during the Depression speculated about the role that innovation might have played in restoring the economy. In his 1935 book, *A Better Economic Order,* Monsignor John A. Ryan, professor of moral theology and Industrial Ethics at the Catholic University of America, includes an interesting footnote in a chapter "Causes of Industrial Depressions." The note reads: "It is curious that Professor Adams does not mention the contribution of the automobile to business activity in this period. If some comparable luxury were now invented which would be within reach only of the rich and the comfortable classes, and for which they had a powerful appetite, consumption would be increased and we might be moved a considerable distance toward the end of the depression."[363]

That footnote raises a valuable economic question, a key to understanding the length of the Great Depression in America. Why was there no new invention, some luxury even for the rich and the fully employed that might have primed the economic pump and brought recovery?

Those who were unemployed had plenty of time, but no discretionary money for the materials necessary for even basic experiments. Young men living in the CCC camps far from home were not in a position to devote time or money to lengthy experiments. Nor was anyone receiving WPA subsistence wages, or unemployment relief payments, likely to afford materials for even basic experiments. Some may have preferred the security of make-work projects even when private-sector work was available.

Even at the deepest part of the Depression, 75 percent of the workforce was employed, although many were working only part-time and therefore struggling to pay bills. Among those who were fully employed, many were helping relatives or friends. So very few might have tinkered in the garage or basement on some new gadget that might become the next dream product or innovative technology.

An idea on the drawing board, or a working sample of a new device, does not become a source of employment until it can be manufactured and sold in a business. That takes money. Who, even among the wealthy, would risk their savings by investing in a new business when business was held in disrepute, and profits were seen as something to be taxed at high rates to pay for the dole? Those who had money to invest chose the steady income from U.S. Treasury bonds, obviously patriotic and above reproach, with payment of interest and principal guaranteed by the full faith and credit of the United States of America, rather than risk their savings for some small after-tax share of the profit—if there were a profit.

The patent application numbers show those decades in which no Henry Ford left the dependable salary of the Detroit Edison, no Wright Brothers invested the profits from the bicycle shop to buy parts for a flying machine or to cover their living expenses at Kitty Hawk. No popular new invention or technology moved us toward the end of the depression, and that drought of innovation continued long after World War II.

---

363 John A. Ryan, *A Better Economic Order,* 24(n).

A modern review of income tax data provides more understanding. Dr. Christina Romer and her husband and fellow researcher Dr. David H. Romer studied the impact of tax changes on economic activity. They reviewed all of the tax changes passed since the end of World War II. They found that tax increases are highly contractionary, i.e., gross domestic product falls when a tax increase is implemented. Some of the key findings:

> Our estimates suggest that a tax increase of 1 percent of GDP reduces output over the next three years by nearly three percent. The effect is highly statistically significant…We find that output responds more closely to the implementation of a tax change than to the news of the change…The most striking finding of this exercise is that tax increases have a large negative effect on investment…The estimated impact of tax increases on consumption in these studies ranges from roughly no effect to a substantial negative effect…In short, tax increases appear to have a very large, sustained, and highly significant negative impact on output…The key results are that both components [investment and consumption] decline, and that the fall in investment is much greater than the fall in consumption…Since most of our exogenous tax changes are in fact reductions, the more intuitive way to express this result is that tax cuts have very large and persistent positive output effects.[364]

Dr. Romer was chair of President Obama's Council of Economic Advisors from January 2009 to August 2010. Her resignation was offered in the same month that her study appeared. This research report by a trusted advisor may have been the intellectual basis for President Obama's decision to break from his earlier pledge to raise tax rates for upper-income households. Instead, he signed the extension of the Bush tax cuts.

Collectively, these economic studies also explain the behavior of investors who favored low-risk, low-reward bonds during the Depression and for decades after. The negative impact that tax rate increases have on investment and consumption explains why total tax revenue sometimes decreases after a rate increase. The studies also suggest reasons for the drought in innovation that might otherwise have produced new technologies and jobs.

---

364 *The Macroeconomic Effects of Tax Changes: Estimates Based on a New Measure of Fiscal Shocks* by Christina D. Romer and David H. Romer, in *American Economic Review 100 (June 2010)* p. 763–801. Available at http://www.aeaweb.org/articles.php?doi=10.1257/aer.100.3.763.

Tax policies for corporations and high-income households also impact non-profit agencies and foundations, as we'll see in future chapters. The experiments with tax rates and the data on patent applications and changes in tax revenue are important to our decisions about innovation, promoting the general welfare, and strengthening the economy.

Chapter Thirteen
Tax Competition

Today, countries use corporate tax rates in their competition to retain existing investment and attract new investment, all of which creates employment for citizens. The competition is not just about low-skill jobs or even skilled manufacturing positions. It's about raising the standard of living for the people—better housing, health care, diet, and the opportunity, if not the guarantee, of financial security, and perhaps, for a few, extraordinary wealth. National governments, interested in promoting the general welfare of their citizens, compete to keep their tax rates applicable to business profits equal to, or lower than, those of other countries that are also interested in jobs and economic growth.

Taxes are a cost of doing business. Every dollar (or Euro, yen, or other currency) collected as corporate tax directly reduces after-tax profits. Those with money to invest seek the highest available after-tax return on their investment that is consistent with the amount of risk they are willing to accept. So tax rates become a consideration for determining where to domicile a corporation and where to locate major facilities, including manufacturing plants.

———

How much *do* major corporations pay in taxes? The following table shows the amount of income taxes paid on profits earned by several large corporations discussed in Part II. The table does not include other taxes paid such as the employer's share of Social Security and unemployment insurance tax (in the U.S.,

6.2 percent of compensation, up to a maximum amount for each employee) and employer's share of Medicare (in the U.S., 1.45 percent of all compensation). Companies involved in oil and gas exploration, mining, and other resource extraction pay royalties to the governments of the nations in which they operate; these figures are not included in the table.

Income Taxes Paid by Selected Large Corporations		
	Pre-Tax Profit 2006 $ Billions	Income Tax Paid or Reserved 2006 $ Billions	Income Tax Rate 2006 %
ExxonMobil	67.7	27.9	41.4
British Petroleum	32.4	11.3	35.4
Royal Dutch Shell	43.1	17.7	41.0
Aetna	2.457	.855	34.8
United Health	6.529	2.369	36.3
Cigna	1.585	.497	33.0
WellPoint	4.915	1.848	37.6
General Motors	5.032	2.833	56.3
Toyota	18.5	4.6	24.9
Honda	7.8	2.8	35.8
Pfizer	19.4	4.4	22.6
GlaxoSmithKline	14.4	4.3	29.5
Merck	7.864	2.4	29.9
Altria	16.3	4.3	26.3
Kellogg	1.470	.466	31.7
General Mills	1.664	.574	34.5
Anheuser-Busch	3.249	1.283	39.5
Heinz	1.124	.332	29.6
Walmart	18.9	6.3	33.6
Target	4.5	1.7	38.0
Sears Holdings	2.3	.907	39.3
JCPenney	1.8	.657	36.7

How much *should* these corporations pay? Business relies on government for a court system that can uphold contracts and resolve disputes, for the maintenance of highways, air traffic control, ports and navigable waterways, and for the protection of international trade routes and ships registered in the United States. Government represents the public's interest in efficient interstate commerce, the safety of consumer products, etc.

The effect of tax rates on business development and employment can be profound. Bermuda, an island nation with limited land mass and natural resources, has long relied on tourism as a major component of its economy. But Bermuda's growing population, and a desire to attract higher-paying jobs suitable to a well-educated workforce, led to its desire to greatly expand its role in the financial services industry. The Bermudian government specifically targeted insurance as a desirable growth industry. In just twenty years, Bermuda has grown from humble beginnings to a major hub that rivals the U.S., and the U.K., including the fabled Lloyd's of London. What is Bermuda's competitive advantage in attracting these companies? Its corporate income tax rate: zero! Investments are an important source of profits for most insurers, so keeping the investment income tax–free is a powerful incentive for insurers and reinsurers to locate in Bermuda. Very little land is required to warehouse money or investments, which are the real "inventory" of an insurance company.

Ireland, similarly, has grown its economy and employment market dramatically by maintaining low corporate taxes, especially compared to its European neighbors. While enjoying the trade benefits of membership in the European Union, Ireland has also reaped rewards from its own initiatives to attract a variety of industries, with especially low tax rates for manufacturers locating there.

The competition is ongoing. KPMG International, a Swiss cooperative of audit, tax, and advisory firms operating in many different countries, publishes an annual survey of corporate taxes, as well as indirect taxes (mainly value added taxes and goods and services taxes) around the world. In the 2007 survey of ninety-two countries, Japan and the United States have the highest corporate tax rates, at 40 percent and 39 percent respectively. The average corporate tax rate among all the countries in the survey is 26.9 percent, down from 38 percent in 1993. The trend is for even lower corporate taxes. China just approved legislation setting its corporate tax rate at 25 percent. The U.K., Germany, and Singapore are considering legislation to reduce their corporate tax rates—all driven by competition. Some countries introduce a tax on consumption, in the form of a sales tax or value-added tax, but the general growth of the economy through more investment and job growth provides a larger and more diverse total revenue to government while raising the standard of living.

The handwriting on the wall is easy to read. Today, many nations recognize the relationships between tax rates, profits, capital formation, job creation, and standards of living for all citizens, as President Kennedy so clearly described them. Countries are competing to keep existing jobs and attract new ones for their citizens by lowering their corporate tax rates. For the U.S., having the second highest corporate income tax rate in the world is a competitive disadvantage.

This affects investment decisions made not only by Americans, but also by foreign companies and investors deciding where to locate their facilities and thus the jobs associated with them.

Earlier, we discussed profits as the reward for risk of investment and ROE as the way to evaluate profits in relationship to the equity that was risked to produce them. With that in mind, let's turn to the quadrennial calls for an excess profits tax, usually raised by politicians who point to the current villain. In the 1936 election, virtually any profitable corporation was a villain. In the 2004 presidential election, pharmaceutical companies were the villains; in 2008, oil companies were villains. We do want to be fair in our tax system, and "excess" or "obscene" profits are not defined in any textbook on accounting, finance, or economics. So let's lay out some numbers to examine the profits in relation to the risk that was involved in earning them.

The Search for Excess or Obscene Profits Ranked by Five-Year Average ROE		
Corporation	ROE 2006	Five-Year Average ROE 2002-2006
Anheuser-Busch	49.8	64
GlaxoSmithKline	55.3	58.8
Kellogg	48.5	48
HJ Heinz	43.0	40
Merck	31.4	35
Cigna	31.4	35
Altria	30.3	33.7
ExxonMobil	35.1	24.7
Walmart	22.0	22.6
United Health	21.5	22.5
Pfizer	21.0	22.5
Royal Dutch Shell	24.1	20.8
General Mills	18.9	20
British Petroleum	24.4	19.2
Target Stores	17.8	18.9
Costco	12.1	17.2
Tiffany	14.1	15.4
Honda	13.2	14.8
Toyota	17	13.9
J C Penney	26.4	12.9
Aetna	17.5	12.7
WellPoint	12.5	9.8

Ranking the companies that have been discussed before, showing highest to lowest ROE based on five-year average, brings some perspective to the discussion. Companies that did not earn any ROE cumulatively over the five years 2002–2006 (General Motors and Ford) have been omitted, as have those with less than five years of history (Sears Holdings and the alternative energy companies). This is, of course, a limited universe. There are lots of corporations.

We need to decide whether "excess" profit is a valid concept for our tax system. If ExxonMobil is guilty of excess profits, based on some apparently secret definition, then all corporations with an ROE higher than ExxonMobil's are also earning excess profits and should be so taxed. If all big oil companies are guilty of earning excess profits, then in our effort to be fair we must consider the profits of General Mills also excessive, since that company's ROE is higher than the ROE of British Petroleum.

By a special tax on the profits of high-ROE corporations, of course, we would, by definition, tax the companies that are the best performers in their own industries. So we remove some of the incentive to invest in our most efficient cereal company, and perhaps other companies, depending on how low we set the threshold for this special tax. Applied fairly, across all industries, we reduce the incentives for the most efficient performers in pharmaceuticals, health insurance, food, oil, and, of course, beer. Handicapping the most efficient player in an industry does nothing to help the competitors (number two and three, and so forth) in these industries. They are already working as hard and as well as they can. But our excess-profits tax would penalize the best performers.

Let's think, for a moment, what that "excess profits tax" would do for job creation and for selection of where to locate manufacturing plants, refineries, corporate headquarters, research and development labs, and so forth. The excess-profits tax may be politically popular, but the economic consequences would be disastrous.

In less than a century, the world has progressed from an era in which nations set their tax rates at any level that was believed necessary and productive in their own self-interest, through a period of learning that excessive taxes can harm entire economies, into a new era in which competition among nations trying to attract jobs is a key factor affecting tax policy.

Where do the after-tax profits go? We'll follow the money.

IV

INVESTORS

Chapter Fourteen

"Show Me the Money"

All other things being equal, people seek to maximize their return of calories, protein, or other specific categories by foraging in a way that yields the most return with the greatest certainty in the least time for the least effort. Simultaneously, they seek to minimize their risk of starving: moderate but reliable returns are preferable to a fluctuating lifestyle with a high time-averaged rate of return but a substantial likelihood of starving to death.[365]

There is nothing uniquely American, or uniquely modern, about people seeking the best possible return on investment and deferring consumption today to secure a better tomorrow. In his epic *Guns, Germs and Steel*, Jared Diamond discusses economic activity in mankind's earliest societies. The gradual development from hunting-gathering to food production (e.g., farming, ranching, herding) took place in numerous bands and tribes on various continents. Food production and hunting-gathering were alternative strategies competing with each other. Mixed economies that added certain crops or livestock to hunting-gathering also competed against both types of "pure" economies, as well as against mixed economies with higher or lower proportions of food production.

Diamond emphasizes the societal impact of this development. The movement to more-efficient food supplies produced benefits far beyond diet. Housing

---

365 Jared Diamond, *Guns, Germs, and Steel, The Fates of Human Societies*, 108.

and settlements became more permanent. Labor became more specialized, leading to improved tool-making and, eventually, to writing.

In modern times, does for-profit business and investment activity benefit the entire community? Who owns the big corporations? Who are the recipients of all those profits that seem to drive corporate behavior? Whose money is behind Wall Street? We need to follow the money to see how this ancient process of investment for highest return plays out in American society.

The variety of investment options expands as societies become more complex. Intercontinental trade gave rise to underwriters at Lloyd's Coffee House in London. The underwriters, on behalf of their partners (known as "names"), accepted the perils of the sea, including risks of shipwreck, piracy, fire, and mutiny, in exchange for a premium. The Lloyd's of London syndicates were partnerships, not corporations. Each partner "name" participated personally as an investor owning a fraction of the business, sharing the profits in good years. If the business borrowed money, the partners were guaranteeing repayment. If the business produced losses instead of profits, each partner was responsible to repay his share of the business debt from his own pocket. Names found the premiums attractive, but the risk was considerable. Each new name was solemnly advised that the responsibility for losses was not limited to the amount of premium collected or to the amount that a member deposited as security. They accepted "unlimited personal liability," pledging their entire personal fortune to the payment of claims, down to "the last button on your shirt." Over the years, some made profits. Others lost their shirts. That same "partnership" model was often used in Europe and in the United States for banks and other businesses. The partners usually knew each other personally, trusted each other, and were active in the management of the business.

By 1900, America's economy included industrial corporations with multi-million dollar investments in plants and equipment. Most of these were "privately held," meaning that the shares of stock were owned by one or a few individuals, and those shares by mutual agreement could not be sold to anyone except another current shareholder. Carnegie Company, Pittsburgh Reduction Company (now known as Alcoa) and Sears, Roebuck and Co. were privately held corporations. All the profits accrued to the benefit of those shareholders, either through dividends or by increased value of the shares. If the business lost money, these same investors earned no reward.

But shareholders of a corporation had no personal liability for the corporation's business losses or bad debts. Creditors to whom the corporation owed money, such as suppliers of raw materials, could take legal action to place the corporation into bankruptcy and thereby force the sale of corporate assets (e.g., factories, vehicles, machinery, inventory, etc.) to satisfy the debts. The shares of stock were then worthless. But the shareholder's property, such as his house, personal bank account, or other investments, could not be seized to satisfy corporate debts. That "corporate veil" separating a business from the investor is a key difference between businesses organized as partnerships and those that are incorporated. The corporate veil allows many people to participate in the ownership of large corporations who would not take the risk of business ownership if it exposed them to the unlimited personal liability of a partnership structure. A corporate shareholder loses the value of his shares if the corporation goes bankrupt, but that is the limit of his loss. The corporation's creditors cannot access a shareholder's other assets. This is a foundation concept of the modern system of capital.[366]

Several situations sometimes induced owners of private shares to convert some or all of their holdings to public shares traded on stock exchanges, available to any purchaser. Building ever-larger plants with ever-more-expensive manufacturing equipment required access to more and more capital for investment. The construction and start-up of a new plant might take a year or more before any product could be sold. The business owners might want to buy another business, perhaps a competitor or supplier, but need money to accomplish the transaction.

Banks were at times unable or unwilling to lend enough money. Banks or other lenders want to be sure there is a substantial amount of owners' "skin in the game"—equity—to keep the owners committed to the success of the business. Lenders also might want a short repayment schedule or insist on covenants that constrain the owners' discretion in running the business.[367]

---

366 Since the mid-twentieth century, a hybrid form of business organization known as a limited liability corporation (LLC) has been recognized, which provides the business owners with a corporate veil shielding their personal assets, while allowing the profits to be distributed to the owners and taxed as partnership income. Professional advice should be obtained when selecting the appropriate "style" of ownership for any business.

367 Covenants are binding agreements set forth in the loan document in which the lender and borrower agree to specific conditions under which the loan is granted and which will be maintained until the loan is repaid. Typical covenants require maintaining a certain minimum cash reserve or keeping

Corporations needed large amounts of cash—long term, patient cash—without a requirement to repay principal or interest and without restrictive covenants. In exchange for their cash paid into the corporation, shareholders received a right to share proportionately in the eventual profits of the corporation. Each share of stock also entitled the holder to one vote in elections of the board of directors and on certain other matters such as mergers.[368] If the business succeeded and earned a profit, the new "equity" owners (shareholders) would be rewarded with dividends and potentially higher share price. If a shareholder later found a better investment, or needed cash for some other purpose, the shares could be sold on the "public" exchange, at whatever price a buyer would pay. That price might be higher or lower than the original share price, producing a gain or loss for the shareholder.

General prosperity in the last few years of the nineteenth century produced growing number of households with discretionary money—cash not needed for the basic necessities, which could be either spent on extras or invested. Some chose real estate as their investment. Others chose to invest in the growing industrial corporations. The needs of corporations for new capital met the desire of savers willing to risk some of their savings for the opportunity to share in the growth.

Lincoln Steffens was one of these investors. Steffens was a reporter who covered the Wall Street beat during the severe recession of 1893–1896. His wife was a published novelist. They were already financially comfortable when Steffens unexpectedly received an inheritance of $12,000 from one of his former university roommates. Half of this sum he invested in Wall Street, and the gains, he reports, left him independently wealthy.[369] He continued working as a reporter. He wrote for *McClure's* as one of the leading muckrakers outing crooked officials in city and state governments in the early years of the new century.

In 1901, the largest corporation in the world was established when J. P. Morgan led a group of investors to form United States Steel. Two years later,

---

debt below a certain ratio to equity. Violation of the covenant may allow the lender to demand immediate repayment of the entire loan or an immediate increase in the interest rate, etc.

368 Most modern corporations follow the "one share, one vote" formula, but there are exceptions, such as Ford Motor Company and The New York Times Company. In each of these corporations, two separate classes of common stock are entitled to share in financial results, but only one class conveys voting rights.

369 *The Autobiography of Lincoln Steffens,* 310.

a share purchase plan was established for company employees. Neither large corporations nor publicly traded shares were new, but the launching of United States Steel seemed to mark the opening of a new century of innovation in the ownership of major corporations.[370] In 1906, Sears, Roebuck and Company sold shares to the public to raise capital for expansion. Throughout the century, corporations "going public" raised new capital, creating new investment opportunities while raising funds to expand operations and create new jobs.

Small corporations also needed shareholders. A few months before the new century, a group of investors in Detroit pooled their savings to entice an amateur race-car enthusiast to leave his supervisory position at Edison Illuminating Company. They offered him a salary of $1,800 per year plus a 10 percent ownership share in the new company. That chance to share in the company profits and be an owner, not just a manager on a salary, trumped the utility's offer of promotion to general superintendent at a salary of $1,900 per year. Thus Henry Ford left the security of his utility career to become technical superintendent of the newly established Detroit Automobile Company, responsible for producing a line of delivery vans powered by gasoline engines.[371] He had been tinkering with automobiles as a hobby for several years. This was a chance to work at his passion. This was an opportunity, but not a guarantee, of an enhanced income and possible wealth.

Detroit Automobile Company failed in less than a year. Henry's stock was worthless, along with all the other shares. At least he had collected his salary. The investors who had paid cash for their shares lost their money—almost $90,000—when the company closed its doors. By 1903, Ford's second company, a partnership with Alex Malcomson, was quickly running out of cash. Borrowing was not an option. No bank would lend to such a speculative business. There were hundreds of start-up ventures in this new industry, but they seemed to cater to the founder's enthusiasm for the new technology, with little plan for developing a business that could pay back the loan. Henry Ford's business failure was typical.

But Henry and his partner in the second failing business, Alex Malcomson, convinced eleven other individuals to take a risk. With Henry Ford's prior business failures, and the questions about the viability of any automobile business,

---

370 The first sale of a corporation's stock to the public on a stock exchange is today referred to as an initial public offering, or IPO.
371 Douglas Brinkley, *Wheels for the World*, 32.

these investors were not interested in making loans at a fixed rate of interest. These investors wanted control. They would put their own savings or services at risk as shareholders in exchange for a share of future profits and direct control over the business. The partnership between Ford and Malcomson was dissolved and they joined the eleven other shareholders to form a new entity, Ford Motor Company.

The automobile and Ford Motor Company were to bring about major advances in American society, but none of that was certain in 1903. The technology was new, the customer base small, and competitors were plentiful. Henry Ford and his fellow shareholders became wealthy men—and one wealthy woman. But without their willingness to risk their savings in pursuit of profit, the automobile might have remained a rich man's toy rather than a transformative technology that spawned new jobs, new incomes, and new wealth.

———

Not all investors have the same goals. Investors primarily seeking a reliable flow of cash income often invest by lending money to a corporation. Investors do this by buying bonds, notes, or commercial paper.[372] Corporations that issue these "debt instruments" are pledging a series of interest payments at prescribed times and the return of principal at the end of the loan period (the maturity date). If the corporation encounters financial difficulty, debt holders enjoy a higher priority of payment. Interest and principal payments on debt instruments are due even if the company has to suspend its dividend payments to stockholders. Also, debt holders have a higher call upon the assets of the firm if it becomes insolvent (not enough cash to meet current payment obligations) or bankrupt (the shortage of cash and other assets is so great that debt holders force the company to liquidate, or sell off, its properties to repay the debt holders). In a bankruptcy, debt holders may recover some or all of the interest and principal owed to them even if shareholders receive nothing, i.e., the stock price drops to

---

372 The principal difference between bonds, notes, and commercial paper is the length of the loan period. Corporate bonds often have maturity dates ten, twenty, or more years from issue date, while notes are usually issued for a period of thirty days but less than one year. Commercial paper may be for durations as short as one week. To compensate for the greater risk associated with longer duration, a corporation's bonds on a certain issue date will offer higher interest rate than notes issued the same day, and notes will offer rates higher than commercial paper.

zero and becomes worthless. However, debt investors do not share in the growth of profits, and over long periods of time, inflation reduces the purchasing power of dollars received in future years. The amount of interest payment is fixed when the instrument is first issued and does not change.

Retirement sometimes leads to a shift in investment preferences from stocks to bonds, as it did for Andrew Carnegie. In 1901, he was sixty-five years old and ready to retire. Steel sales and profits had been growing for the past four years, but Carnegie knew the cyclical nature of business. Selling his business in good times would be far more lucrative than selling later if a recession occurred and profits fell, reducing the value of the company. At the same time, J. P. Morgan was acquiring companies in the steel business and aimed to put together a large entity with its own iron ore mines, blast furnaces, and a wide range of steel products. Morgan already had a group of interested investors who would partic-ipate in the venture. If Carnegie Company could be purchased, it would be the perfect core holding in the new entity, United States Steel Corporation. Morgan sent an emissary to ask Carnegie to set a price. All thirty-two of Carnegie's fel-low shareholders had to agree since all their shares were subject to the same agreement not to sell to an outsider except by mutual agreement. All agreed, and the deal was done.

Carnegie and his fellow shareholders sold Carnegie Steel, with its subsidiary businesses, for $400 million. The price represented a modest multiple of the $40 million profit the company had earned in 1900, especially since profits had grown at an average annual rate of 133 percent for the previous five years.[373]

Carnegie wanted a complete break from his business interests. He wanted no board seat or worries about the performance of the new company. He was also not interested in stock that would be traded on the public market, with the price changing with the mood swings of hundreds or even thousands of inves-tors. He wanted a low-risk investment providing reliable income to support his family, extensive travel, and philanthropic activities. So he insisted that payment for his shares of Carnegie Company be in the form of fifty-year, first-mortgage bonds, paying 5 percent annual interest. If the new corporation defaulted on the interest payments, Carnegie could foreclose on all the steel plants and other real estate of the new company. The bonds contained a gold clause, allowing Carn-egie to demand his payments in gold if he became concerned about declining value of the U.S. dollar.

---

373 Charles R. Morris, *Tycoons*, 321–330.

Andrew Carnegie and his fellow shareholders sold to Morgan, and in April 1901, United States Steel was born. Morgan's investors had invested a total capitalization of $1.4 billion—the first corporation to exceed one billion in capitalization. The common shares were traded on the New York Stock Exchange, available to the general public. Carnegie retired and collected the interest payments from his bonds.

––––––

A third major investment vehicle is government instruments— but these are debt only; government entities do not offer equity. Federal, state, and local governments and some quasi-government entities such as housing authorities, school districts, and bridge and turnpike authorities issue debt instruments in the form of bonds, notes, and bills. These are sought by investors seeking a steady, reliable cash flow. In fact, debt obligations of the United States government are considered the most reliable available. With this high level of safety (very low risk), the interest rate offered (the reward) is lower than for other investments. Traditionally, debt issued by state and local governments has been considered relatively safe, though there have been defaults (missed or delayed payments). Many investors allocate at least a small portion of their savings to government debt because of the reliability of the payments.

Investors also have the option to keep cash on deposit at a bank. Cash savings are the starting point for any new investment program and represent the basic building block and emergency reserve in established programs. Since the Depression, money in bank savings accounts or certificates of deposit has been insured, up to a specified limit, by agencies of the federal government. The risk to these cash holdings is loss of purchasing power through inflation, since the interest rate paid on savings is usually lower than the rate of inflation. That risk is subtle, almost unnoticed in years of low inflation, but can be substantial over years or decades. Periods of high inflation can produce disastrous loss of purchasing power for those relying mainly on cash or debt instruments, as we'll see in later chapters. Some invest in real estate, fine art, gold or other precious metals, and a host of other opportunities, each with their own characteristics. But those are beyond the scope of this book.

––––––

The market crash of October 1929 and the Great Depression had a direct effect on the relatively few investors who owned publicly traded stocks and bonds at the time. As fear spread during the 1930s, thousands of individuals decided independently, each in their own time, to move their money to the relative safety of U.S. Treasury bonds, rather than buying stocks or putting money into their own businesses.

Institutional investors, who had legal and ethical obligations to properly invest funds on behalf of others, were also fleeing the stock market. Yale University's Treasurer Laurence Tighe dramatically reduced the share of equities in Yale's portfolio, observing that higher taxes were likely to expropriate any corporate profits that shareholders might otherwise get even if an economic recovery were to take place. In these circumstances, bonds would be a better investment than stocks. His decision to invest two dollars in fixed-income securities, generally bonds, for every one dollar in equities was a huge departure from traditional asset allocation patterns, but it proved to be the proper action for preserving the university's funds. Yale's preference for bonds over stocks lasted well into the 1960s.[374]

Investors shifted so much money into U.S. Treasury bonds after the 1932 tax increase that the interest rate fell from 4.26 percent to 3.22 percent one year later, and it continued to fall until November 1941, when bond rates bottomed at 1.85 percent.[375] Rates for U.S. Treasury bonds have been set at auction since 1930. This competitive bidding process assures that the Treasury is paying the lowest possible rate of interest on the money borrowed. The flight of capital from high-risk, low-reward (in view of the weak economy and higher taxes) business investment into low-risk government bonds with highly reliable interest payments was a widespread stewardship decision under the circumstances.

The drop in bond interest rates from 1932 to 1941 directly reflected the widespread investor preference for safety. Bond rates dropped even as the national debt tripled from $16.8 billion in June 1930 to $49 billion in June 1941 (six months before the Pearl Harbor attack).[376] As investment in business remained low, unemployment remained high.

---

374 Harvard Business School, Case 9-807-073, "Yale University Investment Office: August, 2006," by Josh Lerner.
375 *Banking and Monetary Statistics, 1914-1941* by the Board of Governors of the Federal Reserve System. Section 12, Table No. 128.
376 Historical Debt Outstanding, United States Treasury, available at <u>www.treasurydirect.gov</u>.

———

Today, a total of 2.5 million individual shareholders own about 40 percent of ExxonMobil. The remaining 60 percent of shares are owned by institutional investors, i.e., mutual funds, pension funds, university endowments, charitable foundations, etc. Combined, these individual and institutional shareholders placed at risk in ExxonMobil's business a total of $111 billion as of December 31, 2005. They expect the corporation to continue to grow profitably and thus reward investors with dividends and higher share prices. The dividends and higher stock prices are key to achieving the long-term goals of these investors.

Buying a share of stock is the acceptance of the risk of failure and loss of the invested funds, in exchange for the opportunity for reward through increased stock price if the business grows in value. Stockholders literally own a share of the corporation, and they have the right to vote for the members of the board of directors. Stockholders also vote on certain major activities of the corporation, such as mergers.

Who are the stockholders? In the U.S., 45 percent of households participate in this ownership of corporate stocks.[377] That percentage, by definition, includes a large number of middle class households. These "equity" investments are one method of growing funds that are not needed for today's expenses, but will eventually be needed for college tuition, retirement, or similar purposes. Is it greed that motivates their participation in the ownership of big businesses, or thoughtful stewardship? Some people buy stocks at a brokerage firm or bank (in which case they are actually buying from another stockholder who wants to sell) or from the corporation issuing the stock. Others buy mutual funds, thereby letting a professional manager choose which stocks to buy or sell. Employees at many firms can acquire stock in the corporation through an employee stock ownership plan (ESOP). Many employers offer 401(k) plans, and some match employee contributions, in effect giving the employee a raise for participating in the plan. Any taxpayer can open an individual retirement account (IRA), which offers tax-deferral features that help the account grow more quickly.

Many others at various economic levels benefit indirectly, for example, if their union or pension funds invest in the stock market. Whether they own the stock directly or indirectly, people buy stocks or invest in mutual funds that buy

---

377 *Equity Ownership in America, 2008.* Investment Company Institute and Securities Industry and Financial Markets Association.

stocks for them to make their money grow. That is the only rationale for buying stock in a corporation.

No single class of investments is inherently better or worse than the others. Each has its own risk/reward characteristics. There are risks and rewards involved in investing in either stocks or bonds. There is risk in relying too heavily on cash (inflation) and a reward in just the right amount of cash (sleeping at night). Investors with different needs and objectives will allocate their funds among these classes, and perhaps others, in an effort to achieve a risk/reward balance that is most consistent with their goals. The proportion of equity, debt, and cash may be shifted as an investor's needs, or risk appetite, change over time.

————

One of the largest "institutional" owners of shares of U.S. corporations is the trust fund of the California Public Employees Retirement Systems (CalPERS). It is the largest public pension fund in the U.S. and third largest in the world. The trust funds are invested to provide future benefits to municipal employees including police officers, firefighters, teachers, and administrators. These 1.4 million working people and retirees are relying on CalPERS trust funds to pay retirement benefits owed them under their contracts. Money deducted from the workers' paychecks, along with funds paid in by the state, county, and municipal government agencies that employ them, are invested by CalPERS. The trust funds totaled $166 billion in June 2004, and a large percentage of the total is invested in corporate stocks (equities). If the trust fund's investment results are inadequate, the burden of meeting these pension obligations would legally fall to California taxpayers, most of whom are businesses or working people already dealing with significant burdens. Clearly, millions of working Californians rely on the ability of CalPERS to obtain excellent financial results from the invested funds. All of these employees, retirees, and citizens of California directly benefit from the investments in profitable corporations.

CalPERS is recognized as a standard-bearer in the corporate governance movement and has published a paper to explain its investment objectives and fiduciary duties. A central thesis is that stockholders must act like owners and take an active interest in the performance of their stock portfolio. CalPERS acknowledges, among other duties as a stockholder investing funds for the benefit of others, legal duties of loyalty and care:

The duty of loyalty requires the Board and other CalPERS fiduciaries to act solely in the interest of members and beneficiaries. Under the duty of care, the Board and other CalPERS fiduciaries must manage Fund assets as a "prudent investor." Essentially, this requires the exercise of care, skill, and diligence that a prudent person, familiar with the matters, would exercise under similar circumstances in managing a pension fund of like size. More explicitly, CalPERS fiduciaries must seek to maximize investment returns, while minimizing risk of loss. The duty of care safeguards the payment objectives of the Fund, to ensure that the defined benefits can be paid when due at the time of retirement or death. The Board also has a duty to maximize the value of its investments, in order to avoid increases in state and local government taxes that might otherwise be needed to pay the employer's share of costs.[378]

CalPERS has also established its Global Principles of Accountable Corporate Governance, and the investment staff is directed to vote for or against proxy questions in accordance with these principles. CalPERS Emerging Equity Market Principles require the staff and external investment managers to consider such issues as civil liberties, democratic accountability, an independent judiciary, free trade unions and collective bargaining, a legal framework that honors contracts and clearly delineates ownership, freedom of the press, government monetary and fiscal policies and transparency, accounting standards, and environmental sustainability when investing in less-developed countries.[379] But the objective of the entire investment program—the duty of the board and other fiduciaries—is to maximize investment return while minimizing risk. That is vital. Generating the funds for reliable retirement benefits and avoiding increased tax burdens for the citizenry would seem to be aspects of prudent stewardship.

Harvard Management Company, a wholly owned subsidiary of Harvard University, was established in 1974 to manage the university's endowment, pension assets, working capital, and deferred-giving accounts. The company is governed by a board of directors appointed by the president and fellows of the university. At year-end 2005, Harvard's endowment totaled $25.5 billion. The endowment exists for the benefit of Harvard University, and each year approximately 5 percent of the endowment fund is used to supplement the university's budget.

---

378 *Statement of Investment Policy for Global Proxy Voting, April 21, 2008.* Copyright ©2008 by CalPERS.
379 *Statement of Investment Policy for Emerging Equity Market Principles, November 13, 2007.* Copyright © 2007 by CalPERS.

Part of this amount is spent to provide tuition assistance to graduate and under-graduate students. Harvard recently adopted a policy that assures that parents in families with income less than $60,000 per year will no longer be expected to contribute to the cost of their children attending Harvard. Also, Harvard will reduce the contributions of families with incomes between $60,000 and $80,000. Two-thirds of Harvard's students receive financial aid, and the average grant award for the 2006–07 year was $33,000, or 70 percent of the cost of at-tendance. Harvard's purpose is to ensure that economic hardship is not a barrier to well-qualified students. Certainly the university benefits from being able to attract the very brightest students, which is part of maintaining its reputation for academic excellence. But society benefits also from the assurance that the finest academic opportunities are not reserved for the wealthy and in fact are open to all on the basis of academic merit.

Harvard Management Company came under scrutiny in recent years be-cause of the very large incentive awards to its president and other financial managers. The investment results were substantially better than benchmarks established earlier by the board of directors, while staying within portfolio risk parameters also set by the board. The endowment's investment gains exceed-ed (in some years substantially) the amount moved into the university's annual spending budget, so the total value of the endowment continued to grow. The president and fellows of Harvard University were willing to reward those whose investment skill brought about that growth.

Harvard's multibillion-dollar endowment fund is divided among a variety of investments to provide the optimal balance between risk and reward. This mix of investments is established by the company board of directors and is known as the Policy Portfolio. The Policy Portfolio sets forth the long-term asset mix that is most likely to meet the university's long-term return goals with the ap-propriate level of risk. The portfolio includes real estate, foreign and domestic bonds, investments in emerging markets (including developing countries), and commodities (timber, precious and nonprecious metals, etc.), but the largest component is equities (stocks of corporations), with 15 percent of the portfolio typically in domestic (U.S.) corporations and 10 percent in foreign corpora-tions. The significant concentration of investment dollars into stocks demon-strates the company directors' interest in companies that grow their profits and thereby raise their share price. Every dollar of improved stock price improves Harvard's ability to carry out its mission. The inclusion of so many other asset classes, besides stocks, is the board's acknowledgement that there is risk in any equity investment, however skillful or diversified, and other investments are appropriate to hedge, or offset, this risk. When stocks in general fall in value (recessions or even depressions), other asset classes may still provide some growth and reduce the loss to the overall portfolio. But the financial performances of corporations and the growing value of stocks inescapably play a major role in funding Harvard's mission in coming years.

The Yale University endowment, totaling $22.5 billion in June 2007, is diversified into asset classes similar to Harvard's. The Yale endowment's 2007 Annual Report provides several insights into the objectives and methods of the investment portfolio:

> The need to provide resources for current operations as well as preserve purchasing power of assets dictates investing for high returns, causing the endowment to be biased toward equity. In addition, the University's vulnerability to inflation further directs the Endowment away from fixed income and toward equity instruments. Hence, 96 percent of the Endowment is targeted for investment in assets expected to produce equity-like returns, through holdings of domestic and international securities, real assets, and private equity.

Yale quantifies, for its purposes, the expected real return of equities at 6 percent, meaning that the value of the equity portfolio is expected to grow, on average, 6 percent annually, in addition to the rate of inflation. So if inflation is running at 3 percent, Yale targets its equity portfolio to produce a 9 percent return, thus achieving 6 percent *real* return. Interestingly, Yale also quantifies the risks it sees as inherent with these various investments. Risk to the equity portfolio value is quantified as a standard deviation of 20 percent. So in any year, while seeking the average targeted real return of 6 percent, Yale recognizes the risk that its stock portfolio value could fall by 20 percent. Individual stocks can rise or fall much more sharply. For bonds, Yale sees a real return of 2 percent with risk of 10 percent. (Yes, bonds can lose value, especially when interest rates are rising.) Yale's well-respected approach to investing, balancing risk and reward, nonetheless relies on corporate stock investments—equities—for the largest portion of growth in its endowment. In fiscal year 2007 (July 1, 2006, to June 30, 2007), the endowment provided $684 million, or 33 percent, of the university's $2.1 billion current revenue—a vital contribution to the university's operations. Lower return on investment would translate directly to higher tuition, or constrained spending on key university initiatives, including instructor salaries, tuition assistance, maintenance of buildings and grounds, etc.

Yale University Endowment

Balancing Risk and Reward

Asset Class	Expected Real Rate of Return (Average per Year over Many Years)	Risk (Per Year, based on One Standard Deviation)	Allocation to Class As of June 30, 2007
Domestic Equity	6%	20.0%	11%
Fixed Income	2%	10.0%	4%
Foreign Equity	Emerging countries 8% Developed countries 6%	25% 20%	14.1%
Private Equity	11.2%	27.7%	18.7%
Real Assets (Real estate, Oil & gas, Timberland)	6%	13.6%	27.1%
Absolute Return	6%	10.0%	23%
Cash			1.9%
Total Endowment Portfolio	6.3%	12.2%	100%

Endowments, and their successful investment, are increasingly vital to colleges and universities of all sizes. In June 2006, the ten largest university endowments in America totaled $118 billion. Each fund was worth $5 billion or more. These largest funds rely heavily, as does Harvard's, on equity investment gains. Perhaps more significantly, smaller universities, with endowments of $500 million or less, tend to rely even more heavily on stock prices. These smaller colleges tend to invest approximately 60 percent of their endowment funds in equities. More than seven hundred colleges and universities in the U.S. reported having endowments in 2006.[380] You might want to check the status of your own alma mater's endowment, its investment goals, and how much it contributes to your institution. In recent years, private high schools and schools for the disabled are trying to build endowment funds to better secure their ability to fund their own mission in the future. Corporate financial performance, shared among the stockholders, will be vital to many educational institutions in coming years.

Individual shareholders have the same goals as endowments and foundations—to put funds that are not needed now but will be needed later into

---

380 National Association of College and University Business Officers Endowment Study, 2006.

investments that will grow in value, particularly as a hedge against inflation. A man or woman who retires today at age sixty-five has, on average, almost twenty years of life expectancy ahead. For some retirees, these will be years of growing medical expenses and Medicare premiums that grow faster than Social Security payments. College tuitions are also growing faster than the Consumer Price Index, so parents saving for their children's college tuition also need investments that grow faster than the overall rate of inflation. Stocks (equities) are the most likely path to fulfilling these important objectives.

So the emphasis on "bottom line" performance is driven by shareholders—university endowments, pension funds, foundations—that provide grants to thousands of nonprofit organizations, as well as individual investors who need to grow their savings for future needs. All of them are counting on rising corporate profits, and thus rising share prices, to ensure their future ability to provide social benefits. Whether these owners pick their own stocks, buy mutual funds, or employ money managers, their goal is clear: grow the value of the investment portfolio faster than the rate of inflation. Society depends on a growing and profitable corporate sector.

———

Is there really that much linkage between corporate profits and stock value? Why are stockholders so intense about profits? Let's see what the experts have to say.

Benjamin Graham and David Dodd's *Security Analysis*, written in 1934 and now in its fifth edition, is widely considered to be the investment bible. Several passages discuss the relationship between earnings (profits) and stock price:

> The long-term value investor recognizes that purchasing a stock accomplishes the acquisition of existing assets and liabilities, regardless of where they came from or when they were acquired. Since the past cannot be changed, it is not an issue in the purchase decision. What is in issue in the purchase decision is the future earnings that the investor will obtain by buying the stock. It is the ability of the existing assets and liabilities to create future earnings that determine the value of the equity position.

The same Benjamin Graham in 1937 wrote *The Interpretation of Financial Statements*, a smaller and less technically complex book that is still in print today. Some interesting passages:

Broadly speaking, the price of common stocks is governed by the prospective earnings. These prospective earnings are, of course, a matter of estimate or foresight; and the action of the stock market is controlled by the indicated trend.

The price of common stocks will depend, therefore, not so much on past or current earnings in themselves as upon what the buying public thinks the earnings will be.

In the ordinary case the price of a common stock is the resultant of the many estimates of what the earnings are going to be in the next six months, in the next year, or even further into the future."

Do practicing investment managers really believe this, or is this just academic theory? Well, Peter Lynch led the Magellan Fund at Fidelity Investments from 1977 to 1990 and became known as a champion stock picker. He earned enough money that he retired from fund management at age forty-six. He wrote the fascinating and easy to read book *One Up on Wall Street* in 1989. On the importance of earnings, and earnings growth, to rising stock price, he said, "It always comes down to earnings and assets. Especially earnings." During Peter's tenure, Magellan averaged a staggering 29.2 percent annualized return. It seems he knows something about what makes stock prices rise.

––––––

Do CEOs of big corporations act on this, or do they have some other agenda for increasing the stock price? One of the most influential independent advisors to CEOs and corporate directors over the past twenty years has been Ram Charan. He is a Senior Fellow at University of Pennsylvania's Wharton School and guest lecturer at quite a few executive development seminars. In his seminars and in his consultations with corporate boards, Charan has a truly unique ability to get right to the heart of an issue, crystallize the factors that will have the most impact on achieving success, and lead the discussion to a discrete set of action steps. For the benefit of us non-CEOs, Ram has written several books. In *What the CEO Wants You to Know*, he writes:

Shareholders (and employees who receive stock options as part of their compensation) expect a CEO to create wealth for them. The best CEOs understand that money-making and wealth creation are linked through what is known as the *price earnings multiple*—also called the *P-E multiple,* or *P-E ratio*. The P is the price of an individual share of stock. The E is earnings per share—how much profit the company made for each share of stock.

So the mission that all businesses have in common might be summarized as growing stockholder value by increasing profits. As we've seen earlier, this is done by providing a product or service that customers in a competitive market-place find worthwhile at the offered price. Stockholders have put their money at risk in exchange for a share in the profits of the firm. They expect the board of directors and management to conduct the business in a way that will grow profits and thus improve share price.

Why do some corporations seem indifferent to important social issues? Don't the shareholder-owners have something to say about that?

We have already seen the position taken by CalPERS, a major holder of corporate shares and a leader in the promotion of good corporate governance, regarding profits and corporate involvement in social causes.

Other investment managers take a slightly different approach to social is-sues. For example, TIAA-CREF manages more than $300 billion in assets, for workers mainly in the academic, health care, and cultural fields. TIAA-CREF explains that it will consider these issues in discussions with corporate directors and in voting the shares it manages. TIAA-CREF's Policy Statement on Corpo-rate Governance (Appendix A) states:

> TIAA-CREF's voting practices are guided by our mission and fiduciary duty to our participants. As indicated in this Policy Statement, we moni-tor portfolio companies' governance, social and environmental prac-tices to ensure that boards consider these factors in the context of their strategic deliberations.
>
> The following guidelines are intended to assist portfolio companies, participants and other interested parties in understanding how TIAA-CREF is likely to vote on governance, compensation, social and envi-ronmental issues.
>
> We establish voting policies with respect to both management pro-posals and shareholder resolutions. Our proxy voting decisions with respect to shareholder resolutions may be influenced by several ad-ditional factors: (i) whether the shareholder resolution process is the appropriate means of addressing the issue; (ii) whether the resolution

promotes good corporate governance and is related to economic performance and shareholder value; and (iii) whether the information and
actions recommended by the resolution are reasonable and practical. In
instances where we agree with the concerns raised by proponents but
do not believe that the policies or actions requested are appropriate,
TIAA-CREF will generally abstain on the resolution.[381]

———

Can a corporation take any role in promoting charitable works unrelated to
the business? What do the owners say about that?

Corporations donated an estimated $14.5 billion in 2008, or 5 percent of
total giving. The recession that started in December 2007 clearly had an impact;
total corporate giving in 2008 was 4.5 percent less than in 2007. The $14.5 bil-
lion still represents growth (ignoring inflation) over the $12.7 billion donated
in 2006. In that year, corporate giving was 4.3 percent of total estimated giving
in the U.S. Over the past forty years, corporate giving (including funds given
by corporate foundations) has averaged 1.1 percent of corporate profits. Some
corporate giving is not captured in the above figures, since gifts to foreign entities or others not registered with the IRS are not tax deductible.[382]

Some corporate charitable donations are beneficial beyond any doubt. Others raise questions. Does a major gift from a corporation to a university threat-
en to compromise the independence and academic freedom of the university?
Is medical research tainted if it is supported in large measure by donations or
grants from a corporation selling pharmaceuticals? In 2003, the Center for Science in the Public Interest (CSPI) questioned whether organizations receiving
funds from corporations could or would release credible research results, health
guidelines, and environmental recommendations. One implication of CSPI's
concern is a potential decrease in public trust in the work of nonprofits where
corporate funding is thought to compromise the organization's mission. Do
large grants from an oil company (or oil industry group) taint the acceptability
of research on global warming? Do large grants from a pharmaceutical company
(or industry-funded nonprofit group) taint research on food additives or drugs?

---

381 TIAA-CREF Policy Statement on Corporate Governance. Accessed at www.
tiaa-cref.org/ucm/groups/content/@ap_ucm_p_tcp/documents/document/
tiaa01007871.pdf on 9/24/2010.
382 "Giving USA, 2007" by the Giving USA Foundation, researched and written at The Center on Philanthropy at Indiana University.

Do large grants from teachers' unions taint research on best student/teacher ratios? The ethics of each case require careful consideration.

Notwithstanding the shareholder-driven priority of profits in corporate governance, corporations donate billions of dollars to nonprofit organizations. Some businesses donate directly to nonprofit organizations. This direct philanthropy is the norm for small businesses. Owners of small businesses write company checks to support everything from local Little League teams to homeless shelters to American Red Cross disaster relief funds.

Larger corporations often establish their own corporate foundations to channel their philanthropy. The corporation donates funds (which would otherwise be profits for the stockholders) to its foundation, which is a separate legal entity with separate trustees. The foundation donates to nonprofit organizations. This separation of the foundation from its founding corporation allows a more focused and consistent approach to giving, managed by a foundation staff dedicated to this specialized function. Many corporate foundations match, dollar for dollar, donations made by the corporation's employees, in effect letting the employees choose the charities that receive foundation gifts. Corporate foundations do not maintain investment funds. They pay out to nonprofits the donation received each year from their corporate sponsor.

Finally, the fundamental issue: is the donation of corporate cash or property to charitable activities outside of the company's business in the best interest of shareholders, or should these assets be retained in the equity account or dispensed as dividends to the shareholders? It is, after all, their money. The practice is widespread among corporations, usually amounting to one or two percent of profits, and is rarely questioned. Shareholders apparently accept the practice. Possibly, this corporate giving produces intangible value by enhancing the reputation of the corporation they own.

————

Do the after-tax profits that flow to investors as dividend payments or by stock buy-backs, or that are retained in the company's shareholder equity account, just make the investors wealthier, or at least more financially secure? What benefit does society get from business activity, beyond job creation and the taxes paid by corporations and investors? To fully understand the powerful role of corporate profits in society and social justice, we must follow the money further, past one more turn in the trail.

V

PHILANTHROPISTS

Chapter Fifteen

"To Promote the Well-being of Mankind"

Corporate executives (not just the CEOs) and others sometimes accumulate more wealth than they, or their families, will ever need. Anyone who has chaired a capital campaign or tried to raise large sums for charity will acknowledge the critical role that attracting one or more "leadership" gifts will play in attaining the goal. Time and again, a wealthy individual or couple writes that big check that helps not just financially but by strengthening the community's conviction that "We can do this."

In the U.S., individuals and households are the largest sources of giving to churches and nonprofit organizations. Combining the proverbial dollar in the collection basket, the pledge of support for a local walkathon, and the multimillion-dollar gifts to building funds, hospitals, and universities, creates a powerful force for good. In 2006, individuals contributed $223 billion (not including bequests), or 76 percent of total giving in the U.S.[383]

Every gift, of whatever size, is vital. Professional fundraisers hired by churches, colleges, hospitals, and museums recognize that large gifts from wealthy people are important to the success of the community efforts. Prominent

---

383 "Giving USA, 2007," researched and written at the Center on Philanthropy at Indiana University.

businesspeople, corporate executives, and successful professionals are ap-proached and asked to give generously, very early in the fundraising campaign, so that everyone in the community sees a campaign having achieved 20, 30, or 40 percent of its goal at an early date. The inspiration and encouragement from these gifts help to garner widespread community participation.

Successful fundraisers cultivate their relationships with upper-income in-dividuals, not just for the size of each potential donation but because nearly all households with incomes of $100,000 or more give to charity. These eleven mil-lion households (the top 10 percent of incomes) account for approximately 40 to 45 percent of total estimated individual contributions.[384]

Charity and nonprofit institutions have played a role in American society since its earliest days. In colonial times, care of those in need was conducted almost exclusively by faith-based groups. In New York City, probably the first such group was the Hebrew Mutual Benefit Society organized in the 1820s.[385] In Philadelphia, Mary Andrews died in 1761 and left a substantial legacy to Christ Church to endow a permanent fund for care of the needy. That endowment still exists today, after centuries of prudent management, and investment income from it still supports aid to the needy in Philadelphia. Almost all of these efforts were locally funded and managed and aimed at solving local problems.

As the American economy grew, larger fortunes funded larger-scale philan-thropies, often addressing problems neglected by government.

Francis Drexel was one of America's foremost bankers in the nineteenth century. His Philadelphia-based firm often partnered with that of Junius Mor-gan, father of J. P. Morgan. Francis had three daughters, and all three were still single and in their twenties when he wrote his will in March 1883. His wife had died two months earlier. Francis was wealthy, with a city home and a country estate and a prosperous business. He had spent an entire career building his fortune.

The banker's will was testament to his values. It specified that 10 percent of his estate, which totaled over $14 million, be donated immediately to twenty-nine charities, mainly hospitals, schools, and orphanages in Pennsylvania. The remaining 90 percent was placed in a trust. Each of his three daughters would receive one third of the trust's investment income during her lifetime. Any child of a daughter would receive a share of the income upon its mother's death. The

---

384 "Giving USA, 2007," using data released by the Internal Revenue Service.
385 *New York Times,* January 28, 1897.

trust principal, after providing income for the daughters during their lives, was to be disbursed among the same charities when his last daughter (or grandchild, if any) passed away.

To administer the trust, Francis Drexel named three reliable friends and the Pennsylvania Company for Insurance on Lives and Granting Annuities. The will gave these trustees sole discretion over investing the trust funds, the duty of disbursing the income to the daughters, and the task distributing the principal when the last income beneficiary passed away.

Consistent with his objectives for the use of his legacy, Drexel specified in his will that the trustees:

> Shall have the right to invest and reinvest the funds which may at any time come into their hands in first-class mortgage bonds of companies whose railroads are finished and earning interest on their entire bonded debt; also, in state, municipal, or corporation bonds, whether of a public or private character, and in such securities as are considered lawful and valid investments for Trustees in the State of Pennsylvania; but I wish them in all investments to look to the security of the investments rather then the rate of interest.[386]

Here was one of the country's most successful investment bankers, familiar with many businesses and with many types of investments, directing his trustees to prefer safety of principal and income over aggressive risk-taking and potential price appreciation or high yield so that his daughters could maintain the lifestyle to which they were accustomed long into the future.

The daughters had already grown to adulthood with all the comforts that wealth could afford: a city home, a country home, travel to Europe, solid education. They had also learned from their father the importance of careful management of one's income and an obligation to help those in need. Shortly after their father's death, the sisters had been donating to several organizations that worked among various Indian tribes. In 1887, just eleven years after Gen. Custer's defeat at Little Big Horn, the three sisters visited missions in North and South Dakota. The following year, another trip was made. The federal government had formally admitted a responsibility to see to the health and educational needs of the Indians who had been herded onto reservations, often far from their ancestral

---

386 Will of Francis A. Drexel, Archives of the Sisters of the Blessed Sacrament, Bensalem, PA.

homes. The Drexel sisters observed firsthand the results of political patronage and incompetence in the Bureau of Indian Affairs. But they were inspired by the missionary priests and nuns already bringing education and other living improvements, as well as Christian beliefs. Success was limited by the scarcity of funds. The Drexel sisters became heavy contributors to Indian missions in the western states.

The oldest daughter, Elizabeth, married in 1890, but she died as she gave birth to her first child, who also died. As provided in the will, Elizabeth's two surviving siblings, Louise and Katharine, then received her share of the income from the trust. Louise married and became a well-known patroness of many charities.

Katharine Drexel decided to dedicate her own life to the betterment of two neglected minority groups. In 1891, she founded the Sisters of the Blessed Sacrament for Indians and Colored People. The Sisters adopted vows of poverty for themselves and devoted their lifetime work to these missions. Spreading the Catholic faith was central to their mission. Improving the education and health care of Native Americans and blacks was every bit as important. Katharine gave up the big houses and the fancy clothes and took to the convent and the habit and veil of religious life. Her entire income went to the congregation of Sisters. They in turn used the funds to build their own mission buildings. Some were simple buildings for Mass on Sundays and school lessons during the week. Others were boarding schools accommodating up to one hundred students and teachers.

Southern University had been a high school and trade school for black students, until 1912 when the state legislature abandoned the New Orleans site and moved the institution to Baton Rouge. In 1915, the Sisters purchased the buildings at auction and established Xavier University. In 1916, a twelfth grade was added, and in 1917, a two-year "Normal" (teacher preparation) course was started. Over the next decade, an addition to the main building provided more classrooms, laboratories, and a library. In 1924, the Normal school added courses and developed into a college of liberal arts and sciences. In 1927, a College of Pharmacy was added. Student enrollment was so strong that in 1929 land was purchased for a new site for the university. The new campus opened in September 1932.[387]

The income from Mother Katharine's trust was more than enough to finance the work of her Sisters. In a typical year, 1924, her income was $312,000.[388] The

---

387 *Katharine Drexel—A Biography*, Sister Consuela Marie Duffy, S.B.S., 327.
388 Recapitulation, Account Ledger of the Estate of Francis A. Drexel (1955).

excess was used to assist other missionaries, or bishops of dioceses, to build schools and other facilities for work among native Americans and blacks. Mother Katharine and her Sisters brought far more than money to these ventures. Whenever funds were to be committed, the Sisters obtained a written agreement signed by the priest who was in charge of the mission, stating that the building would be used for the direct benefit of Indian or black people, depending on the particular project. Where a multiracial clientele was anticipated, as in an orphanage, the agreement specified that Indians and blacks would be admitted in the same manner as children of other races. If the building was in the future converted to some other use, the funds granted were to be immediately repaid to the Sisters. Each agreement was approved by the bishop of the local diocese or by the provincial of the religious order to further assure its enforceability.[389]

While her father was still alive, Katharine had accompanied him on business trips where he checked on railroads and other companies in which he invested. What she had learned about business she applied to her missionary work. She developed a network of attorneys who acted as her agents when property was being acquired to assure that it was bought at a competitive price. Architects developed prototype plans for buildings that could be used repeatedly with minor adaptations to local building materials and site conditions. Mother Katharine spent about six months of each year touring the facilities where work was being done and where new missions might be useful. In time, the work extended from Boston to Harlem in New York City to New Iberia, Louisiana, to Montgomery, Alabama, to Gary, Indiana, Houck, Arizona, Muskogee, "Indian Territory" (now Oklahoma), and dozens of other locations across the country. The congregation of Sisters grew to six hundred at its peak and is still active today. The founder died in 1955. Today she is known as Saint Katharine Drexel.

A generation after the Sisters entered the field, many school districts in the South still refused to build public schools or provide teachers for black children. Julius Rosenwald, president of Sears, Roebuck and Company, had already been a supporter of higher education for blacks and a trustee of Tuskegee Institute. He was drawn to Booker T. Washington's concept of community-based initiatives to provide elementary education for blacks in rural areas. In the early days of the

---

Archives of the Sisters of the Blessed Sacrament. The trust portfolio was apparently yielding about 4.5 percent interest annually on the principal of $14 million, with Katharine and her sister Louise Drexel Morrell each receiving one half of the income.

389 Agreements Binder, Mother Katharine Drexel Papers, Sisters of the Blessed Sacrament Archives.

effort, 1912–1917, Rosenwald donated $300 per school. The community supplied land and labor, and local officials were persuaded to contribute from the tax coffers.

In 1917, Rosenwald established the Rosenwald Fund, based in Chicago, to carry out his philanthropic work, and he donated $20 million to it.[390] Over the next twenty years, more than five thousand elementary schools were built for black children, with a total capacity of 663,615 students. Rosenwald contributed leadership as well as money. The total cost of the buildings was $28 million, of which 64 percent came from local tax funds, 4 percent from local white residents, 15 percent from the Rosenwald Fund, and 17 percent—an amazing $4.7 million—from black residents.[391]

———

With the new century, philanthropy took a great leap forward. Within the first decade, dollars flowed at unprecedented rates into new charitable foundations and institutions addressing the age-old problems of disease, poverty, ignorance, and prejudice. There was also a new interest in measuring the extent of poverty and studying its root causes.

Robert Hunter graduated from Indiana University in 1896 and moved to Chicago to work in a settlement house as a social worker. His 1904 book, *Poverty*, is one early attempt to bring metrics to the study of poverty. He declares the "extent of poverty in the United States absolutely unknown," but goes on to make some estimates.

He adopted from a contemporary in England a minimum standard of living for a family of five to maintain "physical efficiency"—the ability to go to work and earn a wage at unskilled labor:

A well-drained dwelling with several rooms, warm clothing, several changes of underclothing, pure water, a plentiful supply of cereal food, with a moderate allowance of meat and milk, and a little tea, etc., some education, and some recreation, and lastly, sufficient freedom for his wife from other work to enable her to perform properly her maternal and her household duties.

---

390 Edwin R. Embree, *Julius Rosenwald Fund, Review for the Two Year Period, 1931-1933*, 9.

391 Edwin R. Embree, *Julius Rosenwald Fund, Review of Two Decades, 1917-1936*, 23

Hunter calculated that ten million Americans, about 12 percent of the population, lacked even this subsistence lifestyle. Only about four million of these ten million received any public relief. Hunter used data from the census of 1900 and other government records such as pauper burials to arrive at his conclusions.[392]

Aid to the poor was local and direct, addressing the immediate need. Nathan Straus, one of New York City's most successful merchants, was an early believer in the benefits of pasteurization of milk in preventing tuberculosis. But many milk farmers and merchants rejected the theory, and no health regulations required such treatment. Straus took matters in hand. During the recession of 1893–1895, he opened milk stations in the tenement neighborhoods of the city. At each station, milk from the farm was pasteurized by raising the temperature to 176 degrees for thirty minutes, then cooling it. He sold the milk at no profit: six cents per quart or in eight-ounce bottles with nipples for four cents each, with a refund when the bottle was returned. A thirsty passerby could have a cool glass of milk for two cents.[393] But for anyone unable to pay, the milk was free. Straus was so convinced that children especially needed pasteurized milk that he provided mothers and physicians with coupons exchangeable for milk at any of his stations.[394] The death rate among children in the city dropped steadily as the program grew. Straus had also established depots in several European cities, and in every one the death rate among children dropped sharply as soon as distribution of the pasteurized milk started.[395]

In the summer of 1901, Straus's depots distributed more than one million glasses of milk and 770,000 eight-ounce bottles.[396] By 1910, the United States Public Health Service noted forty similar milk distribution programs in northern and Midwestern cities. All except three were funded by charity.[397] Straus maintained his stations until 1920, using not just his income but some of his capital as well. The New York City Health Department took over the work.[398]

---

392 Robert Hunter, *Poverty*, 7–8, 60, 350–351.
393 "May be Fed for 8 Cents a Day," and "Good Milk for the Poor," *New York Times*, June 2, 1893 and June 21, 1893.
394 "The Straus Milk Depots," *New York Times*, September 15, 1902.
395 "16 Years' Success of Straus Milk Plan," *New York Times*, September 22, 1908.
396 "Nathan Straus Charity Made Greatest Distribution in its History," *New York Times*, September 16, 1901.
397 J. W. Kerr, *Infant Milk Depots in the United States, 1910*. Public Health Service Reporter 25: 1227–1245. August 18, 1911.
398 It is interesting to speculate about the role of these milk depot programs in preventing the spread of pellagra in cities that had them, especially in the

In 1905, one million immigrants entered the United States—more than in any previous year. New language and new customs made them easy prey for any landlord, merchant, or employer seeking an easy mark. Then there were the politicians, those nice men who, for a fee, provided citizenship papers without delay and who paid two dollars for each vote duly cast by these new citizens. Every city had its political machine, and its "boss," not the mayor, but the man who "gets things done," who doled out jobs in the streets department or, for a fee, in the police department.[399] Settlement houses were established to help immigrants learn the workings of democracy and their power as voters in this strange new land. Hull-House was established in Chicago in 1890. By 1910, there were settlement houses in all the big cities. These were the safe havens for the new arrivals. Social workers offered advice on the crises that seemed to change by the hour. There was a hall in which to celebrate the holidays of the "old country" or to learn some homemaking skills. English language classes helped the adults catch up with their children, who learned the new language quickly. Some were financed by wealthy benefactors, some were supported by church congregations, and a few were operated by college student-volunteers.

The social safety network had its challenges. Jacob Riis wrote of the elderly widow who sat quietly in her tenement apartment dying of no disease save loneliness, of children pressed into petty crimes by older street-gang members, and the dismal fate of teenage mothers widowed or abandoned with their babies. He watched able-bodied men accepting food and lodging for the unemployed, only to slip away once a job was presented to them. On one occasion, 70 percent of the men taking charity proved to be malingerers.[400]

———

In the first years of the century, Russell Sage was one of the wealthiest men in America. Sage had built a fortune through a series of investments in railroads. He was more financial manipulator than operating executive. He made ample use of some of the most volatile market vehicles, including options. At times, he issued worrisome bulletins about companies, which others took as a reason to sell while he bought up the shares. In some cases, he collaborated with other wealthy individuals; at other times, he undercut their strategies. He and his wife

years 1909 to 1916 and 1921, when it spread so alarmingly elsewhere.
399 *Autobiography of Lincoln Steffens.*
400 Jacob Riis, *The Battle with the Slum*, 65, 85, 118, 161.

were, at the same time, contributing to local charities and to development campaigns at colleges and universities.[401] Sage died in 1906, leaving his fortune to his wife, Margaret. The following year, she established the Russell Sage Foundation and donated $10,000,000 to endow it. Her letter to the trustees announced its mission:

> I have transferred to Russell Sage Foundation...a fund, the principal of which...shall be held, and the income thereof applied to the improvement of social and living conditions in the United States of America...
>
> The scope of the Foundation is not only national but is broad. It should, however, preferably not undertake to do that which is now being done or is likely to be effectively done by other individuals or by other agencies. It should be its aim to take up larger and more difficult problems, and to take them up so far as possible in such a manner as to secure co-operation and aid in their solution...[402]

The Russell Sage Foundation focused on understanding the causes of poverty and developing methods that would be effective in combating it, rather than direct aid to the poor, which many agencies were addressing. As one of its first projects, the foundation set out to document the employment and living conditions of workers in one of America's large industrial cities. Data and photographs in the six-volume Pittsburgh Survey provided a base line for reformers. The foundation provided important resources in the effort to rationalize the operations and methods of private social service agencies.

Russell and Margaret had no children. When Margaret Sage died in 1918, she left the bulk of her estate to be divided among numerous charities. The Sage Foundation received an additional $5.6 million; gifts of $1.6 million each were left to Troy Female Seminary (Margaret's alma mater), Women's Hospital of the State of New York, several mission agencies of the Presbyterian Church, Children's Aid Society, the Charity Organization Society, and the Metropolitan Museum of Art. Gifts of $1 million or more went to Syracuse University and the American Museum of Natural History. Gifts of $800,000 were left to numerous institutions, including the New York Public Library, Troy Polytechnic Institute, the State Charities Aid Association, Tuskegee Institute, Union College

---

401 *New York Times,* July 23, 1906.
402 Letter of Margaret Olivia Sage to the Trustees of Russell Sage Foundation, April 19, 1907, at the foundation's website www.russellsage.org.

(Schenectady, New York), Amherst, Williams, Bryn Mawr, Barnard, Vassar, Smith, Wellesley and Dartmouth Colleges, New York University, and Yale University.

———

At the beginning of the twentieth century, aid to those in need was becoming more formal. The American Red Cross, which had aided troops during the Civil War and conducted relief efforts in numerous natural disasters, still relied heavily on the founder, Clara Barton. She was personally involved in each relief effort, while also trying to deal with the administrative complexities of a growing organization. Barton knew the importance of the organization to the country—and so did others. She was aging. While still vigorous, she seemed unwilling to delegate authority or prepare the organization for her inevitable retirement. Congress recognized the American National Red Cross as a perpetual corporation in 1900 and issued a new charter in 1905. Under terms of the 1905 charter, the Red Cross was to support its activities through donations. Six of eighteen members of the governing central committee, including the chairman, were to be appointed by the president of the United States. They included representatives from the Departments of State, War, Navy, Treasury, and Justice. The revenues and expenses of the organization were to be reviewed annually by the War Department.[403]

There was another discussion in Congress five years later, when John D. Rockefeller requested a Congressional charter for his proposed Rockefeller Foundation. Charitable foundations were not new, nor were trusts established to fund particular benevolent organizations such as individual schools, colleges, and hospitals. But Rockefeller was proposing a foundation that would have a universal mission, with its trustees empowered to direct its activities and grants as new issues and needs emerged.

Rockefeller's attorney described his client's reason for allowing such broad discretion: "The charities of the twenty-first century will not be the charities of the twentieth century. The dead hand should be removed from charitable bequests, and they should be left in the hands of living men. It is impossible to define the scope of the work proposed, and it is his desire to avoid limitations." All of this raised new questions that the Senate Committee for the District of

---

403 Central Files of the American Red Cross, RG 200, Box 9, 101.221, NARA II.

Columbia explored in hearings. Dr. Edward Devine of the New York Charity Organization Society suggested that the charter require that the government select some of the trustees and that the foundation be required to spend its entire annual income each year. Further, Devine wanted Congress to require that the foundation disburse its entire income and principal after one hundred years, thereby concluding its activity.

The Senate Committee decided that any public official serving as a trustee or able to appoint trustees would inevitably be pressured by individuals or groups seeking grants for their favorite causes. The committee chairman acknowledged that, since the hearings were announced, he had received more than one hundred letters asking assistance. The senators decided to spare the foundation's trustees from the predictable political pressures. There would be no government role in trustee selection. Rockefeller's attorney, pointing to the experience of other trusts, explained that requests for aid inevitably exceeded the amount of money available. The challenge confronting the trustees would be one of strategy—to decide which projects or organizations would make the most effective use of the funds available to the foundation. The senators also decided that future trustees and a future Congress would be best able to determine when, and under what circumstances, the foundation might be dissolved.[404] The hearing, and the decisions reached, marked an important development in the interaction between America's government and nonprofit sectors. America would have not just religious charities, but diverse, secular organizations funded by donations and managed by independent trustees free of political or government influence in grant-making.

The variety of foundations existing today reflects the wisdom of that policy. Lynn Fritz sold his own corporation, Fritz Cos., to United Parcel Service, Inc., in 2001. Using some of the $200 million proceeds from the sale, he founded the Fritz Institute, which is devoted to applying modern logistics techniques to the delivery of disaster relief. As reported in the *Wall Street Journal*, Fritz met with the CEOs of Parsons Brinckerhoff, a major engineering firm, and DHL, the giant international shipping firm, and established the Disaster Resource Network. In this consortium, multinational firms donate time and expertise to address major disaster relief supply challenges. The Fritz Institute has provided free software programs to allow aid groups to manage emergency shipments. The International Red Cross used the software in responding to the 2005 tsunami in Southeast Asia. One Red Cross official stated there was a fivefold increase in efficiency compared to earlier procedures. In addition to the critical benefit of

---

404 *New York Times,* March 10, 1910.

moving supplies quickly into disaster areas, the software allows the tracking of donated goods from reception point to destination, allowing donors to ascertain how their supplies were used and thereby encouraging future donations.[405]

Jon Huntsman, who built one of the largest chemical companies in the world, sold it to the public in an initial public offering in 2005. Huntsman has used much of the proceeds to establish the Huntsman Foundation, which is focused on cancer research projects.

James Simons, a world-class mathematician, runs Renaissance Technologies Corp., one of the world's most successful hedge funds. He and his wife, through their family foundation, have committed $38 million to find causes of autism, and they have said they will spend $100 million more in what is rapidly becoming the largest private investment in the field. In addition to an array of multimillion dollar grants to leading universities and laboratories, Simons brings his own considerable knowledge to review grant applications, suggest new avenues for research, and engage star researchers from other specialties.[406]

The Great Depression presented unique challenges to charitable organizations. As unemployment spread, family savings were exhausted. In almost four hundred cities, the Community Chest was the main fund-raising organization. Donations raised in this annual appeal were distributed to "character building" institutions such as Boy and Girl Scouts, YM/YWCA clubs, recreation centers, and dispensaries. Other beneficiaries were counseling services for youth or families in crisis and nongovernment social agencies providing food, clothing, or cash assistance to those in temporary need. Caseworkers evaluated each request for aid and were careful to authorize only the minimum needed to address the specific problem. City or county government took responsibility only for those who were institutionalized on account of obvious, long-term disability.

Rural areas relied more on church-related organizations. Only three hundred of the 3,074 counties in the United States had government social service or welfare agencies. One third of all counties had no general hospital; 75 percent of the population earned less than $2,000 per year and thus could afford neither hospitalization nor any significant amount of private care.[407] In the summer of

---

405 *Wall Street Journal,* November 22, 2005.
406 *Wall Street Journal,* December 15, 2005.
407 Annual Report of the American Red Cross, 1930, 59. Record Group 200, 494.1. NARA II.

1930, a drought affected a wide swath of farm states. In the fall, diminished harvests brought pleas for aid from many rural areas.

Automobile production through the first seven months of 1930 was 44 percent below the level of the same months in 1929.[408] By August, the impact had rippled across the country to suppliers. At some factories, work hours were reduced to spread the available work. That seemed a more humane approach than laying some off completely while others worked full-time. Fewer hours, in some cases only two or three hours per week, meant less money in the pay envelope. Relief applications surged. In the same month, the number of families applying for relief jumped 20 percent in Detroit, 17 percent in Toledo, Akron, and Dayton, 18 percent in Canton, 23 percent in Milwaukee, and 49 percent in Duluth, the city closest to the large iron ore deposits that supported the steel industry.[409] The drought, and less demand from cash-poor city-dwellers, meant hard times in farm areas.

During the winter of 1930–1931, the Red Cross was asked to provide emergency assistance in one third of the counties in the country. Most of the recipients were individual farmers with single cash crops that had failed. The Red Cross stretched its resources to provide drought relief in addition to responding to floods, major fires, and other local disasters. In January 1931, President Hoover appealed to the public for additional funds for the Red Cross drought relief efforts. Donors responded with $10.6 million, plus six hundred rail carloads of food, clothing, and fuel valued at another one million dollars, in addition to the annual membership and donations.[410] As months passed, breadlines formed in the cities. "Hoovervilles" of tents and shacks appeared. Veterans marched in Washington for advances on their bonuses.

In August 1931, President Hoover established the President's Organization for Unemployment Relief, "for cooperation with industry, and especially cooperation with the local welfare bodies, State authorities..." Owen Young, chairman of General Electric Company, was appointed chairman, and Walter Gifford, chairman of AT&T, was director.

---

408 Report of Economic Conditions, Government Finance and United States Securities, September 1930, National City Bank of New York. President's Organization for Unemployment Relief, Central Files, Record Group 73, NARA II.
409 Monthly Statistics of Outdoor Relief, August, 1930, Russell Sage Foundation. Available in President's Organization for Unemployment Relief, Central Files, Record Group 73, NARA II.
410 Annual Report of the American Red Cross, 1931. RG 200, 494.1. NARA II.

A series of four Sunday evening radio broadcasts encouraged greater participation in the local Community Chest drives that fall. Entertainment by leading musicians was interspersed with brief speeches by prominent individuals urging every listener to donate generously to local fund drives. Gen. John Pershing, humorist Will Rogers, and the actress Mary Pickford endorsed the campaign. Across the country, thirty-five thousand billboards carried the same message supporting the local Community Chest as the focal point for relief contributions, enabling local agencies to make the best use of funds to aid local residents. One hundred thirty colleges extended their football season to play exhibition games, with admission funds going to local relief. Theaters held benefit shows and donated the ticket sales to relief agencies. Corporations found their own ways of helping. ITE Circuit Breaker Company donated 2 percent of the gross sale price of any order received over the next five months to the local relief organization serving the town or city in which the order originated.

The nation responded generously. The four hundred Community Chests in the 1931 drive collected a record $82 million, compared to $67 million raised in 1928, the last full year of prosperity.[411]

Harvests were bountiful in 1931, but many had no cash to buy food. Local Save the Surplus committees accepted unmarketable fruits and vegetables from farmers, often using donated trucks and paying hourly wages to collection drivers otherwise unemployed. Women's groups, PTAs, and home economics students used church and school kitchens to cook and can the surplus food and give it to community food pantries to meet their increased demand.[412] In Birmingham, Alabama, where five hundred families qualified for relief, canning groups included the Young Women's Hebrew Association, the Women of the Eastern Star, and Girl Scouts earning service badges. Expenses were covered by the local Community Chest, and the program was initiated and supervised by the Red Cross Food Conservation Committee. County farm agents carried donated canning equipment to rural towns. In some of the remote hollows of Kentucky, this campaign introduced canning to families that had relied for generations on dried foods to get through the winter.[413]

---

411 "Community Chests Near Record Total," *New York Times,* January 3, 1932.
412 First-time canning can be hazardous. After a few early mishaps, many groups hired experienced chefs to supervise the work to reduce the chances of food poisoning.
413 President's Organization on Unemployment Relief, August 1931–June 1932, Record Group 73, Box 141, NARA II.

The bituminous coal regions of Pennsylvania and West Virginia had been plagued by high unemployment during the 1920s. Higher demand for coal during the war had caused an expansion of mining capacity. The end of the war brought a decline in demand, and the rising unemployment in the northern cities after 1930 had further reduced demand for coal. At Hoover's request, the American Friends Service Committee joined forces with the Red Cross to start a feeding program there.

———

As the Depression continued, some businesses failed, and many more suffered reduced sales and profits. Dividends to shareholders were reduced at first, then suspended later. Some corporations could not meet the obligation to pay the interest on their bonds. Some cities and counties defaulted on bond payments. University endowments, charitable foundations, and trust funds, as well as individual investors, depended on those sources of investment income. As businesses failed and cities lost tax income, even the largest charities were crippled.

The Julius Rosenwald Fund had been established with the founder's initial gift of $20 million of common stock in Sears, Roebuck and Company. As the company's business and profits grew, especially after the recession of the early 1920s, the value of the fund's principal grew while income was dispensed for the school building program. By 1928, the value of the fund's 227,874 shares of stock exceeded $40 million. The fund's activities were expanded by contributing to new initiatives in black communities, including library service, health and medical services, and programs to improve race relations. Funds were established to help promising black scholars attend prestigious universities including Harvard, Yale, Columbia, University of Pennsylvania, London School of Economics, and University of Chicago, as well as historically black private colleges and universities.

The fund's trustees had not significantly diversified the investment portfolio. As profits fell at Sears, Roebuck and Company, the company cut its dividend. In 1931, the company paid shareholders a total of $12 million in dividends; in 1932, they paid $6 million. In 1933 and 1934, there were no dividends paid, so the fund had no investment income in those years.[414] To meet its commitments, some shares were pledged as collateral for bank loans, others were sold

---

414 Emmet and Jeuck, *Catalogues and Counters*, 657.

at Depression prices. By 1936, the fund had sold almost two-thirds of its securities to meet commitments to various grantees and repay the bank loans. The $20 million original capital gift, which had grown to $40 million in the late 1920s, had been reduced to $7 million.[415]

Even conservatively managed portfolios were affected. The trust that supplied income to the daughters of Francis Drexel was no exception. Mother Katharine Drexel had been using her trust income to support schools, community centers, and churches serving Native Americans and blacks. As business conditions worsened, the trust's investment income declined. Many of the bond issuers, including cities and electric and gas utilities, had found it impossible to pay their interest obligations and were reorganized with new, reduced debt payments. Some simply failed. By 1934, Mother Katharine was writing to some of the priests and others whose work she helped finance, advising them that her diminished income would leave her unable to continue to contribute to their projects.[416] Her trust income for 1934 was $269,645, down 7 percent from 1927's figure, and requests for aid were increasing, not falling. Under the terms of Francis Drexel's will establishing the trust, there was no authority to use the principal or sell these bonds and other assets for current use—they were pledged to the twenty-nine institutions named in Francis's will. By 1939, Katharine's trust income had fallen to $234,805.[417] The weak economy reduced the capabilities of the most generous donors.

———

America's wealthiest made extraordinary contributions to alleviate unemployment. Beginning in the late 1920s, John D. Rockefeller Jr. funded a restoration of the colonial town of Williamsburg, Virginia. The reconstruction with

---

415 Edwin R. Embree, *Julius Rosenwald Fund, 1917-1936*, 3–9.
416 Letters of Mother M. Katharine Drexel, Archives of the Sisters of the Blessed Sacrament. See especially letter to Rev. G. Caldi, S. J., Omak, Washington, July 9, 1934, and letter to Miss Elizabeth Finigan, Rochester, New York, August 16, 1934.
417 Accounting Ledger (card file) of trust payments to Louise Morrell (Katharine Drexel's sister), SBS Archives. After the death of their sister, Elizabeth, in 1890, Katharine and Louise each received equal halves of the trust income. Louise died suddenly in 1945. She had no children. Her share of the ongoing trust income then went to Mother Katharine, who died in 1955. The principal of the trust was then distributed to the twenty-nine charities as prescribed in the will of Francis Drexel.

historical and architectural accuracy, along with the modern conveniences tourists would need, cost $55 million, but work continued until completion in 1934, when President Franklin Delano Roosevelt officially opened the site. To raise cash for the Rockefeller Center and Williamsburg projects, Junior sold large blocks of Standard Oil stock, at Depression prices, and saw the projects through to completion. Between 1931 and 1933, Rockefeller paid for construction of five of the stone bridges that are now part of Acadia National Park in Maine.[418] In 1931, the Rockefeller family bought a sixty-acre estate on the northern tip of Manhattan for $1.7 million and donated it to New York City. The family donated an additional $3.6 million for landscaping and buildings, including the Cloisters, as a museum for the preservation and display of medieval art. The city added $800,000 for sewer and lighting systems. The park, with its extensive new trees, lawns, walkways, and stone bridges, was completed in October 1935 and dedicated as Fort Tyron Park, with the Cloisters completed several years later.[419]

In the fall of 1931, Henry Ford initiated a program for improvements to Inkster, a village populated by blacks, many of whom were Ford employees who had been laid off when sales of the Model A collapsed. The work allowed many to pay off their debts to local merchants and continue feeding their families. The school was reopened and electric power restored to the community. Sewing machines and seeds were distributed so the community might become self-sufficient at least for the basics of life.[420] Ford also continued, with his personal funds, the construction of Greenfield Village, a complex of buildings and displays intended to celebrate American history, culture, and invention. The campus and core buildings had been dedicated in October 1929, just days before the crash. President Hoover and the aging inventor Thomas Edison attended the ceremony. Construction of buildings and the collection of antique furnishings continued until 1937.[421] Ford had to reach deep into his personal savings to do this, since Ford Motor Company lost $132 million in the years 1931–1937.[422]

Andrew Mellon, while serving as secretary of the Treasury, donated $4 million between 1931 and 1937 for building a new home for the Mellon Institute in Pittsburgh. His brother, Dick, contributed an equal amount. Recognizing the unemployment problem was not to be cured by a few construction projects, (building the Gulf Building also continued, although that had been

418 Robert A. Thayer, *Acadia Carriage Roads*, 13, 48.
419 *New York Times*, October 4, 1935.
420 Robert Lacey, *Ford—The Men and the Machine*, 307–308.
421 Robert Lacey, *Ford—The Men and the Machine*, 248–9.
422 Arthur J. Kuhn, *GM Passes Ford, 1918-38*, 317.

planned before the crash) Andrew contributed $50,000 to the Allegheny County Emergency Association, $20,000 to the American Red Cross, and made similar contributions to several other relief organizations in 1931. His brothers made similar contributions. Dick separately donated $4 million for the complete reconstruction of the East Liberty Presbyterian Church, also in Pittsburgh. Funds from his estate completed the project after his death in 1933. In 1932, Andrew gave another $325,000 to the Welfare Fund and $75,000 in 1933. Andrew Mellon was a wealthy man, indeed, but the Depression seriously reduced his income from stock dividends. To maintain his lifestyle and continue the larger charitable commitments, he borrowed $9 million between 1932 and his death in 1937. He pledged his stock certificates as collateral for the loans.[423]

Rockefeller, Ford, and Mellon were the wealthiest families in America in the early 1930s.[424] Many others with lesser fortunes made extra contributions to alleviate the suffering that came with the Depression.

————

President Hoover's effort to boost Community Chest donations with a national publicity campaign was repeated in 1932. Contributions reached a new record total of $101 million.[425] Hoover's Reconstruction Finance Act made $300 million available for loans to municipalities and state governments that had exhausted their own relief funds.

Franklin Roosevelt's New Deal programs were intended to replace the Red Cross and other philanthropic approaches to unemployment relief. As the president of the American Red Cross noted early in 1934:

> The nature of their [Red Cross chapters] work however has considerably changed, as has the work of all private agencies. The extensive Federal program for the relief of unemployment has greatly decreased the case load of the private agencies like the Red Cross...The assumption of primary responsibility on the part of National, State and local Governments for relief needs which result from economic and industrial ills has released Red Cross chapters for case work services.

---

423 David Cannadine, *Mellon*, 403, 493.
424 Liaquat Ahamed, *Lords of Finance: The Bankers Who Broke the World*, 142.
425 "Gifts to Chest Show Slight Drop," *New York Times*, September 6, 1938.

Chapters are now providing service and relief to families not eligible to public aid...where difficulties have developed, such as family conflicts causing disorganized or broken homes...neglected children, school situations and health conditions. Many such families have benefited from the attention of a skilled case worker.[426]

The Red Cross maintained its lead role in relief in natural disasters, first aid, and water safety training. Other nonprofit agencies were expected to carry on their traditional roles. Roosevelt, following Hoover's example, lent his own support to the Community Chest campaigns. The 1933 Mobilization for Human Needs produced $77 million; in 1934 and 1935, the total fell to $70 million each year. The 1936 Mobilization collected $77.4 million and 1937 funds totaled $81.7 million. The 1938 total was again larger, just under $84 million.[427] The ability of citizens generally to aid their less fortunate neighbor had finally recovered. But the requests for assistance had grown far beyond pre-Depression levels.

By 1938, leaders of the Mobilization for Human Needs, the national umbrella group for local Community Chests, expressed frustration that millions of employable people were still unemployed and administration policy was pushing relief of these unemployed onto local resources. The able-bodied without work became "doubly underprivileged" since the aid they received was far less than the WPA wage, and they were often stigmatized as "unemployables" in spite of their abilities and interest in work. Many nonprofit leaders were now pressing for federal block grants to be sent to state governments, which they believed would be more resourceful and effective than federal bureaucracy.[428] The centralized industrial planning of the NRA, the public works stimulus of the CCC and PWA, and even the later more aggressive jobs programs of the WPA, farm relocation, and urban redevelopment never fully met the needs of the unemployed.

———

John Jacob Raskob, vice president of the DuPont Powder Company and chairman of the finance committee of General Motors Corporation, had donated one million dollars to the Catholic Foundation of the Diocese of Wilmington

426 Annual Report of the American Red Cross, 1933–1934, 55. RG 200, 494.1. NARA II.
427 "Gifts to Chests Show Slight Drop," *New York Times*, September 6, 1938.
428 "Relief: Which Program?" *New York Times*, March 14, 1938.

to jump-start a program for building new churches and schools in 1928. New churches were built in towns on Maryland's eastern shore and in Wilmington during 1933—jobs that were particularly important in the depths of the Depression.

A few months after their major donation to the diocesan foundation, Raskob and his wife Helena lost their son, Bill, in an automobile accident. Bill was a sophomore at Yale University. His parents established the Bill Raskob Foundation for the "relief of poor orphans and other poor children, for their education and to help them get started in life and business." They opened the foundation with a gift of one million dollars. The foundation is still active today as a small family foundation making loans to college students. The impact of its work is best described by a letter received by the foundation from a 1929 Bill Raskob recipient:

Dear Madame or Sir:

In 1929 I was a sophomore at the University of Iowa. As did millions of Americans, my parents suffered a major financial setback. We lost the home my father had designed and his company had built. I was the first female member of my family on either side (and except for my father, the only member of my family) to attend a university. I would have been forced to drop out of college. My aunt, Rose Duffy, contacted the Bill Raskob Foundation and asked for educational loan assistance for me. I was granted an education loan of, I think, $3,000 to complete my university education. I was never asked to sign a note. I was never charged any interest. It took me a long time to pay back the loan. But eight years later, before I married in 1940, I did pay back my obligation in full.

I recall one family discussion long ago. A relative questioned the wisdom of spending money on my education rather than a male relative's. My mother said, "Margaret will always have it in her head." John and I were blessed with five children. We raised our family in South Bend, Indiana. Our daughters include: a special education teacher in Wisconsin, with a master's degree, and three children. An advertising executive living in New York City with two children. And a retired General Accounting Office/Foreign Service Officer living in McLean, VA, with a master's degree and three children. Our sons include: a highly decorated Vietnam War Veteran, New York attorney with two children, and a San Francisco plastic surgeon with one child. I have told each of my children of the benefit that your foundation has provided to our family.

My younger brother Ed also benefited from your good works. Because of your generosity, he was able to complete his study of medicine at Cornell University Medical Center in New York City. He spent much of World War II as a doctor in the jungles of New Guinea. Ed contracted malaria there. Following the War, and for more than a third of a century, Dr. Edward Carey was the only ophthalmologist in the entire northeast quarter of the State of Iowa.

John died in 1994. As a paraplegic for the last fifteen years of his life, he was an inspiration to those of us with milder disabilities. He taught us how to live with strength and dignity. I was 91 three weeks ago. This is a letter I have long intended to write. Certain health issues come with the territory. My children helped produce this letter, but all of the words are mine, as is my signature.

Thank you for the opportunities you have provided to me and in turn, to my family.

Margaret Christine Carey
Graduate of the University of Iowa, Class of 1932

Raskob had been responding to requests for help from individuals, families, and charitable groups since the beginning of his business career. As the Depression wore on, and high tax rates on higher-income households took a larger share of his income, he was less able to respond. In 1937, Raskob poured out his frustration in his response to a priest who had requested assistance. This man with more than thirty-five years in business and philanthropy made clear the proximate cause of his present incapability:

Dear Father Roe:

I have your letter of the fifteenth and, in reply, would advise that it will be quite impossible for me to comply with your request.

It is difficult for me to understand why so few people appreciate that the policy of the Government in confiscating such a huge portion of larger sized incomes makes it impossible for supposedly well-to-do men to do much charitable work. With high taxes, a man with the expenses of a large family just cannot add to obligations he is already under. The rank and file of people ought to call a halt to the policy of the Government in taking such huge slices of income away from men that know how to use money to not only do charitable work but employ gardeners, maids, chauffeurs, sailors, etcetera, etcetera, and make this help get value received, as against having the Government take the money and dole it out in a manner that tends to pauperize the people that are receiving it.

Sincerely yours,[429]

Raskob would meet ongoing commitments to the best of his ability. But he could no longer afford to help new causes and organizations, or to fund new approaches for aid to those in need. Innovation in charity suffered in the same bed with business innovation.

———

Are charitable donations influenced by tax legislation? Research over several decades and through various changes in income tax laws shows that the powerful factors influencing charitable giving are economic conditions, particularly changes in gross domestic product, and changes in individuals' financial circumstances, especially personal income and stock prices. When business is thriving, individuals tend to give more. For corporations, the most important factor affecting year-to-year levels of philanthropic giving are profitability and stock price. In this way, charitable organizations and those who receive their services benefit directly from economic growth, rising personal incomes, and higher stock prices.[430] Actions that boost economic growth (GDP growth), rising personal incomes and higher stock prices lead to increased charitable giving. Actions that restrain or derail GDP growth, personal incomes and stock prices have a negative impact on giving.

During the Great Depression, high taxes on corporate profits, personal incomes, dividends, and capital gains had a serious negative impact on charitable work by weakening the economy, thus destroying asset value in foundations and endowments and reducing the discretionary funds available to high-income earners. Many people who had previously given generously had to reduce the amount of their donations as more of their income went to the government.

---

429 John Jacob Raskob letter to Rev. J. J. Roe, May 27, 1937, Raskob Papers. Hagley Library and Museum.
430 Giving USA Foundation, *Giving USA 2004*, p. 57-58.

Five decades later, the reduced income tax rates of the 1980s boosted innovation and economic growth, accompanied by a dramatic increase in the growth rate of donations.

From 1971 to 1980, charitable donations by individuals to all causes had increased at an average annual rate of 1.3 percent. From 1981 to 1990, donations by individuals increased at an annual rate of 2.3 percent. As their after-tax income grew, people were giving more of that income to charitable causes. Corporate giving also grew more quickly. Donations by corporations had grown at an average annual rate of 3.0 percent from 1971 to 1980. But from 1981 to 1990, corporate giving grew 4.4 percent annually.[431]

Charities were getting more donations from an economy that grew 29 percent from 1981 to 1990, compared to growth of just 21.6 percent from 1971 to 1980.[432] The data from the experiments point to a relationship between income tax rates and charitable giving. The sustained lower income tax rates of the 1980s produced rapid growth in charitable donations. A virtuous cycle of lower income tax rates, more innovation, and stronger economic growth was producing faster growth in donations to charity. As we saw in an earlier chapter, economists have recently confirmed that tax increases have negative impact on GDP, and tax reductions boost GDP.

Estate taxes also impact charitable giving and the economy. In 2001, George W. Bush was about to begin his first term. He had campaigned on a promise to end the estate tax, also known as the death tax. This was one element of what became known as the Bush tax cuts, most of which were enacted with automatic expiration dates in 2010. When the estate tax elimination was discussed, many charities and fundraisers in the philanthropic world were concerned that the repeal, or significant reduction, of the estate tax would remove an important driver of charitable donations and bequests. But Paul Schervish, professor of sociology and director of the Social Welfare Research Institute at Boston College, urged a different view.

Schervish pointed to research by his colleague, John Havens, which showed "a growing number of wealthy Americans already are shifting their financial legacies from heirs to charity" over the prior decade. Estates valued at $20

---

431 *Giving USA 2009*, a publication of Giving USA Foundation, researched and written by the Center on Philanthropy at Indiana University, 211. The figures are inflation-adjusted, thus the growth in donations represents real growth in purchasing power for the educational and charitable institutions that received these donations.

432 Gross Domestic Product (GDP) data from Bureau of Economic Analysis, March 26, 2009.

million or more showed the strongest movement in that direction. Charitable bequests from this group increased 246 percent, while the value of estates rose 135 percent and bequests to heirs rose 75 percent. Heirs were getting less; charities were getting more.

Schervish cited other studies that demonstrated similar trends. He further pointed to research by Aldona and Gary Robbins, at the Institute for Policy Innovation in Dallas, who estimated that abolishing the estate tax would increase the gross domestic product—a measure of economic activity—by nearly $1 trillion during the next decade and create 275,000 jobs. Schervish's conclusion was that doing away with estate taxes "would increase not only the amount of giving, but also the quality of giving…making the voluntary act of charity far more fully a work of liberty and humanitarian care, and less the windfall of a convoluted tax strategy."[433]

Since 1963, total giving in the U.S. has grown faster than the gross domestic product, corporate giving has grown faster than corporate profits, and individual giving has grown faster than personal income and disposable personal income. These trends are consistent with the motivation described by many individuals and corporate boards as a desire to "give back." In 2007, total giving in the U.S. reached $326 billion.[434]

The available evidence indicates a strong positive relationship between healthy economic activity, including growing corporate profits, and donations to charity. But we have not fully answered the question, "What happens to all that money accumulated by wealthy individuals and families?" That is part of answering the larger question, "Where do all those big-business profits go, and who gets the benefit?"

History provides the answer. For this we can look to the disposition of the five largest fortunes that existed about one hundred years ago, in 1905. Three of these megafortunes were accumulated by ownership of shares in industrial corporations. One was assembled over several generations in real estate, and one was created in a retailing empire built by one man. All five fortunes were created before the federal income tax was enacted in 1913. We'll follow the money to learn what happened to all this wealth— business profits accumulated by owners. We'll see who ultimately got the benefit of all those profits.

---

433 *Chronicle of Philanthropy*, January 11, 2001.
434 *Giving USA 2009,* a publication of Giving USA Foundation, researched and written by the Center on Philanthropy at Indiana University, 216.

Chapter Sixteen

Jay Gould

J ay Gould is the most notorious of the robber barons of the late nineteenth century. He amassed a fortune mainly through buying, developing, and selling railroads. He enhanced it with aggressive transactions in railroad stocks. Thomas Edison complained that Gould failed to pay him $250,000 for patent rights on telegraph equipment.[435] His boldest venture was his attempt to corner the gold market in 1869. That attempt failed when the U.S. Treasury became aware of his scheme and released additional supplies of gold into the market, foiling the plan and leaving Jay with a huge loss. But he recovered over the next few years and went on to build a new, larger fortune.

Born Jason Gould in 1836, he had only a few years of formal schooling. As a teen, he worked part-time in his father's store. He taught himself enough book-keeping to get a part-time job in that field. By seventeen, he had learned the basics of surveying and was hired to survey a site for a new tannery operation, actually a small town with its own bark-crushing plant, a water race for power, living quarters, and general store. The tannery owner was impressed with Gould's competence and put him in charge of the fifty-man work crew. In 1860, he moved to New York City and opened a leather brokerage with a partner.

Physically, he never commanded attention. He was barely five feet tall, quite thin, and never in robust health. But hard work and a determination to complete

---

435 Matthew Josephson, *Edison*, 125.

whatever he started would get him through a lifetime of glorious triumphs followed by disastrous setbacks, which in turn were followed by even greater successes. He was twenty-four when he used his savings to purchase the bonds of a small and decrepit rail line between Troy, New York, and Rutland, Vermont, for ten cents on the dollar. He spent the next few years reorganizing the railroad and buying shares of its stock. When Gould's railroad merged with a larger operation, the bonds were back at par value, and the stock price had risen dramatically. He sold his interest for a huge gain.[436]

Very little is recorded regarding charitable donations by Jay Gould, except for two donations to New York University. Those donation helped NYU acquire the University Heights campus in the Bronx. Some biographers contend that Gould kept his money to himself and his family, although one more recent account of his life asserts that he quietly helped those in need through direct support, rather than through institutions. Gould died in 1892 of tuberculosis, leaving a fortune appraised at $74 million in stocks, bonds, and New York real estate, plus land in Louisiana that was subsequently sold for $12 million.[437] (These estate values are based upon independent appraisals accepted by the tax authorities or the courts and are described as such in the text or notes. Appraised values often differ from estimates reported in the media, which often proved to be quite inaccurate once the appraisals were completed.)

Jay's wife had died earlier. His will left specific provisions for his brother and sisters. Jay's oldest child, George Jay Gould, who had handled many of his father's business arrangements in Jay's final years, was left a lump sum payment of $5 million as compensation for those years of service. He was twenty-eight years old at his father's death. Jay's namesake-grandchild, Jay Jr., received a trust of $500,000. A son, Edwin, received a townhouse in Manhattan. Jay's older daughter, Helen, received the Manhattan home where Jay had lived. The remainder was left in trust to be divided into six equal shares, one for each of Jay's children, with the income going to each during his or her lifetime and the residual then going to the child's heirs. There were no bequests to any charitable, religious, or educational institutions; the fortune would stay in the Gould family. Helen was granted the right to use the country mansion, Lyndhurst, at Irvington-on-Hudson until the youngest child, Frank, who was fourteen when Jay died, reached age twenty-one. The estate would also pay $6,000 per month

---

436 Charles R. Morris, *The Tycoons.*
437 *New York Times,* January 8, 1895, November 12, 1925. Also, letter from John H. McCracken to *New York Times,* published December 27, 1938.

for upkeep of the mansion. This would enable Helen to care for her younger siblings there. Then the mansion reverted to the estate. Helen bought the mansion from the estate in 1899.[438]

In his will, Jay had named his eldest four children as trustees.[439] By 1905, the trust for Jay Gould's children represented one of the five largest fortunes in the country.[440]

In 1916, the two youngest of Jay Gould's children initiated a legal suit, charging that the four trustees had mismanaged the trust funds, and in some cases used the trust funds to boost the value of their individual stock holdings, over a period of years. Multimillion dollar loans had been extended to corporations without security. Deals that were obviously speculative had been financed with trust funds. These misadventures and the Panic of 1907 had done substantial damage to the investments in the trusts.

One trustee, George Jay Gould, was found to have acted in a manner that violated specific instructions of the trust document and had commingled trust funds with his personal funds. The court found all four trustees liable, since the inactive trustees had failed in their duty to properly monitor and safeguard the trust funds. The court found that the trusts had suffered a loss of as much as $50 million. Since George had burned his personal records in 1914, the amount of personal profit derived from all this was impossible to determine precisely. The court allowed the family members to negotiate a settlement wherein the trustees, out of their personal wealth, reimbursed the trust a total of $18 million. The legal battle had lasted eleven years. Attorney fees totaled $2.7 million. At one hearing, there were forty-five lawyers, representing various members of the extended Gould family. By 1925, after the settlement and reimbursements, the trust left by Jay Gould for his children totaled $66.5 million.[441]

One of Jay Gould's daughters, Helen, was twenty-four when Jay died. She had already attended law school at New York University. The income from her share of the trust and the two fine homes available for her use left her with no financial worries, but she was responsible for raising two siblings to maturity after their father's death. Helen took an active interest in the railroad investments that were the major part of her inheritance. Every year she toured the

---

438 *New York Times,* November 18, 1924.
439 *New York Times,* December 13, 1892.
440 *Fortune,* October 1936, names the five largest fortunes of 1905, which are traced in this and subsequent chapters.
441 *New York Times,* November 12, 1925; June 1, 1927.

railroads. Because the family trust was a major shareholder, an executive from the railroad escorted her on these tours. In 1912, her assigned escort was Finley Shepard, the handsome, unmarried assistant to the president of the railroad and a veteran railroad executive. Helen and Finley married in 1913. The wedding at Lyndhurst was a major social event for New York City's high society. It was also a memorable day for the city's less fortunate. While planning her wedding, Helen had also arranged for a free dinner to be served to one thousand poor people on her wedding day at a mission in the Bowery section of New York City.[442]

At the time of their wedding, Helen and Finley were both in their mid-forties. They adopted a child who had been abandoned on the steps of St. Patrick's Cathedral, named him Finley Jay Shepard, and raised him as their son. Over the next few years, they took in two girls and another boy, raising them as their own children.

From the time of her father's death, Helen was a generous supporter of numerous causes. Between 1895 and 1901, she had contributed more than $2 million to New York University.[443] She contributed $100,000 to support troops embarking for the Spanish American War. Bibles were awarded as prizes to girls who could memorize a series of verses. Helen's philanthropy continued throughout her life. By the time of her death in 1938, she had donated the vast majority of her fortune. At a memorial service at New York University, she was acknowledged by the University Council as "a steadfast friend of the University for more than forty years, and…the foremost benefactor of New York University throughout its history." Rutgers, Vassar, and Mount Holyoke Colleges also received generous gifts. A home for crippled children, Woody Crest, received $150,000. Her estate, appraised at $3.3 million, was left to Finley, who died in 1942. His estate, including the remainder of Helen's fortune, totaled $3.9 million. After gifts to his former secretary, a few friends, and several churches, the remainder was divided among the children of Helen and Finley.

George Jay Gould, oldest son of Jay, had been his father's alter ego in business during Jay's final years. George shared his father's dream of putting together a coast-to-coast railroad system under Gould control. For the first few years after Jay's death, all went well, and George prospered. He built a magnificent country estate in Lakewood, New Jersey, known as Georgian Court, and mar-

---

442 *New York Times,* August 23, 1942.
443 Letter from John H. McCracken to the *New York Times,* published December 27, 1938.

ried an actress, Edith Kingdon. Just as he was planning to put the final pieces of the coast-to-coast rail system in place, the Panic of 1907 caught him short of cash and forced him to liquidate some of the key investments. Over the next ten years, much of the rest of his fortune slipped away. Then came the lawsuit over management of the family trusts, in which most of the siblings pointed to George as the wrongdoer. In 1921, Edith collapsed and died while playing golf on the private course at Georgian Court, leaving him to raise their seven children. Her will provided that George could reside at Georgian Court until his death and then the property was to be sold, unless George remarried, in which case it was to be sold immediately. In either case, their children would receive the proceeds. Six months after Edith's death, George married Guinevere Sinclair. Georgian Court was sold. A year after the wedding, George died. In his will, he acknowledged that he was the father of the three children born to Guinevere before their marriage and left equal inheritances for all ten of his children.[444] Guinevere remarried. Her children filed lawsuits to get a larger share of George's estate.

At the time of his death in 1923, several sources estimated his wealth at $30 million. But settlement of the lawsuit against George for misconduct in handling the trusts established by Jay Gould, payment of various other expenses, and recognition that several stocks in the estate were worthless depleted the estate. The appraisal completed in 1933 showed an estate worth just over $5 million, including George Jay Gould's share of the trust that Jay Gould had established for his children. This was to be divided among George Jay Gould's widow and ten children, leaving them all quite comfortable but far from the pinnacle of wealth that Jay Gould had reached.

Edwin, Jay's second son, earned his own fortune on Wall Street while Jay was still alive. Then he inherited his share of his father's money. He continued to work and invest wisely, organizing the Continental Match Company, which later merged with Diamond Match Company (a great business in an era when cigarette smoking was considered a social grace), and he became president of Bowling Green Trust, which later merged with Equitable Trust. He sold the last of his railroad holdings in 1925. Edwin and his wife Sarah had been donating generously for years to the Harlem Ear and Eye Hospital, and they had established the Edwin Gould Foundation for Children in 1923. They had had two sons, Edwin Jr., who died at seventeen in a hunting accident, and Frank Miller Gould.

444 Verbatim text of George Jay Gould's Will, *New York Times,* June 5, 1923.

In 1933, Edwin collapsed and died at home, with his wife of forty years at his side. His will left half of his estate to his widow and the other half to the Edwin Gould Foundation, although the investment income from the foundation's half would be paid to the widow during her lifetime. The foundation focused on helping youth. Today, it is best known for funding the Edwin Gould Academy, which provides services to young men and women who have aged out of the foster care system, or have had contact with the juvenile justice system, as they begin to establish themselves as adults in the community. At the main Multi-Service Center/Residence facility in the East Harlem area of New York City, academy staff members provide counseling, employment advice, and access to additional services, and they maintain low-income residences for fifty-one tenants and their sixteen children.

Frank Jay Gould was Jay's youngest son. He graduated from New York University's College of Engineering in 1899. Frank inherited his father's keen interest in railroads, and he had some success investing his inheritance. He also succeeded in suing his older siblings for their handling of the trust that Jay Gould had established. In 1910, he moved to France and established several hotels and gambling casinos along the French Riviera. During World War II, he had to hide from the Nazis, who suspected he was Jewish. In the early 1950s, he made several gifts of $1 million dollars to NYU and donated his estate in Ardsley, New York, to the university. At his death, he left gifts to relatives, his valet, chauffer, caretaker, and several others. The bulk of his wealth, consisting of properties in France, was left to his widow, who lived in France. He left $100,000 to each of his two daughters, one in Switzerland and the other in Mexico, and left them to share the residual of the trust that his father had established for him. The value of the French estate is unknown, and in any event, upon Frank's death all of his wealth passed into foreign hands.

Howard Gould, the last surviving son of Jay, died in 1959 at age eighty-eight. He never married. His estate was appraised at $64 million. Out of that sum, the State of New York received estate taxes of $12.9 million, and the federal government collected $37 million. Howard's will specified one charitable bequest, $100,000, for the Jay Gould Memorial Reformed Church in Roxbury, New York. He left the remainder of his estate to be divided equally among twenty-five relatives, and three additional relatives were to share equally in one twenty-sixth of the estate. These heirs were grandchildren and great-grandchildren of Howard's brother, George Jay, and sister, Anna, who had become Countess de Castellane and Duchesse de Talleyrand. In round numbers, each of the favored twenty-five received one twenty-sixth of $14 million, or $538,000, and the three less-favored heirs each received one seventy-eighth of $14 million, or $179,000. With that accomplished, Howard's fortune was effectively transfused into the fortunes, great or small, of his surviving relatives, for them to invest, spend, or donate as they deemed best.

The last of Jay's children, Anna, died in 1961 at age eighty-six. She left an estate appraised at $5.8 million to her daughter and three grandchildren, all of whom resided in France.

A few of Jay Gould's heirs of later generations raised their own fortunes, using their own wits and making their own decisions, in ventures that had nothing to do with railroads. But those are not the object of this review. The bulk of the fortune that Jay Gould built in the second half of the nineteenth century found its way back into society within one generation. Some of the wealth was dissipated in unsuccessful investments. Not all railroads were profitable, and the Panic of 1907 took its toll. The remaining wealth returned to society through a combination of spending to support lifestyles of the various heirs, some grand and some simple, through donations to universities and charities, and through taxes.

Chapter Seventeen

Astor

Born in Walldorf, Germany, in 1763, John Jacob Astor received a basic education, then went to work in his father's butcher shop. Two years later, he moved to England to work for his brother George in a musical instrument store. He learned English and saved enough money for passage to the new United States of America, landing in Baltimore in 1784. According to family legend, he arrived with little money, a good suit, and seven flutes from the London store. He made his way to New York City. There he was aided by his brother Henry, who had immigrated earlier. John had little to offer an employer except a strong back and willingness to work hard. He found work selling baked goods from a tray in the streets. Next he was hired at a fur shop, for $2 per week plus board, to beat the dust and bugs out of the pelts before packing them into bales. His employer discovered John's quick mind and tremendous energy and began sending him into upstate New York and Canada to trade with the Native Americans. The work was dangerous. Animals, injuries, and disease posed constant threats. But the business was lucrative.[445]

Consumer demand for furs was strong in this era long before synthetic fibers, central heating systems, and motorized transportation. The Native Americans had more than enough furs, but they needed manufactured tools and cloth, and they valued tobacco. These were plentiful in the American cities. So both parties gained in the trade. Then came stage two of the fur business. A single

---

445 Arthur D. Howden Smith, *John Jacob Astor: Landlord of New York*, 36.

beaver fur brought back to New York, then shipped to London, could be sold for 40 shillings. The total profit made in the two transactions was about 900 percent. John decided he could make far more money as a trader and merchant than as a wage earner, and he set up his own business.[446]

The powerful Hudson Bay Company had a near-monopoly on North American furs in that era. But Astor sent his workers far into the Great Lakes region to establish networks of buyers who traded with Native American trappers. He invested in his own fleet of ships to carry furs to Europe and China, accepting products of those lands in exchange for the furs. Routes and cargoes changed to meet the demands of each market. With his global perspective on trade, Astor became America's first millionaire by the early 1800s. His agents followed Lewis and Clark into the Louisiana Purchase and established a trading and shipping post at Astoria where the Columbia River flows into the Pacific. He continued to reinvest profits, buying up small fur companies throughout the west. By 1831, the company was earning profits of at least one half million dollars a year.[447]

During a trip to London, he saw that fashions were changing. Hat makers were using more silk and less beaver. Astor was also aware that intense trapping had led to a declining beaver population. Sensing that the fur trade had reached its peak, John Jacob Astor sold his American Fur Company in 1834.

At Henry's urging, John had been buying land in Manhattan as a sideline investment, as Henry had already been doing. Both brothers could see the tremendous growth in this major port city. Even as he was building the fur business, John used excess cash to buy tracts of undeveloped land on Manhattan Island. When it came to real estate, John was no trader. His approach was to buy land in the path of development, which was obviously to the north of the settled areas. He divided the tracts into individual building lots and leased each lot, usually for twenty-year periods, to anyone who wanted to build on it. John collected rent and retained title to the land. The tenant could build at his own expense. At the end of the lease, a new rent could be negotiated, or John could buy the building at its appraised value. John was rarely, if ever, a seller. This "buy and hold" method of investing was the Astor approach for generations into the future. As the city's population swelled from thirty-three thousand in 1790 to three hundred thousand in 1840, the need for housing grew rapidly. John Jacob Astor's land was right in the path of development.

---

446 Lucy Kavaler, *The Astors—A Family Chronicle of Pomp and Power.*
447 Arthur D. Howden Smith, *John Jacob Astor: Landlord of New York,* 224.

When he died in 1848, Astor left an estate of $20 million, the largest personal fortune in America at the time. He specified $400,000 of his wealth to fund the Astor Library and left the balance—all those acres of New York real estate—in a trust to one of his sons, William Backhouse Astor. Under terms of the trust, William received the rental income from the properties, but not the principal. That was preserved for the next generation.

Over the next few decades, the principal of the Astor fortune was passed down through generations of males. "Generation-skipping" trusts promoted the idea of preserving and adding to principal, spending only the trust income for living expenses, however grand. Daughters received only a modest inheritance, in the expectation they would marry well and be supported by their husbands. For minor daughters, a trust would be established to supply an income until they were married, or perhaps during their lifetime, but the principal of the trust would then revert to an Astor male. This was widespread custom well into the twentieth century. To this, the Astor men added a practice of securing, from their prospective brides, a prenuptial agreement in which the bride, on her wedding day, accepted a large sum of money in exchange for signing away any dower rights—any right to inherit Astor money or property now or later in her husband's ownership or control.

By the late 1800s, two great-grandchildren of the original John Jacob Astor were sharing the real estate fortune that had built up over a century. One half was in a trust providing income to William Waldorf Astor. He moved to England in 1890, thus starting the English Astor branch of the family. The rest of the properties were in a trust for Col. John Jacob Astor IV. Astor wealth was at the core of old money society.

Col. Astor, as he came to be known for his rank in the Spanish-American War, lived a life of luxury, next door to his mother, Caroline Shermerhorn Astor. She was the center of the New York social clique known as "the Four Hundred" and preferred to be known as "the Mrs. Astor." Her dinner and dancing party on the first Monday of each January was the annual high point of society life in New York City. She hosted a similar ball in Newport, Rhode Island, where she spent her summers. Many well-born, mature women, as well as debutantes, would wait desperately, sometimes for years, for an invitation to Mrs. Astor's grand events. To this famous group, spending money on lavish entertainment was just another competitive sport; building large mansions and collecting expensive art and jewelry were also important pastimes. The only criterion for acceptance in this social circle was family history. One's ancestors had to have been in America for at least three generations. That definitely excluded the nouveau-riche industrialists such as Gould, Carnegie, and Rockefeller. The Van Rensselaers, Van Cortlandts, Jays, Livingstons, Roosevelts, Whitneys, Delanos, and, after some thought, the Vanderbilts, were proper company. No Jews or Catholics were acceptable, regardless of wealth or talent.

Colonel Astor's annual income was estimated at $3 million, and there was no federal income tax. By 1905, Col. John Jacob Astor IV was the fourth wealthiest man in America. The real estate fortune that provided his income had grown to $87 million by the time he perished in the *Titanic* sinking in April 1912.[448] He was forty-seven years old. The *Titanic* cruise was the return trip from his European honeymoon with his second wife, Madeline. They had married the previous August, then set sail for Europe. The Colonel had signed a new will nine days after the wedding.[449]

Most of the fortune ($69 million) was left to his first son, Vincent, age twenty, who left his studies at Harvard to assume management of the real estate fortune. Vincent's sister, Ava Alice Muriel Astor, received $3 million; the Colonel's first wife, mother of Vincent and Muriel, received nothing. His second son, John Jacob Astor VI, was born four months after his mother, Madeline, was rescued from the sinking *Titanic*. Under the Colonel's will, "VI" (in his adult years he preferred to be known as "3d") would receive income from a $3 million trust until age twenty-one, and then he would inherit the principal and any accrued investment gains. This amounted to $5 million by the time he reached twenty-one and received the full inheritance, in 1933.[450]

Madeline Force Astor, a widow at age twenty, received the investment income from a $5 million trust established for her, for life or until she remarried. At her death or remarriage, the principal would go to Vincent or his heir. In 1916, Mrs. Astor married a friend from childhood, thereby forfeiting any further distributions of Astor money.

Vincent took a different approach to the family business. His ancestors had generally rented land to anyone who could pay the rent, under twenty-year or longer leases. The tenant would build on the land, at his own expense, but title to the land always remained with the Astors. As Vincent inspected his holdings, he was appalled at the poor condition of some buildings on Astor land. In some cases, he deeded the land to the city for use in new, low-income housing. Some lots were donated for neighborhood parks and playgrounds. On others,

---

448 "Col. Astor Left $85,311,228 Net," *New York Times*, June 14, 1913.
449 "Astor Fortune Goes to Vincent," *New York Times*, May 7, 1912.
450 "Astor 3d Accepts Will Settlement," *New York Times*, November 24, 1959.

he commissioned the construction of apartment buildings with amenities such as garden courtyards. A few of these are still in use, and in demand, early in the twenty-first century. His ancestors had bought land, but rarely sold it. Vincent was more of a trader, buying or selling as he believed best suited the situation.

He also diversified his investments, using proceeds from the real estate sales to purchase stocks and bonds of major corporations. The $69 million Vincent had inherited in 1912 had been increased to $127 million by the time of his death in 1959. Over a period of forty-seven years, he had increased the value of his assets by 89 percent, or 1.8 percent per year, maneuvering through two world wars and the Great Depression, while carefully balancing his time between work and leisure. When not at one of his estates, he could be found cruising on his yacht *Nourmahal*, which had been built in Germany in 1928. When Franklin Delano Roosevelt was ready to vacation after winning the presidential election in 1932, he was Vincent's guest for a ten-day cruise. The 263-foot-long vessel, complete with large gun mounts, was not a typical weekend cabin cruiser. During World War II, the United States Navy acquired *Nourmahal* and placed it in service with the Coast Guard. After the war, it was decommissioned, and in 1968 was sold for scrap.[451]

Vincent's involvement with social causes and charities also started early. One week after the *Titanic* sank, he donated $10,000 to a fund for relief of families who were left destitute by the disaster. As he settled into his real estate duties, he was well aware of the social problems of the era, especially as they affected New York. He conferred frequently with leaders of the American Federation of Labor, as well as leaders of the railroad unions, to obtain their views on the issues and possible solutions. In 1914, as socialism was attracting many followers in Europe and not a few in America, the social critic Upton Sinclair wrote to Vincent, urging him to study socialism and contribute to the socialist cause. Vincent had already been receiving advice from union leaders and sociologists, and he invoked their counsel in his letter rejecting the socialist dogma.[452]

In 1948, Vincent established the Vincent Astor Foundation, "for the alleviation of human suffering." Upon his death in 1959, he left half of his $127 million estate to the foundation to fund its philanthropy. He also established a trust, funded with an equal amount, for the care of his widow, Brooke, and left her an outright inheritance of $2 million. The income from the trust would be paid to

---

451 Dictionary of American Naval Fighting Ships. Department of the Navy, Naval Historical Center.
452 "Astor Sees No Value in Socialist Creed," *New York Times*, January 12, 1914.

her throughout her lifetime, and she was to appoint, in her own will, the disposition of the assets of that trust.[453]

Brooke Astor became actively involved in the Vincent Astor Foundation. She visited every institution or charity that received its donations to ensure that the money would be properly and effectively used. Because of her considerable knowledge of charitable works in the New York area, other foundations began to follow the "lead grants" by the Vincent Astor Foundation. At times, Mrs. Astor would use her own money to supplement grants by the foundation or to support a cause when the foundation's directors declined an application. The New York Public Library was her favorite cause, but her grants supported the city's museums and zoo, churches, homes for the elderly, and a wide variety of other organizations. Under her leadership, the foundation contributed to many neighborhood projects, helping blighted neighborhoods to recover. Among these were the Abyssinian Development Corporation, which built housing for low- and moderate-income residents of Harlem, and a separate organization that provided furniture to people moving from homelessness into permanent housing. She showed her interest and support not just by donating money and serving as chairperson of fund drives but also by her personal involvement. She spent days, dressed in her fashionable clothes, visiting any neighborhood in any borough where her funds were put to use, meeting directly with the people involved. After a paper-plate lunch at a community center, she would offer warm words to a janitor cleaning a clinic or a librarian sorting books. Evenings were for social events, often fundraisers, dining with the rich and powerful, invariably seated as the guest of honor. Weekends were for resting at her country home.[454]

In 1997, Mrs. Astor decided to distribute the remaining assets of the Vincent Astor Foundation. By the time this was completed, the foundation had disbursed almost $200 million—clearly the result of prudent stewardship and investment of the original $60+ million.[455]

When Brooke Astor died on August 13, 2007, at age 105, the *International Herald Tribune* acknowledged her as an eminent New York philanthropist. The governor and the mayor delivered official statements mourning her death and praising the many contributions she had made to improve New York. Flags at many institutions she had supported flew at half mast. While "the Mrs. Astor"

---

453 "Vincent Astor Left $127 Million Estate," *New York Times,* July 1, 1960.
454 Information on Brooke Astor's philanthropy and social contacts is from numerous articles in the *New York Times,* 1959 to 2007.
455 "The Fortune She Inherited and the Fortune She Gave to Philanthropy," *New York Times,* July 28, 2006.

of the late 1800s had a few hundred friends and little time for anyone outside of that social circle, the Mrs. Astor of the late 1900s had made a difference in the lives of thousands, through generous donations and unwavering respect for individuals regardless of their circumstances.

At this writing, the disposition of her personal assets and the investments of the trust established by Vincent for her care and support, which totaled approximately $131 million[456] just before her death in 2007, is not resolved. Questions concerning her will and several codicils to it are being resolved in the courts. But much of the fortune assembled nearly two hundred years ago and husbanded over the centuries has already benefited society through the Vincent Astor Foundation and Brooke Astor's personal philanthropy. It is uncontested that the remainder of the fortune is also destined for charitable use, as specified in Brooke Astor's will.

———

Vincent's younger half-brother, John, born after his father died in the sinking of the *Titanic* and referring to himself as John 3d in his adult years, received the principal of his trust fund at age twenty-one, in the midst of the Great Depression. It had grown from $3 million in 1912 to $5 million in 1933. He did work at one job, briefly, in a company where Vincent exerted some influence, but eventually he gave that up. The inheritance allowed John 3d to live a life of expensive leisure. There were all the household expenses of a townhouse in Manhattan with twenty-five servants, an estate in Newport (fourteen servants inside, plus six gardeners), a fleet of ten automobiles, and a large yacht. Over the years, he made several trips around the world.[457]

In 1959, when Vincent died, John 3d filed suit seeking to break Vincent's will, claiming that it had been signed under "undue influence" by the widow and two executors. As the jury was about to be empanelled, the case was settled with a payment of $250,000 to John from the foundation funds. The will was then probated, and John 3d was required to pay his own legal fees. Then there were the legal fees involved in obtaining two divorces and an attempt to get a third. There were settlements with the ex-wives, in addition to the prenuptial payments he had given to each wife in exchange for the waivers of their right

---

456 "Inventory Details Mrs. Astor's $131 Million Estate," *New York Times,* March 27, 2007.
457 Lucy Kavaler, *The Astors: A Family Chronicle of Pomp and Power,* 284.

to inherit his Astor money. John 3d's marital arrangements were so complicated that the United States Supreme Court was petitioned to decide one basic question on which the courts of two states had issued contradictory decisions: Who is the legal wife of John Jacob Astor, 3d? The Supreme Court declined to get involved. In 1954, a Florida court noted his net worth at $4.75 million—close to the amount he had inherited twenty-one years earlier. Adjusted for inflation, the $4.75 million in 1954 dollars had less than one half of the purchasing power of $4.75 million in 1933.[458] He died in 1992, leaving two children and three grandchildren.[459]

Where did all the purchasing power go? Whatever may have been the investment acumen of John Jacob Astor, 3d, obviously the expensive lifestyle was pumping much of his Astor fortune back into society, creating gainful employment for servants, gardeners, yacht builders, car salesmen, lawyers, and so many others.

———

What became of the "British half" of the Astor fortune? After moving to England in 1890, William Waldorf Astor purchased Cliveden, an eighteenth century estate, and the thirteenth century Hever Castle, and settled into the life of the landed gentry, receiving the rental income from his real estate assets in New York. Astor was determined to be accepted into the highest level of English society. He entertained lavishly and became an important patron of charity and civic organizations. He became a British citizen in 1899. In 1916, he achieved his highest goal when King George raised him to the House of Lords, with the title Baron Astor of Hever Castle. The following year, he was made a viscount. His wife, Nancy, was elected to the House of Commons. William Waldorf Astor died in 1919.

His two sons, Waldorf and John Jacob Astor V, inherited a life interest in two trusts that contained almost all of the American properties that had been left to their father.[460] Each son also owned several properties in his own name,

---

458   Lucy Kavaler, *The Astors—A Family Chronicle of Pomp and Power*, 293–295.
459   "John J. Astor 5th, 79; Son of Builder of Hotel," *New York Times,* June 27, 1992.
460   Generally, a life interest in a property or trust entitles the beneficiary to receive investment income or some other benefit, such as the right to occupy the property, during the beneficiary's life, however the beneficiary does not have power to sell the property or to dispose of the property during his life-

which the viscount had given them long before his death. While the trusts had been established in 1911, title to most of the real estate was transferred to the trusts only a few months before Waldorf died.[461] Then came a major challenge to William Waldorf Astor's estate plan. The federal government took the position that these transfers were made in anticipation of death and therefore subject to estate tax. That real estate in the U.S. was appraised at $46 million. Perhaps anticipating the need for cash to pay the estate tax, the trust sold about $21 million of the real estate during the early 1920s and reinvested the proceeds into Liberty bonds and other U.S. Treasury notes.[462] Appeals lingered in the courts until 1939, when the U.S. Supreme Court declined to hear the case and the federal government collected $11 million in estate tax.[463]

At William Waldorf Astor's death in 1919, Waldorf became the Second Viscount of Cliveden and his brother John Jacob became Second Baron of Hever Castle. They, like their father, lived in England. They received the investment income from the properties in the trusts, net of U.S. and British income taxes. Cliveden was donated to the British government in 1942, though the viscount and his family continued to live there as tenants while tourists paraded through most of the estate.

Waldorf, the Second Viscount of Cliveden, died in 1952. His interest in the New York properties was divided among his five children.[464] His oldest son, William Waldorf Astor, became Third Viscount.

In 1962, the "English Astor" properties in New York were believed to be worth about $100 million. In the same year, Britain enacted a new estate tax aimed at discouraging foreign investments and promoting investment in the U.K. Under the new law, foreign assets owned by a U.K. resident would be subject to an estate tax at 80 percent of value. All the New York real estate owned by the English Astors would be subject to this tax.[465]

Baron Astor of Hever, son of the original Baron, and his wife exercised their inalienable right to avoid taxes by avoiding the taxed activity, which in this case would be dying in England while owning foreign assets. They took up residence

---

time or by will.
461 "Big Astor Estate Here Goes to Sons," *New York Times*, August 16, 1919; "Capt. Astor's Bride Got $4,000,000 Gift," *New York Times*, September 3, 1921.
462 "Astor's Heirs Sold $21,073,983 Realty Here in Five Years," *New York Times*, May 17, 1925.
463 "Astor State Tax Put at $1,775,155," *New York Times*, July 18, 1944.
464 "Astor Will Is Probated," *New York Times*, October 28, 1952.
465 "Leasehold Cornucopia," *New York Times*, November 11, 1962.

in the south of France. As a consequence, the British government never collected the estate tax. Britain also lost the income taxes it had previously been collecting on the substantial rental income flowing from America. That went to France, at a much lower tax rate than Britain's.[466]

In 1983, Hever Castle was sold. It is now an amusement park. Cliveden, the eighteenth century estate, is now a luxury hotel. By the 1960s, there were eight adult grandchildren of the first baron-viscount, and most of them already had their own children. The English Astor wealth has been divided many times, and the trail runs cold.

———

The last of the American Astor fortune, the real estate-based wealth handed down when Col. John Jacob Astor died on the *Titanic*, is the personal legacy of Brooke Astor, widow of Vincent. Prior to his death in 1959, Vincent had converted much of it from real estate to other investments, primarily stocks and bonds.[467] Brooke Astor's $131 million legacy is, in terms of purchasing power, quite small compared to the 1905 fortune of Col. John Jacob Astor. It is no longer among the largest American fortunes listed in *Forbes*. We marvel at the lasting power of such wealth over the past century and enjoy the good that it is funding through philanthropy. The inescapable fact is that most of this great fortune has already found its way back into society, and the remainder is destined to do so under the terms of Brooke Astor's will.

---

466 Lucy Kavaler, *The Astors: A Family Chronicle of Pomp and Power*, 300–302.
467 "Vincent Astor Left $127 Million Estate," *New York Times*, July 1, 1960.

Chapter Eighteen

Marshall Field

M arshall Field (1834–1906) established a wholesale distribution business that supplied local retail stores and general stores around the country. Many of the goods sold to local merchants were actually made in Marshall Field plants. Field was one of nine children born on a farm near Conway, Massachusetts, in 1834. He received little formal schooling and started work at age sixteen as a clerk in a local store. At age twenty-two, he moved to Chicago and took a job as a clerk at the wholesale dry goods house of Cooley, Wadsworth & Co. Four years later, in 1860, he became general manager, with a small financial stake in the business. Some biographers report that Marshall consistently saved one-half of his wages. In 1865, he and a partner, Levi Leiter, were invited to join one of Chicago's other prominent merchants, Potter Palmer. Field put $160,000 into the deal, Levi Leiter $130,000, and Potter Palmer kept a $450,000 interest in the new firm, called Field, Palmer & Leiter. In 1866, this firm hired a twenty-three-year old Montgomery Ward. Six years later, Ward left and established the first mail-order retailer in America.[468] In 1868, Palmer, suffering from tuberculosis, sold his interest to Field and Leiter.[469]

Success was not easy. The new State Street store built by Field and Leiter in 1868 was destroyed, along with a major part of Chicago, in the Great Fire

---

468 *New York Times* obituary of Montgomery Ward, December 8, 1913.
469 "Marshall Field Dead; His Fortune $150,000,000," *New York Times,* January 17, 1906.

of 1871. Another fire destroyed the rebuilt building in 1877. Once again, the partners rebuilt and reopened. As the business grew, the two partners had serious disagreements about strategy for the business. Eventually, Field bought out Leiter's interest, and the firm became Marshall Field & Co. The business was tremendously successful. He reinvested his profits into areas beyond the wholesale/retail empire, buying up every available piece of downtown Chicago real estate and buying enough shares to have controlling interest in Pullman Co., maker of railroad cars. Both the man and the store became icons. In 1890, Field donated the land for the newly established University of Chicago. In 1896, Field's wife passed away.

By 1905, Marshall Field was the third wealthiest man in the U.S. Local newspapers estimated his wealth at $100 million to $125 million. In September 1905, he married his new love. By January 1906, he was dead. Six months after Field died, the Cook County Board of Review, the Chicago Corporation Counsel's Office, and executors of the estate agreed to a provisional assessment value of $180 million.[470]

His twenty-two-thousand-word will was, at the time, the longest ever written. Field left $8 million to establish the Field Museum of Natural History. To his wife, he left their mansion on Prairie Avenue, his personal belongings, and $1 million. She had received a gift of $2 million from him at their wedding just four months earlier. His only daughter, already married, received $8 million. Field's only son, Marshall Field II, had died two months before his father's death of an accidental gunshot wound, leaving a widow and three children: Henry Field, Gwendolyn Field, and Marshall Field III.[471]

Gwendolyn and her brothers shared income from a $5 million trust. Gwendolyn married Archibald Charles Edmonstone in 1923. The groom's parents presented the newlyweds a castle in Scotland as a wedding present. The remainder of the grandfather's estate was in a separate trust to be doled out to the brothers over a period of many years. Field had also specified in his will that the trustees were to keep at least 50 percent of this fortune left to his grandsons invested in real estate. Henry Field died in 1917 at age twenty-two. His share of the Field fortune would go to his brother under terms of the grandfather's will.[472]

Marshall Field III was just twelve years old when his father and grandfather died within weeks of each other. He spent much of his remaining youth in Eng-

---

470   *Chicago Daily Tribune,* July 26, 1906
471   *New York Times,* November 23, 1905; November 21, 1956
472   *New York Times,* January 24, 1906, July 9, 1917, May 15, 1920, April 6, 1923.

land, where he attended Eton College and Cambridge University. He served as an artillery captain in the U.S. Army in World War I, receiving the Silver Star for gallantry in France. In 1917, the trustees of the estate of Marshall Field, including Marshall Field III, sold the company in which the fortune had been made to the officers who were then running the firm. The estate accepted 178,000 shares of preferred stock in exchange for its common stock, thereby allowing the Field estate trustees to step out of management decisions.[473]

During the 1920s, Marshall Field III enjoyed the life of leisure that his inheritance provided and purchased a twenty-two-hundred-acre country estate, Caumsett, on the north shore of Long Island. He owned and piloted his own plane, and he owned racehorses. During the Depression, the decline in business forced a suspension of dividends on the preferred stock.

As directed in the will, he inherited $100 million from his grandfather's estate at age forty-five, in 1938, and received his full inheritance in 1943, when he reached age fifty. At that point, the estate was worth about $75 million, and Marshall Field III already had holdings of about $93 million. The inheritance, added to his existing wealth, made him one of the world's wealthiest men in 1943.[474]

During the Great Depression, Marshall III was a major supporter of President Franklin Roosevelt's New Deal programs, including those that gave greater bargaining strength to unions. There were limits to Marshall's liberality, however. In late 1947 and early 1948, members of the International Typographical Union engaged in a series of work slowdowns, which their own leaders warned them were outside of their contract rights. Finally, the union struck one of the two Field-owned Chicago newspapers. Field merged his two newspaper companies and continued publishing both by simply bypassing the strike-bound composing room.[475]

Marshal Field III established the Field Foundation in 1940 and recruited leading social scientists, scholars, business leaders, and judges to serve on the board of advisors. The foundation's mission was to discover "a few ideas and social techniques [that may] germinate and eventually prove to be of enough value to be adopted by the community." In just the first four years, the foundation paid out grants of $4.5 million to major institutions in Chicago and to smaller groups working to improve race relations and child welfare.[476]

---

473 "Marshall Field & Co.," *Fortune*, October 1936.
474 *New York Times*, September 29, 1938; September 28, 1943.
475 *New York Times*, October 29, 1947; February 5, 1948
476 "Marshall Field Dies at Age of 63," *New York Times*, November 9, 1956.

Marshall Field III died in 1956 at age sixty-three. Newspapers at the time reported that, during his lifetime, Marshall III had already given much of his inheritance to the Field Foundation and to family members over the years. His estate was valued at $160 million. His will designated a $30 million bequest to the Field Foundation. His widow received the family homes—Caumsett, the Long Island country estate, and a co-op apartment in New York City, and a thir-teen-thousand-acre estate in South Carolina—plus $1.1 million cash. Each of his eleven grandchildren received $100,000, and there were specific bequests to many of his business and personal employees, some of whom received as much as a full year of salary. The remainder was left to his only son, Marshall Field IV.[477]

Four years later, the foundation was divided into two entities: the Field Foundation of New York, directed by his widow, Ruth, and the Field Foundation of Illinois, led by his son, Marshall Field IV.[478] The New York foundation, as Ruth had directed, donated the last of its remaining assets and closed in 1989. The Il-linois foundation, with net assets of $62.7 million in 2006, continues to support numerous local organizations active in health, education, community welfare, culture, and the environment, with total grant payments of $3.5 million in 2005 and 2006.

Marshall Field IV, son of Marshall Field III and great-grandson of the original Marshall Field, died September 18, 1965, and left an estate estimated at $25.5 million in trust to his six children. Apparently, he had already given much of the fortune he had inherited nine years earlier to charities and possibly to his children. He had been editor and publisher of the *Chicago Daily News* and the *Chicago Sun-Times* and publisher of the World Book Encyclopedia.[479]

Marshall Field V sold the *Chicago Sun-Times* to Rupert Murdoch in 1984. Marshall manages his own investments and has been a leader in Chicago phi-lanthropy, including the Field Museum, and a supporter of environmental and conservation organizations for many years.

Here the trail runs cold on the fortune of the first Marshall Field, preserved in a trust that was carefully balanced between real estate and securities until its termination in 1943. Much of the current Field fortune is no doubt the result of the numerous major investments made since that time, which is beyond the scope of this work.

---

477 "Field Fund Gets $30 Million in Will," *New York Times,* November 21, 1956.
478 Field Foundation of Illinois website www.fieldfoundation.org contains a biennial report including lists of grants and audited financial statements.
479 "Marshall Field's Estate Valued at $25.5 Million," *New York Times,* September 29, 1965.

Chapter Nineteen

Andrew Carnegie

An immigrant who never lost his Scottish accent or his sense of thrift, Andrew Carnegie worked his way up from telegraph operator to railroad manager, then he jumped into the iron industry. He retired in 1901 as the wealthiest man in the world. Carnegie is widely remembered as a man of enormous wealth. Few know him as a globe-trotting peace activist with direct access to princes and presidents or know that he planned to give away his entire fortune before he died. And he largely accomplished that.

Carnegie was born in Scotland in 1835. Just two years later, his father lost his job as a weaver when factories with steam-powered looms moved into the area. This new technology quickly displaced one thousand handloom weavers in the area, driving the unemployment rate to almost 40 percent. The financial impact was devastating. The weavers lost not only their home-based jobs; the hand-operated looms they owned personally were rendered almost worthless by the new technology. From age eight, Carnegie received some schooling at the local Rolland School, where the school's headmaster taught 180 children in a single classroom.[480] By age thirteen, he had been introduced to Latin and algebra and demonstrated a prodigious memory.[481]

---

480 David Nasaw, *Andrew Carnegie*, 16.
481 *The Autobiography of Andrew Carnegie*, 27.

When Carnegie was thirteen, his mother borrowed the money for the family's passage to America. The Carnegies' first years in America were typical of the thousands of immigrants in that era. They lived in a two-room apartment. Andrew's father found work in a factory. His mother worked at home binding shoes, sometimes working till midnight after a day of housekeeping. Andrew went to work also.

Carnegie's first jobs were in cotton mills. He hated it. Pungent vapors from the soaking vats made him nauseated. He failed as a boiler operator. He and some friends took accounting courses at night. That led to an office job at the mill. A friend told him about a job as a runner, carrying messages from the local telegraph office to the home or business of the recipient. While waiting for his next assignment, Andrew listened to the operators clicking away at their keys and gradually learned Morse Code. He was given several opportunities to fill in temporarily for other operators and did well. He was soon promoted as a telegraph operator, his first "man's job," earning one dollar per day.[482]

Carnegie often lamented his lack of formal education, and he improvised methods of building his knowledge. He organized friends and acquaintances into a debating society, and they used their Sunday afternoons for formal discussions and debates of the news and philosophical questions. He read constantly and memorized long poems and passages from Shakespeare and others. As his business responsibilities grew to involve more social functions, he found coaches to help him learn the social graces that had not been part of his early life.[483] Humble beginnings were not a barrier to success, in Carnegie's view. In a speech he gave to the 1885 graduating class of Bellevue Hospital Medical School in New York, he observed, "Being born poor was a virtue, not a deficit, as it forced a young man to be self-sufficient at an early age."

As his skills improved, his reputation for speed and accuracy spread through the business community. The man in charge of the nearby railroad office eventually needed a full-time telegraph operator to handle railroad messages, and he hired the best operator he could find—Andrew Carnegie. His job as telegraph operator in the railroad office soon grew into that of an all-purpose executive assistant. The more energy and initiative he showed, the more his duties expanded. In a few years, he was filling in as temporary superintendent whenever his boss was away from the office. The job was no longer one of regular hours. Advancement brought responsibility for the work of others, for schedules met

---

482 Ibid, 36, 52–56.
483 Ibid, 69–76, 89.

and cargoes delivered, for accidents and repairs at all hours. When his boss was promoted to vice president, Andrew was promoted to full-time superintendent, responsible for all of the railroad's operations in his geographic area. He was twenty-four years old.[484]

Carnegie had unusual, perhaps unequaled, ability to identify major changes in market demand for products. Those changes are now called strategic inflection points. As described by Andy Grove, former CEO of Intel Corporation, "An inflection point occurs where the old strategic picture dissolves and gives way to the new." Grove goes on to write:

> Strategic inflection points can be caused by technological changes, but they are more than technological change. They can be caused by competitors, but they are more than just competition. They are full-scale changes in the way business is conducted, so that simply adopting new technology or fighting the competition as you used to may be insufficient.

Grove provides additional comments that show how difficult it is to deal with these inflection points:

> We can't stop these changes. We can't hide from them. Instead we must focus on getting ready for them. The lessons of dealing with strategic inflection points are similar whether you're dealing with a company or your own career...You need to plan the way a fire department plans: It cannot anticipate where the next fire will be, so it has to shape an energetic and efficient team that is capable of responding to the unanticipated as well as to any ordinary event...when companies no longer have lifetime careers, how can they provide one for their employees?[485]

Many fine business leaders recognize and deal successfully with one strategic inflection point in their career. Carnegie managed his own career, and his companies, to triumph in at least three. First, he picked a great time to enter the iron business and leave the railroad, in 1864–1865. Carnegie had concluded that it was far better to supply materials to the railroads than to be an investor in them. In contrast, his mentor at the Pennsylvania Railroad, Tom Scott,

---

484 Ibid, 58, 61–68, 83.
485 Andy Grove, *Only the Paranoid Survive,* 4–6.

remained there and lost a great deal of money and all his railroad stock in the Panic of 1873. Carnegie also recognized early that iron would give way to steel as the material for railroad tracks. The railroads wanted steel rails to hold heavier freight loads and more powerful locomotives. In the 1880s, when the railroads were still buying rails for their expansion across the continent, Carnegie foresaw that the market for rails was reaching its peak. He converted many of his plants to making structural components for buildings. His timing was perfect. Architects and engineers wanted steel for taller buildings, longer bridges, and bigger ships. Between 1883 and 1890, the market for rails grew 62 percent, but the market for structural parts grew 808 percent! Recognizing that access to coke was essential to the growing steel business, Carnegie formed an important alliance with Henry Clay Frick, acquiring in that deal not just access to coke, but partnership with another experienced executive fourteen years younger than Carnegie. His foresight was excellent.

Andrew Carnegie was not the only person making an immense fortune at the time. In 1888, a reporter for the *New York Times* compiled a list of 134 millionaires living in Pittsburgh alone. Some of these fortunes may have been smaller than they appeared, since the income tax did not yet exist and there was little public disclosure of profits or executive compensation by most businesses. Whatever the precise numbers, numerous very large fortunes were being made. At the same time, the middle class was rapidly expanding, with sufficient discretionary income to support the retailing fortunes of Marshall Field, Montgomery Ward, Irving Straus (Macy's), and at the turn of the century, Messrs. Sears, Roebuck, and Rosenwald.

Some of Carnegie's success depended upon his selection of well-trained, energetic managers, and setting them up as financial partners in his businesses. Carnegie went so far as to lend money to his key managers so they could afford to buy into the company and share in its profits. Early on, he hired Alexander Holley, the foremost steel engineer in the U.S., to design a new steel plant at Braddock Field in Pennsylvania, strategically close to supplies of bituminous coal (for coke) and low-phosphorous iron ore. It proved to be the most efficient mill in the U.S. Ever focused on his customers, Carnegie named the mill "Edgar B. Thomson," after the president of the Pennsylvania Railroad.

Carnegie recognized basic truths that applied, then and now, in process industries. The cost of plants and equipment were huge fixed costs that did not subside when sales were slow. Customers constantly sought the lowest available price, so prices of finished products were subject to large swings driven by shifts in supply and demand. Only the most efficient operations could survive during the inevitable periods of low prices in these cyclical industries. Just before the Panic of 1873, steel was selling for $120 per ton. By 1875, it was selling for $66 per ton; in December 1876, $52/ton; one year later, $42/ton; and in May 1878, it sold for $40/ton. Reinvestment of profits, especially in the "good years," was key to long-term survival in the highly cyclical iron and steel businesses. Rather than dividing and paying out all the profits at the end of each year, Carnegie and his partners usually reinvested 75 percent of the profits into new equipment and mills to keep the competitive advantage of ever-greater efficiency. In a downturn, they could make a profit, however thin, while their less-efficient competitors were losing money and possibly going broke. Carnegie and his partners would sell steel at whatever price they could get to keep the mills running. When overproduction or periodic business recessions drove down steel prices and profits, Carnegie's companies were able to buy up the mills and equipment of struggling competitors. When the economy recovered and demand for steel resumed, they reaped the benefit of their long-term planning, financial discipline, and reinvestment in the business.

Carnegie kept the wages of his workers as low as possible and constantly compared wages at his mills to wages paid by competitors. He considered unions to be desirable as social and fraternal organizations for his workers and allowed his executives to negotiate with a union as bargaining agent for the workers. Union reps and workers could read the ever-changing steel prices in the business news or in data supplied by the company. But if a negotiating deadline passed without agreement, then the company's new wage scale would be posted at the mill gate. Any worker who wanted employment was to individually sign a new contract.[486] Strikes were not uncommon, and he accepted the costly inefficiencies of shutting down and restarting the huge mills whenever strikes occurred. The darkest days of Carnegie's business career involve the 1892 labor strike and lockout at the Homestead Plant in Pennsylvania.

At the time, Homestead was the most technologically advanced steel mill in the nation, with almost four thousand employees. The population of the nearby town was twelve thousand, and almost everyone's livelihood depended on the plant. The Amalgamated Association of Iron and Steel Workers, the strongest union in the area and the largest metalworkers union in the world, represented the workers.[487] But labor costs were rising faster than productivity. Early in 1892, Carnegie decided to merge the Homestead Plant and several other non-

---

486 David Nasaw, *Andrew Carnegie*, 412.
487 "A Mighty Struggle Ahead," *New York Times*, June 27, 1892.

union plants into a single company, Carnegie Steel. He wanted the same wage structure at all the plants, and that structure had to recognize recent plant modernizations. Over the next few months, as the July 1 contract expiration approached, positions hardened, especially on wages. Carnegie was in Scotland, but he was informed of the escalating tensions by his on-site president, Henry Clay Frick.

When negotiations broke down on July 24, the company closed the plant and hired three hundred Pinkerton security guards to protect the property. Workers became concerned that the company would hire new workers to replace them and set up patrols in the area to detect any new arrivals. In fact, Carnegie supported a plan to import such scab workers.[488] Workers forced the local sheriff and deputies out of town, believing they were likely to sympathize with the company. Local authorities asked the governor to send militia to keep order, but he declined. When the Pinkerton security guards arrived at the plant on July 6, a pitched battle broke out. Six workers and two guards were killed. The Pennsylvania militia was dispatched and restored order. The strike continued until late November, when the workers accepted the company wage structure. Homestead remained a nonunion plant. In the deep recession that started in 1893, Carnegie Steel remained profitable each year, and employment at Homestead remained steady.[489] Two decades later, Andrew Carnegie was still haunted by the events of 1892 and devoted a chapter of his autobiography to exorcising the demons.

―――――

Carnegie's financial management of the companies mirrored his management of his personal finances. As a young man, he had always saved a large portion of his wages, rather than spending whatever he had. He invested the savings in promising ventures beyond the companies he managed. As early as 1863, not yet thirty years old, his annual income was $47,860 (equal to about $8.5 million today), from fifteen different investments. Carnegie was doing quite well before he entered the iron and steel business. Years later, Carnegie would reach into his personal savings to buy back shares from partners who had been less thrifty with their own finances and found themselves short of cash. Even after he had amassed a huge fortune, he sought bargains. Carnegie bought Skibo, a

---

488 David Nasaw, *Andrew Carnegie,* 396–407, 413–420.
489 Ibid, 420–427, 456, 469.

dilapidated Scottish castle, at a steep discount as a summer home and put money into repairs and improvements.[490] In 1898, near the apex of his career, he was looking for a site for his new home in New York City. Ever the bargain hunter, he bought land far north of the established mansion district, and therefore less expensive. Within a few years, the well-to-do were paying much higher prices to be his neighbor.

While Carnegie gave millions to causes for the benefit of people in general, he fiercely resisted almsgiving—providing subsistence to the poor. His position was clear: "There should be no failures in the world, and no poor. The man who is poor has himself to blame. I would be the last to lend him money."[491] Carnegie was equally critical of those who are wealthy but lazy: "Why should not an honest, worthy, educated man, even though he be a coachman, be better than a worthless profligate, even though the latter be a Duke?"[492]

In a speech in London in 1902, Carnegie gave his thoughts on how best to assist those in need:

It is so easy to create poverty and pauperism by giving, so difficult to lessen it. Curative measures seem ineffective and of little moment; we must get at prevention, and that is probably only to be reached through the instruction of the people leading to better habits, for much of the extreme poverty of the people comes from lack of sobriety, prudence, and thrift. Where it arises from other causes, such as disability or indisposition to work or confirmed intemperance causing permanent pauperism, then such persons become the proper care of the State, not of the individual. If all the money devoted to charitable ends were wisely given and wisely administered we should make some headway, but much of that which well-meaning people give is not only useless; some of it may be positively harmful, widening the area of the misery which they fondly hope to contract.

Indiscriminate charity works evil, and that continually, and, generally speaking, individual charity is beneficial only when it helps people to help themselves... We must attend to the causes of poverty and crime and strike at the roots, and not keep forever chopping at the branches of

---

490 David Nasaw, *Andrew Carnegie*, 85, 523.
491 *New York Times*, August 31, 1919
492 *New York Times*, April 27, 1905

the Upas tree. No man can be pushed up a ladder who does not do some of the climbing himself.[493]

Carnegie's comments were in tune with many leading social workers of the time. The influential Charity Organization Societies (COS) had lobbied during the 1880s and 1890s for the abolition of all "outdoor aid"—assistance to people not in institutions.[494] In 1894, Amos Warner, professor of economics and social science at Stanford University, after reviewing the available literature on aid programs, published his conclusion that "as administered in the United States... outdoor relief educates more people for the almshouse than it keeps out of it, and that therefore it is neither economical nor kindly."[495]

In 1901, Carnegie, then sixty-five years old, was looking forward to retirement as an opportunity to spend even more time on his other activities. Investment banker J. P. Morgan was planning to put together the new steel-making corporation that would become known as United States Steel. Carnegie, the largest shareholder of Carnegie Company, received $226 million for his 56 percent share—approximately $120 billion today.[496] The capitalization of the new U.S. Steel would total $1.4 billion, including the bonds that Carnegie received in exchange for his stock in Carnegie Company. The 5 percent interest rate provided an income stream of $11.3 million each year. If the new corporation defaulted on these payments, Carnegie could foreclose on all the real estate of the new corporation.

When they shook hands after agreeing on the deal, J. P. Morgan congratulated Andrew Carnegie on becoming the richest man in the world. Morgan would know. He was a leading investment banker in the New York, London, and European financial markets.[497]

———

493 Verbatim text of speech, *New York Times,* June 1, 1902.

494 James T. Patterson, *America's Struggle Against Poverty in the Twentieth Century,* 20

495 Amos Warner, *American Charities—A Study in Philanthropy and Economics,* 171

496 Charles R. Morris, *Tycoons,* contains detailed analysis of the Carnegie Steel buyout, including valuation considerations such as book value and profits of the company.

497 David Nasan, *Andrew Carnegie,* 586.

Fully retired, Carnegie became a full-time philanthropist and publicly announced his plan to give all of his fortune to charity before he died. He worked hard at it and maintained a full-time staff to efficiently handle this major work in a manner that ensured that funds were achieving the desired objectives. But the idea of giving away his entire fortune during his lifetime was not new to him. Prior to his marriage in 1887, he had made known his intentions to his fiancée, Louise. The planned wholesale philanthropy was clearly written into their prenuptial agreement, signed by both of them on their wedding day, in which Louise accepted an annual income of $20,000 (more than $3 million today) in exchange for acknowledging and agreeing to Andrew's plan "to devote the bulk of his estate to charitable and educational purposes."[498] The document not only sets forth their shared intention with regard to the fortune, but also establishes that the philanthropy was not some self-administered penance for the harsh labor practices that would later tarnish his reputation, nor a response to social activists decrying the wide gap between rich and poor. In fact, Carnegie was ahead of his time, and his widely published essays "Gospel of Wealth" called on his fellow millionaires to begin giving away their fortunes as well.

Carnegie believed that libraries, open to the public and free of charge, would be valuable to anyone interested in improving his or her own education. He embarked on a program to make libraries available. Any town or city that would provide suitable land and commit to supporting the staff and maintenance of the library would receive a grant from Carnegie for the total cost of the building. More than sixteen hundred libraries were built in the U.S., another nine hundred overseas, including locations in South Africa, New Zealand, Fiji, Mauritius, the Seychelles, and the West Indies. In New York City alone, sixty-seven libraries were built, forming the major part of what became the branch library system for the city. The buildings were so well designed and constructed that a study of the New York City libraries conducted in 1996 found that fifty-seven were still standing, and fifty-four were still serving as libraries.[499] Many of them serve recent immigrants, as they did when they opened a century ago. The libraries are Carnegie's quiet legacy; there are no plaques or monuments honoring the benefactor.

In 1905, he established the Carnegie Foundation for the Advancement of Teaching. The original mission of this foundation was "to provide retiring pen-

---

498 Ibid, 297.
499 Kirk Johnson, "Carnegie Descendant Finds Personal Stake in Historical Study," *New York Times*, November 28, 1996.

sions for the teachers of universities, colleges, and technical schools in our country, Canada and Newfoundland...without regard to race, sex, creed or color." State-supported institutions and those affiliated with churches were excluded. For this endeavor, he enlisted a board of directors consisting of presidents of leading universities and colleges. Pensions quickly became a major factor in attracting the best professors, since their salaries were often so low that saving for retirement was impossible. The board of directors set standards for institutions that would be eligible for pensions, declaring that the college or university must already have an endowment fund of at least $200,000 (to prevent hastily established or marginally financed operations from applying) and that students have completed a minimum number of academic courses in high school prior to admission. The foundation became the first unofficial national accreditation agency for colleges and universities. As independent colleges and universities grew in number and size, it became apparent that not even Carnegie could afford to finance all the pensions that would be needed. In response, the trustees established and provided initial funding for a new contributory pension plan. Today it is known as the Teachers Insurance and Annuity Association—College Retirement Equities Fund (TIAA-CREF).

The Carnegie Foundation for the Advancement of Teaching also had dramatic impact upon the training of American physicians. In 1908, the foundation commissioned a study of medical schools in the United States and Canada. Two years later, the report, now known as the Flexner Report for its principal author, Abraham Flexner, rocked the medical and academic communities. Flexner had visited all of the 155 medical schools operating in the U.S. and Canada, measuring them in detail against the well-established medical schools of Germany and a few newer schools in the U.S., particularly Johns Hopkins in Maryland. The report was devastatingly honest. It was not unusual for medical schools to admit students who had not completed high school, and a few admitted students with only grade school–level training. Laboratories, microscopes, and medical instruments were optional. Many of the medical schools were diploma mills. The country already had more than enough practitioners with an MD degree. Some towns of a few hundred people had several physicians, none of them adequately trained and all of them hustling for business. Meanwhile, the number of people graduating from medical schools each year was four times the number needed to replace physicians who died or retired and to minister to the nation's growing population.

The report urged the buildup of a much smaller number of schools directly tied to universities, the immediate tightening of admission standards to require documented completion of high school, including biology, chemistry, and physics courses, and a roll-in of requirements for a complete college degree as a prerequisite to medical school admission. Instructors were to be full-time physician-researchers, rather than moonlighting general practitioners looking for supplemental income. The schools would be allied with hospitals to give students properly managed clinical training. In some states, the medical licensing exams used the same questions every year and thus could be passed by anyone with an average memory. The foundation's report urged adoption of exams that tested a graduate's understanding of scientific methods and clinical diagnosis, rather than repetition of facts.[500] The importance of the Flexner Report in establishing the modern system of medical education in America was recognized in a *New England Journal of Medicine* article, "American Medical Education 100 Years After the Flexner Report," in September 2006.

———

Long before his retirement, Carnegie became an outspoken advocate of naval disarmament and lobbied for treaties that would require arbitration of international disputes. As early as 1887, he brought a delegation of British MPs to the White House to press President Cleveland for an arbitration treaty. According to Carnegie's plan, arbitration treaties would establish a commission that would listen to the disputing countries, and then render a decision. Carnegie realized that some parties would be unwilling to abide by the commission's decision, and in some cases, military action might be needed to enforce the decision. He was well aware of the limitations in his proposal. But Carnegie still saw value in establishing a track record of precedents that would give interpretation to international law, just as court decisions within countries become precedents that add to the understanding of state and national laws. The precedents, Carnegie believed, would be valuable in helping future disputants resolve their own differences peacefully.

Carnegie pursued these policies as passionately as he had pursued his business plans. He gave speeches to numerous pacifist organizations, and he paid the travel expenses of ministers visiting Washington to meet with their senators to discuss disarmament. There were letters to the editors of newspapers in the

---

500 *Medical Education in the United States and Canada Bulletin Number Four (The Flexner Report).* Available at www.carnegiefoundation.org/sites/default/files/library/Carnegie_Flexner_Report.pdf

U.S. and abroad, plus massive distribution of pamphlets written by Carnegie himself, explaining his proposals. As one of America's wealthiest citizens and leading industrialists, he wrote often to every U.S. president to hold office from 1887 until his death in 1919. He lobbied against U.S. annexation of Cuba and the Philippines, which had been ceded to the U.S. by Spain at the end of the Spanish-American War. As a major contributor to political campaigns, he had easy access to the White House. Lunch with the president of the United States was just another opportunity for Carnegie to present his position. His articles and letters to the editor were carried in newspapers in the U.S. and abroad. He visited British foreign secretaries and prime ministers, who were also guests at his summer home in Scotland.

Congress was apparently unimpressed by the naval disarmament idea. In January 1900, the U.S. had 5 battleships and 133 active navy vessels. Five years later, there were 12 battleships and 177 vessels. By 1910, there were 25 battleships and 187 vessels. And by 1915, with Europe at war, the U.S. fleet had expanded to 34 battleships and 224 vessels.[501] During the same period, Britain had been upgrading its navy with more heavily armed battleships and cruisers. Germany, widely recognized as the strongest military force in the world, was leading the arms race.

The leaders Carnegie courted listened patiently and nodded appreciatively, but they ignored his advice. If Kaiser Wilhelm paid any attention to Carnegie's plan, he was also aware of Carnegie's numerous speeches highlighting the superiority of the English-speaking race. The Kaiser would also have noted Carnegie's well-publicized calls for close union between Britain and America, as well as his specific discussion of a naval alliance between the two. Carnegie even flew a "united flag," a Union Jack sewed to the Stars and Stripes, from his Scottish castle and his yacht.[502] In 1910, Carnegie enlisted former President Theodore Roosevelt to visit the German Kaiser and advance the Carnegie agenda. Roosevelt had solid credentials as a peacemaker. He had convinced Britain and Venezuela to submit a dispute to the newly established Hague Tribunal in 1902, and he received the Nobel Peace Prize in 1906 for negotiating an end to the Russo-Japanese War. But the Kaiser surely knew that the same Theodore Roosevelt had, as president from 1901 to 1909, built up the American naval fleet to one of the

---

501 Data from Naval Historical Center.
502 "Mr. Carnegie on the Anglo-American Ideal" *New York Times,* June 1, 1902.

largest in the world. Carnegie never realized the mixed messages he was giving the German leader.[503]

In a press conference in 1913, Carnegie lamented, "It is a pity that we have to spend so much money on warships. For the price of one battleship we could build sixty American embassies at $250,000 each."[504] For all his familiarity with people in power, on both sides of the Atlantic, Carnegie seemed unable to read political developments. In 1914, when Europe erupted into full-scale war, Carnegie was completely surprised. He became somber and reclusive for several years.[505]

In 1911, Carnegie made his big move in philanthropy. He established the Carnegie Corporation of New York[506] as a grant-making foundation to promote "the advancement and diffusion of knowledge and understanding." His initial gift was $25 million in U.S. Steel first mortgage gold bonds, which he had obtained in his sale of Carnegie Steel to J. P. Morgan in 1901. By the time of his death in 1919, he had endowed this foundation with a total of $125 million, and under terms of his will, the corporation received another $10 million in 1923–1924.[507] As specified by Carnegie, the grants must benefit the people of the United States, although up to 7.4 percent of the funds could be used for the same purpose in countries that are or have been members of the British Commonwealth, with a current emphasis on sub-Saharan Africa. Carnegie also set up and funded a parallel United Kingdom Trust in 1913.

This tremendous concentration of wealth, in the form of highly secure corporate bonds backed by the real estate of America's largest corporation, is worth tracking. Carnegie specified in the organization's charter that the capital he had donated was to be a permanent fund, and only the income (interest or dividends) from it could be spent. Both realized and unrealized capital gains (profits from selling or holding securities that had increased in value) were to remain

---

503 Roosevelt, who had no official position at that time, did visit the Kaiser, but never brought up disarmament or arbitration treaties.
504 "Carnegie Derides Abbott's Panacea," *New York Times,* May 25, 1913.
505 *The Autobiography of Andrew Carnegie,* preface by Louise Whitfield Carnegie.
506 The use of the word corporation in the name of this organization, which is clearly a foundation, is most unusual. It arises from the fact that Carnegie had already established so many philanthropic organizations and foundations that naming the new organization became a challenge. For lack of an agreeable alternative, Carnegie and the trustees agreed on this name.
507 Carnegie Corporation of New York, memo of R. Sullivan, treasurer, to the Board of Trustees, January 22, 1980

with the principal. Carnegie's primary concern was safety of the principal. Unfortunately, the concentration in bonds, while consistent with prevailing investment methods of the time, exposed the corporation's principal and income to the ravages of serious inflation during and immediately after World War I. By 1920, inflation had cut the purchasing power of a dollar to half of its value in 1913. In other words, if the corporation paid a grant of $5,000 to an organization in 1913, and then awarded another grant of $5,000 to the same organization in 1920, the second grant would buy only half as much in goods or services as the first grant.

One important weakness of bonds, from an investment perspective, is the erosion of purchasing power from inflation, especially during periods of high inflation rates.[508] During periods of deflation, when prices are falling, the purchasing power of fixed income from bonds actually rises. This was a benefit to the corporation during the Great Depression, and by 1936, the purchasing power of the principal had recovered to 91 percent of its 1913 level. By 1953, although the corporation had shifted part of its principal into stocks beginning in 1933, the purchasing power of the principal, and thus of grants paid out of the income, had dropped to 51 percent of the 1913 level. By 1979, purchasing power had again dropped to 29 percent of 1913 levels, because of inflation rates that averaged 8.5 percent annually from 1972 to 1979.

Treasurer Richard Sullivan explained the situation to the corporation's board of trustees in 1980:

> Let me turn this about to be sure that the long-term effect is understood. At the close of the last fiscal year (9/30/79) the market value of invested assets was just under $295 million. For those assets to be as valuable in purchasing power as the endowment was in 1913, they would need to be slightly over $1 billion in 1979. The cumulative effect of the Corporation's own policies and strategies, of market patterns, and of inflation has been very large indeed."[509]

---

508 The serious problem of rising costs is well-known to individuals retiring on a fixed income, such as a defined-benefit pension. Fortunately, Social Security payments are adjusted each year for inflation, using a "cost of living adjustment," or COLA. With longer life expectancies, the need for individuals to have inflation-resistant investments becomes more acute. Thus the importance of properly invested 401(k) and IRA accounts and the recent government interest in individual investment accounts to supplement Social Security.
509 Carnegie Corporation of New York, memo of R. Sullivan, treasurer, to the

The message was clear. Without improved investment results, produced through higher corporate profits, the corporation's ability to fund the organizations depending on it would diminish. This contradicted Carnegie's instruction that the corporation continue in perpetuity. Unless the trend were reversed, there could come a day when the corporation would close its doors. These problems arose in spite of the best efforts of a diligent board and officers, its investment committee, and professional investment advisors retained by the corporation.

The board invoked competition to assure that the outside investment managers were effective. The board divided the portfolio into thirds in 1971 and hired three investment managers, each to invest one third of the assets. Knowing that their future fees were at stake, no doubt all three investment managers aggressively sought the best performing stocks. After measuring the performance of each manager for five years, the finance and administration committee dismissed the manager whose cumulative results had been the weakest, and the investment portfolio was divided evenly between the two surviving investment management firms.[510] But during the 1970s, high tax rates and an Arab oil embargo depressed corporate profits and led to the grim message in Sullivan's memo.

Grants awarded during 2007 by the Carnegie Corporation of New York included $200,000 to the National Association of State Universities and Land Grant Colleges toward an initiative to increase the number of high-quality science and mathematics teachers; $1 million to Teach for America, Inc., toward providing high-quality teachers for New Orleans schools; and $970,000 to the Chattanooga-Hamilton (Tennessee) County Public Education Fund toward the development of a comprehensive assessment system in mathematics and improved mathematics instruction.

Toward peace and improved international relations, grants included $25,000 to promote an intranet website for dialogue among Israeli and Palestinian journalists; $50,000 to the John F. Kennedy Library Foundation toward a conference on challenges in Iraq; and $45,000 to the Women's Foreign Policy Group for a seminar series on Islam, highlighting Carnegie scholars.

In the same year, more than six hundred grants were awarded to local organizations in the arts and social services, ranging from $10,000 to $100,000. A

---

board of trustees, January 22, 1980
510 Christian readers may note the competitive process set up by the corporation matches that described in Matthew's Gospel, Chapter 25. The quest for high return on investment is an ancient component of stewardship, and competition is a way of enlisting best efforts.

total of $14 million was awarded to universities and libraries in New Orleans, under the Revitalizing New Orleans Initiative. Altogether, $133 million was disbursed in grants by the corporation in 2007, and an additional $37 million was paid in taxes. Foundations, including those recognized as "tax exempt" 501(c)(3) organizations by the IRS, must pay an excise tax of 1 or 2 percent of their investment income each year. Presumably, the tax money also benefits the public, but it reduces the financial resources available for the foundation's work.

At the end of 2007, the corporation's net assets totaled $2.9 billion, reflecting stewardship of the funds Carnegie had donated. The corporation's website includes an interesting article, "Investing for the Long Term," written in 2000 by D. Ellen Shuman, vice president and chief investment officer, discussing the many challenges that confront the corporation in stewarding assets to meet the donor's original mandate to operate as a perpetual trust paying dividends to society forever. The corporation's investment strategy needs to overcome the erosion of purchasing power that inflation brings and allow a high degree of stability and predictability in funds available for grant-giving each year, while navigating the bull and bear years of investment markets.

Under federal law, private foundations must spend—in grants and administration—an amount equal to at least 5 percent of their assets each year. With inflation averaging, over the long term, 3 percent per year, a foundation needs to earn more than 8 percent annual return on its invested assets to avoid exhausting its funds and going out of business. Excise taxes add to that challenge.

———

When Carnegie died in 1919, at age eighty-three, he had nearly attained his goal of donating his entire fortune to charity during his lifetime. In his will, he left all his real estate, works of art, automobiles, and similar possessions to his wife. He had already provided for her financial needs and entrusted her with providing for their daughter, who married four months before Andrew died. There were numerous gifts to old friends, employees at his various residences, and the widows of former U.S. presidents. All the residual estate was left to the Carnegie Corporation of New York. His estate was appraised at just over $23 million, after debts and estate taxes. Since New York law at the time limited charitable bequests to a maximum of 50 percent of the estate's value, the gift to the Carnegie Corporation was limited, and his wife's inheritance was thereby increased.

Mrs. Carnegie maintained the homes in New York City and Scotland, spending her summers at Skibo. She set about giving away the funds that she had inherited by virtue of the New York estate law at her husband's death. She was an avid supporter of the American Red Cross, the Young Women's Christian Association, and numerous scholarship funds. She remained active until just before her death in 1946, at age eighty-nine.

Her will specified a bequest of $1 million to be divided equally among her four grandchildren. The oldest granddaughter, Louise Carnegie Miller Thomson, received her inheritance outright.[511] The three youngest would receive their inheritance in steps, as each attained ages twenty-one, thirty, and fifty. The Brick Presbyterian Church, near Mrs. Carnegie's New York City mansion, received $200,000. Several New York charities received gifts of $25,000 to $50,000. Several relatives received gifts of $50,000 to $250,000 each, and approximately eighty other individuals received gifts of between $250 and $25,000. Each servant employed at the New York mansion, at Skibo, or at her other residence in Scotland received a sum equivalent to one month's salary. She specified that all these gifts would be paid free and clear of inheritance taxes (the estate would pay them on behalf of the gift recipient). The balance of her wealth was left to her daughter, Margaret Carnegie Miller.[512]

Margaret, the only child of Andrew and Louise, died in 1990 at age ninety-three, at her home in Connecticut. She had served for almost forty years as a trustee of the Carnegie Corporation of New York. Her marriage had ended in divorce. Only one of her four children outlived her, along with thirteen grandchildren, twenty-six great-grandchildren, and two great-great-grandchildren.[513]

Through major philanthropies and foundations, and in lesser ways through bequests to so many friends, employees, and relatives, and through the expenses of long life, the Carnegie fortune has found its way back into society, at a value much greater than it had during the lifetimes of Andrew, Louise, and Margaret. Wealth in America is transient.

---

511 Just fourteen months later, Mrs. Thomson died at age twenty-seven of infantile paralysis after a brief illness, leaving behind her husband and four children.
512 *New York Times,* June 29, 1946
513 *New York Times,* April 21, 1990

Chapter Twenty
John D. Rockefeller

John D. Rockefeller's fortune in our "base line" year 1905 totaled more than $200 million. By that time, he had received approximately $120 million in dividends over the preceding years from his ownership of approximately 25 percent of Standard Oil stock. That stock would have been worth between $88 million (.25 x $316 million book value in 1905) and $144 million (.25 x 57.5 million profits in 1905 x P/E ratio of 10).[514] Rockefeller's other investments included an $80 million stake in United States Steel, received in exchange for his vast holdings of land rich in iron ore, and his investments in railroad and steamship companies.[515] Carnegie, who was still accumulating interest income from his United States Steel bonds faster than he was spending or donating, was probably in that year the wealthiest American and the wealthiest man in the world. But Carnegie's wealth peaked a few years later as he started to give it away in earnest. Rockefeller's wealth continued to grow. A few years after the forced breakup of the Standard Oil Trust in 1911, Rockefeller's fortune was reported to be more than $1 billion dollars.[516] It may have been multiples of that.[517]

But there is more to understanding the magnitude, and the subsequent impact, of Rockefeller's fortune. *Forbes* magazine estimates that Rockefeller's

---

514 Charles R. Morris, *The Tycoons*, 332.
515 Ron Chernow, *Titan*, 393.
516 *30 Richest Americans of 1918, Forbes* (Reprinted September 27, 2002.)
517 Charles R. Morris, *The Tycoons*, 332–333.

fortune, at its peak value in 1917, would now be worth more than $300 billion, and Carnegie's about $280 billion.[518] The wealth of John D. Rockefeller Sr. in the early decades of the twentieth century exceeded the *combined* wealth of Warren Buffett and Bill Gates one hundred years later. Economists caution that the use of simple inflation-adjustment factors, such as the Consumer Price Index, to convert dollars of a century ago into current dollars will not yield precise results. These estimates are made by trending the individual's wealth valued a century ago with growth of America's gross domestic product. The method is particularly relevant because Rockefeller and Carnegie, at the peak of their careers, owned a significant part of the country's productive capacity. Rockefeller remains the wealthiest person in history by a very wide margin. As we follow the money to learn what happens to the profits from large corporations, we must track this, the largest fortune ever assembled in America or the world.

John D. Rockefeller was born in 1839. John's early years included moving several times. His father, William, had difficulties in his business ventures, which included the sale of patent medicines, and in his personal life. William had two wives in two different towns. While the bigamist father balanced his time between his business pursuits and his two families, John's mother raised her six children in the Baptist faith, and John's lifestyle reflected that upbringing. Throughout his adult life, John attended church regularly, frequently taught Bible classes, and strictly avoided alcohol, card-playing, dancing, and theater.[519]

John acquired a basic education in the public schools of Cleveland, Ohio, and then a few courses at a business college. His first job search at age sixteen involved weeks of walking the streets of Cleveland and sitting through numerous fruitless interviews before landing a job as a clerk and bookkeeper at a warehouse on the Cleveland waterfront. Years later, Rockefeller still marked "Job Day," September 26, as one of the most important dates in his life. His pay was $50 total for the first three months. He must have impressed the boss, for his salary was increased effective January 1, 1856, to $25 per month.[520]

Two years later, John was restless and believed that he was not being paid enough. He had received a promotion, and his predecessor had been paid $2,000 per year in that position. John asked for a raise, to $800 per year, but the boss was not responding. John saw an opportunity, and he was willing to take a risk in order to improve his situation. With $800 he had saved from his pay (about one

---

518 "The All-Time Richest Americans," *Forbes,* September 14, 2007.
519 Ron Chernow, *Titan.*
520 John D. Rockefeller, *Some Random Reminiscences of Men and Events,* 45–50.

half of his total salary of the past two years!) and a thousand dollars borrowed from his father (at 10 percent interest!), he partnered with M. B. Clark in a new produce commissioning business. The total investment by the two partners was $4,000. John D. Rockefeller was now a businessman and entrepreneur. The new firm did almost $500,000 in sales in the first year and cleared a profit of $4,400—a magnificent ROE for the first year in business. Initially, John handled the office and financial aspects of the business, but later he got involved in dealing with customers' questions and making sales visits to get new business.[521]

In 1862, Clark and Rockefeller met Samuel Andrews, who owned a small refinery near Cleveland. Andrews had ideas for modernizing and expanding the plant, but he needed money for the work. Rockefeller and Clark invested $4,000 in Andrews's business. Andrews was a mechanical genius. He devised new processes, improved the quality of his products, and obtained higher yields from the crude oil he refined. The refinery grew and became much more profitable. Clark and Rockefeller saw their initial investment grow to $100,000. By 1865, Rockefeller sold his interest in the produce business and formed Rockefeller and Andrews. In 1870, Rockefeller, Andrews, and four other investors formed the Standard Oil Company (Ohio). This, and its corporate successors, would be the vehicle for building the Rockefeller oil fortune.[522]

Much of that fortune was earned before the automobile was invented. Kerosene for lighting and lubricating greases were the key refinery products when Rockefeller was growing his business. Candles had been the common source of lighting until whale oil became available in the early 1800s. Customers who could afford it wanted its brighter illumination and convenience. By the mid-1850s, however, the whale population was being rapidly depleted. Whatever environmental damage Rockefeller and his competitors caused, their success in producing inexpensive illuminating oil must be credited with saving the whales. By 1898, when Rockefeller was almost completely retired from business, there were only eight hundred automobiles registered in America. In what must be the greatest coincidence in economic history, sales of gasoline for the mass-marketed automobile would more than compensate for the declining sales of lamp oil as electric lighting spread to cities, towns, and even remote homesteads. Rockefeller's fortune would grow even larger, not only through his ownership of more than 25 percent of Standard Oil stock, but through appreciation of his extensive holdings in other corporations, including U.S. Steel and General Motors.

---

521 Ron Chernow, *Titan,* 59–64
522 Ibid, 77, 86–88.

Several excellent biographies include detailed accounts of Rockefeller's business career, his buildup of the Standard Oil, and the eventual breakup of the Standard Oil Trust. There is also the detailed *History of the Standard Oil Company*, by the investigative reporter Ida Minerva Tarbell. Published in 1904, it remains today one of the most influential pieces of business journalism in history. Ida Tarbell was probably the most knowledgeable person in the country regarding Rockefeller's business—she had spent years studying court transcripts, interviewing customers and competitors, and meeting on numerous occasions with senior executives of Standard Oil. She also had tremendous personal animosity toward Rockefeller because her father and brother had sold their barrel-making business to Rockefeller on terms they later regretted.

So what did Ms. Tarbell write about Mr. Rockefeller? Regarding the man in his early days in the oil business, around 1860:

> He was demonstrating that he possesses other qualities even more essential than the fundamentals with which he started out—he was showing he had the instinct for opportunities, the courage to seize them…the power to persuade men to lend him money, the patience to stick by enterprises until they had justified his faith…frugal, calculating, money-bent—cautious in trade yet daring, quick to seize yet ready to wait.[523]

Regarding Standard Oil, which certainly reflected Rockefeller's management capabilities, she devoted an entire chapter to "The Legitimate Greatness of the Standard Oil Company," noting:

> …everybody worked. There was not a lazy bone in the organization, nor an incompetent hand, nor a stupid head. It was a machine where everybody was kept on his mettle by an extraordinary system of competition, where success met immediate recognition, where opportunity was wide…[524]

> The very day-labourers were picked men. It was the custom to offer a little better day wages for labourers than was current and then… those men were advanced as they showed ability…The efficiency of the

---

523 Ida Tarbell, "John D. Rockefeller: A Character Study," *McClure's*, July 1, 1905, 226–49.
524 Ida Tarbell, *History of the Standard Oil Company*, vol. 2, 126.

working force was greatly increased…by the opportunity given to the employees of taking stock. They were urged to do it, and where they had no savings money was lent them on easy terms by the company.[525]

Without dismissing the significant financial contribution from railroad rebates, Standard Oil's competitive success derived in no small measure from continuous process improvements and rapid increases in volume at the refineries. Rockefeller hired the best chemists and established a research lab. The research enabled Standard to make a marketable product out of sulfur-heavy crude, which competitors considered almost worthless. In 1890, Standard opened the largest refinery in the world at Whiting, Indiana. Dr. William Burton of Standard Oil developed a cracking process that produced a much higher gasoline yield, and Standard held that patent until 1921.

Refinery operations are most profitable when they are interrupted only for maintenance at planned intervals. Any unscheduled outage, or a fire or accident that disrupts operations, is a serious drain on profits. Keenly aware of this, Standard paid its employees well and maintained good labor relations.[526] There was no union. During the decades of John D. Rockefeller's leadership of Standard Oil, there was hardly a flutter of labor strife. This was a tremendous record, especially since the railroads and steel mills in the same era experienced major strikes and more than a few fatal confrontations between labor and management.

How complete was the Standard Oil monopoly, and what forces finally broke it? Plenty of information exists about the worldwide oil industry since its beginning in the 1850s. By 1877, Standard Oil controlled about 90 percent of the refining capacity in America, and by the 1880s it controlled 90 percent of the refineries and pipelines.[527] By the late 1880s, Standard Oil sold about 84 percent of the oil products sold in America and pumped about one-third of its crude.[528]

But by 1895, there was effective competition in the U.S. from two significant companies, Producers' and Refiners' Oil Company and Pure Oil Company. During the late 1890s, Russia produced 35 percent of the world's crude oil. Shell Oil and Royal Dutch formed a new alliance late in 1901, joined by the Rothschilds, creating a powerful competitor, especially for European and Asian markets.

In 1901, oil was discovered in Texas, a state where Standard Oil had only limited operations and elected not to expand. The Texas discovery quickly

---

525 Ibid, vol. 2, 253.
526 Charles R. Morris, *The Tycoons*, 203.
527 Ron Chernow, *Titan*, 205, 226–227.
528 Ibid, 430.

changed the oil business in America. By 1905, about one-fourth of the crude oil pumped in America was Texas oil. Among the numerous competitors that would arise from this development were Gulf Oil Company and Texas Oil Company, which was later renamed Texaco. Additional wells were established in California, Oklahoma, Kansas, and Illinois. Standard was certainly not crippled, but competition was alive and well.

With serious, well-financed competitors taking the field, and politicians less easily co-opted, Standard's management took notice and substantially improved its own performance. ROE had been stable since 1886, ranging from 13.5 percent to 16.7 percent, but was drifting below 12 percent in 1893–1894. A serious recession in 1893 no doubt contributed to the weaker results. But complacency, the predictable result of monopoly and lack of competition, had also set in. The Standard shareholders at this point included not only the original partners, but also many of those whose companies had been acquired by Standard and more than a few employees. As they watched that critical measure of their own results fall short, and read the ever-growing list of competitors, they were energized.

A new president was installed at Standard Oil, William Archbold. Within two years, the ROE was improved. By 1896, it was 23 percent and by 1900 an impressive 27 percent, and it would remain high long into the future.[529] The government case to break up the Standard Oil Trust, initiated at the end of 1906 and not decided until 1911, produced competition among the various Standard corporations, which then had separate boards and separately traded stocks. But normal economic forces had clearly destroyed the trust's monopoly more than fifteen years before the government acted. There is nothing like competition to focus attention and improve corporate performance and benefit customers.

The focus here is on what became of Rockefeller's fortune. Where did all the profits go?

Rockefeller had started giving to charities and to needy individuals when he received his first pay as a clerk. In 1855, he started a detailed record of all his income and expenditures in a small book labeled "Ledger A" and kept it all his life. The record shows a frugal approach to personal expenses, preferring good quality but not extravagant business suits, simple living quarters, and a generous approach to charitable giving. In most weeks, his donations equaled about 6 percent of his income. By 1859, at the age of twenty, his donations were regularly

---

529 ROE figures are shown in Morris, Charles R. *The Tycoons*, Appendix II, p. 332, credited to Nevins, Allan. *John D. Rockefeller.*

10 percent of his income.[530] At the same time, he was supporting his mother and siblings, since by then John's father had abandoned the family.

In 1881, two Baptist teachers had opened a school for black women in Atlanta—the first such facility in Georgia. The following year, traveling to Cleveland to raise funds for their school, the two teachers met with Rockefeller, his wife Cettie, and members of her family. The group listened patiently to the two women, who were obviously dedicated to their work. Rockefeller and his wife saw many opportunities to assist others and heard plenty of requests for money. John was known to discreetly hand envelopes to people in need. But before committing to significant financial support for a new cause, he posed one central question: "Will you stick?" He wanted to evaluate whether these two women had the stamina and professionalism to attract others to work with them and build an enduring institution, or would they simply burn themselves out after a few years of concentrated effort?

The two teachers must have made quite an impression, for the Rockefellers adopted the school as a favorite charity. Over the next twenty years, the school received frequent donations, usually pledged as matching gifts, to encourage others to donate as well. In addition, several main buildings were built with Rockefeller donations. In gratitude for this major support, the school was named Spelman Seminary in honor of Cettie Rockefeller's maiden name. It was later changed to Spelman College.[531] It became one of the leading schools for women in the South, and many alumnae today hold distinguished positions in medicine, government service, law, education, and several major corporations. But perhaps the graduate who had the greatest influence on life in the twentieth century was Alberta Williams King, mother of Dr. Martin Luther King Jr. During the same period, Rockefeller made a series of donations to Indian University, today known as Bacone College, serving Native Americans in Oklahoma.[532]

In 1890, working in concert with the American Baptist Education Society, Rockefeller founded the University of Chicago with an initial gift of $600,000, equal to $9.5 million today. From the beginning, the university's trustees realized the importance of getting the best available professors for the new institution, and they offered higher salaries to lure leading academics from their posts in eastern universities. Although the university was established by Baptists, it

---

530 Ron Chernow, *Titan*, 50.
531 Ibid, 240–242, 482.
532 Ibid, 238.

was nondenominational and welcomed women and minority students at a time when many universities did not. By 1910, Rockefeller had contributed $35 million, a massive sum at a time when full professors earned $2,500 per year. At his insistence, no building, department, or academic chair carried the Rockefeller name. Still, there was the widespread sentiment that the school needed no financial support other than Rockefeller, and there were unspoken questions about whether he might exercise control over academics, professor tenures, and similar matters. In 1910, he advised the university's board that his desire was to see the school continue to flourish, noting that "the property of the people should be controlled, conducted and supported by the people." Over the years, there would be donations from time to time from several Rockefeller foundations, and from John D. Rockefeller Jr., but the university grew, as designed, free of any Rockefeller influence. It remains today one of America's foremost universities.[533]

During the 1890s, as he moved into retirement, Rockefeller began to look for ways in which his tremendous wealth might be used to address major health problems of the day. Very likely, the final impetus for action was the death of his three-year-old grandson, Jack, in January 1901. Jack died of scarlet fever while staying with his grandparents. Rockefeller, the stern businessman of quiet demeanor and reserved disciplinarian of his own children, was a doting grandfather who played lively games with his grandchildren. The impact of Jack's death was profound. Six months later, the Rockefeller Institute for Medical Research was founded. Dr. Simon Flexner, a pathology professor from the University of Pennsylvania and brother of Abraham Flexner (author of the Carnegie Foundation's Flexner Report), was chosen as the institute's first president.

The institute was the first biomedical research center in the United States. Rockefeller pledged $20,000 per year for ten years to set up the institute. As the facilities grew, he donated $55 million as an endowment to fund its ongoing work. The institute, still active today, is known as Rockefeller University. Its long history of accomplishments includes developing a serum for treating meningitis (1908), determining that cancer can be caused by a virus (1911), finding the Rh factor in blood, discovering that DNA is the basic material of heredity (1944), demonstrating the connection between cholesterol and heart disease (1950s), and developing the AIDS "cocktail" drug therapy in the 1990s. Work at this research center has contributed to twenty-three Nobel Prizes. Today, the university collaborates with Columbia University and Sloan-Kettering Institute

---

533 Ibid, 309–318.

to offer graduate studies, including MD and PhD programs. Current projects seek to solve public health problems, and research focuses on treatments for AIDS, genetic causes of cancer, Alzheimer's, human genetics, molecular biology, neuroscience, and protein chemistry.

In 1903, Rockefeller established the General Education Board (GEB) to improve and standardize education in the U.S. "without distinction of race, sex or creed." While grants were made to schools across the country, the emphasis was on the south. The need there was acute. Almost no four-year high schools existed in the former Confederate states, and not a single one would accept Negro students. Without four-year high schools, only the children of the very rich, taught by private tutors, could hope to attend universities; there was also no source of well-trained teachers for the elementary schools. Lack of funds for school buildings and teacher salaries was only part of the problem. There was little public interest in secondary education, so there was no political motivation for government to levy taxes to support education. To change attitudes, the GEB paid for professors from state colleges to tour their states, select potential sites for high schools, and build support among local citizens. The state education departments were also engaged in the effort.

Some find fault in that only about 10 percent of GEB funding went to education for blacks, although this was a key concern when the GEB was established. Consistent with his father's strategy of getting expert advice before committing major funds, John D. Rockefeller Jr.—an 1897 graduate of Brown University— had participated in the Millionaire Special, a chartered train ride through the South for millionaires in April 1901. It was designed to solicit donations for the support of education for blacks. The trip was organized by Robert C. Ogden, a department store magnate. Along the train's journey through the South, Henry St. George Tucker, president of Washington and Lee University, delivered some profound advice:

> If it is your idea to educate the Negro you must have the white of the South with you. If the poor white sees the son of a Negro neighbor enjoying through your munificence benefits denied to his boy, it raises in him a feeling that will render futile all your work. You must lift up the "poor white" and the Negro together if you would ever approach success.[534]

---

534 Ron Chernow, *Titan*, 481–482.

The Rockefellers also sought advice from Booker T. Washington. His counsel was to focus on technical schools that would teach skills matched to the jobs available to blacks, rather than academic courses.

Race relations in that era were extremely volatile, and the Rockefellers were aware of that. Just seven months before the Millionaire Special train left Manhattan, the *New York Times* had reported the lynching of four black men in Ponchatoula, Louisiana. These were among the 115 lynchings in the United States that year.[535] In August 1901, a United States senator from South Carolina defended lynching before a large audience in Wisconsin and proclaimed that Booker T. Washington's education of blacks for industrial trades would intensify race hatred in the South.[536] The reports were not rare, and the occasional news of a Southern sheriff saving a black prisoner from a threatening mob was scant evidence of social stability. Even the ministers recruited by Rockefeller to lead the GEB were comfortable only with a "separate but equal" approach to education of the races, no doubt reflecting the general sentiment.[537] But the establishment of eight hundred Southern high schools by 1910 is a success that should not be dismissed. The widespread grants for teacher training, certification, and salaries improved the quality of education for generations of students of all races in many areas of the country.

In addition to major obstacles, there were nuisances that might have discouraged people with less determination or foundations with less money. One New York state senator introduced a resolution calling for a committee of senators and assemblymen, with an appropriation of $10,000 for its expenses, with power "to investigate generally the activities, objects, purposes, and accounts of the Rockefeller Foundation, the General Education Board of such foundation, the Public Education Association connected therewith, and all similar bodies." The proposed measure had the support of the State Federation of Labor.[538] Fortunately, the New York legislature never passed the legislation. Building public-private partnerships for social change continued as a core process in Rockefeller philanthropies.

---

535 "Four Negroes Lynched," *New York Times*, September 22, 1900; "Fewer Lynchings," *New York Times*, March 4, 1913.

536 "Tillman Favors Lynching," *New York Times*, August 5, 1901. Lynching was not unique to the deep South. There were lynchings as far north as Wilmington, Delaware, in 1903 and Annapolis, Maryland, in 1906, and Springfield, Illinois, in 1908. See the *New York Times*: "One Arrest Made for Delaware Lynching," June 24, 1903; "Annapolis Lynchers Hang and Shoot Negro," December 22, 1906; "The First Lynching," August 16, 1908.

537 Ron Chernow, *Titan*, 483.

538 *New York Times*, February 8, 1916.

In 1905, the GEB received additional millions from Rockefeller and extended its efforts to colleges and universities. But the GEB's greatest impact would be in the education of physicians. The GEB was the agent of change that would bring American medical schools to a higher level of professionalism and overcome the problems noted in the Flexner Report. The University of Rochester received a $5 million dollar grant in 1920 for its medical school. Baltimore Provident Hospital received support for training black interns and nurses and providing post-graduate work for black doctors. Funds went to Howard University for its endowment, and for construction, fellowships, and clinical teaching. Money flowed to all parts of the country. By 1928, the GEB had distributed $78 million to achieve an impact that was nothing short of complete transformation of physician training in America.

By 1964, the objectives identified for the GEB in its early years were largely met. The desirability of secondary education was clearly established, and taxpayer-supported public school systems were the norm. The remaining GEB funds were exhausted in a final round of appropriation by the board. In the end, 90 percent of the GEB's expenditures went to white schools or to promote medical education. Most would acknowledge the universal benefits of improved medical education. But some see a major disappointment in this philanthropic effort since it failed to focus singularly and directly on the education of blacks. Others see a culturally realistic approach that, over time, improved the lot of all Southerners and that of the nation.

In 1913, Rockefeller, well into his seventies, established the Rockefeller Foundation "to promote the well-being of mankind throughout the world" and funded it with initial donations totaling $100 million. The foundation funded on-site research into reducing the spread of hookworm and other intestinal parasites in the Southern states and throughout the world, and it provided public health education in the methods of effectively reducing these contagions and curing those afflicted. The work was of major importance. Hookworm prevents the intestines from properly absorbing the nutrition in food, stunting growth in children and leaving adults without energy. The foundation also provided funds to send instructors from Harvard and Yale to teach at new medical schools in China.

One of the Rockefeller Foundation's earliest grants, in 1915, was to help establish an endowment fund at Wellesley College. The college's goal for this initial endowment campaign was $2 million. The Rockefeller Foundation's donation of $750,000 was a major part of the campaign's success. Wellesley College has thrived over the years and has been a major factor in the advancement of women in America. Today its endowment fund has investments of about $1.6 billion, and the income from the endowment covers about 33 percent of the university's annual expenses, directly supplementing tuition in the college's operating budget. The endowment also allows Wellesley to continue to admit students on a competitive academic basis, granting tuition aid to any qualified student who needs the assistance. Some of the distinguished and influential graduates of Wellesley include Madeline Albright in '59, Diane Sawyer in '67, and Hillary Rodham Clinton in '69. Could Rockefeller have dreamed, in an era when women could not yet vote, that his foundation's gift to a women's college would help educate two future secretaries of state and a senator from New York? Surely, twenty years before the introduction of television, he never imagined educating the future co-anchor of "Good Morning America" and ABC World News.

———

During the Great Depression, the foundation continued its grants along the strategic lines already well established. As early as 1930, major grants were made to the Emergency Employment Committee of New York. In the spring of 1933, the board of trustees appointed three of its members to investigate ways to address two major challenges: the continuing worldwide economic depression and the displacement of many eminent scholars in Europe as the Nazi influence spread. Between 1933 and 1940, the foundation provided funds to universities in free countries so that more than two hundred European professors and scientists could escape from Nazi-controlled countries, where their work was suppressed and their personal safety threatened. The grants covered travel expenses, and up to two years of salary at the hiring university, to give the school time to incorporate the refugee-scholars into their regular budgets. Numerous activities were undertaken to address Depression conditions. Foundation staff helped municipal officials preparing proposals for relief and work projects to apply for federal funds. Economists and urban planners from Europe were brought to the U.S., at foundation expense, to exchange ideas with American relief officials.[539]

---

539 All of the information on investment income, disbursements, and the investment portfolio is from the Foundation's Annual Reports, which are available at the Rockefeller Foundation website, www.rockfound.com. The annual President's Review in these reports provides a rich history of the events and issues confronting the foundation during this era.

The foundation's investment income was significantly reduced by the Depression. At the end of 1929, the $177 million investment portfolio was split between 36 percent bonds and 64 percent stocks. Investment income that year was $14.3 million. As business profits deteriorated, many corporations were unable to continue paying dividends on either their common or preferred stock, and some companies failed to make the interest payments on their bonds. During 1930, investment income fell to $12.4 million, and the decline continued until 1935, when income for the year was $7.9 million. Income rose in 1936 and 1937 as business briefly improved, but in 1938, income fell to $7.1 million. It would not again reach pre-crash levels until 1952, when the stock market fully recovered to its pre-Crash level. If adjusted for inflation to match the pre-Crash purchasing power, the recovery of investment income arrived still later.

The economic policies of the Depression years, particularly the ever-higher corporate and personal income taxes on dividends and capital gains, had stifled both demand and investment. The direct effect, in addition to widespread unemployment, was drastically reduced investment income (dividends and bond interest) to foundations, endowments, and nonprofits generally.

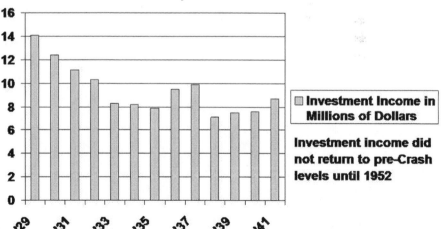

Rockefeller Foundation
The Depression Years

Investment Income in Millions of Dollars

Investment income did not return to pre-Crash levels until 1952

To continue as best as possible to meet the needs of all the organizations and causes it had been aiding, plus the emergency situations brought on by the Depression and persecution in Europe, the board used the discretion given to it by its founder to spend principal as well as interest. This was an authority not enjoyed by the trustees at the Carnegie Corporation of New York or many other foundations of the era.

The board's aggressive action, spending principal at a time of falling investment values, helped maintain cash flow to many nonprofit organizations that depended on the foundation, but it reduced the foundation's resources. At the end of 1930, the investment portfolio was valued on the foundation's ledgers, perhaps optimistically (probably reflecting a belief that the business downturn would soon right itself, as earlier panics and recessions had) at $193 million. By 1940, the ledger value had shrunk to $149 million, and actual market value of the securities was $142 million.

Wealth was not transferred in the Depression, it was destroyed. Factories sitting idle, or operating at a fraction of their full capacity, are worth little more than the cost of bricks and steel and the value of the land. The machinery inside, regardless of its original cost, has nothing more than scrap value if it cannot be used to make products for sale or be sold to another firm to produce a saleable product. The corporations that own these plants and equipment are worth less because idle plants and equipment produce no current profits, and expectations of future profits are diminished. The price of the stock falls, and then falls even more dramatically when the corporation reduces or eliminates the dividend because there are no profits.

The impact of underutilized capital spreads to people in all sections of the economy. A man or woman who loses a week's wages may, over time, recover from the financial setback. But the loss of wages for six months, a year, or several years will have impact for a lifetime. For foundations and endowments, the loss of investment income, and the reduced value of securities, means that less aid can be given at a time of greater need to all the causes and charities that depend upon them. When business fails, there is no safe ground.

Rockefeller Foundation—The Depression Years Income and Disbursements ($ in millions)												
Year 19-	29	30	31	32	33	34	35	36	37	38	39	40
Investment Income	14.1	12.4	11.1	10.3	8.3	8.2	7.9	9.5	9.9	7.1	7.5	7.6
Grants + Admin. Expenses	19.0	15.7	17.5	13.7	14.8	12.7	12.7	13.4	10.6	12.8	12.9	10.8
As dividends and interest fell and grants and expenses exceeded income, principal was used, selling securities at Depression prices												

While Rockefeller gave millions to his foundations and, through them, to various charitable causes, he was far more restrained in distributing wealth to his children. Even as adults, each received an allowance, and each was required periodically to provide a written account of expenses. In the case of John Jr., the allowance came in the form of a salary for his work at the Rockefeller family office, where Junior worked as a director of several Rockefeller companies and more actively as day-to-day overseer of the burgeoning philanthropies. The allowances were generous, but Senior maintained control.

Then, in 1917, there was a sudden change. Rockefeller started giving assets to his children. The largest share by far was given to his only son, John Jr., who received outright gifts of stocks and bonds worth roughly $450 million. For each of his surviving daughters, Alta and Edith, Senior established a trust with $12 million, at Equitable Trust Company. By 1922, the wealthiest man in the world had reduced his own fortune to $25 million, having donated over the past decades about $475 million to his various charities and, more recently, approximately the same amount to his children.

Why the sudden rush to transfer so much wealth that had been so closely controlled? At this point, Rockefeller was in robust health and often spoke of living to be one hundred. His dear Cettie had died in 1915. Some have speculated that Senior was influenced by the federal income tax, enacted in 1913, or the federal inheritance tax passed in 1916. Others hold that Senior had finally concluded that Junior, now age forty-three, was mature and sophisticated enough as a businessperson to responsibly manage such a fortune. Prudent stewardship of money was a bedrock issue to Rockefeller. Even in his will, written in 1925, Senior specifically instructed his trustees that the funds distributed to any beneficiary "shall not exceed such amount as my said trustees may believe the life beneficiary has at the time...sufficient character and ability to manage and use with wisdom and discretion."[540] But this line of reasoning ignores the fact that Junior's finest hour in the Standard business had been the successful sale of ore resources to J. P. Morgan in 1901 and Junior's decision to withdraw almost completely from business activities in 1910–11, with Senior's full knowledge.

There is a more likely explanation of Senior's sudden rush to hand off his wealth to his heirs. In 1916, the two youngest children of Jay Gould had filed

---

540 "Text of the Will of John D. Rockefeller," *New York Times,* June 6, 1937.

suit alleging massive mismanagement of the trusts that had been created by Jay's will for their benefit. They sought tens of millions of dollars in damages from the older children, who were the trustees under the will. Newspapers carried all the latest developments. Details of Gould family life and financial dealings were on public display. For the very private Rockefeller, who had always sheltered his family from the press, even the remote chance of such a media circus affecting the Rockefellers at some future date would be horrifying.

Gould's will had been clear and specific, no doubt drafted by the best available attorneys. If such careful preparations could not prevent a squandered fortune and a divided family, then Rockefeller would use a different strategy for dispensing his wealth and protecting the family. Gifts made and documented during his lifetime would be much harder to challenge. While Gould had left a trust that held a major part of his estate and required investment management for many decades after his death, Rockefeller decided to distribute virtually all of his vast fortune, including the house he lived in, while he still lived. Only a small remainder would go into trusts. Gould had written detailed instructions for his trustees; Rockefeller trustees—four trusted associates, no family members—would have extremely broad discretion to act "upon the sole and absolute judgment and discretion," a freedom that he broadened in a 1934 codicil to "use their own best judgment and discretion as fully and completely as I might do if living, and entirely untrammeled by the usual rules laid down by law or statutory provision." By giving away his fortune while alive, and writing the broadest possible discretion for trustees into his will, Rockefeller was acting to spare his family any repetition of the Gould debacle.

Of all the fortunes made in the oil industry, and there were many, why was John D. Rockefeller's so exceptionally large? There was no guaranteed fortune in the oil business. Many of Rockefeller's competitors and suppliers sold their companies to him for cash, rather than accept Standard Oil stock, which was also offered. Ida Tarbell's father and brother took the cash, instead of stock, for their barrel-making operation. Even some of Rockefeller's long-time partners sold the stock when the best years, as it turned out, were still ahead. In the 1890s, Henry Flagler sold large blocks of Standard Oil stock back to Rockefeller to raise money for his Florida real estate developments and extravagant lifestyle, just before the automobile arrived to boost oil and gasoline demand. Flagler died in 1913, reportedly leaving $60 million to a widow half his age.[541] Henry Rogers, an early associate and technical guru of refining, became caught up in

---

541 *New York Times,* November 20, 1917.

other business investments and found himself short of cash in 1907. At a meeting of the Standard Oil board of directors, Rogers wanted the company to buy out some of his shares in a railroad. Rockefeller voted against that. Standard Oil was in the oil business. A railroad in West Virginia was not part of the strategy and therefore a poor use of capital. Rogers, in a fit of temper, insisted that Rockefeller personally buy his Standard Oil stock. Rockefeller calmly asked him to name his price and bought the stock with a certified check the next day.[542] When Rogers died in 1909, he left a fortune appraised at $41 million, and he was still a major shareholder and director of the Standard Oil he had helped build.[543] Rockefeller made not just one right decision, but an incredibly long series of decisions, all of which involved placing his money at risk.

Senior died in 1937, at age ninety-eight. During his lifetime, he had donated $530 million to various foundations and charities, with $450 million of that sum going directly or indirectly into medicine.[544] At his death, his remaining estate was appraised at $26.4 million, from which the state and federal estate taxes of $16.6 million were collected. Most of the remainder was left to Senior's granddaughter, Margaret, whose mother, Bessie, had died in 1906. The Rockefellers, father and son, had collaborated for almost forty years to discover and develop grand causes, international in scope, in which monetary grants of unprecedented scale could make a difference by addressing root causes of problems affecting the world.

John D. Rockefeller Jr., only son of the oil magnate, graduated from Brown University in 1897. He worked in the Standard Oil office for several years, involved in his father's various investments and involved in the family's growing philanthropies. His responsibilities grew as his father took a less active role in business. But he became completely disillusioned by the business practices revealed in Ida Tarbell's 1904 exposé and by revelations of payments to senators and congressmen by Standard Oil executives. In 1910, he resigned his board seats at Standard Oil and U.S. Steel. His decision to remain on one corporate board, Colorado Fuel and Iron Company, led to his involvement in the most

---

542 Ron Chernow, *Titan*, 380–381.
543 *New York Times*, May 20, 1909; February 3, 1914.
544 Ron Chernow, *Titan*, 570.

deadly labor-management confrontation in American history in the 1914 mining strikes in Colorado.[545]

The largest shareholder of CF&I was John D. Rockefeller Sr. He had purchased 40 percent of the stock of CF&I, and 30 percent of its bonds, in 1902. As the largest shareholder of this profitless company, he installed a new management team led by a veteran executive from Rockefeller's Great Lakes ore-shipping business. From the early days of their ownership, the Rockefellers had insisted that no union be recognized as a bargaining agent or even as informal negotiator for the workers.[546] That had been the policy at Standard Oil from the beginning. Relations with the sixty-five thousand oil workers were stable. To the Rockefellers, that policy seemed equally appropriate for the second largest steel company in the nation after U.S. Steel and one of the largest employers in the western states. Since 1903, Rockefeller Junior had been corresponding with executives at the mining company's Colorado offices. After the management change, Junior accepted without question the executive's written reports and never visited the mines. Photos of employee housing added to the assurance that workers were well treated.

The workers' most serious grievances were below ground: frequent disabling injuries and fatalities, rigged scales that cheated the men of tonnage-based pay, and arbitrary work rules. When the miners voted to strike in September 1913, recognition of the United Mine Workers of America topped the list of their demands. A 10 percent pay raise, an eight-hour day, compliance with Colorado's mine safety laws, and fair weighing of the day's tonnage followed. The list ended with above-ground issues: the right to choose their own living places, their own doctor, and abolition of the notorious company guard system.[547]

Junior saw the strike as just another challenge to the prerogatives of a management that he believed already provided well for its employees. To entreaties that he become more personally involved in finding a solution, first by an assistant to the secretary of labor and later by a Congressional committee, Junior responded that he relied completely upon the trusted executives on the scene and supported their position. Behind the scenes, he had the quiet, firm support of Rockefeller Senior, who had retired almost twenty years earlier. Junior still held father's business principles, if not his practices, in high esteem. In March, the company filed suit against the union, seeking one million dollars in damages.

---

545 Ibid, 551
546 Ibid, 571
547 Thomas G. Andrews, *Killing for Coal: America's Deadliest Labor War,* 238.

The suit alleged that union officials had caused large quantities of guns and ammunition to be purchased for use in terrifying employees into striking, making speeches that intimidated workers into joining the strike, and policing the tent colonies in ways that terrified any who wished to return to work.[548] In correspondence eerily similar to the messages between Carnegie and Frick leading to the Homestead violence twenty-two years earlier, Rockefeller supported the tough stand against unionization in frequent contact with CF&I's Colorado executives in the days leading up to the fatal battle of April 20, 1914.[549]

In the aftermath, crowds protested outside his office and home in New York City. Rockefeller considered the fatalities entirely the fault of irresponsible miners, who had continued the strike and initiated the violence while up to ten thousand miners had returned to work. President Wilson sent federal troops into the area to reinforce the Colorado militia. The federal government also offered to mediate the dispute. Even when the strikers agreed to talks without a union, the company declined to participate.[550]

Either worn down by the ongoing crisis, or encouraged by President Wilson's direct invitation to take "some large action which would show the way not only in this case but in many others," Junior sought new counsel. His business associates' "no union representation" stance was fruitless. Advice from the Wilson administration was suspect, since the secretary of labor was a known union supporter. While Henry Ford's Five Dollar Day was enjoying public acclaim, the CF&I conflict had reached the highest level of public scrutiny and critique. Demonstrators publicly accused Rockefeller of murder and threatened his life.[551] Any further work in philanthropy—his real passion—might be shunned if this dark stain could not be lifted. He had to find a way forward.

Junior found his new mentor in William Lyon Mackenzie King, a former minister of labor in the Canadian government who had studied economics at Toronto, Chicago, and Harvard. He had experience with difficult labor negotiations. He stressed fact-finding and gradual change. The Rockefeller Foundation hired Mackenzie King, thereby avoiding any stigma or influence of Colorado Fuel and Iron or Standard Oil. Junior publicly acknowledged that he should have been better informed and more involved as a director of the company. Eighteen months after the April tragedy, Rockefeller and Mackenzie King presented a new labor relations plan to workers and officers of the Colorado Fuel and Iron.

---

548 "Miners' Union Sued," *New York Times*, March 21, 1914.
549 Ron Chernow, *Titan*, 577.
550 "Refuse to Settle Strike," *New York Times*, May 1, 1914.
551 "Leaders Abandon Silence Mourning," *New York Times*, May 10, 1914.

The miners accepted the reforms in a secret ballot. The miners would elect delegates, each one representing 150 miners. The delegates would represent the miners in collective bargaining for multiyear contracts. No specific union would be recognized, and any applicant or employee was free to participate in any union or none. Disputes, and the discussion of any problems, would be brought to district conferences composed of equal numbers of company officers and worker delegates. The eight-hour day was established for underground workers, and a nine-hour day for those above-ground.[552]

Rockefeller Jr. replaced the executive who had led CF&I since 1907, who protested the new arrangement even after long discussion with Rockefeller. Peace was restored in the Colorado mines. The worker representation arrangement, which came to be called the Colorado Plan, was adopted by other firms. In 1933, the United Mine Workers of America won the right to represent CF&I workers, and in 1935, the Wagner Act set aside "company unions" of the type authorized by the plan. William Lyon Mackenzie King was elected prime minister of Canada in 1921. He was re-elected several times and led Canada during World War II.

———

Rockefeller Jr. returned to the work that most satisfied him, devoting his time and wealth to major projects that continue to benefit people today. "Mr. Junior," as he was called in the press during the 1930s, enjoyed visiting the national parks, which the government had purchased during Theodore Roosevelt's administration. He became quite keen on enlarging them. Often, he purchased thousands of acres adjoining the original parklands and donated these to the government. On several occasions, he purchased large stands of ancient redwood trees that were in the path of lumber operations and donated these to the federal government for preservation. His land donations significantly increased the size of several national parks.

To preserve the great vistas along the Hudson River, which were threatened by development, he purchased large tracts of land on both the New Jersey and New York sides of the river, preserving the beautiful Palisades for posterity.

Preservation of art and antiquities were important to Rockefeller Jr., and he donated millions of dollars to the French government to restore important

---

552 Ron Chernow, *Titan,* 581–589.

buildings damaged in the First World War, including the palace at Versailles and the thirteenth century cathedral at Reims.

In July 1936, an informal "audit" by *Fortune* magazine concluded that "Mr. Junior" had already made grants of $125 million of his own money to a wide array of worthy efforts around the world.[553]

Junior's most visible and enduring business accomplishment was the construction of Rockefeller Center, a large tract of office buildings that is still considered prime New York City real estate. Before construction started, the stock market crashed in October 1929. In the subsequent Depression, most businesspeople thought it foolish to proceed. But John D. Rockefeller Jr. had committed to a long-term land lease from Columbia University, and he honored it. He became actively involved in overseeing the construction, and he persuaded many large corporations to lease space in the new buildings, even allowing the Rockefeller name to be associated with the project as a sign of commitment to its completion and adding prestige to the office space. The construction project provided jobs, at union rates, for more than one hundred thousand workers in years when jobs were especially scarce. The Rockefeller Center buildings remain today one of the most prestigious business addresses in America, although the Rockefellers sold their interest in the property long ago.

During World War II, Rockefeller bought large quantities of war bonds to help finance the effort, and at the war's end he donated funds for the land for the United Nations headquarters in New York.

At his death in 1960, John D. Rockefeller Jr. left an estate of $161 million.[554] His wife received $56 million in a trust from which she would receive income, withdraw principal during her life, and dispose of in her will. The Rockefeller Brothers Fund, a nonprofit philanthropic organization, and several other charities received a total of $75 million. The federal government collected estate taxes of $10.4 million (there was no federal tax payable on the portion of the estate that was left to charity) and state taxes totaled $3.1 million. During his lifetime, Junior had contributed $473 million of his personal funds, in addition to guiding the work of the various Rockefeller foundations. Separately, Junior had earlier created trusts for each of his six children, funding them with a total of $200 million. Where Senior had split his fortune roughly in half, giving about $475 million to Junior and just over $500 million to the foundations and charities,

---

553 *Fortune*, July 1936.
554 "Estate of John D. Rockefeller, Jr., Is $160 Million," *New York Times*, December 25, 1964.

Junior apparently gave most of his fortune to philanthropic use and divided considerably less than half among his own six children. It is worth noting that most of Rockefeller Junior's investments at his death were bonds, reflecting the general tendency of investors in that era to avoid stocks. Very high income tax rates, which had prevailed since the Great Depression, gave most of the rewards of stock ownership to the government without reducing the risks inherent with stocks. So the low yield but relative safety of bonds was preferred.

———

Junior's five sons, who became known collectively as "the brothers generation," with too little thought to their sister, followed their father and grandfather in large-scale philanthropy. While enjoying and preserving the comfortable surroundings of great wealth, they devoted their time and much of their treasure to improving the lives of others.[555] Each donated to his own chosen causes, and the five brothers jointly established the Rockefeller Brothers Fund in 1940 to provide major funding to well-researched projects. Since the establishment of the fund, three generations of family members have served as trustees, alongside others who are not members of the Rockefeller family. The current president is Stephen B. Heintz, who assumed office in February 2001.

Abby Rockefeller Mauze, the first child and only daughter of John Jr. and his wife Abby, was born in 1903. In 1977, she established her own Abby Rockefeller Mauze Charitable Trust, with $11.9 million. Through careful investment of the principal, it has made disbursements of $1 million to $4 million each year, for a total of $47.3 million, and it will likely achieve total disbursements in excess of $59 million before it closes in 2011. Major recipients have been Memorial Sloan-Kettering Cancer Center, Rockefeller University, Planned Parenthood of New York City, and the New York Academy of Sciences for its Harbor Project, an initiative that brought together an array of business leaders, scientists, advocates, researchers, and policymakers to better safeguard the harbors of New York and New Jersey from toxic chemicals. The Harbor Project has already won international acclaim for its solutions based on "good science" that can be implemented in the short term.

---

555 Much of the information regarding the members of the Brothers Generation (children of John D. Rockefeller Jr.) is from the Rockefeller Archive Center.

John D. Rockefeller 3d, born in 1906, was the eldest of the five brothers. He devoted his energies to continuing the foundations and philanthropic interests of his father and grandfather. By the time he died in an automobile accident in 1978, he had donated $94 million to a variety of causes. His will dispensed another $36 million to various cultural and educational organizations. He had served as the first president of the Lincoln Center for the Performing Arts, when it was incorporated in 1956, and donated more than $12 million toward construction of its six-building complex. He had actively solicited tens of millions of dollars in donations from others for the $185 million project.[556]

Nelson Rockefeller (1908–1979) graduated cum laude from Dartmouth College with a bachelor's degree in economics in 1930 and married Mary Todhunter Clark. When they returned from their nine-month, round-the-world honeymoon cruise, he went to work at the London and Paris offices of Chase National Bank. Nelson served on numerous commissions for Presidents Roosevelt, Truman, Eisenhower, and Nixon, focusing on government organization, public policy, and foreign affairs. In 1958, he was elected governor of New York, and he was elected to three additional terms. His long tenure was marked by legislative initiatives in education, housing, welfare, environmental regulation, civil rights, and the arts. In 1961, the family suffered a tragedy when their son, Michael, who had just graduated from Harvard, disappeared in New Guinea while on an anthropological expedition. In 1974, in the aftermath of the Watergate scandal, President Ford nominated Nelson to serve as vice president, and he served in that capacity until January 1977. The quiet presence of a respected, four-term former governor in the vice-presidency was part of the healing process for a nation shaken by a long, unpopular war and scandals that had forced resignations of President Nixon and, less than a year earlier, Vice President Spiro Agnew.

Laurance Rockefeller (1910–2004), earned a bachelor's degree in philosophy from Princeton University and studied law for two years at Harvard. Of all the Rockefeller siblings, Laurance was the most active and successful businessperson. His business career included developing several outstanding environmentally oriented resort hotels and investing capital in hundreds of new companies based primarily in scientific and technological development. According to the *New York Times*, his investment acumen led to multiplying his original wealth many times over. He was an original major investor in Captain Eddie Rickenbacker's Eastern Airlines. His investment interests included electronics and biotechnology.

---

556 *New York Times,* articles July 21, 1978; July 10, 1979

His desire was to make a profit in ways that produced something of lasting value. He served on several presidential commissions on environmental quality and played pivotal roles in the establishment of national parks, including Grand Teton in Wyoming and Virgin Islands National Park on the island of St. John. Over the span of his life, he donated hundreds of thousands of acres to governments for conservation. Laurance served as trustee of several major institutions, including the New York Zoological Society and Alfred P. Sloan Foundation, and as chairman of Memorial Sloan-Kettering Cancer Center in New York from 1960 to 1982, overseeing a major expansion and modernization of its facilities.[557] After his death, his Fifth Avenue co-op, a three-story penthouse he had purchased in 1946 as his family's primary residence, was sold to Rupert Murdoch for a reported $44 million, the highest price ever paid for a private residence in New York City.[558]

Winthrop Rockefeller (1912–1973) departed in many ways from the New York–centered family into which he was born. He dropped out of Yale in 1934 and went to work in the oil fields of Texas as a roughneck. He enlisted in the army in January 1941 as a private and participated in assault landings on Guam, Leyte, and Okinawa. He was awarded the Bronze Star with Oak Leaf Cluster and the Purple Heart, and by the end of the war, he had attained the rank of lieutenant colonel. In the early 1950s, Winthrop settled in Arkansas, where he purchased a small ranch and expanded it into the twenty-four-hundred-acre Winrock Farm. This would become a world-class facility for pure-bred Santa Gertrudis cattle.

"Win" Rockefeller advanced civil rights in ways that probably raised eyebrows in the quiet board meetings of the GEB. He appointed James Hudson, a black college graduate, as general superintendent of Winrock Farm. Many of the local vendors quietly objected to conducting business with a black man, until Win let it be known that all business transacted at the farm would be done through Mr. Hudson. Businessmen weighed their desire for sales and profits against their segregationist views, and they soon found James Hudson to be a desirable customer. Hudson also established himself as a competent and effective manager of the farm's large workforce—a delicate task in the rural South in the 1950s. Win offered to help the tiny local school district replace its obsolete buildings. He enlisted community support for higher school taxes and improved curriculum, and he pledged $2.5 million toward construction of new school buildings. But Win made it clear that his gift would not be used to finance segregated schools, which would be inherently wasteful. Citizens came together in

---

557 Rockefeller Foundation website, rf.org.
558 *New York Times,* July 12, 2004; December 17, 2004

favor of integrated and improved schools for all of the community's children. Win brought together business and community leaders to establish a clinic, which brought the first physician to Perry County and provided low-cost health services to the rural population. Win became an active leader of the Arkansas Industrial Development Commission, promoting community improvements that attracted companies to Arkansas and expanded job opportunities beyond the largely agriculture-based economy.[559]

In 1964, he ran for governor and lost. In 1966, he ran again and won, becoming the first Republican governor in Arkansas in ninety-four years. He won reelection in 1968, but he lost the 1970 election. His tenure was marked by reform of the state penal system and passage of the Freedom of Information Act of 1967, which opened official meetings to public scrutiny. In 1956, he established a foundation, now known as the Winthrop Rockefeller Foundation, which is still active today. The primary focus of this foundation is improving the lives of Arkansans by supporting and strengthening the organizations that serve them. The goals are in three areas: economic development; education; and economic, racial, and social justice. At the end of 2006, the foundation's assets were $149 million. Grants that year totaled $9.7 million. Winthrop had one son, Winthrop Paul Rockefeller, who served two terms as Arkansas' lieutenant governor and who served the foundation for thirty-three years until his death in 2006, at age fifty-six, leaving eight children.[560]

At this writing, David Rockefeller, in his nineties, is the sole surviving member of the "brothers generation" and patriarch of the Rockefeller family. He had a long and distinguished career in banking after serving in the U.S. Army during World War II. David joined Chase National Bank in 1946 as an assistant manager in the foreign department. He moved up through the ranks and was responsible for Chase's operations in Latin America in the early 1950s. In 1961, he became president of the bank, and in 1969, he was elected chairman of the board of directors and CEO of Chase Manhattan Corporation. He retired from banking in 1981 but continued his many philanthropic duties, including serving as chairman of the board of trustees at the Museum of Modern Art and trustee of the University of Chicago. He helped establish Harvard University's Center for Latin American Studies, which opened in 1994. Since 2005, David Rockefeller has announced several very large donations, including $100 million to the

---

559 *Saturday Evening Post,* September 29, 1956.
560 Information about the Winthrop Rockefeller Foundation is from the foundation's website, including its annual reports, which are posted there.

Museum of Modern Art and $100 million to Harvard University, most of which will be dedicated to helping more Harvard students to study abroad. He has also announced a gift of $225 million to the Rockefeller Brothers Fund. This will be used to establish the David Rockefeller Global Development Fund to complement the fund's work in sustainable development, poverty eradication, and international trade and finance.[561]

———

The fortune of John D. Rockefeller has been flowing back into society through multiple charities benefiting billions of people around the world. Today, the Rockefeller Foundation established in 1913 remains financially strong, with $3 billion worth of invested assets. Each year, investment income from that fortune is distributed to a wide variety of civic, artistic, charitable, and educational causes. In 2006 alone, the foundation made grants totaling $134.5 million. The foundation's financial reports, including the annual Internal Revenue Service Form 990-T and a list of all grants made, can be viewed at the foundation's website.

The Rockefeller Brothers Fund promotes social change that contributes to a more just, sustainable, and peaceful world, and four pivotal places: New York City, South Africa, Western Balkans, and Southern China. Net assets at the end of 2007 totaled $981 million, allowing the fund to distribute $29 million in grants to organizations that carry out work consistent with these goals. Total program spending, including grants and administrative expenses and excluding investment-related expenses and taxes, was $41.6 million.

The "brothers generation" produced the "cousins generation," of whom twenty-nine lived into adulthood. Many of them became involved in the foundations, and quite a few embarked on their own charitable works.[562] Winthrop Paul Rockefeller, Winthrop's son, was of this generation, as is John D. (Jay) Rockefeller IV, former governor of West Virginia and since 1985 a U.S. Senator from West Virginia. Together the cousins established the Rockefeller Family Fund in 1967 as a major vehicle for the philanthropy of this generation. This fund concentrates its efforts in advocacy in areas such as environmental protection, advancing the economic rights of women, and holding public and private institutions accountable for their actions. This is an obvious departure from the Rockefeller Foundation and the Rockefeller Brothers Fund, which concentrated on grants to uni-

---

561 *New York Times,* June 9, 2005; November 21, 2006; April 25, 2008
562 *New York Times,* December 30, 1984

versities, museums, hospitals, and support of academic or medical research. The Rockefeller Family Fund describes its resources as limited. Typical grants have ranged from $25,000 to $30,000. The fund's trustees are listed on its website; at least half are Rockefeller family members. The cousins' children ("the fifth generation") are now middle-aged or older and more numerous than their parents.

Today, there are seventy-eight adult descendants of John D. Rockefeller. David, at ninety-four, is the last surviving grandchild of Senior; all the others are great-grandchildren or great-great-grandchildren.[563] Each generation has brought about a wider distribution of inherited wealth, and differences in interests, priorities, and investment skills have no doubt brought about growing gaps in personal fortunes. Even in the brothers' generation, marriage mixed other family fortunes with Rockefeller money. A number of Rockefellers of various generations have been very successful in business or the professions and may well have added to their own fortunes, rather than living off of their inheritances. Newspapers no longer report the assessed value of estates or the details of wills. Money has been passed down by gifts and trusts, out of the public eye. The heirs have their own interest in privacy. Thus the trail begins to run cold on that portion of Rockefeller money that has not gone into philanthropy.

But the *Forbes* lists do provide some insight. *Forbes* estimates David Rockefeller's personal net worth at $2.7 billion. Adjusted for inflation, this sum represents less than 1 percent of the purchasing power of John D. Rockefeller's personal fortune a century ago. Before his death in 2006, Winthrop Paul Rockefeller's net worth was estimated at $1.2 billion, less that one-half of one percent of the founder's fortune. It is safe to assume that members of the "cousins" generation and their children, now grown, are quite comfortable, but the concentration of wealth has been diminished by the sheer number of heirs over the years, and by each generation's personal philanthropy.

―――

We could easily fall into the assumption that Rockefeller wealth—the original fortune and its direct descendant fortune, if that can be isolated—represents a major block of economic power with one common purpose. Many of the descendants came together to present shareholder resolutions to ExxonMobil's Annual Meeting in 2008. They coordinated their votes to support shareholder resolutions regarding environmental safety. The resolutions were supported by

40 percent of the shares voted at the meeting, including many beyond the Rockefeller family, but they failed to obtain a majority of shares voted. The extended family, even when acting together, is not an irresistible force. The theory of a hereditary concentration of power derived from great fortunes was disproven. The widely disbursed ownership of ExxonMobil and many of America's other large corporations is a dilution of economic power that had no precedent one hundred years ago. Millions of individual and institutional investors share the profits of the corporate successors of the Standard Oil companies.

Perhaps our greater concern should be with the autonomy of the various foundations to which a great deal of Rockefeller wealth has been given over the past century. Each of these is led by a board of trustees. The members of the Rockefeller Foundation's board are identified on the foundation's website. The board includes only one Rockefeller, plus fourteen people of independent accomplishment and competence in a variety of disciplines. The president is Judith Rodin, PhD, formerly the president of the University of Pennsylvania and provost of Yale University. The website contains every Annual Report since the inception of the foundation, including detailed accounting of invested assets, income, and disbursements. The Rockefeller Brothers Fund has sixteen trustees, including several Rockefeller family members, from varied backgrounds. The website contains a biography of each trustee and officer.

How did one man set all this in motion? Rockefeller Senior's methods in business and philanthropy were similar. In both areas, he employed the smartest people he could find and valued their advice. His own analytical powers were strong. Data, carefully collected and analyzed, were valued more than instinct. In business and philanthropy, he pondered major decisions, sometimes for months, to the frustration of his high-energy associates. He gave long thought to discovering the root cause of a business opportunity or a problem in public health, education, or any of his other interests. In business and philanthropy, patient, long-term effort pursued enduring gain, rather than the speculative move or quick fix that soon fades.

There is ample evidence that Rockefeller Senior was a gifted negotiator. His ability to convince bankers to lend money in the early years, his ability to buy out the businesses of many competitors and suppliers, his audacious negotiations with the railroads, and even his ability to launch so many philanthropic efforts demonstrate a prodigious talent for inspiring people to accept his propositions. Rockefeller also went to great lengths to avoid disputes or controversy. Buying out a competitor is conciliatory; building a new facility in a competitor's territory is competitive. His labor practices, including high-er-than-competitor wages, were in line with his appreciation that process in-dustries are most profitable when they operate smoothly, without unplanned interruption. This conciliatory labor policy may account, more than any other single factor, for the difference between Carnegie's fortune and Rockefeller's. Rockefeller was usually a buyer, a consolidator, especially in the early decades. His estate plan—giving his wealth away during his lifetime rather than relying heavily on wills and trusts, with all the potential difficulties—reflects a strong aversion to controversy.

Once decisions were reached and direction chosen, the message was sent in clear terms to all who needed to hear it. The organizations he founded were living, thinking organisms, designed to be self-perpetuating and enabled to carry on without him. The business organization of the Standard Oil, from its origin as a company in 1870 to the forced dissolution of the Standard Oil Trust in 1911, was more of a confederation of companies with common goals and coordinated strategy than a hierarchical monarchy. The same organizational model is found in the Rockefeller Foundation, the GEB, and Rockefeller's other charitable ven-tures. Rockefeller's organizations looked for the best available practices in each area of their work and quickly made these available throughout the organization. In business and philanthropy, his organizations had a corporate culture similar to modern-day Toyota's and little in common with the mind-numbing factories of early twentieth century Ford Motor Company.

Why did this happen? The motivation of any thinking person is complex and evolves as life experience accumulates. A powerful need to achieve may have de-veloped at an early age.[564] Rockefeller wrote of his father's interest in the young man's early business ventures. His mother, raising six children alone, set high standards. Biographers note that Rockefeller, throughout his life, read and pon-dered the Bible, and he listened every Sunday to preachers of his Baptist tradi-tion. He left no written compendium of his Bible reflections. He taught Sunday school and gave guest lectures, but the very few talks that were written down discuss his own childhood thrift and work ethic. His career and philanthropy were not based on celebrity. He rarely granted interviews, did not attend char-ity balls or fundraising events, and did not accept seats on the boards of charity organizations that received his support.

Some comments from Rockefeller himself:

---

564 For a psychologist's discussion of "need to achieve," see David C. McClel-land, *Human Motivation*, 224-267.

You hear a good many people of pessimistic disposition say much about greed in American life…To lay too much stress upon the reports of greed in the newspapers would be folly, since their function is to report the unusual and even the abnormal. When a man goes properly about his daily affairs, the public prints say nothing; it is only when something extraordinary happens to him that he is discussed…It is by no means for money alone that these active-minded men labour—they are engaged in something better than the accumulation of money…

Many men of wealth do not retire from business even when they can. They are not willing to be idle, or they have a just pride in their work and want to perfect the plans in which they have faith, or, what is of still more consequence, they may feel the call to expand and build up for the benefit of their employees and associates, and these men are the great builders up in our country. Consider for a moment how much would have been left undone if our prosperous American business men had sat down with folded hands when they had acquired a competency …our institutions devoted to helping men to help themselves need the brain of the American business man as well as part of his money.[565]

A century later, Steve Jobs, co-founder of Apple Inc., gave his thoughts:

You've got to find what you love, and that is as true for work as it is for your lovers. Your work is going to fill a large part of your life. The only way to be satisfied is to do what you believe is great work, and the only way to do great work is to love what you do. If you haven't found it yet, keep looking, and don't settle. As with all matters of the heart, you'll know when you find it, and like any great relationship it just gets better and better as the years roll on.[566]

––––––

Some look askance at the philanthropy of the Rockefellers, Carnegie, Astors, Fields, Goulds, or others as tainted by their profit-oriented business activities. The same dilemma exists when we consider Alfred Nobel. His will established and funded the Nobel Prizes in medicine, physics, chemistry, literature, and peace.

---

565 John D. Rockefeller, *Some Random Reminiscences of Men and Events,* 67, 70.
566 Steve Jobs, Commencement Address, Stanford University, June 12, 2005.

Nobel made his fortune, also from the 1850s through the 1890s, by supplying arms to the Russian government in the Crimean War and selling dynamite and other explosives. Nobel increased his fortune by competing against Rockefeller, the Rothschilds, and others in the oil business in Europe and Asia. The sale of Nobel's stock in the various companies he established provided the initial endowment, which as prescribed in his will, "invested in safe securities by my executors, shall constitute a fund, the interest on which shall be annually distributed in the form of prizes…"[567] Without accumulated corporate profits there would be no Nobel Prizes.

Some, but not all, of these nineteenth century fortunes were accumulated using business practices that were deplorable then and illegal now. In that era, there were few unions, no Interstate Commerce Commission until 1887, no Sherman Anti-Trust Act until 1890, no Federal Reserve Bank (1913), no Securities and Exchange Commission (1934), no National Labor Relations Act (1935), and no Occupational Safety and Health Act (1970). Workers compensation insurance was not established in the states until 1911 and later. There were conspiracies to fix prices and avoid competition. Some labor negotiations were settled using armed thugs. This dilemma of dealing with wealth obtained by means now unacceptable is not new. George Washington, Thomas Jefferson, and others professed that all men are created equal, but they used slave labor on their own plantations. The end does not justify the means. We condemn the evils of slavery and celebrate the great legacies of our early political leaders.

––––––

The philanthropy of wealthy people sometimes encounters quiet skepticism. "Shouldn't the wealthy give generously, when they have so much more than they will ever need?" or "Perhaps some guilt goes along with all the greed," or "Sure, they gave up some money, but it's a fraction of what they kept for themselves." These comments reflect the "two buckets" way of thinking about money. This financial strategy allocates wages to two main uses: current living expenses and charitable contributions. Many people allocate their income carefully between these two purposes. But this strategy neglects the opportunity and the need to build for the future. It reflects a lack of knowledge about the origins of wealth and large-scale philanthropy. Our century of observation is valuable.

567 Information about the Nobel Prizes, and a complete English translation of Nobel's will, are available at www.Nobelprize.org. The Nobel Prize in Economics was established in 1968 by a Swedish bank and operates in the same manner as the other Nobel Prizes.

At the start of their careers, Rockefeller, Carnegie, and many other builders of large fortunes earned no more than their contemporaries in similar
entry-level jobs. They had opportunity, nothing more. But they used a "three
buckets" financial strategy for allocating that income. They donated to churches
or charities—the first bucket. They made a choice to use a selected portion of
every pay check to fill a second bucket—savings. Whatever money remained—
the third bucket—determined their lifestyle. From an early age, Rockefeller
and Carnegie used only the third bucket portion of their humble wages for their
own living expenses and to help support their siblings and mothers. Carnegie,
Rockefeller, and our other mega-wealthy were not born rich. They started on
the road to wealth by careful planning and discipline: they gave, they saved, and
they lived on what was left.

At the start of their careers, they deliberately limited themselves to basic
necessities: food, necessary clothing, decent housing. Amusements and recreation were infrequent and inexpensive. In the early years, they took no elaborate
vacations. The savings were not just coincidence, accumulating whatever happened to be left over at the end of the week. Nor were their savings achieved by
neglecting family duties or charities. The savings resulted from recognizing three
proper uses of income and setting priorities.

The planning and self-discipline of the three-bucket approach set them on
a different path from their peers. The savings enabled them to invest in their
early business ventures. Some of these included borrowed money, but the core
investment was savings, and without that core, there would have been no loan.
The savings, once invested in business, allowed them to offer jobs to others. The
businesses started small and grew larger, creating employment for thousands.
Throughout their careers, Rockefeller, Carnegie, Field, Ford, and the others
maintained savings that enabled them to deal with financial panics, recessions,
and partners who wanted to sell.

That second bucket—saving and investing for the future—allowed them the
opportunity, but never the assurance, of wealth. Their savings, investment, and
the skill with which they ran their businesses over many decades produced great
wealth. That wealth became their gift to the world. The foundations they established and funded enable the trustees to pursue projects helpful to mankind.
Careful stewardship of the original funds, including successful investment over
the long term, allows the trustees to continue the good works. Even today, funds
from these foundations support the activities of local, regional and worldwide
charities. That three-bucket strategy is available to individuals and households
today. It is part of the way forward.

Chapter Twenty-one

Ancient Problems, New Approaches

Field and Astor philanthropies focused on, respectively, Chicago and New York. Carnegie and Rockefeller had a global view, and the foundations they established continue to work on a grand scale. Are these simply vestiges of the Gilded Age of American enterprise, or are they early demonstrations of the power of accumulated profits to advance the common good? The current assets of both the Rockefeller Foundation and the Carnegie Corporation of New York, after a century of investment results and grant-making, are valued at less than 5 percent of their original assets. How does our society build new purchasing power to fund good works?

In 1905, when Carnegie and Rockefeller were retired and donating vast fortunes to their foundations, Henry Ford and his family were still living in a rented house, enjoying the early success of the two-year-old Ford Motor Company. William Durant had not yet organized General Motors. Andrew Mellon was just turning fifty years old. He was already a wealthy banker, planning a round-the-world cruise for himself and his wife. But the companies in which he had invested were just beginning to pay dividends to shareholders, after years of costly investment in equipment and plants. These companies and many others built a new generation of wealth by delivering new products to a new generation of customers. These new fortunes funded vast new foundations at midcentury.

The Ford Foundation, established in 1936, inherited almost all the nonvoting class A shares of Ford Motor Company (valued for estate purposes as more than $417 million) plus $95 million in U.S. Government securities when Henry, Clara, and Edsel had passed away.[568] Thus it became the wealthiest foundation in America in 1950. In 1956, the foundation began to diversify its investment portfolio. The trustees recognized that concentrating the foundation's assets so heavily in the stock of any one corporation was inconsistent with their responsibilities as stewards of the foundation's resources. This prompted the first sale of Ford Motor Company stock to the public.[569] Until then, only the original shareholders from 1903 and then the family of Henry Ford and then the Ford Foundation had been in possession of company stock. Ford Motor Company became, for the first time, a publicly traded company. The $641 million raised in the sale of approximately 22 percent of the foundation's stock was reinvested in other securities. The foundation's remaining shares of Ford Motor Company, if assigned the same per-share price as the shares sold, had an assumed market valuation of $2.2 billion. In subsequent years, the foundation sold additional shares and reinvested in order to diversify income sources and reduce the foundation's dependence on the success of any one business.

The Ford Foundation's charter sets forth its purpose: "To receive and administer funds for scientific, educational and charitable purposes, all for the public welfare." The trustees recognized that other foundations, institutions, and government agencies were already working toward this same general objective. They also realized their own responsibility to see that the foundation's resources were wisely used in ways that actually advanced the public welfare. The trustees assembled a study committee to provide independent advice on how best to carry out the foundation's work. Eight distinguished leaders in the fields of education, public health and medicine, political sciences and government, the natural sciences, social sciences, the humanities, and business and industry served on the committee. More than one thousand interviews were conducted to get the best available insights. University presidents, business and professional leaders, representatives from state and federal government and the United Nations, and heads of private organizations concerned with world affairs gave their advice.

The result was the Gaither Report, which was adopted by the trustees as the formal strategy for the foundation's activities. The major themes to be advanced

---

568 "Most of Ford $200,000,000 Estate Is Given to Foundation in His Will," *New York Times,* June 4, 1943; "Ford Tax Indicates $70,000,000 Estate," *New York Times,* October 29, 1948.

569 "Ford Fund Faces Cash Indigestion," *New York Times,* November 13, 1955; "Ford Foundation, Largest in Nation, Holds Bulk of Motor Company's Stock," *New York Times,* November 7, 1935.

were peace, education, the behavioral sciences, democratic institutions, and economic stability. Initial financial backing was given to programs ranging from disarmament studies to agricultural extension work in India, from research into human behavior to programs for raising the competence of teachers. The foundation would work toward long-term social gains rather than support projects that meet only current crises or temporary needs, however worthy.

In 2009, the Ford Foundation approved $490 million in grants to programs in pursuit of social justice in the United States and around the world. The Ford Foundation's impact might be more fully appreciated when considering that disbursements since 1980 have totaled $12.7 billion, more than four times the value of the endowment in 1980. Investment of the foundation's endowment portfolio produces this bounty.[570]

Other fortunes were donated to charitable purposes as this new generation of investors made their own decisions about financial legacies. Charles Marsh started his newspaper career in 1909 as a reporter for a small newspaper in Oklahoma, earning $25 per week. He saved $2,500 and formed a partnership with brothers Charles and E. S. Fentress. Together, they built a chain of newspapers and became enormously wealthy.[571] Marsh established the Public Welfare Foundation in 1947. When he died in 1964, the foundation received an unusual gift—ownership of three active newspapers. All profits from the papers would flow into the foundation, to be distributed as charitable grants.[572]

The Public Welfare Foundation also had a novel approach to grant-making. During his life, Charles Marsh had practiced what he called an "agency" approach to giving. He gave money directly to individuals who were doing good work in their community. The "agents" received funds to be used at their own discretion during the year. Marsh required very little documentation of the work beyond an annual letter from each agent reporting what had been done and indicating a willingness to continue. Marsh sought to minimize the paperwork and administrative structures that he felt distracted from the accomplishment of direct aid to the disadvantaged. His foundation followed that practice in its early years. But in the 1960s, the IRS challenged the foundation regarding its ownership of the for-profit newspapers and the donation of funds to individuals with little

---

570 Annual Report, 2010, The Ford Foundation, 44.

571 Philip Kopper, *Anonymous Giver: A Life of Charles E. Marsh*, Public Welfare Foundation, 2000.

572 Peggy Dillon, *Seeking the Greatest Good: The Public Welfare Foundation*, Public Welfare Foundation. 2000.

accountability. The newspapers were sold, and the proceeds of sale were re-invested, mainly into publicly traded stocks and bonds. The agency system of giving was replaced with grants to nonprofit organizations for specific purposes, and record-keeping was improved to meet the government's standards.

Today, the Public Welfare Foundation actively supports local and state nonprof-its working in the areas of criminal and juvenile justice, health reform, and workers' rights. In 2007, the Public Welfare Foundation approved grants totaling more than $19 million. The unrestricted assets of the foundation in 2007 were $589 million.

Andrew Mellon, secretary of the treasury from 1921 to 1932, became one of the richest people in America before entering government service. From his early days working at the bank his father had established in Pittsburgh, Andrew Mellon had invested his own money as a stockholder in companies that needed large amounts of cash to buy mineral resources, build plants, and expand until operations were large enough to generate profits. Mellon's large equity invest-ments provided the long-term, "patient" money for these companies. Bank loans supplied the balance of the funds needed.

Mellon invested for the long term in companies he felt had new technologies that would be important and profitable in time, but needed large amounts of cash investment to build their first commercial-sized plants and begin operations. This was not the quest for a quick stock gain in six months or a year, or even five years. In fact, he invested mainly in companies that were not publicly traded. He was not active in the day-to-day management of these corporations, but he relied upon the founders of the businesses, mainly young people with new ideas, who impressed him with their competence and perseverance. He stayed with the investments, even through the Panic of 1907 and the years of the Great War. By the 1920s, Mel-lon was on sixty boards. When he resigned these positions to take up the duties of treasury secretary, his brother stepped into many of the board seats. A few of Andrew's early investments had become very successful, especially Gulf Oil, Pitts-burgh Reduction Company (later renamed Aluminum Company of America and now Alcoa), and of course Union Trust, which owned Mellon National Bank (now Bank of New York Mellon).[573] Not all of his investments were so rewarding, but these few big, long-term successes had made him one of America's wealthiest men.

Andrew Mellon died in 1937. Each of his two adult children, Ailsa Mellon Bruce and Paul Mellon, received major gifts of corporate stock from their father during his lifetime. They had also developed their own sense of philanthropy.

Ailsa founded the Avalon Foundation, and Paul founded the Old Dominion Foundation. In 1969, these were merged, and the name was changed to The Andrew

---

573 David Cannadine, *Mellon.*

W. Mellon Foundation, honoring the former treasury secretary. Later in the same year, Ailsa passed away. She was survived by three grandchildren, to whom she left her jewelry and a small amount of cash. Most of her fortune was left to the foundation. This inheritance of $400 million more than doubled the foundation's assets, enabling a much larger flow of annual grants. A major part of the legacy was 8,570,124 shares of Gulf Oil Company (market value $277 million), 600,000 shares of Aluminum Company of America ($34 million), 616,980 shares of Mellon National Bank and Trust Company ($34 million), and 150,000 shares of Carborundum Company ($7.3 million). These were shares that Andrew Mellon had purchased decades earlier and given to his daughter, who gave them to the foundation.[574]

A small sample of the $279 million in grants awarded by the Andrew W. Mellon Foundation in 2008 reflects the breadth of projects supported at numerous institutions.

Grants in the higher education and scholarship category assist many small but excellent liberal arts colleges as well as the largest universities. Southern Education Foundation, Inc., received an appropriation of $915,000 to support reaccreditation preparation for historically black colleges and universities. Appalachian College Association received $500,000 to support faculty career enhancement and expansion of the Central Library online catalogue; Smith College in Massachusetts, $1.4 million to support the first-year program, advanced interdisciplinary seminars, and faculty advising. Sarah Lawrence College, New York, received $700,000 for faculty revitalization. The New School, New York, received $400,000 to add curricula for the environmental studies program. Stanford University, California, $75,000 to develop a program to evaluate interventions to increase the pool of well-qualified, low-income students at leading universities. Earlham College, Indiana, $300,000 to support development of an Islamic studies program. Bowdoin College, Maine, $1.7 million to support enhanced sabbatical leaves. This is only a partial list. In total, more than 250 grants totaling $160 million were appropriated to more than 120 colleges and universities—a tremendous boost that enables them to improve in ways that would otherwise require higher tuitions. Every year, a new round of grants supports activity at institutions of higher education.

In addition, $33 million was appropriated to institutions working in the field of libraries and scholarly communications, including $557,000 to the Northeast Document Conservation Center, Inc., in Massachusetts for development of digitized services that would be offered to libraries, archives, historical societies, and museums. Johns Hopkins University, Maryland, received $792,000 to support an initiative to increase scientific expertise in conservation programs of libraries and archives.

574 Andrew W. Mellon Foundation, Annual Reports, 1969, 1970.

In the same year, the Andrew W. Mellon Foundation appropriated more than $29 million to museums and art conservation, including $2 million to the Art Institute of Chicago to establish an endowment for the position of associate scientist in the Department of Conservation and to sustain essential elements of the collaboration with Northwestern University. The Denver Art Museum received $1.75 million to establish an endowment for the position of paintings conservator and to support essential equipment purchases. Additional appropriations were made to support the performing arts, conservation, and the environment.

The grand total of grants in 2008, $279 million, supported this broad variety of projects. Each grant was important to the mission of the recipient organization. Cumulatively over forty years, such a wide variety of grants has certainly improved the general welfare. In spite of significant investment losses in the recent financial crisis, the foundation remains strong, with more than $4 billion in invested assets. [575]

The board of trustees consists of nine members, including the president Don M. Randel, former president of the University of Chicago. The backgrounds of the board's nine members reflect the purposes for which the foundation was established, to "aid and promote such religious, charitable, scientific, literary, and educational purposes as may be in the furtherance of the public welfare or tend to promote the well-doing or well-being of mankind." Five trustees have extensive experience as professors or presidents in universities or major cultural institutions, while four trustees are drawn from corporate backgrounds, including investment banking. These backgrounds provide talent consistent with conducting two major functions inherent with continuing the foundation's work: well-informed decisions about the numerous applications seeking grants, and stewardship of the foundation's assets.

After his father's death, Paul Mellon led the effort to complete the National Gallery of Art. He served as president of the National Gallery of Art from 1938 until the building was finished in 1941, when President Roosevelt accepted the gallery on behalf of the nation. Paul continued to serve the gallery as a trustee until 1985, except during his military service in World War II. As Andrew Mellon had intended, many art collectors donated important pieces that filled out the gallery's space. Andrew also anticipated the need for eventual expansion, and at his insistence Congress had reserved land adjacent to the original building for that purpose. In the late 1960s, Paul and Ailsa agreed to provide the funds for a major addition by direct contributions and through the foundations each had established earlier. Unusually high inflation rates in the 1970s drove construction costs, origi-

---

575 Annual Report, 2008, The Andrew W. Mellon Foundation. The financial crisis of 2008 had reduced the value of the assets from $6.0 billion one year earlier.

nally estimated at $20 million, to almost $100 million by the time of its completion in 1978.[576] But the pledge to contribute the entire cost of construction was fulfilled, and the foundation provided additional millions to fund an endowment to pay the salaries of the gallery staff. During his lifetime, Paul Mellon contributed more than nine hundred works to the National Gallery, including important works by Cezanne, Monet, Degas, and van Gogh. Today, the National Gallery of Art remains open daily to the public. There is no charge for admission.

Separately, he donated to Yale University the building, numerous art works, and funds for the endowment of the Center for British Art. This has become the largest collection of British art in the United States.

Over the course of his lifetime, Paul Mellon became one of Yale's most generous benefactors. His donations have funded numerous deanships, professorships, and fellowships in the colleges and in the Schools of Medicine, Divinity, Forestry, and Environmental Studies. The medical school fellowships helped make possible the trend toward specialization in the 1970s, an innovation that improved treatment quality and effectiveness.

Paul Mellon lived on a large estate in Virginia and supported many community projects in Richmond. The West Wing of the Virginia Museum of Fine Arts, built in 1985, was heavily underwritten by Mellon and his wife, and they contributed many of the paintings that occupied the new wing.

The Ford Foundation, Public Welfare Foundation, and Andrew W. Mellon Foundation are just three of the legacies of the wealth assembled in the first half of the twentieth century and now committed to the public welfare. The trustees of each of these foundations select the areas of social action in which the foundation concentrates its grants. Universities and hospitals continue to be major recipients of funds. But these newer foundations have also channeled significant funds and attention to newer areas of concern, such as working with troubled teenagers, early childhood development, and funds for medical schools to provide teaching and research opportunities for young faculty members.

Corporations that did not exist fifty years ago have created new fortunes. That wealth is now funding a new generation of foundations to meet new needs and to bring new thinking and new funds to promote the general welfare.

---

576 In eight of the ten years between 1969 and 1978, the Consumer Price Index rose more than 5 percent. In 1974 alone, the Index rose 11 percent.

Bill Gates, currently one of the wealthiest individuals in the world with a personal net worth of $58 billion,[577] has founded the largest philanthropic foundation in the world—the Bill and Melinda Gates Foundation—and donated $26 billion to it. While the foundation does make grants to local and regional organizations in the northwestern U.S., Bill and Melinda Gates have announced that a priority for the foundation will be to work with the United Nations and various nongovernment organizations (NGOs) to eradicate certain diseases that currently afflict the least developed countries of the world. The foundation has already directed major funding to vaccination programs and public health education. The founders are very keen on using this major wealth to accomplish world-scale goals that would be otherwise unattainable. As just one indication of the power that such large funding brings to solving world-scale problems, the foundation, in February 2006, hired Dr. Tadataka Yamada, formerly chairman of research and development at GlaxoSmithKline, as executive director of the foundation's Global Health program. The foundation's annual report is available at www.gatesfoundation.org and makes for inspiring reading.

Warren Buffett, chairman of Berkshire Hathaway, and also one of the wealthiest people in the world,[578] long ago established the Buffett Foundation and used it as a vehicle for major philanthropy. In 2006, Buffett announced that he would donate the bulk of his fortune to the Bill and Melinda Gates Foundation by transferring his shares of Berkshire Hathaway stock to the foundation in installments over the next ten years.[579] Buffett has often discussed, in interviews, his conviction that his children should receive some of his wealth, but that society in general should be the major beneficiary. This is a motivation found frequently among the very rich, as reported by several studies of philanthropy.

So it is that the largest fortunes in the world and many smaller fortunes—accumulated profits from corporate activity—continue to be inherited mainly by foundations, whose directors or trustees exercise stewardship of this wealth while dispensing it to benefit those in need.

---

577 *Forbes* 400 list, 2009.
578 *Forbes* 400, 2009. Many books have been written explaining how Warren Buffett became the wealthiest person in the world, mainly by buying publicly traded stocks and holding them as long term investments. The books are interesting. But if you want to save some money and learn directly from Warren Buffett, go to the Berkshire Hathaway website and read the annual Chairman's Letters, which are widely considered camp art by business leaders. Buffett explains it all in simple, clear terms.
579 The letter conveying this pledge is available on the Berkshire Hathaway website.

VI
CONCLUSION

Chapter Twenty-two

Legacies

Customer-driven business activity produces profits and accumulations of wealth, and it funds vigorous philanthropy in America and beyond. Has that process brought measureable benefits to the poor and to the man or woman who works for wages, living paycheck to paycheck?

Important changes benefit the entire population. The infant mortality rate in America shows dramatic improvement. In 1900, one child in ten died within a year of birth. By 1950, fewer than three in one hundred would die so young (29.2 per 1,000). In 2006, the rate was one child in 150 (6.7 per 1,000) dying before age one.[580]

Life expectancy has increased from forty-seven years in 1900 to seventy-eight years in 2007. Today, a man in average health at age sixty-five has a life expectancy of seventeen more years; a woman has twenty years. For blacks, the improvement has been much more dramatic. At birth in 1900, a black American had a life expectancy of thirty-three years. Today, a black newborn has a life expectancy of seventy-three years.[581]

Our longer life expectancy is influenced by many factors. Today, large numbers of public health officials are trained and empowered to prevent conditions that so often spread avoidable diseases just a century ago. Those unsanitary conditions and resultant diseases were far more prevalent among the poor. Many Americans

---

580 National Center for Health Statistics, U.S. Department of Health and Human Services. *Health, United States, 2010.* Table15.
581 National Center for Health Statistics, U.S. Department of Health and Human Services. *Health, United States 2010.* Table 22.

early in the twentieth century suffered diseases related to deficient diets and poor sanitation: rickets, pellagra, tuberculosis. Today's health problems, even among low-income households, are symptoms of prosperity: obesity, high cholesterol, diabetes. Another major improvement is the availability of well-trained physicians. In 1900, as the Flexner Report documented, physician training was spotty. Some were well trained, but many others were well-intentioned quacks. By 1975, there were thirteen active patient care physicians per ten thousand people in the U.S. Today, there are twenty-four per ten thousand.[582] Medical research at many universities and corporate research laboratories, often building on each other's findings, has produced vaccines and cures for a host of ailments. Reduced infant mortality and longer life expectancy are broad improvements in the general welfare.

———

The lifestyle of today's poorest in America far surpasses the basic lifestyle affordable at the $721 that Louise Bolard More calculated in 1904–1905 to support a family of five in Gramercy Park, or at the $800 annual income that John Curtis Kennedy found was the minimum required to provide for a family of five in the Chicago stockyard district in 1909–1910.

More and Kennedy studied urban areas. In rural areas, where most Americans still lived, expenses for food may have been lower. But sanitary conditions, diet, medical care, and access to education were often much worse.

James T. Patterson, a professor of history at Brown University, has studied the history of poverty and welfare in the United States, focusing on the twentieth century. Patterson's estimate that 40 percent of Americans lived in poverty in 1900 is based on the $800 per year income figure needed to attain a subsistence lifestyle.[583] By the late 1950s, the poverty rate for all Americans had dropped to 22.4 percent. In 2000, the rate hit an historic low at 11.3 percent, but rose to 13.2 percent in 2008[584] and 15.3 percent in 2010.[585]

Referring specifically to developments between 1900 and 1929, Patterson described a phenomenon that persists through modern times:

---

582 National Center for Health Statistics, U.S. Department of Health and Human Services. *Health, United States 2010.* Table 106.

583 James T. Patterson, *America's Struggle with Poverty in the Twentieth Century.*

584 U.S. Bureau of Census, Current Population Survey, Table 19.

585 U.S. Bureau of Census, 2010 American Community Survey, Table S1701. For 2010, the poverty income threshold for a family of four is defined as $22,314.

Improved communications by 1930 made many of the needy a little less isolated than they had been and more aware of what they were missing. Above all, economic growth was real, and it inevitably led some of the poor to share in the improved standards of living. Social scientists and social workers thought the poor needed more, and they constructed slightly more generous budgets (in real dollars) for poor families in the 1920s than they had in the 1890s. The liberalization of such budgets over time, like the rising of the poverty line, reflected the experts' awareness that poor people themselves expected a little more in 1929 than they had thirty and fifty years before.[586]

Patterson also observed that:

Statistics, of course, need some comparative dimension...Americans in the 1930s did not expect to own many gadgets (fully 40 percent of all households in 1940 lacked bathtubs, and 58 percent lacked central heating). By the 1960s, however, the poor thought they had to have phones, television sets, electricity, and cars.[587]

Patterson's point is not to push the poverty threshold back to some former level. He points out the improvements that the poor have obtained in their living standard because these products have become available at ever-lower prices. Radios, televisions, telephones, computers, and most recently camera-equipped cell phones have raised awareness of poverty. All these devices, as well as refrigerators, microwave ovens, and air conditioners are increasingly owned by the poor.

———

Ownership of America's productive capacity has also changed. Forty-seven percent of American households now own equities, either common stock or stock mutual funds, compared to 32 percent in 1989 and just 3 percent in 1929.[588] These fifty-four million shareholder-households are, in every sense of the word, owners of capital. They share in the profits of ExxonMobil, Coca-Cola Company, Aetna, Bank of America, Apple, Inc., or other corporations whose shares they own. Some

586 James T. Patterson, *America's Struggle Against Poverty in the Twentieth Century*, 18.
587 Ibid, 42.
588 *Equity Ownership in America, 2008*, by the Investment Company Institute and Securities Industry and Financial Markets Association.

of these shares are purchased directly, others by purchasing mutual funds. Many workers also participate in employee stock ownership plans (ESOP) or 401(k) plans where they work. Similarly, government pension funds, unions, universities, and other institutions benefit from this ownership of corporate securities.

United States Steel offered one of the earliest employee stock purchase plans, beginning in 1903. That plan included many of the key features of modern plans, including employer matching funds.[589] These plans offer opportunities to accumulate sizeable savings over the long term. The larger implication for society is the participation, by labor, in the ownership of capital. This is no assurance of wealth—opportunity always involves risk. But the ownership stake of workers in corporate wealth has grown larger and more diverse. After-tax corporate profits are flowing to those who work for wages and choose to participate.

This broader distribution of the profits of large corporations to workers aligns the interests of labor and management. Workers participate in the growth of capital to improve their financial circumstances. It is voluntary. For employee stock plans and 401(k) plans, employers pay the costs of pamphlets, booklets, and meetings to explain the plan features and encourage enrollment. Fortunately, the Pension Protection Act of 2006 provides that employees at corporations that have such plans are automatically enrolled when they become eligible, although they retain the right to opt out. There are also appropriate default investment funds for employees who may be skittish about making their own choices. The path of opportunity along which Rockefeller, Carnegie, Astor, Gould, Field, and many others walked, starting out poor and building wealth by saving and investing in business, is broader now than it has ever been in history. There is no guarantee of wealth, nor has there ever been. For many workers, the road to better financial security begins with enrollment in their 401(k).

———

The gap between the richest and poorest has grown narrower, not wider. The largest fortune ever accumulated in this country was that of John D. Rockefeller at its peak in 1917. His fortune then, adjusted for inflation, was greater than the present-day wealth of Warren Buffett and Bill Gates combined. The richest American today is far less rich than his counterpart of a century ago, and the poor have possessions and lifestyle beyond the imagination of their counterparts.

This narrowing of the wealth gap between rich and poor is documented by Wojciech Kopczuk of Columbia University and Emmanuel Saez of the University of California at Berkeley. The sharpest decline in share-of-wealth has been

589 "Steel Trust New Year," *New York Times,* January 1, 1903.

incurred by those at the very top of the economic pyramid—the top one half of one percent. In 1916, this small group owned almost 12 percent of the nation's total wealth. This percentage dropped sharply during the Great Depression and World War II and then fell again noticeably in the 1970s. In 2000, this group owned about 7 percent of the nation's wealth. These researchers also documented the downward trend for a slightly larger group, the wealthiest 1 percent of the population. That group owned almost 40 percent of the country's wealth in 1916 versus about 22 percent in 2000.[590] Depression, war, and high inflation were economic setbacks for rich and poor alike. On the positive side, broader ownership of equities has elevated workers' share of the country's wealth.

Innovation provides financial mobility in our society. Of the five wealthiest Americans from 1905, only one has an heir among the wealthiest four hundred people in 2009, as listed in *Forbes* magazine. David Rockefeller, grandson of John D. Rockefeller, is ranked 147, with a net worth of $2.2 billion.[591] No Carnegies, Astors, Goulds, or Fields appear among the list of the top four hundred personal fortunes. The *Forbes* 400 list is populated with fortunes made in businesses that did not exist one hundred or even fifty years ago. The *Forbes* 400 list fifty years hence will most likely be dominated by names we have not yet heard, who started businesses we do not yet know. Wealth, in America, is transient. That opportunity to advance one's financial circumstances through profitable innovation is part of our legacy.

––––––

Literacy is the entry point to opportunity in America. In 1900, just 72 percent of those aged five to seventeen were enrolled in school. New York and Pennsylvania reported just under 70 percent while Ohio reported 75 percent. Iowa, Maine, and the state of Washington had close to 90 percent enrolled. Alabama, New Mexico, and both Carolinas hovered just over 60 percent. In Louisiana, only 44 percent were enrolled.[592] The average student was present for classes 99 days during the school year. In the same year, 11 percent of American adults were illiterate. Among blacks, the rate was 45 percent. Ten states, including New York and Pennsylvania, counted more than three hundred thousand illiterate adults in their populations.[593]

590 *Top Wealth Shares in the United States, 1916-2000: Evidence from Estate Tax Returns.* National Bureau of Economic Research Working Paper 10399, by Wojciech Kopczuk and Emanuel Saez, © 2004 Wojciech Kopczuk and Emanuel Saez.
591 *Forbes,* 400 Richest Americans, listed September 30, 2009, at www.forbes. com/lists/2009/54/rich-list-09_The-400-Richest-Americans_rank.html.
592 *Statistical Abstract of the United States, 1929,* Table 122.
593 *Statistical Abstract of the United States, 1910,* Tables 34, 35.

Over the century, taxpayer-supported free education through high school prepared many for the skilled trades and shop-keeping jobs as people moved from rural areas to the cities. Public schools expanded to offer college-preparation curricula. Private school systems, supported in large part by donations, offered a parallel educational system—a form of consumer choice. Community colleges since the 1960s and the expansion of the colleges and universities throughout the country have opened doors for high school graduates from every neighborhood. Today's child, even in poverty, has educational opportunity beyond the imagination of his peers a century ago. Teachers and parents today are the trustees of that inheritance as they disburse to each child a wealth of knowledge, analytical skills, and effective communication methods, and encourage every child to participate fully in this legacy.

Not all children receive that benefit. One public school district recently explained in a glossy-paged Annual Report to the county taxpayers that, two years hence, it would require each student to demonstrate proficiency in tenth grade algebra, English, and civics in order to obtain a high school diploma.[594] A sense of stewardship might lead taxpayers to rebel at financing the buildings, supplies, books, utilities, and salaries for a twelve-year education system when only ten years of performance are required. Employers no doubt wonder why they should hire high school graduates from this school district, rather than from schools with higher standards. Those students are being deprived of their full legacy, to their lifelong detriment. Parents are left to improvise ways to assure that their own children receive a decent education.

The high dropout rates in many large city school districts reveal that many young people do not benefit from the educational legacy. Equally troubling, many high school graduates—those who have passed the tests required by their local school districts—have been awarded a useless piece of paper. The Education Trust, a nonprofit organization concerned with the education of youth, reported on the results of tests administered by the U.S. Army to 350,000 high school graduates seeking enlistment between 2004 and 2009. As explained in *Shut Out of the Military,* the army's test measures aptitude in word knowledge, paragraph comprehension, arithmetic reasoning, mathematics knowledge, general science, mechanical comprehension, electronics information, auto and shop information, and assembling objects. The combined results determine whether or not candidates have the aptitudes, skills, and knowledge needed to enlist and to qualify for the occupational specialties needed in today's military forces.

Twenty-three percent of the test-takers in this very large sample failed to achieve the minimum qualifying score for enlistment. While professionals debate

594 Annual Report 2006-2007, Cecil County (Maryland) Public Schools.

the merits or relevance of the No Child Left Behind testing, many schools promote and graduate young people lacking the ability to qualify for basic jobs in the military—jobs that can provide specialized training and experience leading to solid civilian careers. Warfare is not a forgiving or nurturing environment. Lowering enlistment standards to accommodate lower graduation standards would serve no one well. Those who might attribute underachievement problems to race, ethnicity, illegal immigration, or certain regions of the country must explain the ineligibility rates of whites who took the test: Maryland (27 percent), New Jersey (20.6 percent), District of Columbia (23.1 percent), Rhode Island (21.3 percent), Kentucky (22.2 percent), Arizona (21.2 percent), and Hawaii (20.1 percent).[595] Graduates who fail this test are hardly prepared to take their place in civilian society. The educational gaps leave them ill equipped to read an apartment lease or credit card charges or to understand an employee benefits booklet. Not every student needs to attend an academic college. But every student needs to train for a job that ultimately serves customers or clients. For too many in our society, public education is failing.

Educational deficits are barriers to economic advancement. A study of adult literacy in 2003 presents a strong correlation between literacy skills and income.[596] In a sampling representative of the American adult population, approximately 20 percent were unable to perform basic tasks involving printed material. Specifically, they have trouble completing a job application form, understanding written instructions, reading a basic health bulletin or apartment lease. They may be unable to locate numbers and use them in simple operations such as addition, even when the math information is very concrete and familiar. This 20 percent demonstrated, in the report's terminology, Below Basic literacy skills. Some experts use the term "functionally illiterate" to describe this skill level.

The connection between literacy skills and household income is straightforward. Of the adults with Below Basic literacy, most (54 percent) lived in households with income less than $20,000. The poverty threshold that year was $18,810 for a family of four. Higher literacy skills correlate to higher incomes. For adults demonstrating Intermediate literacy skills, 63 percent lived in households with incomes greater than $40,000. Among adults with Proficient literacy (the highest skill level), 65 percent enjoyed household income greater than $60,000. Lower skill levels confine people to lower pay scales, but the more

---

595 The Education Trust, *Shut Out of the Military*, December, 2010. Available online at www.edtrust.org/publication/shut-out-of-the-military. Accessed December 26, 2010.

596 U.S. Department of Education, National Center for Education Statistics, *Literacy for Everyday Life: Results of the National Assessment of Adult Literacy. NCES 2007-480.*

devastating impact of lower literacy skills is inability to get work at any pay level. A staggering 50 percent of those with Below Basic literacy skills described themselves as not in the labor pool—no job, and no hope of a job. The percentage of adults so describing themselves declined at each higher level of literacy skill.[597]

There are impacts on families and on society. Those with Below Basic skills were far more likely to be dependent upon public assistance than those with higher skill levels, and three times more likely to be long-term dependent (receiving assistance for more than three years) than those with Intermediate skills.

A study in 2005 by the Pew Foundation found 15 percent of households with zero net worth or negative net worth.[598] This is the group at the lower end of the wealth gap. This study and the *National Assessment of Adult Literacy* above, considered together, point to connections between Below Basic literacy skills, chronic unemployment and low-wage jobs, and the low end of the income and wealth gaps.

———

Our post-secondary educational system is very different from the public school systems that serves almost all elementary and high school students. Public schools enjoy a near-monopoly in their geographic district. Students who can afford to attend private school can exercise some choice. All others attend a school based on geographic districting. On the other hand, most colleges and universities compete to attract students from around the world. This competition for customer dollars affects the selection of professors, curriculum design, and extracurricular programs. Successful graduates are often generous benefactors. The college that does well by its students by educating them to make positive contributions to society is likely to thrive.

Broader access to college education is, in major part, the legacy of Rockefeller, Carnegie, Rosenwald, Mellon, Marsh, and so many others whose donations built important elements of the modern university system. Our most prestigious universities rely heavily on donors, especially for their building campaigns and endowment funds.

---

597 The national unemployment rate that year (2003) averaged 6 percent.
598 Pew Research Center, *Wealth Gaps Rise to Record Highs Between Whites, Blacks and Hispanics.* Available at www.pewsocialtrends.org. This report contains the statistics from the similar study in 2005, before the Great Recession. Household wealth, or net worth, is the accumulated sum of assets (houses, cars, savings and checking accounts, stocks and mutual funds, retirement accounts, etc.) minus the sum of debt (mortgages, car loans, credit card debt, etc.) It is different from household income, which measures the annual inflow of wages, interest, profits and other sources of earning.

Universities today are reaching out to their communities to attract potential students from economically disadvantaged neighborhoods. The Ignatian College Connection at Saint Joseph's University is one of the most comprehensive of these programs. The university works closely with public and parochial school officials in Philadelphia and in Camden, New Jersey, to identify high-aptitude students as early as the sixth grade. Parental support and encouragement are critical to student success, so students and their parents or guardian attend a series of workshops to discuss the importance of education in future career opportunities, as well as study methods and the importance of good grades in elementary and high school. The workshops and meetings continue through high school, with coaching, tutoring, mentoring, and summer academic sessions. For students who qualify for admission to the university, substantial financial aid is made available. On campus, students participate fully in the various academic, cultural, and social programs that increase the likelihood of success for all students. Funding for the ICC program is mainly from the university's general operating funds, supplemented by income from a small endowment fund dedicated to this program. The first five students to complete this program graduated in May 2009.

Tremendous change comes to a family when their first-ever graduates from college. With the awarding of that one diploma, not only the graduate but all those generations who preceded him or her have completed a long march, a relay race in which each contributed to the eventual victory marked by that one who finally crossed the finish line. That college education admits the graduate to better career opportunities; it allows a more robust role as an informed citizen and participant in our economic system. It provides the graduate the opportunity to do so much more for his own family and for others.

———

We are heirs also to an economic system capable of replenishing and growing philanthropy that funds the nonprofit sector of American society. The ever-larger scale of business in the nineteenth century made possible a grand scale of philanthropy. Rockefeller and Carnegie used their wealth to bring improvements to people in every level of our society. The foundations they established have now been disbursing funds for more than a century. The Astors and Fields concentrated their giving locally and remain active today. Gould wealth brought benefits long into the twentieth century.

By mid-twentieth century, newer corporations had produced new wealth. The Ford Foundation endowment surpassed that of the Rockefeller Foundation as the largest in the country, bringing vast new funds to humanitarian efforts. Sloan, Mellon, Raskob, and many others similarly committed their fortunes. Foundations are not solely the work of a few mega-wealthy individuals. Today, there are more than sixty-eight thousand grant-making foundations in America (seventy-five thousand if corporate foundations are included) supporting a vast array of organizations and causes.[599] We rely on wealth-builders in every generation.

Many wealthy individuals use their innovative talents along with their financial resources to confront the most difficult problems in our society. Thousands of nonprofit organizations address, in novel ways, problems that have defied solution. That is the progressive genius of America's nonprofit sector. Philanthropy returns corporate profits and personal wealth to society over time, often at a value that greatly exceeds their original worth, with a vision and creativity that reflects the donor's imagination, often addressing causes that voters neglect with a passion and practicality that government agencies do not possess.

———

We are heirs to these legacies: intellectually independent institutions of higher education, improved living standards and longer life-spans, a customer-driven business sector, voting and other civil rights without regard to race or sex, activist nonprofit organizations and foundations that steward the wealth to support them, and stable government institutions. We are a nation with challenges: chronic unemployment, energy dependency, the environment, access to health care, aging Baby Boomers, chronic disease management, rising high-school dropout rates, and rapidly increasing college tuitions, just to name a few.

For households, businesses, governments, and nonprofits, resources are always finite. We need to manage our resources and pick the most effective strategies. Good decisions boost innovation, which is key to promoting the general welfare and balancing the scales of social justice. Wrong moves cause real misery. The decisions we make as customers, managers and employees, voters, investors and donors have impact. They tip the scales of social justice.

Our most valuable legacy is the knowledge from one hundred years of ex-preiments, *if* we let it inform our decisions. Physicians early in the century knew from Goldberger and his colleagues how to alleviate suffering, if they would accept the evidence from the experiments. We know how to alleviate suffering.

---

599 *Giving USA, 2009,* a publication of Giving USA Foundation, researched and written by the Center on Philanthropy at Indiana University, 69, Table 2.

Chapter Twenty-three

Looking Forward

Today we look for innovation—new products or technologies—to create new jobs and strengthen a weak economy. We're back to the quandary noted by the ethicist in 1935: that a new invention attractive at first only to the rich, perhaps like the automobile in the first decade of the century, would help the recovery. How then do we promote innovation? How do we move forward? Guglielmo Marconi had an interesting comment about discovery:

Science demands a flexible mind. It's no use interrogating the universe with a formula. You've got to observe it, take what it gives you and then reflect upon it with the aid of reason and experience…I like to be out in the open looking at the universe, asking it questions, letting the mystery of it soak right into the mind, admitting the wonderful beauty of it all, and then think my way to the truth of things.[600]

We have observed our universe in which corporate, government, and non-profit sectors interact, a universe in which customers, executives and workers, voters and their elected officials, investors and philanthropists are constantly experimenting. We must take what our century of experiments has given us.

---

600 Calvin D. Trowbridge Jr., *Marconi: The Story of the Race to Control Long-Distance Wireless,* 273.

Customers drive corporate decisions. We choose from competing products or decide to save our money. As each of us implements our own energy plan, and takes better care of our health, corporations will rush to make even more choices available for these efforts. Consumer choice brought plenty of profit-seeking fast-food restaurants into low-income neighborhoods while profit-seeking supermarkets disappeared for lack of customers. In any neighborhood, a change in consumer choices can reverse that.

The previous chapter discussed the linkage between literacy skills, income and wealth. America has a literacy crisis. We should employ the healthy forces of competition. Vouchers could bring the powerful force of consumer choice to drive innovation—change—in public education. There is also a need for leadership, in families and communities.

In fifth grade, Ben Carson was regarded as the "class dummy" in an underachieving, dysfunctional public school. He and his brother were being raised in Detroit tenements by their single mom, who had a third grade education and could not read. Concerned about her sons' lack of progress, Mrs. Carson established her own learning regime for her sons. First she assured them that they could accomplish any goal they chose if they worked toward it. Then she limited their television to a few programs each week. She insisted that they read two books from the Detroit Free Library each week and that they submit written book reports to her. The boys did not know she could not read. Neighbors and relatives criticized Mrs. Carson for being so strict. She held her ground. Confronted with their mother's "no excuses" mandate, the boys soon became proficient readers with expanding vocabularies and interests. Ben went to public high school, then to Yale on a scholarship, medical school, etc.

Dr. Ben Carson Sr. has been directing pediatric neurosurgery at the Johns Hopkins School of Medicine for more than twenty-five years. He has led surgical teams that completed many newsworthy operations, including the first separation of craniopagus (Siamese) twins joined at the back of the head. His brother is an engineer. Today, Dr. Carson credits his mother's persistence with getting him onto the right track. You may have seen his story in the book and movie *Gifted Hands*.

In the fall of 1960, twenty-five-year-old Sister Regina Ancilla, IHM,[601] presided alone over a classroom of sixty eighth graders in a working-class suburban parish school. In those days, as now, a parish would rejoice if just one of its sons were admitted to St. Joseph's Prep, a Jesuit high school in Philadelphia. Admis-

---

601 IHM is the suffix used by members of the congregation, "Sisters, Servants of the Immaculate Heart of Mary." The congregation was founded in the 1840s.

sions were by competitive exam. The widely accepted status quo was that only the smartest boy in any parish could possibly qualify for the Prep. Sister spoke to the parents of her students and told them she would like to step up the curriculum to get more boys and girls eligible for private high schools. The parents agreed. She added a class in Latin, a class in algebra, and a long list of new vocabulary words to the normal weekly agenda. Every night there were three hours of homework. In the spring of 1961, twenty-nine boys were admitted to St. Joseph's from that parish, and quite a few boys and girls were admitted to other prep schools.

Mrs. Carson and Sister Regina Ancilla showed real leadership: positive attitude, specific assignments, challenging goals, no excuses. Parents and teachers show children how to accept the legacy.

In one hundred years we have made progress against the prejudices of race, religion, and national origin. Our corporations have CEOs of every race and both genders. America's president is the son of a bi-racial couple. One disenfranchised minority remains: those with poor literacy skills. These deficits are barriers to using computers and the internet. Those with poor reading skills get no benefit from the many warning labels and consumer and financial disclosures required by law. They have little opportunity to be well-informed about community and national issues. They are limited in employment opportunities, income and wealth. These deficits are at the heart of the income and wealth gap issues. In today's America, if you want justice, work for literacy.

———

We ask questions of our universe. What sparked the great innovators of the century, those Wright Brothers risking not just their savings but also life and limb? Why did Alfred Sloan take a job managing the failing bearing company his father had just purchased, and why did he sell the company to William Durant? What persuaded a dozen people to finance the same Henry Ford who had already let two firms fail? Why did Andrew Mellon take the risk of investing in Pittsburgh Reduction Company and Gulf Oil Company? We must think our way to the truth of things.

Innovation requires both a new, clever idea and money invested to start production. Thomas Edison patented his inventions to bring the new products to market. The innovations were already proven. The patents were his intellectual property. His motivation to experiment, to test his ideas, was probably the same as that expressed by Rockefeller and Steve Jobs. But to finance production facilities and payrolls to get the product to the first customers, he needed investors with cash. Wilbur Wright tackled the problem of heavier-than-air flight to make something of his life, after a "lost decade" in which he seemed to drift aimlessly. All the experiments, the calculations, the test flights, were an intellectual challenge. This was work he loved. As soon as he and his brother had a flying machine, they patented the control systems that their experiments developed. Commercializing the flyer—turning it into a saleable product—would require money. They offered to sell the machine to the governments of the United States, Great Britain, and France. Within a few years, wealthy individuals were buying airplanes and forming flying clubs. The Wrights' actions reveal their motivation. They were not seeking merely to recoup the costs of time and materials. The process they followed was geared to monetary gain.

Alfred Sloan graduated from M.I.T. as an electrical engineer with a high grade-point average. Dozens of firms were seeking electrical engineers. He could have accepted a salaried job at any one of them. But he took up the risky challenge of turning a money-losing manufacturing firm into a profitable venture, to build something of value out of his father's investment and launch his career onto a higher trajectory. There was satisfaction in that, and the work grew better and better as years rolled on. The sale of Hyatt Roller Bearing Company to William Durant shows a second objective clearly. Henry Ford wanted a share of the profits of Detroit Automobile Company. That company failed. In that experience, he learned that innovation depends not just on dreams, but on getting a useful product to customers. The motivation of those first shareholders of the Ford Motor Company, well, you know that story already.

Profit. Do we think less now of Edison, or of Wilbur and Orville Wright, when we understand their motivation? Was Sloan greedy when he took charge of a failing firm for his own gain and in the process saved the jobs of at least some of the firm's employees? Would the world be a better place if Rosetta Couzens, her brother, and ten others had just left their money in the bank? Understanding *why* people try, *why* they attempt, *why* they dare, helps us to understand *how* we might motivate others to do the same today. When we observe these capitalists, we understand how we might best promote new inventions, build new companies, employ more workers, distribute more dividends, produce more wealth, and thus promote the general welfare.

The long-term chart of annual patent applications is data from our experiments. The prevailing circumstances, especially tax rates, when big changes occurred in the number of patent applications link after-tax profits and innovation. Jared Diamond's *Guns, Germs, and Steel, The Fates of Human Societies,* explains the humanity of it. Economists who analyzed the elasticity of taxable income document the universality of it among Americans who earn incomes. All that we know about business leaders and investors is consistent with the theory. The evidence is nonpolitical. The Dark Age of American Innovation persisted through Democratic and Republican presidencies. Congressional majorities changed many times over those years.

Tax credits or subsidies directed to a particular industry or technology presume that invention is neat, orderly, systematic. Our century of experience proves otherwise. Most real innovation occurs in industries and companies not yet born. A bicycle mechanic built the first successful flying machine. The Wright brothers spent months spread over four years living in a shed while they tested a series of glider designs. They were living off the profits of their bicycle shop. Henry Ford built his first automobile with a bunch of friends working in the evenings after their day jobs. No one knew. Even in large companies, innovation is one success out of innumerable efforts, most of which end in failure. Ford rearranging his production process led to the assembly line. That enabled the Five Dollar Day for unskilled workers and made a new product affordable for millions of people. DuPont's rayon and nylon were singular successes arising from a decade of experiments.

To promote innovation, we must promote risk-taking across all industries, known and unknown. For when we subsidize the known industry, technology, or product, even in the early stages, we penalize the truly new and innovative: those unknown experimenters working today on a windy beach or in a cold garage. Inventors need risk-taking investors to bring the innovation to market. Like the hunter-gatherers of ancient times, they seek the highest reward consistent with the amount of risk they are willing to take. After-tax profits are the reward for successful innovation. Almost half the households in America are using investment profits to build a better future. These investors always have options, and they make their own decisions. If the prospects for after-tax profits are poor, then the safety of government bonds becomes more attractive. Risk is avoided. Innovation slows.

We promote innovation by letting more of the profit from business activity stay with the investors who risk their capital. We suppress it by taking more of the profits in taxes.

———

Voters decide what part of those profits and wealth return to society through taxes and what part is left to those who risk their capital for innovation. Every change in tax rules and rates since Woodrow Wilson signed the Underwood Act with its 1 percent tax on large incomes has been an experiment. The results should inform our selection of strategies for recovering from the Great Recession of 2008-2009. Economists agree that tax policy did not *start* the Great Depression. Decline in aggregate demand, brought about by a worldwide contraction in money supplies, was the proximate cause.[602] The money supply contraction resulted from mismanagement of the gold standard monetary system during the late 1920s and early 1930s.[603] Many countries shared in that mismanagement, thus the global spread of the depression.

Both Hoover and Roosevelt experimented with the interactions of the corporate, government, and nonprofit sectors. Modern economic studies explain why this particular recession and stock market crash lasted so much longer than any before or since.[604] Some actions, economists now know, were precisely the opposite of what was needed. The Federal Reserve's erratic interest rate movements made banks skittish. The Smoot-Hawley Tariff caused a serious reduction in exports. Large infrastructure projects and stimulus provided by the Reconstruction Finance Corporation failed to offset the decline in business activity. As unemployment swelled, even the huge increases in charitable donations to community chests, soup kitchens, and the Red Cross were inadequate to provide subsistence aid to all who needed it. The assets and investment income of nonprofits were diminished when they were most needed. Tax increases in 1932 collected money that consumers and businesses might otherwise have spent or invested or donated. Unemployment soared.

Roosevelt's New Deal experiments were bolder and more numerous. Restoring confidence in the banks was perhaps his most effective move. Taking the dollar off of the gold standard was controversial, but important in a world of floating currencies. The Civilian Conservation Corps provided immediate work for hundreds of thousands of men, and the Public Works Administration's infrastructure projects employed many more. All of this stopped the downward spiral of the American economy and employment.

The National Industrial Recovery Act set a strategy for restarting the nation's economy. Industry coordination, mandated by law, reduced competition and raised prices and wages. This was the brainchild of business leaders and it set the stage for recovery. The economy and employment began to grow again.[605] But

---

602 Ben Bernanke, *Essays on the Great Depression*, viii.
603 Ibid, 70–80, 108–115.
604 In comparative economics, researchers assemble data from numerous countries with similar economies, then use mathematical models to determine which changes cause, or at least correlate to, different economic performances.
605 Ben Bernanke, *Essays on the Great Depression*, 8, 78, 250, 278.

the NIRA's bureaucratic complexity stifled attempts to serve bargain-hunting customers and make a profit. Wages and prices set at arbitrarily high levels worked against the natural self-correcting tendencies of the economy. Bank lending to small and midsized businesses remained slow as bank managers remained risk-averse.[606] The higher taxes of 1935 and 1936 further reduced the after-tax reward for investors. Abrupt changes in antitrust enforcement policy, the sham income tax investigations of Mellon and others, the blanket vilification of business and the "fog of uncertainty," and the persistent antibusiness, soak-the-rich agenda left investors clinging to their bonds and business leaders foregoing capital spending. The CCC, PWA, and WPA programs were intended to employ all but the unemployable. All of this, plus college tuition assistance, farm aid, slum clearance, reduced mortgage rates, and subsidized housing construction, were wildly popular with the majority of voters. It produced one of the largest popular election landslides this country has ever seen in a presidential election.

But in terms of correcting the major tragedy of the Depression—large-scale, chronic unemployment—the strategy failed. The unemployment rates and tax returns are unambiguous. These policies left millions working at subsistence-level jobs and more millions still on unemployment relief and charity. The federal deficits grew each year in spite of higher income tax rates and new excise taxes. The unemployment rate did not drop back to pre-Depression levels until 1943 when millions were in uniform and therefore not counted in the civilian workforce.

The same strategies strangled philanthropy as asset values and investment income fell and the Great Depression lingered. Those who had been so generous in good times lacked the funds to continue their gifts.

If we use patent applications as a gage of innovation and economic activity, the Great Depression lasted until the mid-1980s. All the best work of presidents and congressmen, corporate executives and social workers, and economists and ethicists could not replace the lost spark of innovation born of the opportunity for after-tax profit and wealth.

Then, a half-century after the Depression, the majority of voters chose a different strategy. After a landslide election for a second presidential term, income tax rates were radically reduced. Tax revenue grew. Charitable donations increased. Patent applications, our key indicator of innovation, soared.

The recent research of Drs. Christina and David Romer confirms our observations: "The most striking finding of this exercise is that tax increases have a

---

606 Ibid, 63–64, 252–253, 279, 300.

large negative effect on investment."[607] With lower investment, fewer patents are filed for bringing innovations to market. Fewer new jobs are created. Employment, gross domestic product, charitable giving, and tax revenues suffer. The decisions we make as voters taxing income and wealth impact all segments of society. When business fails, there is no safe ground.

Some urge us to change our tax code. Robert Reich served as secretary of labor in President Bill Clinton's administration. He is now Chancellor's Professor of Public Policy at University of California at Berkeley. Reich recommends eliminating the corporate income tax.[608] Warren Buffett, chairman of Berkshire Hathaway, suggests higher personal income tax rates on all households with income in excess of $1 million per year and still higher rates for income in excess of $10 million.[609] These are two very different strategies. We are searching for ways to boost innovation. We should evaluate these proposals, and all others, using the data from our experiments, ready to challenge the axioms we hold dear.

In the Constitution, *we the people* required that tax legislation be introduced only in the House of Representatives, whose members were the only federal officials directly elected by the people, with 2-year terms.[610] Presidents may suggest, promote, recommend or urge tax legislation, and they often do. But the tax process was carefully designed to ensure that we the people get exactly the tax laws we want. We should use that power. Vote!

————

Senator Huey Long gave us an important clue to the problem inherent with government redistributions of wealth. His plan called for new redistributions every seven years. Long knew that, even after the Depression was over, many at the lower end of the income and wealth divide would be unable to properly steward their free gift taken from others, and would need successive redistri-

---

607 *The Macroeconomic Effects of Tax Changes: Estimates Based on a New Measure of Fiscal Shocks"*, by Christina D. Romer and David H. Romer, Department of Economics, University of California, Berkeley, CA. in *American Economic Review 100 (June 2010)* p. 763-801.
608 Robert Reich, *Supercapitalism*, 216–218.
609 Warren Buffett, "Stop Coddling the Super Rich," *New York Times*, August 15, 2011.
610 Under the Constitution, Senators were elected by the Legislature of each state. The Seventeenth Amendment, ratified in 1913, provided for direct election by the people of each state. The President and Vice-President are elected by the Electoral College.

butions. Stewardship of small sums or large requires knowledge, discernment and discipline. Huey Long and Franklin Roosevelt proclaimed redistribution as sound public policy. But they never acknowledged what would happen to innovation, to jobs, to the advancement of society, once investors no longer put their money at risk, knowing that any profits would be periodically redistributed. What then would be the source of that long-term, patient capital that companies of every size need? When we stop wealth creation, we stop the advancement of society. Our century of experiments also reveals that great wealth is continuously redistributed to society, voluntarily. That was true before the income tax, and remains true today. The wealthy do not take their money into the grave.

Some of the great fortunes come back into society by spending, some of which is frivolous. But the spending creates jobs for architects and artists, carpenters and electricians, yacht builders and gardeners, cooks and housekeepers, automobile dealers and lawyers, and tennis pros and golf caddies. By spending on the early, expensive automobiles, radios, refrigerators, and cell phones, wealthy buyers propelled the development of goods and services that soon became mass-market items at ever-lower prices. The same process today is making hybrid vehicles, solar panels, and organic food increasingly affordable. Society advances.

Profits and wealth also come back to society through philanthropy. Early in the twenty-first century, a new generation of wealth is flowing from Gates, Buffett, and others into a new generation of foundations, endowments, and charitable organizations. The cycle of returning wealth to society and providing for its careful stewardship continues. Much of that wealth is the accumulation of after-tax corporate profits.[611] The data from our experiments shows that a strong economy and growing after-tax profits produce larger donations and enhance the investment income of foundations and endowments. Today's new fortunes fund tomorrow's foundations. There is no other source.

———

We have answered our initial questions. We know who gets the benefit of all those corporate profits, and who benefits from the accumulated wealth. When we follow the money, the benefits of corporate activity are clear. Customers find products and services that meet their needs. Workers receive pay and benefits for jobs performed. Governments collect taxes. From whatever is left—profits—investors receive dividends or capital gains as compensation for putting

---

611 *Giving USA 2009,* a publication of Giving USA Foundation, researched and written by the Center on Philanthropy at Indiana University, 69, Table 2.

their savings at risk. Some of those investors accumulate great wealth. Mankind, including those who rely on charity, inherits all that wealth. The benefit to society is real. Could we do better?

The quick recovery from the financial panic of 1907 and from the serious business recession of 1921 stand in marked contrast to the prolonged crash of 1929 to 1933 and the long, anemic recovery that eventually took place—a recovery so weak and so long that we still call it the Great Depression. Some point to the post offices and courthouses built by the WPA, and the bridges and dams erected by the PWA, as measurable gains from that era. How do we weigh that against what was lost in the drought of patents that did not recover until 1986? What did we lose in the inventions never brought forward into commerce, the companies never formed to manufacture and sell them, the jobs never created? How many tax dollars did our government not collect, how much productivity and innovation was not achieved, how many fortunes not made, how much economic status quo was maintained, how much funding was never generated for the nonprofit sector? What was the cost of that quiet fear and the high tax rates that damped the fires of invention and industry?

Lester V. Chandler calculated the economic benefit lost from 1930 through 1941. The actual gross domestic product in those years was more than 35 percent below its "normal" 3 percent compound annual growth rate. He calculates that the missing GNP could have purchased 716,000 schools, 35,800,000 homes, 179,000,000 automobiles, or 3,580,000 miles of highway.[612] That loss was for just twelve years. We have no measure of the longer-term loss from depressed innovation—as measured by patent applications—that lasted from the 1930s until 1986. What was the loss, in advancing the general welfare, from that half-century (leaving aside the warfare innovations of 1941–1945) of lost innovation? If we had avoided the Dark Age of American Innovation, how much better might today's world be?

———

Our century of experimentation has brought us, as a nation, far beyond laissez-faire capitalism. In that century, we also turned away from socialism and witnessed its utter failure in the former Soviet Union. Nor does our observation leave us to a system that secures the gains of capitalism to the wealthy few,

---

612 Lester V. Chandler, *America's Greatest Depression 1929-1941*, 5.

leaving a small remainder to trickle down well-worn valleys propelled only by gravity to those in need.

One hundred years of experiments urge us to admit the working beauty of a universe in which business plays an irreplaceable role in our society, alongside government and nonprofit organizations. More after-tax profits flowing to investors as the return on successful risk-taking produces more innovation. That produces more choices for consumers and new jobs for workers, enabling them to donate, save, invest, and spend as they deem best—all part of a strong economy. A strong economy increases revenue to the government and funds an innovative, passionate and energetic philanthropic sector. The benefits of that system flow with self-replenishing energy in new channels to promote the general welfare and balance the scales of social justice.

Author's Note
&
Acknowledgements

A review of one hundred years of experiments must rely heavily upon others. High on the list of contributors are the numerous archivists and librarians who provided access to primary documents without which the book would simply be impossible. Special thanks in this category to Tab Lewis at the National Archives II, in College Park, Maryland. His knowledge of materials in the archives is supplemented by his knowledge of many other public and private collections. All of this and his willingness, even enthusiasm, for guiding any researcher to relevant material make him a national resource of great value. Similarly, archivists at the Franklin D. Roosevelt Library and Museum at Hyde Park, New York, at the Archives of the Sisters of the Blessed Sacrament in Bensalem, Pennsylvania, and the Hagley Museum and Library in Wilmington, Delaware, were tireless and efficient in providing access to original documents. Officials at the Carnegie Corporation of New York, Medical Association of Georgia, Medical Association of Alabama, the office of the Attorney General of Michigan, and the Bankroft Library of the University of California at Berkley also provided copies of documents that were invaluable to this project.

My thanks also go to the many people who read early drafts of the entire book or parts of it and offered comments for improvement. Some offered many specific notes, others a letter or email with suggestions, and some challenged me to address a particular topic with more vigor. Some gave more of an overview evaluation of what they read. The readers included Rev. Frank Moan, S.J., and Rev. William Byron, S.J.; Sister Rosalie Bertell, G.N.S.H.; Barbara St. Aubrey, Jennie May Witkin; Cathy May; Kareem Govan; Joe Weinbrecht; Gary Underwood; David Willis, President of Whitford Worldwide; Akos Swierkiewicz, Principal of Ircos, LLC.; and Gary Witkin, MD. Gary not only read the manuscript but also answered my uncounted questions about diseases and medical practice. Two intrepid high school students, Jaime Capron and Cade Underwood, found time in their busy college-bound schedules to read and provide valuable comments. A few individuals read more than one draft. All were immensely helpful. Their work improved the book in many areas. However, their contribution of time and energy to help me in this does not in any way convey their endorsement of any facts or interpretations expressed in this book. Also, any errors that remain, or any shortfall in quality, are solely my responsibility.

Several individuals gave generously of their valuable time to share information and discuss potential sources of historical information: Donald Smith, executive director of Christ Church Preservation Trust, Philadelphia, Pennsylvania; Thomas Rzeznik, PhD, assistant professor of history at Seton Hall University; and Eric Johnston, PhD, assistant professor of theology at Seton Hall University.

Several early readers asked why this book does not take a more global view, including areas such as European laws on corporate governance, the impact on foreign workers of jobs outsourced from the United States, state-funded retirement and welfare programs, and tax structures in other countries. Some of these are mentioned in various chapters. No doubt, we live in an increasingly global community. Actions of consumers, workers, investors, voters, and philanthropists in one country have impact in foreign lands.

But several considerations caused me to focus on the American experience. First, the news from other countries gives ongoing evidence that no country has achieved a state of sustained and universal contentment managing its own interactions of corporations, government, and nonprofit (including faith-based) organizations. In politically stable democracies, voters periodically express their discontent by voting out the party they voted in just a few years earlier. In many countries, popular demonstrations of various intensities make clear the discontentment of people with their circumstances. In all of these countries, people are still conducting their own experiments in how best to promote the general welfare, as are we in America. I respect their culture, history, decision-making, objectives that may differ from ours, and especially their right to conduct their own experiments in social advancement. Finally, America is unique among nations in having vested so much hope, hard work, money, and imaginative thinking about its social advancement into nonprofit, nongovernment organizations and associations. Our nonprofit sector includes many of our finest universities, leading medical facilities, great research laboratories, foundations, activist groups, and political think-tanks. The size and scope of this sector's role in our social progress is uniquely American and has been throughout our history. The role of that sector is too little known, even in our own country. Whether that role in American society might have value for other nations is for them to decide.

As a nation of immigrants, we have already adopted much from other lands. We might still learn a thing or two from foreign experience. But why not first learn well about our own century of homegrown experiments? So, for better or worse, this book is about America's century of experiments with corporate profits and wealth and our ongoing quest to promote the general welfare in our society. There is much to learn from our unique story.

By way of disclosure, no corporation, foundation, nonprofit organization, or government agency provided any financial support, grant, stipend, or expense reimbursement (except deduction of expenses for income tax purposes) in connection with this book. The author may from time to time buy, sell, or hold securities of one or more of the corporations discussed herein. The reader is specifically advised not to rely upon information herein as investment advice. All of the information herein has been publicly announced by the corporations. The author may from time to time donate to some of the nonprofit organizations mentioned herein, but this is no endorsement or recommendation of any nonprofit organization or the causes they advance. Readers are encouraged to explore carefully any organization they intend to support to assure the best use of hard-earned funds they choose to donate.

Many an author's family has been pressed into service, as has mine. Our sons, Paul and Steven, did read the book and engaged in many conversations about it. Whether they did all this out of high appreciation for its literary merit or just to help dad get through one of the many moments of uncertainty, I need not probe. Their help has been valuable and is sincerely appreciated. My siblings also read early editions and contributed excellent commentary as well as moral support.

Finally, my wife, Patricia, has read more drafts of chapters, and of the entire book, than anyone. In her comments, she applied the same candor and high standards that account for her success in running our home and managing her own practice as a financial advisor. Pat also demonstrated remarkable patience in allowing my cluttered study to remain untidy with research files, books, and sticky notes, in stark contrast to the rest of our home—a condition that must surely try her patience. For this and her unwavering support of the project, I am very grateful.

This book provides historical information regarding the subjects covered. All of these knowledge areas are complex and constantly evolving, and every reader has unique circumstances and needs. This book does not provide legal, medical, tax, or investment advice. Readers should obtain the services of a professional to help achieve their goals.

The author welcomes comments at After100Years@comcast.net

Bibliography

Published Works

Addams, Jane. *Twenty Years at Hull-House*. New York: Signet Classics, 1909.

Ahamed, Liaquat. *Lords of Finance: The Bankers Who Broke the World*. New York: The Penguin Group, 2009.

Ambrose, Stephen E. *Eisenhower, Soldier and President*. New York: Simon & Schuster.

_____. *D-Day, June 6, 1944: The Climactic Battle of World War II*. Simon & Schuster, 1994.

Anderson, Ray C. *Confessions of a Radical Industrialist: Profits, People, Purpose—Doing Business by Respecting the Earth*. New York: St. Martin's Press, 2009.

Andrews, Thomas G. *Killing for Coal: America's Deadliest Labor War*. Massachusetts: Harvard University Press, 2008.

Arnold, Thurman W. *The Folklore of Capitalism*. New Haven: Yale University Press, 1937.

Axilrod, Stephen H. *Inside the Fed: Monetary Policy and its Management, Martin through Greenspan to Bernanke*. Cambridge, MA: The MIT Press, 2009.

Barbiere, Joseph. *The Tariff in a Nutshell: An Economic View of the Question*. Philadelphia, PA: J.B. Lippincott Company, 1888.

Barkley, Alben W. *That Reminds Me*. New York: Doubleday & Company, Inc., 1954.

Beard, Charles A., and Beard, William. *The American Leviathan: The Republic in the Machine Age*. New York: The Macmillan Company, 1930.

Behrman, Greg. *The Most Noble Adventure: The Marshall Plan and the Time When America Helped Save Europe.* New York: Free Press, 2007.

Berle, Adolph A., and Means, Gardiner C. *The Modern Corporation and Private Property.* New York: Harcourt, Brace & World, Inc., 1932.

Bernanke, Ben (ed.). *Essays on the Great Depression.* Princeton University Press, 2000.

Bernard, Harry. *An Independent Man: The Life of Senator James Couzens.* New York: Charles Scribner's Sons, 1958.

Brinkley, Douglas. *Wheels for the World: Henry Ford, His Company, and a Century of Progress, 1903-2003.* New York: Viking Penguin, 2003.

Brokaw, Tom. *The Greatest Generation.* New York: Random House, 1998.

Bronson, William. *The Earth Shook, The Sky Burned.* San Francisco, CA: First Chronicle Books, 1959.

Brooks, Arthur C. *Who Really Cares: America's Charity Divide, Who Gives, Who Doesn't, and Why.* New York: Basic Books, member of Perseus Books Group, 2006.

Bruner, Robert F., and Carr, Sean D. *The Panic of 1907: Lessons Learned from the Market's Perfect Storm.* Hoboken, NJ: John Wiley & Sons, Inc., 2007.

Burke, Edmund. *Speech on Conciliation with America, March 22, 1775.* London: J. Dodsley, 1775.

Burns, James MacGregor (ed.). *To Heal and to Build: The Programs of President Lyndon B. Johnson.* New York: McGraw-Hill Book Company, 1968.

Burns, Jennifer. *Goddess of the American Market: Ayn Rand and the American Right.* Oxford University Press, 2009.

Bush, George H. W. *All the Best: My Life in Letters and Other Writings.* New York: Touchstone, 1999.

Byron, William J. *The Power of Principles: Ethics for a New Corporate Culture.* New York: Orbis Books, 2006.

Cannadine, David. *Mellon.* New York: Alfred A. Knopf, 2006.

Chandler, Lester V. *America's Greatest Depression, 1929-1941.* New York: Harper & Row, 1970.

Charan, Ram. *What the CEO Wants You to Know: Using Business Acumen to Understand How Your Company Really Works.* New York: Crown Business, 2001.

_____. *Profitable Growth Is Everyone's Business: 10 Tools You Can Use Monday Morning.* New York: Crown Business, 2004.

Chernow, Ron. *The House of Morgan: An American Banking Dynasty and the Rise of Modern Finance.* New York: Grove Press, 1990.

_____. *Titan: The Life of John D. Rockefeller, Sr.* New York: Vintage Books.

Churchill, Winston. *The Gathering Storm*. Boston: Houghton Mifflin Company.

Clifford, Clark with Holbrooke, Richard. *Counsel to the President: A Memoir*. New York: Anchor Books Doubleday, 1991.

Clinton, Bill. *Giving: How Each of Us Can Change the World*. New York: Alfred A. Knopf, 2007.

Coblentz, Edmond D. (ed.). *William Randolph Hearst: A Portrait in His Own Words*. New York: Simon and Schuster, 1952.

Cochran, Thomas B., and Miller, Herman P. (eds.) *Smull's Legislative Handbook and Manual of the State of Pennsylvania, 1905*. State Printer of Pennsylvania.

Cohen, Adam. *Nothing to Fear: FDR's Inner Circle and the Hundred Days that Created Modern America*. New York: The Penguin Press, 2009.

Collier, Paul. *The Bottom Billion: Why the Poorest Countries are Failing and What Can Be Done About It*. Oxford University Press, 2007.

Cottle, Sidney, Murray, Roger F., and Block, Frank E. *Graham and Dodd's Security Analysis, Fifth Edition*. McGraw-Hill Book Company, 1934.

Coughlin, Rev. Charles E. *The New Deal in Money*. Royal Oak, MI: The Radio League of the Little Flower, 1933.

Dawes, Charles G. *Journal As Ambassador to Great Britain*. New York: The Macmillan Company, 1939.

_____. *Notes as Vice President, 1928-1929*. Boston: Little, Brown, and Company, 1935.

_____. *A Journal of the McKinley Years*. Chicago: The Lakeside Press, R.R. Donnelley & Sons Company, 1950.

Diamond, Jared. *Guns, Germs, and Steel: The Fates of Human Societies*. New York: W.W. Norton & Company.

DeSoto, Hernando. *The Other Path: The Economic Answer to Terrorism*. New York: Basic Books, Perseus Books Group, 1989.

Dillon, Peggy. *Seeking the Greatest Good: The Public Welfare Foundation*. Washington DC: The Public Welfare Foundation.

Donald, Aida D. *Lion in the White House: A Life of Theodore Roosevelt*. New York: Basic Books.

Downey, Kirstin. *The Woman Behind the New Deal: The Life and Legacy of Frances Perkins*. New York: Anchor Books, A Division of Random House, Inc., 2009.

Duffy, Sister Consuela Marie, S.B.S. *Katharine Drexel: A Biography*. Cornwells Heights, PA: Mother Katharine Drexel Guild, 1966.

Dutton, William S. *Du Pont: One Hundred and Forty Years*. New York: Charles Scribner's Sons, 1949.

Dyer, Thomas G. *The University of Georgia: A Bicentennial History, 1785-1985.* The University of Georgia Press, 1985.

E.I. Du Pont de Nemours & Company. *Du Pont: The Autobiography of an American Enterprise.* New York: Charles Scribner's Sons, 1952.

Eichengreen, Barry. *Exorbitant Privilege: The Rise and Fall f the Dollar and the Future of the International Monetary System.* Oxford University Press, 2011.

Eisenhower, Dwight D. *The White House Years, A Personal Account 1956-1961, Waging Peace.* New York: Doubleday & Company, 1965.

Ellis, Charles D. *The Partnership: The Making of Goldman Sachs.* New York: Penguin Books, 2008.

Embree, Edwin R. *Julius Rosenwald Fund: Review for the Two-Year Period 1931-1933.* Chicago: The Julius Rosenwald Fund, 1933.

_____. *Julius Rosenwald Fund, 1917-1936.* Chicago: The Julius Rosenwald Fund, 1936.

Emmet, Boris & Jeuck, John E. *Catalogues and Counters: A History of Sears, Roebuck and Company.* Chicago: The University of Chicago Press, 1950.

Etheridge, Elizabeth W. *The Butterfly Castle: A Social History of Pellagra in the South.* Connecticut: Greenwood Publishing Company, 1972.

Everett, Marshall. *Complete Life of William McKinley and Story of His Assassination.* 1901.

Farber, David. *Sloan Rules: Alfred P. Sloan and the Triumph of General Motors.* Chicago: The University of Chicago Press, 2002.

Feingold, M.D., Ben F. *Why Your Child Is Hyperactive.* New York: Random House, 1974.

Ferguson, Niall. *Colossus: The Rise and Fall of the American Empire.* New York: Penguin Books, 2004.

Ferrell, Robert H. (Ed.). *The Autobiography of Harry S. Truman.* Boulder, CO: Colorado Associated University Press, 1980.

_____. *The Eisenhower Diaries.* New York: W. W. Norton & Company, 1981.

Fisher, Douglas A. *Steel Serves the Nation, 1901-1951: The Fifty Year Story of United States Steel.* United States Steel Corporation, 1951.

Fishman, Charles. *The Wal-Mart Effect: How the World's Most Powerful Company Really Works—and How It's Transforming the American Economy.* New York: Penguin Press, 2006.

Flexner, James Thomas. *George Washington: Anguish and Farewell, 1793-1799.* Boston: Little, Brown and Company, 1969.

Ford, Henry. *My Life and Work—An Autobiography of Henry Ford.* New York: Classic House Books, 1923.

_____. *Today and Tomorrow*. New York. Doubleday, Page & Company, 1926.

Freidel, Frank. *Franklin D. Roosevelt: A Rendezvous with Destiny*. New York: Little, Brown and Company, 1990.

Friedman, Milton and Schwartz, Anna Jacobson. *A Monetary History of the United States, 1867-1960*. Princeton, NJ: Princeton University Press, 1971.

Friedman, Milton. *Capitalism and Freedom*. The University of Chicago Press, 1962.

Friedman, Thomas L. *The World Is Flat: A Brief History of the Twenty-First Century*. New York: Farrar, Straus and Giroux, 2005.

_____. *Hot, Flat, and Crowded: Why We Need a Green Revolution and How It Can Renew America*. New York: Farrar, Straus and Giroux, 2008.

Galbraith, John Kenneth. *A Life in Our Times: Memoirs*. Boston: Houghton Mifflin Company, 1981.

_____. *The Great Crash 1929*. Houghton Mifflin Company, 1954.

Geisst, Charles R. *100 Years of Wall Street*. New York: McGraw-Hill, 2000.

Gilbo, Patrick F. *The American Red Cross: The First Century*. New York: Harper & Row, 1981.

Gordon, John Steele. *An Empire of Wealth: The Epic History of American Economic Power*. New York: HarperCollins Publishers, 2004.

Gough, Deborah Mathias. *Christ Church, Philadelphia: The Nation's Church in a Changing City*. Philadelphia, PA: A Barra Foundation Book, University of Pennsylvania Press, 1995.

Graham, Benjamin. *The Intelligent Investor*. HarperCollins, 1949.

_____ and Meredith, Spencer B. *The Interpretation of Financial Statements*. New York: HarperCollins, 1937.

Graham, Katharine. *Personal History*. New York: Alfred A. Knopf, 1997.

Grayson, Theodore B. *Investment Trusts: Their Origin, Development, and Operation*. New York: John Wiley & Sons, Inc., 1928.

Greenspan, Alan. *The Age of Turbulence: Adventures in a New World*. New York: Penguin Press, 2007.

Hager, Thomas. *The Demon Under the Microscope*. New York: Harmony Books, 2006.

Halberstam, David. *The Best and the Brightest*. New York: Random House, 1969.

Harris, Leon. *Merchant Princes: An Intimate History of Jewish Families Who Built the Great Department Stores*. New York: Kodansha International, 1979.

Hayek, F.A. *The Road to Serfdom*. The University of Chicago Press, 1944.

Hessen, Robert. *In Defense of the Corporation*. Hoover Institution Press, Stanford University, 1979.

Hoffecker, Carol E. *Corporate Capital:Wilmington in the Twentieth Century.* Philadelphia: Temple University Press, 1983.

Hoover, Herbert. *The Memoirs of Herbert Hoover:The Great Depression, 1929-1941.* New York: The Macmillan Company, 1952.

Hoover, Irwin Hood. *Forty-Two Years in the White House.* New York: Houghton Mifflin Company, 1934.

Howden Smith, Arthur D. *John Jacob Astor: Landlord of New York.* Cosimo, Inc., 1929.

Hunter, Robert. *Poverty: Social Conscience in the Progressive Era.* New York: Harper & Row, 1904.

Ickes, Harold L. *The Secret Diary of Harold L. Ickes.* New York: Simon and Schuster.

_____. *America's House of Lords: An Inquiry into the Freedom of the Press.* New York: Harcourt, Brace and Company, 1939.

Jablonski, Edward. *Flying Fortress:The Illustrated Biography of the B-17s and the Men Who Flew Them.* New York: Doubleday & Company, Inc., 1965.

James, Marquis. *Biography of a Business 1792-1942.* New York: The Bobbs-Merrill Company, 1942.

Johnson, Lyndon Baines. *The Vantage Point: Perspectives of the Presidency 1963-1969.* New York: Holt, Rinehart and Winston, 1971.

Josephson, Matthew. *Edison.* New York: McGraw-Hill, 1959.

Kaplan, Justin. *When the Astors Ruled New York: Blue Bloods and Grand Hotels in a Gilded Age.* New York: Viking, Penguin Group, 2006.

Katz, Michael B. *In the Shadow of the Poorhouse:A Social History of Welfare in America.* New York: Basic Books, 1996.

Kavaler, Lucy. *The Astors:A Family Chronicle of Pomp and Power.* Lincoln, NE: iUniverse.com, Inc., 1966.

Kehoe, Timothy J., and Prescott, Edward C., (Editors). *Great Depressions of the Twentieth Century.* Federal Reserve Bank of Minneapolis, 2007.

Kennedy, John Curtis. *Wages and Family Budgets in the Chicago Stockyard District: With Wage Statistics.* University of Chicago Press, 1910.

Kiernan, Frances. *The Last Mrs. Astor:A New York Story.* New York: W. W. Norton & Company, 2007.

Kinnane, Adrian. *DuPont: From the Banks of the Brandywine to Miracles of Science.* E.I. du Pont de Nemours and Company, 2002.

Kluger, Richard. *The Paper:The Life and Death of the New York Herald Tribune.* New York: Vintage Books, Random House, 1986.

Kohlsaat, H.H. *From McKinley to Harding: Personal Recollections of Our Presidents.* New York: Charles Scribner's Sons, 1923.

Kopper, Philip. *Anonymous Giver: A Life of Charles E. Marsh*. Washington, DC: Public Welfare Foundation, 2000.

Kuhn, Arthur J. *GM Passes Ford, 1918-1938*. Pennsylvania: The Pennsylvania University Press, 1986.

Lacey, Robert. *Ford, The Men and the Machine*. Boston: Little, Brown and Company, 1986.

Leamer, Laurence. *The Kennedy Men, 1901-1963*. New York: HarperCollins Publishers, 2001.

Lerner, Max (ed.). *The Mind and Faith of Justice Holmes: His Speeches, Essays, Letters and Judicial Opinions*. Boston: Little, Brown and Company, 1945.

Leuchtenburg, William E. *The Perils of Prosperity, 1914-32*. Chicago: The University of Chicago Press, 1958.

Lindley, Ernest K. *Half Way with Roosevelt*. New York: Viking Press, 1936.

Lomborg, Bjorn. *The Skeptical Environmentalist: Measuring the Real State of the World*. London: Cambridge University Press, 2001.

Lynch, Peter. *One Up On Wall Street*. New York: Penguin Books, 1989.

Lyons, Eugene. *Our Unknown Ex-President: A Portrait of Herbert Hoover*. New York: Doubleday & Company, Inc., 1948.

Mallaby, Sebastian. *The World's Banker: A Story of Failed States, Financial Crises, and the Wealth and Poverty of Nations*. New York: The Penguin Press, 2004.

Mangione, Jerre. *An Ethnic at Large*. Syracuse University Press, 1971.

Mason, Alpheus T. *Brandeis and the Modern State*. Princeton University Press., 1933.

McCraw, Thomas K. *Prophet of Innovation: Joseph Schumpeter and Creative Destruction*. Cambridge, MA: Belknap Press of Harvard University Press.

McCullough, David. *Truman*. New York: Simon & Schuster Paperbacks, 1992.

_____. *The Path Between the Seas: The Creation of the Panama Canal, 1870-1914*. New York: Simon & Schuster, 1977.

McElvaine, Robert S. *The Great Depression: America, 1929-1941*. New York: Three Rivers Press, 1984.

Meacham, Jon. *Franklin and Winston: An Intimate Portrait of an Epic Friendship*. New York: Random House, 2003.

Mellon, Paul and Baskett, John. *Reflections in a Silver Spoon: A Memoir*. New York: William Morrow and Company, Inc., 1992.

Mitchell, Broadus. *Depression Decade: From New Era through New Deal, 1929-1941*. New York: Harper & Row, 1947.

Moley, Raymond. *After Seven Years*. New York: Harper & Brothers, 1939.

More, Louise Bolard. *Wage-Earners' Budgets: A Study of Living Standards and Cost of Living in New York City.* Henry Holt and Company, 1907.

Morris, Charles R. *The Tycoons: How Andrew Carnegie, John D. Rockefeller, Jay Gould, and J.P. Morgan Invented the American Supereconomy.* New York: Owl Books, Henry Holt and Company, LLC, 2005.

Morris, Edmund. *The Rise of Theodore Roosevelt.* New York: Random House, Inc., 1979.

_____. *Theodore Rex.* New York: Random House, Inc., 2001.

_____. *Dutch: A Memoir of Ronald Reagan.* New York: Random House, 1999.

Mosley, Leonard. *Blood Relations: The Rise and Fall of the du Ponts of Delaware.* New York: Atheneum, 1980.

Myers, Margaret G. *A Financial History of the United States.* New York: Columbia University Press, 1970.

Nasaw, David. *The Chief: The Life of William Randolph Hearst.* New York: Mariner; Houghton Mifflin Company, 2000.

_____. *Andrew Carnegie.* New York: The Penguin Press, 2006.

Nixon, Richard. *The Memoirs of Richard Nixon.* New York: Warner Books, 1978.

Novak, Michael. *The Universal Hunger for Liberty: Why the Clash of Civilizations is Not Inevitable.* New York: Basic Books, A Member of the Perseus Books Group, 2004.

Odum, Howard W. *Social and Mental Traits of the Negro: Research into the Conditions of the Negro Race in Southern Towns.* Submitted in partial fulfillment of the requirements for the degree of Doctor of Philosophy in the Faculty of Political Science, Columbia University. New York, 1910.

_____. *Southern Regions of the United States.* University of North Carolina Press, 1936.

Osborne, M.D., Oliver T., and Fishbein, M.D., Morris. *Handbook of Therapy.* Chicago: American Medical Association, Seventh Edition, 1923.

Osler, M.D., William. *Principles and Practice of Medicine, Designed for the Use of Practitioners and Students of Medicine.* New York: D. Appleton and Company, Fourth Edition, 1901.

Patterson, Robert T. *The Great Boom and Panic 1921-1929.* Chicago: Henry Regnery Company, 1965.

_____. *America's Struggle Against Poverty in the Twentieth Century.* Cambridge, MA: Harvard University Press, 2000.

Payne, Robert. *The Life and Death of Adolph Hitler.* New York: Praeger Publishers, 1973.

Pelling, Henry. *Modern Britain 1885-1955.* New York: W. W. Norton & Company, Inc., 1960.

Perkins, Edwin J. *Wall Street to Main Street: Charles Merrill and Middle-Class Investors.* Cambridge University Press, 1999.

Persico, Joseph E. *Roosevelt's Secret War: FDR and World War II Espionage.* New York: Random House, Inc., 2001.

Pfister, Joel. *The Yale Indian: The Education of Henry Roe Cloud.* Durham NC: Duke University Press, 2009.

Rand, Ayn. *Capitalism: The Unknown Ideal.* New York: Penguin Putnam, Inc., 1946.

Reagan, Ronald. *An American Life: The Autobiography.* New York: Simon & Schuster, Inc., 1990.

Reich, Robert B. *Supercapitalism: The Transformation of Business, Democracy, and Everyday Life.* New York: Alfred A. Knopf, 2007.

Residents of Hull-House. *Hull-House Maps and Papers: A Presentation of Nationalities and Wages in a Congested District of Chicago Together with Comments and Essays on the Problems Growing Out of the Social Conditions.* Chicago: University of Illinois Press, 1895.

Rhodes, James Ford. *The McKinley and Roosevelt Administrations, 1897-1909.* New York: Macmillan Company, 1923.

Riis, Jacob A. *The Battle with the Slum.* New York: The Macmillan Company, 1902.

Rockefeller, David. *Memoirs.* New York: Random House, 2002.

Rockefeller, John D. *Some Random Reminiscences of Men and Events.* New York: Doubleday, Page & Company, 1909.

Roosevelt, Elliott and Brough, James. *An Untold Story: The Roosevelts of Hyde Park.* New York: The Dell Publishing Company, 1973.

Roosevelt, Franklin D. *Looking Forward.* New York: Simon and Schuster, 1933.

Roosevelt, James and Shalett, Sidney. *Affectionately, F.D.R.——A Son's Story of a Lonely Man.* New York: Avon Book Division, The Hearst Corporation, 1959.

Roosevelt, Theodore. *An Autobiography.* New York: Charles Scribner's Sons, 1925.

Rothbard, Murray N. *America's Greatest Depression,* BN Publishing.

Rothschild, William E. *The Secret to GE's Success.* McGraw-Hill, 2007.

Rottenberg, Dan. *The Man Who Made Wall Street: Anthony J. Drexel and the Rise of Modern Finance.* University of Pennsylvania Press, 2001.

Rubin, Robert E., and Weisberg, Jacob. *In An Uncertain World: Tough Choices from Wall Street to Washington.* New York: Random House, 2003.

Ruoff, Henry W. (Ed.). *The Century Book of Facts: A Handbook of Ready Reference.* Springfield, MA: The King-Richardson Company, 1903.

Russell, Francis. *The Shadow of Blooming Grove: Warren G. Harding and His Times.* New York: McGraw-Hill Company, 1968.

Ryan, Rev. Msgr. John A. *A Better Economic Order.* New York: Harper & Brothers Publishers, 1935.

Sachs, Jeffrey D. *The End of Poverty: Economic Possibilities for Our Time.* New York: The Penguin Press, 2005.

Salter, Sir Arthur. *Recovery: The Second Effort.* New York: The Century Co., 1932.

Schatz, Ronald W. *The Electrical Workers: A History of Labor at General Electric and Westinghouse 1923-1960.* University of Illinois Press, 1983.

Schlesinger, Arthur M. Jr. *The Age of Roosevelt: The Crisis of the Old Order, 1919-1933.* Houghton Mifflin Company, 1957.

_____. *The Age of Roosevelt: The Coming of the New Deal.* Boston: Houghton Mifflin Company, 1958.

_____. *The Age of Roosevelt: The Politics of Upheaval.* Boston: Houghton Mifflin Company, 1960.

Schlesinger, Arthur M. Jr., and Bruns, Roger (eds.). *Congress Investigates, 1792-1974.* New York: Chelsea House Publishers, 1975.

Shlaes, Amity. *The Forgotten Man: A New History of the Greta Depression.* HarperCollins Publishers, 2007.

Sherwood, Robert E. *Roosevelt and Hopkins: An Intimate History.* New York: Harper & Brothers, 1948.

Siegfried, Andre. *America Comes of Age.* (English Translation by H. H. Hemmong and Doris Hemming). London: Jonathan Cape, 1927.

Sinclair, Upton. *My Lifetime in Letters.* University of Missouri Press, 1960.

Sloan, Alfred P., Jr. *My Years with General Motors.* New York: Doubleday, A Division of Bantam Doubleday Dell Publishing, 1963.

Smith, Adam. *The Wealth of Nations.* New York: Random House, 1776.

Smith, Jean Edward. *FDR.* New York: Random House, 2007.

Steffens, Lincoln. *The Autobiography of Lincoln Steffens.* New York: Harcourt, Brace and Company.

Stewart, George C., Jr. *Marvels of Charity: History of American Sisters and Nuns.* Huntington, IN: Our Sunday Visitor, Inc., 1994.

Stiglitz, Joseph E. *Globalization and Its Discontents.* New York: W. W. Norton & Company, 2002.

Taft, Charles P. *You and I—And Roosevelt.* New York: Farrar & Rinehart, Inc., 1936.

Taylor, Nick. *American-Made: The Enduring Legacy of the W.P.A., When FDR Put the Nation to Work.* New York: Bantam Dell, a Division of Random House, Inc., 2008.

Terkel, Studs. *Hard Times: An Oral History of the Great Depression.* New York: The New Press, 1970.

Thirteen Correspondents of the New York Times. *We Saw It Happen: The News Behind the News That's Fit to Print.* New York: Simon and Schuster, 1939.

Thomas, Gordon and Morgan-Witts, Max. *The Day the Bubble Burst: A Social History of the Wall Street Crash of 1929.* Garden City, NY: Doubleday & Company, Inc., 1979.

Townsend, Col. G.W. *Memorial Life of William McKinley*, 1901.

Truman, Harry S. *Memoirs: Year of Decisions. Volume 1.* New York: Doubleday, 1955.

_____. *Memoirs: Years of Trial and Hope, 1946-1952.* New York: Doubleday, 1956.

Tully, Grace. *F.D.R. My Boss.* New York: Charles Scribner's Sons, 1949.

Tumulty, Joseph P. *Woodrow Wilson As I Know Him.* Garden City, NY: Garden City Publishing Co., Inc., 1921.

United States Department of Agriculture. *Yearbook of Agriculture 1931.* United States Government Printing Office, 1931.

Urban, Wayne J., and Wagoner, Jr., Jennings L. *American Education: A History.* Fourth Edition. New York: Routledge Taylor & Francis Group, 2009.

Wachhorst, Wyn. *Thomas Alva Edison: An American Myth.* Cambridge, MA: The MIT Press, 1981.

Wallace, Henry. *New Frontiers.* New York: Reynal & Hitchcock, 1934.

Walsh, John Evangelist. *One Day at Kitty Hawk: The Untold Story of the Wright Brothers and the Airplane.* New York: Thomas Y. Crowell, 1975.

Warner, Amos Griswold. *American Charities: A Study in Philanthropy and Economics.* New York: Thomas Y. Crowell & Co., 1894.

Warshow, Robert Irving. *Jay Gould: The Story of a Fortune.* New York: Greenberg Publisher, Inc., 1928.

Watkins, T.H. *The Hungry Years: A Narrative History of the Great Depression in America.* New York: Henry Holt and Company, 1999.

Webb, R.K. *Modern England: From the 18th Century to the Present.* New York: Dodd, Mead & Company, 1968.

Weinberg, Steve. *Taking on the Trust: The Epic Battle of Ida Tarbell and John D. Rockefeller.* New York: W.W. Norton & Company, Ltd., 2008.

Weiner, Eric J. *What Goes Up: The Uncensored History of Modern Wall Street as Told By the Bankers, Brokers, CEOs and Scoundrels Who Made It Happen.* New York: Little, Brown and Company, 2005.

Welch, Jack. *Jack—Straight from the Gut.* New York: Warner Books, 2001.

Wessel, David. *In Fed We Trust: Ben Bernanke's War on the Great Panic.* New York: Crown Publishing Group, a division of Random House, Inc., 2009.

Widmer, Candace and Houchin, Susan. *The Art of Trusteeship: The Nonprofit Board Member's Guide to Effective Governance.* San Francisco: Jossey-Bass, Inc., 2000.

Williams, T. Harry. *Huey Long.* New York: Vintage Books, a division of Random House, 1969.

Wilson, Woodrow. *The Messages and Papers of Woodrow Wilson. Volumes I and II.* New York: The Review of Reviews Corporation, 1924.

Winkler, John K. *Incredible Carnegie.* New York: Garden City Publishing Company, Inc., 1931.

_____. *Morgan the Magnificent.* New York: The Vanguard Press, 1930.

Worthy, James C. *Shaping an American Institution: Robert E. Wood and Sears, Roebuck.* University of Illinois Press, 1984.

Selected Articles

"One of Two of a Kind," *Fortune,* May 1934.

"Mr. Junior's Beneficences: An Audit," *Fortune,* July 1936.

"Marshall Field & Co.," *Fortune,* October 1936.

"The U.S. Wheat Farmer Gets a Good Price for a Bumper Crop," *Life,* August 2, 1937.

"Senators Bury Their Leader and the Court Bill," *Life,* August 2, 1937.

"Brazil Destroys Its Coffee to Keep Prices Up," *Life,* August 2, 1937.

"Another Vehicular Tunnel Under Hudson River Now Connects New York and New Jersey," *Life,* December 27, 1937.

"The U.S. Budget and Mr. Lacey: The Tax Life of a Connecticut Yankee," *Life,* January 17, 1938.

"General Motors' Knudsen Can't Help the Senate," *Life,* January 17, 1938.

"Up Close to the Rockefellers," *Life,* July 11, 1960.

Berg, Roland H. "Heart Transplants Are Not Enough," *Look.* April 16, 1968.

Index

Made in the USA
Charleston, SC
03 February 2012